4th Workshop on Challenges and Applications of Automated Extraction of Socio-political Events from Text (CASE 2021)

Online
5-6 August 2021

ISBN: 978-1-7138-3313-0

Printed from e-media with permission by:

Curran Associates, Inc.
57 Morehouse Lane
Red Hook, NY 12571

Some format issues inherent in the e-media version may also appear in this print version.

Printed with permission by Curran Associates, Inc. (2021)

For permission requests, please contact the Association for Computational Linguistics at the address below.

Association for Computational Linguistics
209 N. Eighth Street
Stroudsburg, Pennsylvania 18360

Phone: 1-570-476-8006
Fax: 1-570-476-0860

acl@aclweb.org

Additional copies of this publication are available from:

Curran Associates, Inc.
57 Morehouse Lane
Red Hook, NY 12571 USA
Phone: 845-758-0400
Fax: 845-758-2633
Email: curran@proceedings.com
Web: www.proceedings.com

CASE 2021

The 4th Workshop on Challenges and Applications of Automated Extraction of Socio-political Events from Text (CASE)

Proceedings of the Workshop

August 5 - 6, 2021

This workshop is the fourth issue of a series of workshops on automatic extraction of socio-political events from news, organized by the Emerging Market Welfare Project, with the support of the Joint Research Centre of the European Commission and with contributions from many other prominent scholars in this field. The purpose of this series of workshops is to foster research and development of reliable, valid, robust, and practical solutions for automatically detecting descriptions of socio-political events, such as protests, riots, wars and armed conflicts, in text streams. This year workshop contributors make use of the state-of-the-art NLP technologies, such as Deep Learning, Word Embeddings and Transformers and cover a wide range of topics from text classification to news bias detection. Around 40 teams have registered and 15 teams contributed to three tasks that are i) multilingual protest news detection detection, ii) fine-grained classification of socio-political events, and iii) discovering Black Lives Matter protest events. The workshop also highlights two keynote and four invited talks about various aspects of creating event data sets and multi- and cross-lingual machine learning in few- and zero-shot settings.

Organizing Committee

Ali Hürriyetoğlu (Koc University, Turkey)

Hristo Tanev (Joint Research Centre of the European Commission, Italy)

Vanni Zavarella (Joint Research Centre of the European Commission, Italy)

Osman Mutlu (Koc University, Turkey)

Reyyan Yeniterzi (Sabancı University, Turkey)

Erdem Yörük (Koc University, Turkey),

Aline Villavicencio (University of Sheffield, the United Kingdom; and Institute of Informatics, Federal University of Rio Grande do Sul, Brazil)

Deniz Yuret (Koc University, Turkey),

Jakub Piskorski (Polish Academy of Sciences, Poland),

Program Committee

Tommaso Caselli (University of Groningen, the Netherlands),

Osman Mutlu (Koc University, Turkey),

Fırat Duruşan (Koc University, Turkey),

Ali Safaya (Koc University, Turkey),

Bharathi Raja Asoka Chakravarthi (Insight SFI Centre for Data Analytics, the United Kingdom),

Gautam Kishore Shahi (University of Duisburg-Essen, Germany),

Jakub Piskorski (Polish Academy of Sciences, Poland),

Benjamin J. Radford (UNC Charlotte, the United States),

Mark Lee (University of Birmingham, the United Kingdom),

Fredrik Olsson (RISE, Sweden),

Kristine Eck (Uppsala University, Sweden),

Nelleke Oostdijk (Radboud University, the Netherlands),

Francielle Vargas (University of São Paulo, Brazil),

Farhana Liza (University of Essex, the UK),

Nicoletta Calzolari (Institute for Computational Linguistics, Italy),

Milena Slavcheva (Bulgarian Academy of Sciences, Bulgaria),

Harish Tayyar Madabushi (University of Birmingham, the United Kingdom),

Ritesh Kumar (Dr. Bhimrao Ambedkar University, India),

Alexandra DeLucia (Johns Hopkins University, United States),

Jasmine Lorenzini (University of Geneva, Switzerland),

Andrew Lee Halterman (Massachusetts Institute of Technology, the United States),

Marijn Schraagen (Utrecht University, the Netherlands).

Niklas Stoehr (ETH Zürich, Switzerland)

Onur Uca (Mersin University, Turkey)

Tareq Al-Moslmi (University of Bergen, Norway)

Alfred Krzywicki (UNSW Sydney, Australia)

Table of Contents

Workshop Program

Day 1

Challenges and Applications of Automated Extraction of Socio-political Events from Text (CASE 2021): Workshop and Shared Task Report
Ali Hürriyetoğlu, Hristo Tanev, Vanni Zavarella, Jakub Piskorski, Reyyan Yeniterzi, Deniz Yuret and Aline Villavicencio

Keynote Abstract: Events on a Global Scale: Towards Language-Agnostic Event Extraction
Elizabeth Boschee

Keynote Abstract: Machine Learning in Conflict Studies: Reflections on Ethics, Collaboration, and Ongoing Challenges
Kristine Eck

PROTEST-ER: Retraining BERT for Protest Event Extraction
Tommaso Caselli, Osman Mutlu, Angelo Basile and Ali Hürriyetoğlu

ArgFuse: A Weakly-Supervised Framework for Document-Level Event Argument Aggregation
Debanjana Kar, Sudeshna Sarkar and Pawan Goyal

Modality and Negation in Event Extraction
Sander Bijl de Vroe, Liane Guillou, Miloš Stanojević, Nick McKenna and Mark Steedman

Characterizing News Portrayal of Civil Unrest in Hong Kong, 1998–2020
James Scharf, Arya D. McCarthy and Giovanna Maria Dora Dore

Regressing Location on Text for Probabilistic Geocoding
Benjamin J. Radford

Extracting Events from Industrial Incident Reports
Nitin Ramrakhiyani, Swapnil Hingmire, Sangameshwar Patil, Alok Kumar and Girish Palshikar

Automatic Fake News Detection in Political Platforms - A Transformer-based Approach
Shaina Raza

Day 2

Challenges and Applications of Automated Extraction of Socio-political Events from Text (CASE 2021): Workshop and Shared Task Report

Ali Hürriyetoğlu
Koç University
Sarıyer, İstanbul, Turkey
ahurriyetoglu@ku.edu.tr

Hristo Tanev
European Commission
Ispra, Varese, Italy
hristo.tanev@ec.europa.eu

Vanni Zavarella
European Commission
Ispra, Varese, Italy
vanni.zavarella@ec.europa.eu

Jakub Piskorski
Polish Academy of Sciences
Warsaw, Poland
jpiskorski@gmail.com

Reyyan Yeniterzi
Sabancı University
Tuzla, İstanbul, Turkey
reyyan@sabanciuniv.edu

Erdem Yörük
Koç University
Sarıyer, İstanbul, Turkey
eryoruk@ku.edu.tr

Osman Mutlu
Koç University
Sarıyer, İstanbul, Turkey
omutlu@ku.edu.tr

Deniz Yüret
Koç University
Sarıyer, İstanbul, Turkey
dyuret@ku.edu.tr

Aline Villavicencio
The University of Sheffield
Sheffield, United Kingdom
a.villavicencio@sheffield.ac.uk

Abstract

This workshop is the fourth issue of a series of workshops on automatic extraction of socio-political events from news, organized by the Emerging Market Welfare Project, with the support of the Joint Research Centre of the European Commission and with contributions from many other prominent scholars in this field. The purpose of this series of workshops is to foster research and development of reliable, valid, robust, and practical solutions for automatically detecting descriptions of socio-political events, such as protests, riots, wars and armed conflicts, in text streams. This year workshop contributors make use of the state-of-the-art NLP technologies, such as Deep Learning, Word Embeddings and Transformers and cover a wide range of topics from text classification to news bias detection. Around 40 teams have registered and 15 teams contributed to three tasks that are i) multilingual protest news detection, ii) fine-grained classification of socio-political events, and iii) discovering Black Lives Matter protest events. The workshop also highlights two keynote and four invited talks about various aspects of creating event data sets and multi- and cross-lingual machine learning in few- and zero-shot settings.

1 Introduction

Today, the unprecedented quantity of easily accessible data on social, political, and economic processes offers ground-breaking potential in guiding data-driven analysis in social and human sciences and in influencing policy-making processes. The need for precise and high-quality information about a wide variety of events ranging from political violence, environmental catastrophes, and conflict to international economic and health crises has rapidly escalated (Della Porta and Diani, 2015; Coleman et al., 2014). Governments, multilateral organizations, and local and global NGOs present an increasing demand for this data to prevent or resolve conflicts, provide relief for those that are afflicted, or improve the lives of and protect citizens in a variety of ways. For instance, Black Lives Matter protests [1], conflict in Syria [2] and COVID-19 related events [3] are only a few examples where we must understand, analyze, and improve the real-life situations using such data.

A recent report from ReliefWeb [4] clearly demon-

[1] http://protestmap.raceandpolicing.com, accessed on June 2, 2021.

[2] https://www.cartercenter.org/peace/conflict_resolution/syria-conflict-resolution.html, accessed on June 2, 2021.

[3] https://en.wikipedia.org/wiki/Protests_over_responses_to_the_COVID-19_pandemic, accessed on June 2, 2021.

[4] https://reliefweb.int/report/world/trends-armed-conflict-1946-2017, accessed on June 3, 2021.

Proceedings of the 4th Workshop on Challenges and Applications of Automated Extraction of Socio-political Events from Text (CASE), pages 1–9
August 5–6, 2021,

strates that the number of wars and other armed conflicts is on an increasing trend. In particular, the so-called internationalized conflicts are on a rise in the last two decades. In this situation, it is important to provide solutions for situation awareness, using various branches of artificial intelligence (AI), natural language processing (NLP), machine learning (ML), and advanced statistical methods.

In this clue, event detection and extraction plays an important role, because of its capacity to detect conflict developments in news and social media and to extract important information about them. Such information involves the quantity and the profiles of the victims, the participating entities, the conflict dynamics, its spatio-temporal characteristics, the weaponry used, as well as infrastructural, technical and human impact. This information extracted through various NLP methods can throw light on the intensity and the trend development of each conflict, as it is reflected in the media. Event detection has been used by political analysts to write their daily situation reports for decision makers, to create long-term analyses, as well as for conflict forecasting and prediction.

Automation offers scholars not only the opportunity to improve existing practices, but also to vastly expand the scope of data that can be collected and studied, thus potentially opening up new research frontiers within the field of socio-political events, such as political violence and social movements. Event information collection has long been a challenge for the NLP community as it requires sophisticated methods in defining event ontologies, creating language resources, and developing algorithmic approaches (Pustejovsky et al., 2003; Tanev et al., 2008; Emanuela, 2018; Chen et al., 2021). We believe that this workshop and the shared task contribute strongly towards putting emphasis on this important technology, providing a gathering point for scientists and developers in NLP, AI, conflict studies and related areas.

Social and political scientists have been creating event databases such as ACLED (Raleigh et al., 2010), EMBERS (Saraf and Ramakrishnan, 2016), GDELT (Leetaru and Schrodt, 2013), ICEWS (O'Brien, 2010), MMAD (Weidmann and Rød, 2019), PHOENIX, POLDEM (Kriesi et al., 2019), SPEED (Nardulli et al., 2015), TERRIER (Liang et al., 2018), and UCDP (Sundberg et al., 2012) for decades. These projects and the new ones increasingly rely on machine learning (ML) and NLP methods to deal better with the vast amount and variety of data in this domain (Hürriyetoğlu et al., 2021). Nonetheless, automated approaches suffer from major issues like bias, low generalizability, class imbalance, training data limitations, ethical issues, and lack of recall quantification which affect the quality of the results and their use drastically (Leins et al., 2020; Bhatia et al., 2020; Chang et al., 2019; Yörük et al., 2021). Moreover, the results of the automated systems for socio-political event information collection may not be comparable to each other or not of sufficient quality (Wang et al., 2016; Schrodt, 2020).

Socio-political events are varied and nuanced. Both the political context and the local language used may affect whether and how they are reported. Therefore, all steps of information collection (event definition, language resources, and manual or algorithmic steps) may need to be constantly updated. This leads us to a series of challenging questions such as: Do events related to minority groups are represented well? Are new types of events covered? Are the event definitions and their operationalization comparable across systems? We organize the workshop on Challenges and Applications of Automated Extraction of Socio-political Events from Text (CASE 2021) [5] and the shared task Socio-political and Crisis Events Detection [6] to seek answers to these and related questions, to inspire innovative technological and scientific solutions for tackling the aforementioned issues, and to quantify the quality of the automated event extraction systems. Moreover, the workshop aims to trigger a deeper understanding of the performance of the computational tools used and the usability of the resulting socio-political event datasets. The workshop is co-located with the Joint Conference of the 59th Annual Meeting of the Association for Computational Linguistics and the 11th International Joint Conference on Natural Language Processing (ACL-IJCNLP 2021).

We invited contributions from researchers in computer science, NLP, ML, AI, socio-political sciences, conflict analysis and forecasting, peace studies, as well as computational social science scholars involved in the collection and utilization of socio-political event data. Social and political scientists are interested in reporting and discussing

[5] `https://emw.ku.edu.tr/case-2021/`, accessed on June 9, 2021.

[6] `https://github.com/emerging-welfare/case-2021-shared-task`, June 12, 2021.

their approaches and observe what the state-of-the-art text processing systems can achieve for their domain. Computational scholars have the opportunity to illustrate the capacity of their approaches in this domain and benefit from being challenged by real-world use cases. Academic workshops specific to tackling event information in general or for analyzing text in specific domains such as health, law, finance, and biomedical sciences have significantly accelerated progress in these topics and fields, respectively. However, there is not a comparable effort for handling socio-political events. We hope to fill this gap and contribute to social and political sciences in a similar spirit. We invite work on all aspects of automated coding of socio-political events from mono- or multi-lingual text sources. This includes (but is not limited to) the broad topics below.

Data: collecting and annotating data, identifying the qualities, bias and fairness of the sources, handling ethics, misinformation, privacy, and fairness concerns pertaining to event datasets, respecting copyright of the sources at the creation, dissemination, and release phases of an event dataset;

Task: defining, populating, and facilitating event schemas and ontologies, extracting events in and beyond a sentence, detecting event coreference and event-event relations such as subevents, main events, and causal relations, investigating lexical, syntactic, and pragmatic aspects of event information manifestation, determining socio-poltical events pertaining to societal issues such as COVID-19 and BLM, detecting novel events;

Approaches: developing rule-based, machine learning, hybrid, and human-in-the-loop approaches for creating event datasets; and

Evaluation: evaluating event datasets in light of reliability and validity metrics, estimating what is missing in event datasets using internal and external information, utilizing event datasets, releasing of new event datasets.

We provide summaries of the accepted papers, the shared task, keynotes, and invited talks in the sections 2, 3, 4, and 5 respectively. Section 6 concludes this report with main lessons derived from these efforts and interactions.

2 Accepted Papers

The workshop attracted 21 submissions. The competition was high and 7 of them were accepted based on reviewer evaluations, which vary between 4 and 6 for each paper.

Here are brief descriptions of all accepted papers, except from the ones participating in the shared task, which are described in other papers in this proceedings:

de Vroe et al. (2021) present an open domain, lexicon-based event extraction system that captures various types of event modality. The definition of "event" in this work is quite broad, i.e. every predicate construction is taken into consideration. The authors use syntactic parsing to detect the event modality, which is a very important phenomena when making distinction between current, past and just probable events. The system explores conditionality, counterfactuality, negation, and propositional attitude. The achieved accuracy in the modality labelling task is 0.81 F1 that is measured on a small corpus of 100 manually annotated predicates.

Raza (2021) explores the topic of detecting fake news, which is potentially related to the trustability of the sources, from which events are extracted. The main approach in this study is based on a modified version of a pre-trained Bidirectional Encoder Representations from Transformers (BERT) with the capability to receive as input news-related and side information. In particular, each news item is represented by its title (main information) and side information, such as temporal, news-related information, author and source, as well as social contexts (related tweets) which give information about users' reactions on the news. The proposed model is quite promising, considering it outperforms all other state-of-the-art methods. It achieves 96% accuracy in deciding between fake and real news on a test set with fake and real news nearly equally represented.

Caselli et al. (2021) explore how efficiently a retrained BERT model detects protest events. Authors present the PROTEST-ER system, which uses a retrained BERT model for protest event extraction. They use annotated event data from the protest event detection task following the 2019 CLEF ProtestNews Lab (Hürriyetoğlu et al., 2019a,b). A worth-to-mention finding of this work is that PROTEST-ER outperforms a corresponding generic BERT with 8.1 points.

Ramrakhiyani et al. (2021) describe a deep learning approach for detecting incidents from industrial reports. Incidents in industries have huge social and political impacts. However, automated analysis of repositories of incident reports has remained a challenge. Due to absence of event annotated datasets for industrial incidents authors employ a transfer learning based approach. A detailed analysis is provided on how amount of data utilized affect pre-training and why pre-training improves the performance. Data is gathered from aviation and construction incident reports. Different deep learning methods are evaluated for the task, including BiLSTM and transfer learning. Transfer learning consistently outperforms the baseline and achieves F1 measure of 0.81.

Radford (2021) presents a study on geocoding and a new data set. Geocoding is an important subtask of event detection, in which the goal is to find the geographic coordinates associated with event descriptions. The paper presents an "end-to-end probabilistic model" for geocoding from text data. A novel data set has been created for evaluating the performance of geocoding systems. The output of the new model is compared with a state-of-the-art model, called Mordecai. The comparison clearly shows an improvement provided by the proposed model.

Scharf et al. (2021) report on a study on the political bias in Hong Kong published news reporting about protest events. The paper reports on lexical differences between home and Western news sources about protests happening in Hong Kong in the period 1998-2020. Experiments on topic modeling, sentiment analysis, lexical distribution and comparative lexical analysis between Western- and Hong Kong-based sources reveal a bias in the reporting from the Hong Kong press. The evaluation reveals that during the Anti-Extradition Law Amendment Bill Movement reports from Hong Kong made fewer references to police violence compared to the Western media. The study also reveals that the lexical contexts of salient keywords changed in Hong Kong sources when the Movement emerged.

Kar et al. (2021) describe an algorithm for event argument detection and aggregation. The paper reports on document level aggregation of the following argument types: Time, Place, Casualties, After-Effect, Reason, and Participant. The ArgFuse algorithm is based on a BERT based active learning classifier, which identifies whether a pair of event arguments is redundant, and a Biased Text Rank argument ordering function. Authors report F1 measure of 0.61, which beats all the other 5 baseline algorithms with which the ArgFuse performance is compared.

3 Shared Task: Socio-political and Crisis Events Detection

The work on event database creation comprises of three steps that are collecting events, classifying them, and measuring utility of the system output, which is an event database, against ground-truth. Each of these steps contains pitfalls and subject to limitations. For instance, the data source utilized maybe biased or a ground-truth may not be available. Although aforementioned issues in socio-political and crisis event studies have been studied by numerous scholars for decades to date, there are still no answers or solutions to them (Wang et al., 2016; Lorenzini et al., 2016; Schrodt, 2020; Raleigh, 2020; Eck, 2021; Boschee, 2021). Therefore, we aim at contributing to the understanding and resolution of event database creation via quantifying performance of the state-of-the-art text processing systems in the shared task Socio-political and Crisis Events Detection. [7]

The shared task consists of three tasks that are on collection (Task 1), classification (Task 2) (Haneczok et al., 2021), and evaluation (Task 3) of event databases. Shared task and submission details are reported in the overview papers of the tasks (Hürriyetoğlu et al., 2021; Haneczok et al., 2021; Giorgi et al., 2021) and the system description papers in this proceedings respectively. We provide a summary of the tasks and the findings in the following subsections.

3.1 Task 1: Multilingual protest news detection

The task is designed to be both multilingual (having both training and test data in English, Portuguese, and Spanish) and cross-lingual (having data in Hindi only for test). There are four subtasks that are document classification (subtask 1), sentence classification (subtask 2), event sentence classification (subtask 3), and event extraction (subtask 4). Event information is at the center of all of the subtasks, i.e. documents and sentences are classified as containing event information in subtasks

[7] `https://github.com/emerging-welfare/case-2021-shared-task`, accessed on June 9, 2021.

1 and 2, sentences that are about the same event are identified in subtask 3, and event trigger and its arguments are extracted in subtask 4.

13 teams have submitted 238 submissions for the evaluation scenarios specified with subtask and language combinations. The best submissions utilized deep learning approaches that combine the training data in various languages, utilize large models, further re-train the models, and create ensemble models (Awasthy et al., 2021; Hettiarachchi et al., 2021; Re et al., 2021; Hu and Stoehr, 2021; Tan et al., 2021). Although training data was limited in Portuguese and Spanish and not available in Hindi, the best performing participants managed to deliver predictions that are between 77.27 and 93.03 F1-macro in subtasks 1, 2, and 3 for all languages. The performance of the best system for subtask 4 for all languages was between 66.20 and 78.11 for all languages and 4-5 F1-macro points ahead of all other teams in all languages.

3.2 Task 2: Fine-grained Event Classification in News-like Text Snippets

Task 2 aims at evaluating conventional and generalized zero-shot learning event classification approaches to classify short text snippets reporting socio-political and crisis events. The task is divided into three subtasks: (a) classification of text snippets reporting socio-political events, using 25 events classes from the Armed Conflict Location and Event Data Project (ACLED) event taxonomy(Raleigh et al., 2010), for which vast amount of training data exists, although exhibiting slightly different structure and style vis-a-vis test data, (b) enhancement to a generalized zero-shot learning problem, where 3 additional event types were introduced in advance, but without any training data ('unseen' classes), and (c) further extension, which introduced 2 additional event types, announced shortly prior to the evaluation phase. Task 2 focuses on classification of events in English texts and the event definitions of events in this task are not fully compatible with those in Task 1.

8 teams registered, out of which 4 returned system responses, for Task 2. Best performing systems for the subtask 1, 2 and 3 achieved 83.9%, 79.7% and 77.1% weighted F_1 scores respectively. Most of the solutions submitted are built on top of fine-tuned Transformer-based models like BERT and RoBERTa. Given the specific set up of this task, i.e., the training data being some-what different from the test data and inclusion of some unseen classes the top results obtained can be considered good, however, there is place for improvement.

3.3 Task 3: Discovering Black Lives Matter events in United States

Task 3 is only an evaluation task where the participants of Task 1 have the possibility to evaluate their systems on reproducing a manually curated Black Lives Matter (BLM) related protest event list. Participants use document collections, provided by the organizers and different from the documents from where Gold Standard has been extracted, to extract place and date of the BLM events in these collections. The event definition applied for determining these events is the same as the one facilitated for task 1. Participants may utilize any other data source to improve performance of their submissions. The goal of the task is to achieve as high correlation as possible with the events from the Gold Standard, as computed by aggregating events on a regular cell geographical grid..

5 teams that performed the best in Task 1 were invited to participate in this task. In general all participating systems showed low levels of correlation with the Gold standard data, including the baseline system. The low recall at this year's shared task is most probably due to the low coverage of the test corpus, which participating systems have used, and its poor overlapping with manually collected Gold Standard Data. Two systems showed a relatively good performance: NoConflict Hu and Stoehr (2021) and EventMiner Hettiarachchi et al. (2021). The main lesson from this task is that Gold Standard data and test data should be checked for consistency and correlation. Moreover, this evaluation task highlighted some of the current limits on the usability of automatically extracted event datasets for modelling socio-political processes, such as fine-grained geocoding of events.

4 Keynotes

Kristine Eck and Elizabeth Boschee will deliver the keynote talks. Eck (2021) addresses the responsibility of the scholars that create event datasets to define and apply what is right, suggests data sources alternative to news data that may report event information inconsistently, and emphasizes the need for interdisciplinary collaboration for creating data sets that advance conflict studies. Boschee et al. (2013); Boschee (2021) share the concerns addressed by

Prof. Eck and presents a detailed study that compares various approaches for utilizing multilingual data in a cross-lingual zero-shot setting to improve quality of the event datasets.

5 Invited Talks

The workshop contains an invited talks session as well. The authors of the papers published in Findings of ACL and related to workshop theme are invited to present their work in this session. The papers are

Zhou et al. (2021) propose an event-driven trading strategy that predicts stock movements by detecting corporate events from news articles;

Halterman et al. (2021) introduce the IndiaPoliceEvents Corpus—all 21,391 sentences from 1,257 *Times of India* articles about events in the state of Gujarat during March 2002;

Halterman and Radford (2021) show utility of "upsampling" coarse document labels to fine-grained labels or spans for protest size detection; and

Tsarapatsanis and Aletras (2021) discuss the importance of academic freedom, the diversity of legal and ethical norms, and the threat of moralism in the computational law field.

6 Conclusion

This workshop is the fourth event from a series of workshops on automatic extraction of socio-political events from news, organized by the Emerging Market Welfare Project, with the support of the Joint Research Centre of the European Commission, with contributions from many other prominent scholars in this field. The purpose of this series of workshops is to foster research and development in the area of event extraction of socio-political events.

The topics cover a wide range of applications and technologies: event detection via text classification, detection of news bias, fake news detection, modality analysis through syntactic parsing, event argument extraction and aggregation, a new geocoding algorithm and the creation of a new geocoding dataset. Most of the papers are dedicated to protest events, one paper is about industrial reports, and one paper discusses generic events, not related to the socio-political topic.

The papers in this issue of the workshop make use of state-of-the-art NLP technologies, such as Deep Learning, Word Embeddings and Transformers. Most of the papers use the BERT model: some use the pre-trained existing models, others train domain-specific ones, and one of the paper introduces a modified version of BERT. Most papers use BERT embeddings as features in their models and one paper discusses an algorithm, which uses a full syntactic parser. Sentiment analysis is used in one paper, which studies the political bias of the news.

The shared task results shed light on critical aspects of the automated socio-political extraction and evaluation methodology. [8]

Acknowledgments

The authors from Koc University were funded by the European Research Council (ERC) Starting Grant 714868 awarded to Dr. Erdem Yörük for his project Emerging Welfare.

References

Parul Awasthy, Jian Ni, Ken Barker, and Radu Florian. 2021. IBM MNLP IE at CASE 2021 task 1: Multi-granular and multilingual event detection on protest news. In *Proceedings of the 4th Workshop on Challenges and Applications of Automated Extraction of Socio-political Events from Text (CASE 2021)*, online. Association for Computational Linguistics (ACL).

Shraey Bhatia, Jey Han Lau, and Timothy Baldwin. 2020. You are right. i am alarmed–but by climate change counter movement. *arXiv preprint arXiv:2004.14907*.

Elizabeth Boschee. 2021. Keynote Abstract: Events on a Global Scale: Towards Language-Agnostic Event Extraction. In *Proceedings of the 4th Workshop on Challenges and Applications of Automated Extraction of Socio-political Events from Text (CASE 2021)*, online. Association for Computational Linguistics (ACL).

Elizabeth Boschee, Premkumar Natarajan, and Ralph Weischedel. 2013. Automatic Extraction of Events from Open Source Text for Predictive Forecasting. In V.S. Subrahmanian, editor, *Handbook of Computational Approaches to Counterterrorism*, pages 51–67. Springer New York, New York, NY.

[8] Detailed results are summarized in the overview papers (Hürriyetoğlu et al., 2021; Haneczok et al., 2021), and evaluation (Task 3) (Giorgi et al., 2021) of event databases. Moreover, system description papers provide full details

Tommaso Caselli, Osman Mutlu, Angelo Basile, and Ali Hürriyetoğlu. 2021. PROTEST-ER: Retraining BERT for Protest Event Extraction. In *Proceedings of the 4th Workshop on Challenges and Applications of Automated Extraction of Socio-political Events from Text (CASE 2021)*, online. Association for Computational Linguistics (ACL).

Kai-Wei Chang, Vinod Prabhakaran, and Vicente Ordonez. 2019. Bias and fairness in natural language processing. In *Proceedings of the 2019 Conference on Empirical Methods in Natural Language Processing and the 9th International Joint Conference on Natural Language Processing (EMNLP-IJCNLP): Tutorial Abstracts*, Hong Kong, China. Association for Computational Linguistics.

Muhao Chen, Hongming Zhang, Qiang Ning, Manling Li, Heng Ji, Kathleen McKeown, and Dan Roth. 2021. Event-centric natural language understanding.

Peter T Coleman, Morton Deutsch, and Eric C Marcus. 2014. *The handbook of conflict resolution: Theory and practice*. John Wiley & Sons.

Donatella Della Porta and Mario Diani. 2015. *The Oxford handbook of social movements*. Oxford University Press.

Kristine Eck. 2021. Keynote Abstract: Machine Learning in Conflict Studies: Reflections on Ethics, Collaboration, and Ongoing Challenges. In *Proceedings of the 4th Workshop on Challenges and Applications of Automated Extraction of Socio-political Events from Text (CASE 2021)*, online. Association for Computational Linguistics (ACL).

Boroş Emanuela. 2018. *Neural Methods for Event Extraction*. Ph.D. thesis, Université Paris-Saclay.

Salvatore Giorgi, Vanni Zavarella, Hristo Tanev, Nicolas Stefanovitch, Sy Hwang, Hansi Hettiarachchi, Tharindu Ranasinghe, Vivek Kalyan, Paul Tan, Shaun Tan, Martin Andrews, Hu Tiancheng, Niklas Stoehr, Francesco Ignazio Re, Daniel Vegh, Dennis Atzenhofer, Brenda Curtis, and Ali Hürriyetoğlu. 2021. Discovering Black Lives Matter events in the United States - Shared Task 3, CASE 2021. In *Proceedings of the 4th Workshop on Challenges and Applications of Automated Extraction of Socio-political Events from Text (CASE 2021)*, online. Association for Computational Linguistics (ACL).

Andrew Halterman, Katherine Keith, Sheikhand Sarwar, and Brendan O'Connor. 2021. Corpus-level evaluation for event qa: The indiapoliceevents corpus covering the 2002. In *Proceedings of the 59th Annual Meeting of the Association for Computational Linguistics*, Online. Association for Computational Linguistics.

Andrew Halterman and Benjamin J. Radford. 2021. Few-shot upsampling for protest size detection. In *Proceedings of the 59th Annual Meeting of the Association for Computational Linguistics*, Online. Association for Computational Linguistics.

Jacek Haneczok, Guillaume Jacquet, Jakub Piskorski, and Nicolas Stefanovitch. 2021. Fine-grained event classification in news-like text snippets shared task 2, CASE 2021. In *Proceedings of the 4th Workshop on Challenges and Applications of Automated Extraction of Socio-political Events from Text (CASE 2021)*, online. Association for Computational Linguistics (ACL).

Hansi Hettiarachchi, Mariam Adedoyin-Olowe, Jagdev Bhogal, and Mohamed Gaber. 2021. DAAI at CASE 2021 Task 1: Transformer-based Multilingual Socio-political and Crisis Event Detection. In *Proceedings of the 4th Workshop on Challenges and Applications of Automated Extraction of Socio-political Events from Text (CASE 2021)*, online. Association for Computational Linguistics (ACL).

Tiancheng Hu and Niklas Stoehr. 2021. Team "NoConflict" at CASE 2021 Task 1:Pretraining for Sentence-Level Protest Event Detection. In *Proceedings of the 4th Workshop on Challenges and Applications of Automated Extraction of Socio-political Events from Text (CASE 2021)*, online. Association for Computational Linguistics (ACL).

Ali Hürriyetoğlu, Osman Mutlu, Farhana Ferdousi Liza, Erdem Yörük, Ritesh Kumar, and Shyam Ratan. 2021. Multilingual protest news detection - Shared Task 1, CASE 2021. In *Proceedings of the 4th Workshop on Challenges and Applications of Automated Extraction of Socio-political Events from Text (CASE 2021)*, online. Association for Computational Linguistics (ACL).

Ali Hürriyetoğlu, Erdem Yörük, Deniz Yüret, Çağrı Yoltar, Burak Gürel, Fırat Duruşan, and Osman Mutlu. 2019a. A task set proposal for automatic protest information collection across multiple countries. In *Advances in Information Retrieval*, pages 316–323, Cham. Springer International Publishing.

Ali Hürriyetoğlu, Erdem Yörük, Deniz Yüret, Çağrı Yoltar, Burak Gürel, Fırat Duruşan, Osman Mutlu, and Arda Akdemir. 2019b. Overview of CLEF 2019 Lab ProtestNews: Extracting Protests from News in a Cross-Context Setting. In *Experimental IR Meets Multilinguality, Multimodality, and Interaction*, pages 425–432, Cham. Springer International Publishing.

Ali Hürriyetoğlu, Erdem Yörük, Osman Mutlu, Fırat Duruşşan, Çağrı Yoltar, Deniz Yüret, and Burak Gürel. 2021. Cross-Context News Corpus for Protest Event-Related Knowledge Base Construction. *Data Intelligence*, 3(2):308–335.

Debanjana Kar, Sudeshna Sarkar, and Pawan Goyal. 2021. ArgFuse: A Weakly-Supervised Framework for Document-Level Event Argument Aggregation. In *Proceedings of the 4th Workshop on Challenges *and Applications of Automated Extraction of Socio-political Events from Text (CASE 2021)*, online. Association for Computational Linguistics (ACL).

Hanspeter Kriesi, Bruno Wüest, Jasmine Lorenzini, Peter Makarov, Matthias Enggist, Klaus Rothenhäusler, Thomas Kurer, Silja Häusermann, and Altiparmakis Patrice Wangen. 2019. Poldem–protest event dataset 30.

Kalev Leetaru and Philip A Schrodt. 2013. GDELT: Global data on events, location, and tone, 1979–2012. In *ISA annual convention*, volume 2, pages 1–49. Citeseer.

Kobi Leins, Jey Han Lau, and Timothy Baldwin. 2020. Give me convenience and give her death: Who should decide what uses of NLP are appropriate, and on what basis? In *Proceedings of the 58th Annual Meeting of the Association for Computational Linguistics*, pages 2908–2913, Online. Association for Computational Linguistics.

Yan Liang, Khaled Jabr, Christan Grant, Jill Irvine, and Andrew Halterman. 2018. New techniques for coding political events across languages. In *2018 IEEE International Conference on Information Reuse and Integration (IRI)*, pages 88–93.

Jasmine Lorenzini, Peter Makarov, Hanspeter Kriesi, and Bruno Wueest. 2016. Towards a Dataset of Automatically Coded Protest Events from English-language Newswire Documents. In *Paper presented at the Amsterdam Text Analysis Conference*.

Peter F. Nardulli, Scott L. Althaus, and Matthew Hayes. 2015. A Progressive Supervised-learning Approach to Generating Rich Civil Strife Data. *Sociological Methodology*, 45(1):148–183.

Sean P. O'Brien. 2010. Crisis Early Warning and Decision Support: Contemporary Approaches and Thoughts on Future Research. *International Studies Review*, 12(1):87–104.

James Pustejovsky, José M Castano, Robert Ingria, Roser Sauri, Robert J Gaizauskas, Andrea Setzer, Graham Katz, and Dragomir R Radev. 2003. Timeml: Robust specification of event and temporal expressions in text. *New directions in question answering*, 3:28–34.

Benjamin J. Radford. 2021. Regressing Location on Text for Probabilistic Geocoding. In *Proceedings of the 4th Workshop on Challenges and Applications of Automated Extraction of Socio-political Events from Text (CASE 2021)*, online. Association for Computational Linguistics (ACL).

Clionadh Raleigh. 2020. Keynote abstract: Too soon? the limitations of AI for event data. In *Proceedings of the Workshop on Automated Extraction of Socio-political Events from News 2020*, page 7, Marseille, France. European Language Resources Association (ELRA).

Clionadh Raleigh, Andrew Linke, Håvard Hegre, and Joakim Karlsen. 2010. Introducing acled: an armed conflict location and event dataset: special data feature. *Journal of peace research*, 47(5):651–660.

Nitin Ramrakhiyani, Swapnil Hingmire, Sangameshwar Patil, Alok Kumar, and Girish Palshikar. 2021. Extracting Events from Industrial Incident Reports . In *Proceedings of the 4th Workshop on Challenges and Applications of Automated Extraction of Socio-political Events from Text (CASE 2021)*, online. Association for Computational Linguistics (ACL).

Shaina Raza. 2021. Automatic Fake News Detection in Political Platforms - A Transformer-based Approach . In *Proceedings of the 4th Workshop on Challenges and Applications of Automated Extraction of Socio-political Events from Text (CASE 2021)*, online. Association for Computational Linguistics (ACL).

Francesco Re, Daniel Vegh, Dennis Atzenhofer, and Niklas Stoehr. 2021. Team "DaDeFrNi" at CASE 2021 Task 1: Document and Sentence Classification for Protest Event Detection. In *Proceedings of the 4th Workshop on Challenges and Applications of Automated Extraction of Socio-political Events from Text (CASE 2021)*, online. Association for Computational Linguistics (ACL).

Parang Saraf and Naren Ramakrishnan. 2016. Embers autogsr: Automated coding of civil unrest events. In *Proceedings of the 22nd ACM SIGKDD International Conference on Knowledge Discovery and Data Mining*, KDD '16, page 599–608, New York, NY, USA. Association for Computing Machinery.

James Scharf, Arya D. McCarthy, and Giovanna Dore. 2021. Characterizing News Portrayal of Civil Unrest in Hong Kong, 1998–2020. In *Proceedings of the 4th Workshop on Challenges and Applications of Automated Extraction of Socio-political Events from Text (CASE 2021)*, online. Association for Computational Linguistics (ACL).

Philip A. Schrodt. 2020. Keynote abstract: Current open questions for operational event data. In *Proceedings of the Workshop on Automated Extraction of Socio-political Events from News 2020*, page 8, Marseille, France. European Language Resources Association (ELRA).

Ralph Sundberg, Kristine Eck, and Joakim Kreutz. 2012. Introducing the ucdp non-state conflict dataset. *Journal of Peace Research*, 49(2):351–362.

Fiona An Ting Tan, Sujatha Das Gollapalli, and See-Kiong Ng. 2021. NUS-IDS at CASE 2021 Task 1: Improving Multilingual Event Sentence Coreference Identification With Linguistic Information. In *Proceedings of the 4th Workshop on Challenges and Applications of Automated Extraction of Socio-political Events from Text (CASE 2021)*, online. Association for Computational Linguistics (ACL).

Hristo Tanev, Jakub Piskorski, and Martin Atkinson. 2008. Real-time news event extraction for global crisis monitoring. In *Natural Language and Information Systems*, pages 207–218, Berlin, Heidelberg. Springer Berlin Heidelberg.

Dimitrios Tsarapatsanis and Nikolaos Aletras. 2021. On the ethical limits of natural language processing on legal text. In *Proceedings of the 59th Annual Meeting of the Association for Computational Linguistics*, Online. Association for Computational Linguistics.

Sander Bijl de Vroe, Liane Guillou, Miloš Stanojević, Nick McKenna, and Mark Steedman. 2021. Modality and Negation in Event Extraction. In *Proceedings of the 4th Workshop on Challenges and Applications of Automated Extraction of Socio-political Events from Text (CASE 2021)*, online. Association for Computational Linguistics (ACL).

Wei Wang, Ryan Kennedy, David Lazer, and Naren Ramakrishnan. 2016. Growing pains for global monitoring of societal events. *Science*, 353(6307):1502–1503.

Nils B. Weidmann and Espen Geelmuyden Rød. 2019. *The Internet and Political Protest in Autocracies*, chapter Coding Protest Events in Autocracies. Oxford Studies in Digital Politics, Oxford.

Erdem Yörük, Ali Hürriyetoğlu, Çağrı Yoltar, and Fırat Duruşan. 2021. Random Sampling in Corpus Design: Cross-Context Generalizability in Automated Multicountry Protest Event Collection. *American Behavioral Scientist*, 0(0):00027642211021630.

Zhihan Zhou, Liqian Ma, and Han Liu. 2021. Trade the event: Corporate events detection for news-based event-driven trading. In *Proceedings of the 59th Annual Meeting of the Association for Computational Linguistics*, Online. Association for Computational Linguistics.

Keynote Abstract: Events on a Global Scale: Towards Language-Agnostic Event Extraction

Elizabeth Boschee
University of Southern California
CA, California, U.S.A.
boschee@isi.edu

Event extraction is a challenging and exciting task in the world of machine learning & natural language processing. The breadth of events of possible interest, the speed at which surrounding socio-political event contexts evolve, and the complexities involved in generating representative annotated data all contribute to this challenge. One particular dimension of difficulty is the intrinsically global nature of events: many downstream use cases for event extraction involve reporting not just in a few major languages but in a much broader context. The languages of interest for even a fixed task may still shift from day to day, e.g. when a disease emerges in an unexpected location.

Early approaches to multi-lingual event extraction (e.g. ACE) relied wholly on supervised data provided in each language of interest. Later approaches leveraged the success of machine translation to side-step the issue, simply translating foreign-language content to English and deploying English models on the result (often leaving some significant portion of the original content behind). Most recently, however, the community has begun to shown significant progress applying zero-shot transfer techniques to the problem, developing models using supervised English data but decoding in a foreign language without translation, typically using embedding spaces specifically designed to capture multi-lingual semantic content.

In this talk I will discuss multiple dimensions of these promising new approaches and the linguistic representations that underlie them. I will compare them with approaches based on machine translation (as well as with models trained using in-language training data, where available), and discuss their strengths and weaknesses in different contexts, including the amount of English/foreign bitext available and the nature of the target event ontology. I will also discuss possible future directions with an eye to improving the quality of event extraction no matter its source around the globe.

Bio: *Elizabeth Boschee is the Director of the Boston office of the University of Southern California's Information Sciences Institute and a Senior Supervising Computer Scientist in the Emerging Activities division. Her current efforts focus on cross-lingual information extraction, retrieval, and summarization, specifically targeting low or zero-resource settings, e.g. cross-lingual settings with <1M words of bitext or event extraction from non-English languages with only English training data. Prior to joining ISI, Boschee spent 17 years at BBN Technologies. As a Lead Scientist there, she was the chief architect of the BBN ACCENT event coder, the technology behind the W-ICEWS event data, which more than doubled the precision (while still increasing recall) of the previously deployed solution for CAMEO event coding.*

Proceedings of the 4th Workshop on Challenges and Applications of Automated Extraction of Socio-political Events from Text (CASE), page 10
August 5–6, 2021, ©2021 Association for Computational Linguistics

Keynote Abstract: Machine Learning in Conflict Studies: Reflections on Ethics, Collaboration, and Ongoing Challenges

Kristine Eck
Uppsala University
Uppsala, Sweden
kristine.eck@pcr.uu.se

Advances in machine learning are nothing short of revolutionary in their potential to analyze massive amounts of data and in doing so, create new knowledge bases. But there is a responsibility in wielding the power to analyze these data since the public attributes a high degree of confidence to results which are based on big datasets.

In this keynote, I will first address our ethical imperative as scholars to "get it right." This imperative relates not only to model precision but also to the quality of the underlying data, and to whether the models inadvertently reproduce or obscure political biases in the source material. In considering the ethical imperative to get it right, it is also important to define what is "right": what is considered an acceptable threshold for classification success needs to be understood in light of the project's objectives.

I then reflect on the different topics and data which are sourced in this field. Much of the existing research has focused on identifying conflict events (e.g. battles), but scholars are also increasingly turning to ML approaches to address other facets of the conflict environment.

Conflict event extraction has long been a challenge for the natural language processing (NLP) community because it requires sophisticated methods for defining event ontologies, creating language resources, and developing algorithmic approaches. NLP machine-learning tools are ill-adapted to the complex, often messy, and diverse data generated during conflicts. Relative to other types of NLP text corpora, conflicts tend to generate less textual data, and texts are generated non-systematically. Conflict-related texts are often lexically idiosyncratic and tend to be written differently across actors, periods, and conflicts. Event definition and adjudication present tough challenges in the context of conflict corpora.

Topics which rely on other types of data may be better-suited to NLP and machine learning methods. For example, Twitter and other social media data lend themselves well to studying hate speech, public opinion, social polarization, or discursive aspects of conflictual environments. Likewise, government-produced policy documents have typically been analyzed with historical, qualitative methods but their standardized formats and quantity suggest that ML methods can provide new traction. ML approaches may also allow scholars to exploit local sources and multi-language sources to a greater degree than has been possible.

Many challenges remain, and these are best addressed in collaborative projects which build on interdisciplinary expertise. Classification projects need to be anchored in the theoretical interests of scholars of political violence if the data they produce are to be put to analytical use. There are few ontologies for classification that adequately reflect conflict researchers' interests, which highlights the need for conceptual as well as technical development.

Bio: *Kristine Eck is an Associate Professor at the Department of Peace and Conflict Research at Uppsala University, where she serves as the Director of the Uppsala Rotary Peace Center. Her research interests concern coercion and resistance, including human rights, police misconduct, state surveillance, and conflict data production. She served as the Director of the Uppsala Conflict Data Program (UCDP) 2017-2018 and has been a Visiting Researcher at Oxford University, Copenhagen University, the University of Notre Dame, and Kobe University. Dr. Eck's research has been funded by the Swedish Research Council, the Swedish Foundation for Humanities and Social Sciences, and the Norwegian Foreign Ministry.*

Proceedings of the 4th Workshop on Challenges and Applications of Automated Extraction of Socio-political Events from Text (CASE) , page 11
August 5–6, 2021, ©2021 Association for Computational Linguistics

PROTEST-ER: Retraining BERT for Protest Event Extraction

Tommaso Caselli[⋆], **Osman Mutlu**[†], **Angelo Basile**[◇], **Ali Hürriyetoğlu**[†]
[⋆]University of Groningen [†]Koç University [◇]Symanto Research
t.caselli@rug.nl, angelo.basile@symanto.com
{ahurriyetoglu,omutlu}@ku.edu.tr

Abstract

We analyze the effect of further pre-training BERT with different domain specific data as an unsupervised domain adaptation strategy for event extraction. Portability of event extraction models is particularly challenging, with large performance drops affecting data on the same text genres (e.g., news). We present PROTEST-ER, a retrained BERT model for protest event extraction. PROTEST-ER outperforms a corresponding generic BERT on out-of-domain data of 8.1 points. Our best performing models reach 51.91-46.39 F1 across both domains.

1 Introduction and Problem Statement

Events, i.e., things that happen in the world or states that hold true, play a central role in human lives. It is not a simplification to claim that our lives are nothing but a constant sequence of events. Nevertheless not all events are equally relevant, especially when the focus of attention and analysis moves away from individuals and touches upon societies. In this broader context, socio-political events are of particular interest since they directly impact and affect the lives of multiple individuals at the same time. Different actors (e.g., governments, multilateral organizations, NGOs, social movements) have various interests in collecting information and conducting analyses on this type of events. This, however, is a challenging task. The increasing availability and amount of data, thanks to the growth of the Web, calls for the development of automatic solutions based on Natural Language Processing (NLP).

Besides the good level of maturity reached by NLP systems in many areas, numerous challenges are still pending. **Portability** of systems, i.e., the reuse of previously trained systems for a specific task on different datasets, is one of them and it is far from being solved (Daumé III, 2007; Plank and van Noord, 2011; Axelrod et al., 2011; Ganin and Lempitsky, 2015; Alam et al., 2018; Xie et al., 2018; Zhao et al., 2019; Ben-David et al., 2020). As such, portability is a **domain adaptation** problem. Following Ramponi and Plank (2020), we consider a domain to be a *variety* where each corpus, or dataset, can be described as a multidimensional region including notions such as topics, genres, writing styles, years of publication, socio-demographic aspects, annotation bias, among other unknown factors. Every dataset belonging to a different variety poses a domain adaptation challenge.

Unsupervised domain adaptation has a long tradition in NLP (Blitzer et al., 2006; McClosky et al., 2006; Moore and Lewis, 2010; Ganin et al., 2016; Ruder and Plank, 2017; Guo et al., 2018; Miller, 2019; Nishida et al., 2020). The availability of large pre-trained transformer-based language models (TLMs), e.g., BERT (Devlin et al., 2019), has inspired a new trend in domain adaptation, namely **domain adaptive retraining** (DAR) (Xu et al., 2019; Han and Eisenstein, 2019; Rietzler et al., 2020; Gururangan et al., 2020). The idea behind DAR is as simple as effective: first, additional textual material matching the target domain is selected, then the masked language modeling (MLM) objective is used to further train an existing TLMs. The outcome is a new TLM whose representations are shifted to better suit the target domain. Fine-tuning domain adapted TLMs results in improved performance.

This contribution applies this approach to develop a portable system for **protest event extraction**. Our unsupervised domain adaptation setting investigates two related aspects. The first concerns the impact of the data used to adapt a generic TLM to a target domain (i.e., protest events). The second targets the portability in a zero-shot scenario of a domain-adapted TLMs across protest event datasets. Our experimental results provide additional evidence that further pretraining TLM on

Proceedings of the 4th Workshop on Challenges and Applications of Automated Extraction of Socio-political Events from Text (CASE), pages 12–19
August 5–6, 2021, ©2021 Association for Computational Linguistics

domain-related data is a "cheap" and successful method in single-source single-target unsupervised domain adaptation settings. Furthermore, we show that fine-tuned retrained TLMs results in models with a better portability.

2 Task and Data

We focus on the protest event detection task following the 2019 CLEF ProtestNews Lab (Hürriyetoğlu et al., 2019).[1] Protest events are identified as politically motivated collective actions which lay outside the official mechanisms of political participation of the country in which the action takes place.

The lab is organised around three non-overlapping subtasks: (a.) document classification; (b.) sentence classification; and (c.) event extraction. Tasks (a.) and (b.) are text classification tasks, requiring systems to distinguish whether a document/sentence is referring to a protest event. The event extraction task is a sequence tagging problem requiring systems to identify event triggers and their corresponding arguments, similarly to other event extraction tasks, e.g., ACE (Linguistic Data Consortium, 2005).

The lab is designed to challenge models' portability in an unsupervised setting: systems receive a training and development data belonging to one variety and are asked to test both against a dataset from the same variety and a different one. We report in Table 1 the distribution of the markables (event triggers and arguments) for event extraction across the two varieties. We refer to the same variety (or source) distributions as India and to the different variety (or target) as China.

		India		China
Markable	**Train**	**Dev.**	**Test**	**Test**
Triggers	844	126	215	144
Arguments	1,895	288	552	295

Table 1: Distribution of event triggers and arguments. India is source. China is target.

The data are good examples of differences across factors characterising language varieties. For instance, although they belong to the same text genre (news articles), they describe protest events from two countries that have historical and cultural differences concerning what is worth protesting (e.g., caste protests are specific to India) and the type of protests (e.g., riots *vs.* petitions). Differences in the political systems entail differences in the actors of the protest events which is mirrored in the named entities describing person or organization names. Language is a further challenge. Both datasets are in English but they present dialectal and stylistic differences.

We quantified differences and similarities by comparing the training data (India_{train}) against the two test ones (India_{test} and China_{test}) using the Jensen-Shannon (J-S) divergence and the out-of-vocabulary rate (OOV) that previous work has shown to be particularly useful for this purpose (Ruder and Plank, 2017). The figures in Table 2 better show how these data distributions occupy different regions in the variety space, with India_{test} being closer to the training data than China_{test}. Tackling these similarities and differences is at the heart of our domain adaptation problem for event extraction.

	J-S		OOV	
↓Train / Test→	**India**	**China**	**India**	**China**
India	0.703	0.575	44.33%	53.82%

Table 2: J-S (Similarity) and OOV (Diversity) between train and test distributions for the event extraction task.

A further challenge is posed by the limited amount of training material. A comparison against the training portion of ACE shows that ProtestNews has 5 times less triggers and 4 times less arguments.[2] Unlike ACE, event triggers are not further classified into subtypes. However, seven argument types are annotated, namely *participant*, *organiser*, *target*, *etime* (event time), *place*, *fname* (facility name), and *loc* (location). The role set is inspired by ACE Attack and Demonstrate event types but they are more fine-grained. The markables are encoded in a BIO scheme (Beginning, Inside, Outside), resulting in different alphabets for triggers (e.g. B-*trigger*, I-*trigger* and O) and each of the arguments (e.g. O, B-*organiser*, I-*organiser*, B-*etime*, I-*etime*, etc.).

3 Continue Pre-training to Adapt

We applied DAR to English BERT `base-uncased` to fill a gap in language variety between BERT, trained on the BooksCorpus and Wikipedia, and the ProtestNews's data.

We collected two sets of domain related data from the TREC Washington Post Corpus version

[1] `https://emw.ku.edu.tr/clef-protestnews-2019/`

[2] The training portion of ACE has 4,312 triggers and 7,811 arguments.

Model	Input Format	Overall			Triggers			Arguments		
		P	R	F1	P	R	F1	P	R	F1
BERT	Document	$51.52_{4.20}$	$42.68_{4.98}$	$46.23_{1.98}$	$78.97_{4.32}$	$63.72_{4.76}$	$70.25_{1.87}$	$31.50_{17.54}$	$29.61_{16.09}$	$29.94_{16.49}$
NEWS-BERT	Document	$36.11_{3.77}$	$33.63_{7.79}$	$34.18_{3.48}$	$69.96_{5.18}$	$52.00_{10.32}$	$58.87_{5.41}$	$22.61_{4.69}$	$20.96_{9.62}$	$19.96_{6.95}$
PROTEST-ER	Document	$\mathit{54.56}_{3.18}$	$48.47_{3.69}$	$51.11_{0.87}$	$70.48_{1.35}$	$67.90_{3.51}$	$69.08_{1.24}$	$37.59_{20.28}$	$40.20_{17.91}$	$37.86_{18.42}$
BERT	Sentence	$32.85_{6.27}$	$25.18_{6.61}$	$27.41_{4.19}$	$\mathit{80.01}_{5.98}$	$29.30_{13.03}$	$41.16_{12.81}$	$18.95_{15.46}$	$22.79_{17.38}$	$19.74_{15.43}$
NEWS-BERT	Sentence	$52.86_{8.83}$	$10.76_{1.94}$	$17.67_{2.32}$	$\mathbf{92.92}_{1.84}$	$9.83_{3.08}$	$18.24_{5.90}$	$29.47_{6.16}$	$10.15_{1.12}$	$14.46_{0.85}$
PROTEST-ER	Sentence	$49.91_{1.99}$	$\mathit{54.13}_{0.63}$	$\mathit{51.91}_{0.97}$	$77.63_{1.41}$	$\mathit{68.93}_{1.75}$	$\mathit{72.99}_{0.80}$	$\mathit{39.82}_{17.61}$	$\mathit{46.13}_{17.86}$	$\mathit{41.98}_{17.26}$
Best CLEF 2019	Sentence	**66.20**	**55.67**	**60.48**	79.79	**69.77**	**74.44**	**56.55**	**48.66**	**51.54**

Table 3: India data (source). Results for TLM are averaged over five runs. Standard deviation is reported in subscript. *Best* results correspond to the best system in the 2019 CLEF ProtestNews Lab tasks. Best scores are in bold. Second best scores are in italics.

Model	Input Format	Overall			Triggers			Arguments		
		P	R	F1	P	R	F1	P	R	F1
PROTEST-ER	Document	$\mathbf{64.48}_{5.01}$	$36.53_{2.76}$	$\mathit{46.39}_{1.02}$	$74.07_{4.74}$	$\mathit{69.30}_{5.66}$	$\mathit{71.23}_{1.05}$	$\mathit{42.70}_{18.68}$	$20.11_{14.83}$	$25.19_{14.71}$
PROTEST-ER	Sentence	$52.62_{5.34}$	$\mathit{39.18}_{3.25}$	$44.62_{1.97}$	$\mathit{74.08}_{3.20}$	$64.86_{7.44}$	$68.73_{2.75}$	$39.06_{16.03}$	$\mathit{23.56}_{11.99}$	$\mathit{27.02}_{11.81}$
Best CLEF 2019	Sentence	*62.65*	**46.24**	**53.21**	**77.27**	**70.83**	**73.91**	**49.64**	**33.57**	**39.56**

Table 4: China data (target). Results for TLM are averaged over five runs. Standard deviation is reported in subscript. *Best* results correspond to the best system in the 2019 CLEF ProtestNews Lab tasks. Best scores are in bold. Second best scores are in italics.

3[3] (WPC). The first collection (WPC-Gen) contains 100k random news articles. The second collection (WPC-Ev) contains all news articles related to an ongoing or past protest event for a total of 79,515 documents. The protest news articles have been automatically extracted with a specific BERT model for document classification trained and validated on an extended version of the document classification task from the ProtestNews Lab (Hürriyetoğlu et al., 2021). The model achieves an average F1-score of 90.15 on both India and China. We explicitly excluded as data for further pre-train BERT the CLEF 2019 India and China documents.

	J-S		OOV	
↓**DAR / Test**→	**India**	**China**	**India**	**China**
WPC-Gen	0.583	0.594	12.17%	4.38%
WPC-Ev	0.562	0.569	11.61%	4.46%

Table 5: J-S (Similarity) and OOV (Diversity) between the DAR datasets WPC-Gen and WPC-EV and the and test data distributions for the event extraction task.

We apply each data collection separately BERT `base-uncased` by further training for 100 epochs using the MLM objective. The outcomes are two pre-trained language models: NEWS-BERT and PROTEST-ER. The differences between the models are assumed to be minimal but yet relevant to assess the impact of the data used for DAR. To further support this claim we report in Table 5 an analysis of the similarities and differences of the DAR data materials against the India and China test data. As the figures show, the DAR datasets are equally different from the protest event extraction ones. Furthermore, we did not modify BERT original vocabulary by introducing new tokens. More details on the retraining parameters are reported in the Appendix A.1.

[3] `https://trec.nist.gov/data/wapost/`

4 Experiments and Results

Event extraction is framed as a token-level classification task. We adopt a joint strategy where triggers' and arguments' extent and labels are predicted at once (Nguyen et al., 2016). We used $India_{test}$ to identify the best model (NEWS-BERT *vs.* PROTEST-ER) and system's input granularity. With respect to this latter point, we investigate whether processing data at document or sentence level could benefit the TLMs as a strategy to deal with limited training materials. We compare each configuration against a generic BERT counterpart. We fine-tune each model by training all the parameters simultaneously. All models are evaluated using the official script from the ProtestNews Lab. Triggers and arguments are correctly identified only if both the extent and the label are correct. We apply to China only the best model and input format.

India data Results for India are illustrated in Table 3. In general, PROTEST-ER obtains better results than BERT and NEWS-BERT. Sentence qualifies as the best input format for PROTEST-ER, while document works best for NEWS-BERT and

BERT.

The language variety of the data distributions used for DAR has a big impact on the performance of fine-tuned systems, with NEWS-BERT being the worst model. The extra training should have made this model more suited for working with news articles than the corresponding generic BERT. This indicates that selection of suitable data is an essential step for successfully applying DAR.

Globally, the results show that DAR has a positive effect on Precision, especially when sentences are used as input for fine tuning the models. Positive effects on Recall can only be observed for PROTEST-ER.

With the exclusion of NEWS-BERT, the systems achieve satisfying results for the trigger component. Argument detection, as expected, is more challenging, with no model reaching an F1-score above 50%. PROTEST-ER always performs better, especially when processing the data at sentence level. In numerical terms, PROTEST-ER provides an average gain of 11.74 points. [4] We observe a relationship between argument type frequency in the training data and models's performance where the most frequent arguments, i.e., *participant* (26.43%), *organizer* (18.31%), and *place* (14.45%), obtain the best results. However, PROTEST-ER improves performances also on the least frequent argument types, i.e., *loc* (6.49%) and *fname* (5.85) of, respectively, 12.00 and 5.38 points on average, when compared to BERT.

China data Results for China are reported in Table 4. We applied only PROTEST-ER keeping the distinction between document *vs.* sentence input. Although using sentences as input leads to the best results for India, we also observe that the results of the document input models are competitive, leaving open questions whether such a way of processing the input could be an effective strategy for model portability for event extraction. The results clearly indicate that PROTEST-ER is a competitive and pretty robust system. Interestingly, we observe that on the China data, the best results are obtained when processing data at document level.

Looking at the portability for the event components, it clearly appears that arguments are more difficult than triggers. Indeed, the absolute F1-score of the best models for triggers is in the same range of that for India. When focusing on the arguments, the drops in performances severely affect all argument types, except for *fname*. We also observe that the biggest drops are registered in those arguments that are most likely to express domain specific properties. For instance, the absolute F1-score difference between the best models for India and China for *place* is 39.79 points, 36.29 for *organizer*, and 27.11 for *etime*. On the contrary, only a drop of 9.84 points is observed for *participant*, suggesting that ways of indicating those who take part to a protest event (e.g. protesters, or rioters) are closer than expected.

5 Discussion and Conclusions

Our results indicate that DAR is an effective strategy for unsupervised domain adaptation. However, we show that not every data distribution matching a potential target domain has the same impact. In our case, we measure improvements only when using data that more directly target the content of the task, i.e., protest events, possibly supplementing limitations in training materials. We have gathered interesting cues that processing data at document level can actually be an effective strategy also for a sequence labeling task with small training data. We think that this approach allows the TLMs to gain from processing longer sequences and acquire better knowledge. However, more experiments on different tasks (e.g., NER) and with different training sizes are needed to test this hypothesis.

A further positive aspect of DAR is that it requires less training material to boost system's performance, pointing to new directions for few-shot learning. We projected the learning curves of BERT and PROTEST-ER using increasing steps of the training data. PROTEST-ER achieves an overall F1-score ~30% with only 10% of the training data, while BERT needs minimally 30% to achieve comparable performances (see Appendix A.3).

Disappointingly, PROTEST-ER falls way back the best model that participated in Protest-News. Skitalinskaya et al. (2019) propose a Bi-LSTM-CRF architecture using FLAIR contextualized word embeddings (Akbik et al., 2018). They also adopt a joint strategy for trigger and argument prediction. PROTEST-ER obtains a better Precision only on China for the overall evaluation and for trigger. Quite surprisingly, on India it is BERT that achieves better results on trigger, although the model appears to be quite unstable, as shown by the standard deviation. At this stage, it is still unclear whether these disappointing performances are due to the retraining (i.e., need to extend the number of documents used) or the small training corpus.

[4] This figure has been obtained by grouping the scores of all models using the retrained version, regardless of the input format.

Future work will focus on two aspects. First, we will further investigate the impact of the size of the training data when using TLMs. This will require to experiment with different datasets and tasks. Secondly, we will explore solutions for multilingual extensions of PROTEST-ER.

Acknowledgments

The authors from Koc University were funded by the European Research Council (ERC) Starting Grant 714868 awarded to Dr. Erdem Yörük for his project Emerging Welfare.

References

Martín Abadi, Paul Barham, Jianmin Chen, Zhifeng Chen, Andy Davis, Jeffrey Dean, Matthieu Devin, Sanjay Ghemawat, Geoffrey Irving, Michael Isard, Manjunath Kudlur, Josh Levenberg, Rajat Monga, Sherry Moore, Derek G. Murray, Benoit Steiner, Paul Tucker, Vijay Vasudevan, Pete Warden, Martin Wicke, Yuan Yu, and Xiaoqiang Zheng. 2016. Tensorflow: A system for large-scale machine learning. In *12th USENIX Symposium on Operating Systems Design and Implementation (OSDI 16)*, pages 265–283, Savannah, GA. USENIX Association.

Alan Akbik, Duncan Blythe, and Roland Vollgraf. 2018. Contextual string embeddings for sequence labeling. In *Proceedings of the 27th International Conference on Computational Linguistics*, pages 1638–1649, Santa Fe, New Mexico, USA. Association for Computational Linguistics.

Firoj Alam, Shafiq Joty, and Muhammad Imran. 2018. Domain adaptation with adversarial training and graph embeddings. In *Proceedings of the 56th Annual Meeting of the Association for Computational Linguistics (Volume 1: Long Papers)*, pages 1077–1087, Melbourne, Australia. Association for Computational Linguistics.

Amittai Axelrod, Xiaodong He, and Jianfeng Gao. 2011. Domain adaptation via pseudo in-domain data selection. In *Proceedings of the 2011 Conference on Empirical Methods in Natural Language Processing*, pages 355–362, Edinburgh, Scotland, UK. Association for Computational Linguistics.

Eyal Ben-David, Carmel Rabinovitz, and Roi Reichart. 2020. PERL: Pivot-based domain adaptation for pre-trained deep contextualized embedding models. *Transactions of the Association for Computational Linguistics*, 8:504–521.

John Blitzer, Ryan McDonald, and Fernando Pereira. 2006. Domain adaptation with structural correspondence learning. In *Proceedings of the 2006 conference on empirical methods in natural language processing*, pages 120–128. Association for Computational Linguistics.

Hal Daumé III. 2007. Frustratingly easy domain adaptation. In *Proceedings of the 45th Annual Meeting of the Association of Computational Linguistics*, pages 256–263, Prague, Czech Republic. Association for Computational Linguistics.

Jacob Devlin, Ming-Wei Chang, Kenton Lee, and Kristina Toutanova. 2019. BERT: Pre-training of deep bidirectional transformers for language understanding. In *Proceedings of the 2019 Conference of the North American Chapter of the Association for Computational Linguistics: Human Language Technologies, Volume 1 (Long and Short Papers)*, pages 4171–4186, Minneapolis, Minnesota. Association for Computational Linguistics.

Yaroslav Ganin and Victor Lempitsky. 2015. Unsupervised domain adaptation by backpropagation. In *International conference on machine learning*, pages 1180–1189. PMLR.

Yaroslav Ganin, Evgeniya Ustinova, Hana Ajakan, Pascal Germain, Hugo Larochelle, François Laviolette, Mario Marchand, and Victor Lempitsky. 2016. Domain-adversarial training of neural networks. *The Journal of Machine Learning Research*, 17(1):2096–2030.

Jiang Guo, Darsh Shah, and Regina Barzilay. 2018. Multi-source domain adaptation with mixture of experts. In *Proceedings of the 2018 Conference on Empirical Methods in Natural Language Processing*, pages 4694–4703, Brussels, Belgium. Association for Computational Linguistics.

Suchin Gururangan, Ana Marasović, Swabha Swayamdipta, Kyle Lo, Iz Beltagy, Doug Downey, and Noah A. Smith. 2020. Don't stop pretraining: Adapt language models to domains and tasks. In *Proceedings of the 58th Annual Meeting of the Association for Computational Linguistics*, pages 8342–8360, Online. Association for Computational Linguistics.

Xiaochuang Han and Jacob Eisenstein. 2019. Unsupervised domain adaptation of contextualized embeddings for sequence labeling. In *Proceedings of the 2019 Conference on Empirical Methods in Natural Language Processing and the 9th International Joint Conference on Natural Language Processing (EMNLP-IJCNLP)*, pages 4238–4248, Hong Kong, China. Association for Computational Linguistics.

Matthew Honnibal, Ines Montani, Sofie Van Landeghem, and Adriane Boyd. 2020. spaCy: Industrial-strength Natural Language Processing in Python.

Ali Hürriyetoğlu, Erdem Yörük, Deniz Yüret, Çağrı Yoltar, Burak Gürel, Fırat Duruşan, Osman Mutlu, and Arda Akdemir. 2019. Overview of clef 2019 lab protestnews: Extracting protests from news in a cross-context setting. In *Experimental IR Meets Multilinguality, Multimodality, and Interaction*, pages 425–432, Cham. Springer International Publishing.

Ali Hürriyetoğlu, Erdem Yörük, Osman Mutlu, Fırat Duruşan, Çağrı Yoltar, Deniz Yüret, and Burak Gürel. 2021. Cross-Context News Corpus for Protest Event-Related Knowledge Base Construction. *Data Intelligence*, pages 1–28.

Linguistic Data Consortium. 2005. *ACE (Automatic Content Extraction) English Annotation Guidelines for Events*, 5.4.3 2005.07.01 edition.

David McClosky, Eugene Charniak, and Mark Johnson. 2006. Reranking and self-training for parser adaptation. In *Proceedings of the 21st International Conference on Computational Linguistics and 44th Annual Meeting of the Association for Computational Linguistics*, pages 337–344, Sydney, Australia. Association for Computational Linguistics.

Timothy Miller. 2019. Simplified neural unsupervised domain adaptation. In *Proceedings of the 2019 Conference of the North American Chapter of the Association for Computational Linguistics: Human Language Technologies, Volume 1 (Long and Short Papers)*, pages 414–419, Minneapolis, Minnesota. Association for Computational Linguistics.

Robert C. Moore and William Lewis. 2010. Intelligent selection of language model training data. In *Proceedings of the ACL 2010 Conference Short Papers*, pages 220–224, Uppsala, Sweden. Association for Computational Linguistics.

Thien Huu Nguyen, Kyunghyun Cho, and Ralph Grishman. 2016. Joint event extraction via recurrent neural networks. In *Proceedings of the 2016 Conference of the North American Chapter of the Association for Computational Linguistics: Human Language Technologies*, pages 300–309, San Diego, California. Association for Computational Linguistics.

Kosuke Nishida, Kyosuke Nishida, Itsumi Saito, Hisako Asano, and Junji Tomita. 2020. Unsupervised domain adaptation of language models for reading comprehension. In *Proceedings of the 12th Language Resources and Evaluation Conference*, pages 5392–5399, Marseille, France. European Language Resources Association.

Barbara Plank and Gertjan van Noord. 2011. Effective measures of domain similarity for parsing. In *Proceedings of the 49th Annual Meeting of the Association for Computational Linguistics: Human Language Technologies*, pages 1566–1576, Portland, Oregon, USA. Association for Computational Linguistics.

Alan Ramponi and Barbara Plank. 2020. Neural unsupervised domain adaptation in NLP—A survey. In *Proceedings of the 28th International Conference on Computational Linguistics*, pages 6838–6855, Barcelona, Spain (Online). International Committee on Computational Linguistics.

Alexander Rietzler, Sebastian Stabinger, Paul Opitz, and Stefan Engl. 2020. Adapt or get left behind: Domain adaptation through BERT language model finetuning for aspect-target sentiment classification. In *Proceedings of the 12th Language Resources and Evaluation Conference*, pages 4933–4941, Marseille, France. European Language Resources Association.

Sebastian Ruder and Barbara Plank. 2017. Learning to select data for transfer learning with bayesian optimization. In *Proceedings of the 2017 Conference on Empirical Methods in Natural Language Processing*, pages 372–382, Copenhagen, Denmark. Association for Computational Linguistics.

Gabriella Skitalinskaya, Jonas Klaff, and Maximilian Spliethöver. 2019. Clef protestnews lab 2019: Contextualized word embeddings for event sentence detection and event extraction. In *CLEF (Working Notes)*.

Thomas Wolf, Lysandre Debut, Victor Sanh, Julien Chaumond, Clement Delangue, Anthony Moi, Pierric Cistac, Tim Rault, Remi Louf, Morgan Funtowicz, Joe Davison, Sam Shleifer, Patrick von Platen, Clara Ma, Yacine Jernite, Julien Plu, Canwen Xu, Teven Le Scao, Sylvain Gugger, Mariama Drame, Quentin Lhoest, and Alexander Rush. 2020. Transformers: State-of-the-art natural language processing. In *Proceedings of the 2020 Conference on Empirical Methods in Natural Language Processing: System Demonstrations*, pages 38–45, Online. Association for Computational Linguistics.

Shaoan Xie, Zibin Zheng, Liang Chen, and Chuan Chen. 2018. Learning semantic representations for unsupervised domain adaptation. In *International Conference on Machine Learning*, pages 5423–5432.

Hu Xu, Bing Liu, Lei Shu, and Philip Yu. 2019. BERT post-training for review reading comprehension and aspect-based sentiment analysis. In *Proceedings of the 2019 Conference of the North American Chapter of the Association for Computational Linguistics: Human Language Technologies, Volume 1 (Long and Short Papers)*, pages 2324–2335, Minneapolis, Minnesota. Association for Computational Linguistics.

Sicheng Zhao, Bo Li, Xiangyu Yue, Yang Gu, Pengfei Xu, Runbo Hu, Hua Chai, and Kurt Keutzer. 2019. Multi-source domain adaptation for semantic segmentation. In *Advances in Neural Information Processing Systems*, volume 32, pages 7287–7300. Curran Associates, Inc.

A Appendices

A.1 BERT-NEWS/PROTEST-ER Further Training

Preprocessing The unlabeled corpora of (protest related) news articles from the TREC Washington Post version 3 are minimally preprocessed prior to the language model retraining phase. We use the full text, including the title, of each news article. Document Creation Times are removed. We perform sentence splitting using `spaCy` (Honnibal et al., 2020).

Training details We further train the English BERT `base-uncased` for 100 epochs. We use a batch size of 64 through gradient accumulation. Other hyperparameters are illustrated in Table 6. Our TLM implementation uses the `HuggingFace` library (Wolf et al., 2020). The pretrainig experiment was performed on a single Nvidia V100 GPU and took 8 days.

Hyperparameter	**Value**
optimizer	adam
adam_epsilon	1e-08
learning rate	5e-05
logging steps	500
mlm probability	0.15
gradient accumulation steps	4
per gpu train batch size	16
max grad norm	1.0
pretrained model	bert-base-uncased
max-tokens	512
max epochs	100
random seed	42

Table 6: Hyperparameter configuration used for generating PROTEST-ER.

A.2 BERT/PROTEST-ER Fine-tuning

Table 7 shows the values of the hyperparameters used for fine-tuning BERT and PROTEST-ER. We used Tensorflow (Abadi et al., 2016) for the implementation and the `Huggingface` library (Wolf et al., 2020) for implementing the BERT embeddings and loading the data. We used the CRF implementation available from the Tensorflow Addons package.

The models are trained for a maximum of 100 epochs, using a constant learning rate of 2e-5; if the validation loss does not improve for 5 consecutive epochs, training is stopped. The best model is selected on the basis of the validation loss. We manually experimented with the learning rates 1e-5, 2e-5, 3e-5. No other hyperparameter optimization was performed.

Hyperparameter	**Value**
learning rate	2e-5
learning rate schedule	constant
clipnorm	1.0
optimizer	adam
dropout	0.1
max-tokens	512
max epochs	100
random seed	42

Table 7: Hyperparameter configuration used for task finetuning.

We used the original train, validation, and test splits of the event extraction task of the 2019 CLEF ProtestNews Lab.

We conducted all the experiments using the Google Colaboratory platform. The time required to run all the experiments on the free plan of Colaboratory is approximately 20 hours. Figure 1 graphically illustrates the base architecture.

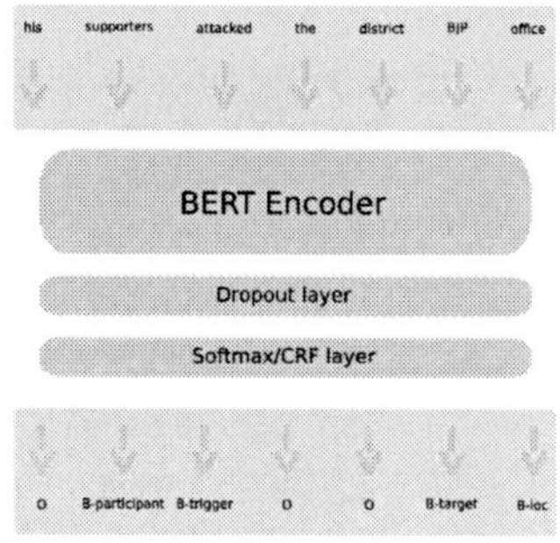

Figure 1: The base model architecture for the token classifier.

A.3 BERT/PROTEST-ER Learning Curves

In the following graphs we plot the learning curves of the BERT and PROTEST-ER model on the India and China dataset. In both cases, we observe that PROTEST-ER obtains competitive scores just using 10% of the training data, suggesting that the TLM's representations are already shifted towards the protest domain. To obtain the same results, the generic BERT models need minimally 30% of the training data, when using documents as input, and 70% of the training, when using sentences.

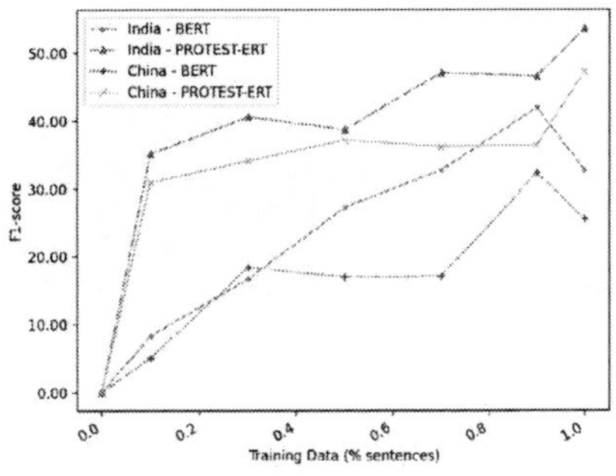

Figure 2: Learning curve for event extraction (triggers and arguments) for BERT and PROTEST-ER models on India and China, according to different portions (percentages) of the training materials (input granularity: **sentence**). Input data are randomly selected.

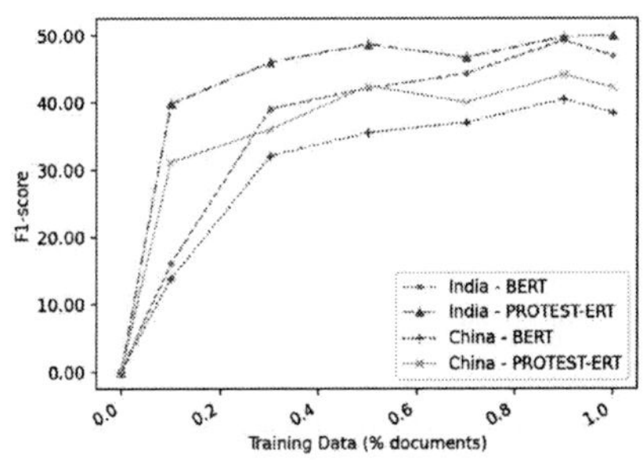

Figure 3: Learning curve for event extraction (triggers and arguments) for BERT and PROTEST-ER models on India and China, according to different portions (percentages) of the training materials (input granularity: **document**). Input data are randomly selected.

ArgFuse: A Weakly-Supervised Framework for Document-Level Event Argument Aggregation

Debanjana Kar[1], **Sudeshna Sarkar**[2], and **Pawan Goyal**[3]

Department of Computer Science & Engineering
Indian Institute of Technology, Kharagpur.
[1]debanjana.kar@iitkgp.ac.in
[2,3]{*sudeshna, pawang*}@*cse.iitkgp.ac.in*

Abstract

Most of the existing information extraction frameworks (Wadden et al., 2019; Veyseh et al., 2020) focus on sentence-level tasks and are hardly able to capture the consolidated information from a given document. In our endeavour to generate precise document-level information frames from lengthy textual records, we introduce the task of Information Aggregation or Argument Aggregation. More specifically, our aim is to filter irrelevant and redundant argument mentions that were extracted at a sentence level and render a document level information frame. Majority of the existing works have been observed to resolve related tasks of document-level event argument extraction (Yang et al., 2018; Zheng et al., 2019) and salient entity identification (Jain et al., 2020) using supervised techniques. To remove dependency from large amounts of labeled data, we explore the task of information aggregation using weakly-supervised techniques. In particular, we present an extractive algorithm with multiple sieves which adopts active learning strategies to work efficiently in low-resource settings. For this task, we have annotated our own test dataset comprising of 131 document information frames and have released the code and dataset to further research prospects in this new domain. To the best of our knowledge, we are the first to establish baseline results for this task in English. Our data and code are publicly available at `https://github.com/DebanjanaKar/ArgFuse`

Indonesia cyclone death toll more than doubles to 41

JAKARTA: A tropical cyclone that pounded Indonesia's main island of Java has killed 41 people, the country's disaster agency said on Tuesday - more than double the initial toll with tens of thousands displaced by severe flooding and landslides. Among the victims of Cyclone Cempaka were 25 people killed by a single landslide in east Java last week the agency said. Some 28000 people have been displaced by the cyclone which hit Indonesia's most populous island last week. Almost five thousand homes have been damaged and more than three thousand others were inundated by flooding said agency spokesman Sutopo Purwo Nugroho. Cempaka has moved away from Indonesia but Nugroho warned that more flooding and landslides still could happen. Indonesia is prone to natural disasters and is often hit by floods and landslides. A landslide on Bali in February killed 12 people including three children.

TIME-ARG: last week
PLACE-ARG: Indonesia's main island of Java
CASUALTIES-ARG: killed 41 people
AFTER_EFFECTS-ARG: 28000 people have been displaced, Almost five thousand homes have been damaged and more than three thousand others were inundated

Figure 1: Example document excerpt from our corpus highlighting the different challenges of the aggregation task. The phrases highlighted in red, blue and green denote the redundant, irrelevant and exclusive sentence-level arguments respectively. The document level arguments are as reported at the end of the example.

1 Introduction

Extraction of event argument information at a document level is an important non-trivial task that requires a system to have advanced natural language understanding capabilities. Most of the existing event-argument extraction systems (Nguyen et al., 2016; Luan et al., 2019; Wadden et al., 2019; Veyseh et al., 2020) pertain to a sentence-level focus, often circumventing to capture information at a document-level. Among the few existing works that have researched the task of document-level event argument extraction, we observe that unsupervised techniques like (Hamborg et al., 2019) lack the capacity to identify complex argument mentions, while sophisticated supervised mechanisms like that of (Yang et al., 2018; Zheng et al., 2019) rely on large amounts of annotated corpus and present domain-specific solutions.

While supervised techniques may often produce highly accurate systems, in real life, annotating a large corpus can be both very expensive and time consuming. In order to surmount the existing shortcomings coupled with the challenging scenario of data scarcity, we propose our model *ArgFuse*. ArgFuse focuses on extraction of relevant and non-redundant event arguments at a document

Proceedings of the 4th Workshop on Challenges and Applications of Automated Extraction of Socio-political Events from Text (CASE), pages 20–30
August 5–6, 2021, ©2021 Association for Computational Linguistics

level scope. The task of document level event argument extraction typically focuses on extracting argument mentions associated with an event type or event trigger from a document. It does not involve checking extracted arguments for irrelevant and redundant mentions. Through our work, we also propose the related task of Argument Aggregation which focuses on assessing extracted arguments for irrelevance and redundancy to produce a precise aggregated document-level information frame. Figure 1 provides an illustrative example of our task while highlighting the different challenges the task presents.

The task presents itself with multiple challenges and avenues to explore. To produce a precise document-level information frame, we focus on sieving irrelevant and redundant sentence-level argument mentions. Irrelevant argument mentions, as illustrated in Figure 1 refer to argument mentions that do not contribute to the topical focus of the document. A category of irrelevant arguments often encountered in real life news articles are past event records mentioned in narratives to provide a comparative perspective to the reader, much like the arguments in blue mentioned in Figure 1. While irrelevant arguments are usually mentions that refer to past, future or unrelated events; redundancy in arguments manifests in diverse forms. Redundant arguments can either be i) duplicate argument mentions (e.g. *last week*), ii) arguments with similar surface form (e.g. *Indonesia, Indonesia's main Island Java)*, iii) re-worded (e.g. *killed 41 people, death toll more than doubles to 41*), or iv) subsuming information of the other argument(s) (e.g. *killed 41 people, 25 people killed*). While the first two types of redundancy can be tackled by simple heuristics, the detection of the remaining types of redundancy requires implicit natural language understanding and coreference reasoning capabilities. To filter such arguments effectively, we realised that contextual information of a document is imperative. The argument mentions in green illustrated in Figure 1 highlight arguments which impart unique information with respect to the context of the document. These argument mentions cannot be aggregated and are directly added to the output information frame. We refer to such argument mentions in our work as *exclusive argument* mentions.

Based on the different types of arguments we encounter, we propose an extractive algorithm that aggregates sentence-level argument or entity mentions to produce precise document-level information frames from lengthy text articles effectively. In our work, we present an end-to-end framework to extract events and arguments from English news articles and present an aggregated information frame at the document level. Given that we introduce a novel task with no prior labeled dataset, we present a weakly-supervised algorithm to achieve our task with a good accuracy. Our contributions in this work are two fold:

1. We propose a novel task of document-level event-argument aggregation and establish baseline for the same. We also release the first annotated test dataset for this task with 131 aggregated document information frames.

2. We propose a weakly supervised model to aggregate event-arguments at a document-level. We deeply analyse the task, dataset and algorithm proposed in this paper, thus highlighting areas of future research and development.

In the following sections, we discuss our dataset, algorithms and findings in detail. Our analysis emphasizes on the importance of having document level information extraction frameworks for the task of argument aggregation and we invite the research community to further investigate this task.

2 Related Work

Event argument extraction is a well researched information extraction task which has seen a lot of work at the sentence-level (Wang et al., 2019; Wadden et al., 2019; Nguyen et al., 2016; Luan et al., 2019; Veyseh et al., 2020) but a scarce amount of research has been carried out at the document level. Recent literature on event argument extraction at a document level include the works of (Yang et al., 2018) and (Zheng et al., 2019). While (Zheng et al., 2019)'s work explores supervised transformer based techniques to extract events and arguments from Chinese financial documents, (Yang et al., 2018) employs Bi-LSTM based classifiers on a subset of the same dataset to extract events first at the sentence level followed by a document level extraction similar to our framework. (Jain et al., 2020) employs a BiLSTM-CRF classifier to finetune SciBERT(Beltagy et al., 2019) on various document-level information extraction tasks including the related task of salient entity clustering. All of these methods employ supervised techniques which call for a large corpus of annotated dataset, making it difficult to adopt to domains and tasks with no labelled annotations. (Hamborg et al., 2019) presents an unsupervised approach of extracting document level information from news documents, but the heuristics adopted in their work do not extend well to our task which involves more complex argument mentions. The limited amount of research that exists in this domain does not explore the task of aggregation in particular, where, given a set of arguments referring to the same concept, the most informative argument is selected to represent that knowledge. We propose a novel task and present an end-to-end baseline solution to extract and aggregate document-level arguments which presents a complete overview of the document without minimal loss of information. In our work, we employ ranking strategies as part of our aggregation process. Some of the classic works related to the task of ranking text snippets are that of PageRank (Page et al., 1998) and TextRank (Mihalcea and Tarau, 2004).

3 Dataset

One of the main challenges that we faced was the unavailability of annotated resources for this task. For our auxiliary task of sentence level event argument extraction, we use the dataset adopted by (Kar et al., 2021). The dataset is available in five Indian languages but for this task, we only use the English dataset. The dataset covers 32 event types at a fine grain level and 12 event types at a coarse level. The dataset contains annotations for 14 argument types, but in our work we focus on 6 main argument types which are, *Time, Place, Casualties, After-Effect, Reason* and *Participant*. In the sections to follow we discuss regarding the scarcely available document-level annotated resources and the details of the annotated dataset we release with this work.

3.1 Existing Document-Level IE Datasets

Information Extraction (IE) is a well-researched domain albeit mostly at the sentence-level. Event-Argument Extraction, the IE task most related to the task of aggregation has a number of well-documented and reliable datasets annotated at the sentence level in different languages like ACE 2005 and TAC KBP (Mitamura et al., 2015) datasets. IE tasks with a document-level focus have gained attention in recent times but there are hardly any document-level event argument annotated datasets. We discuss two recent works that include document-level event argument or entity mention annotations here; the RAMS (Ebner et al., 2020) and the SciREX (Jain et al., 2020) dataset. The RAMS dataset is not particularly document-level, but explores the task of extracting argument roles beyond sentences. In a 5-sentence window of a news article around each event trigger, they annotate the closest span for each argument role. Their ontology consists of 139 event types and 65 argument roles. The SciREX dataset is a comprehensive dataset comprising of document-level annotations for a variety of IE tasks. The dataset consists of annotations for related tasks like entity recognition and coreference on 438 scientific articles. However, none of these datasets provide consolidated argument annotations for an entire document. To the best of our knowledge, we are the first to introduce a document-level event-argument annotated dataset in English which provides an aggregated overview of the document, that is, the first annotated dataset for the task of Event-Argument Aggregation in English.

3.2 ArgFuse Dataset

Most of our work employs weakly-supervised techniques for curation of document level information frames but for sound testing of our final model we manually aggregate document-level arguments for each argument type from the 131 English documents in the test set of the above mentioned dataset. Each information frame for a document contains the event-type and the corresponding relevant arguments for each argument type from the document. During curation of the test set, we followed certain annotation guidelines defined for each argument type. The guidelines contain detailed instructions for identifying relevant arguments at a document level. For example, if the *Time* arguments of a document mention different degrees of temporal expressions like day, month and hour of the day, all the arguments are to be considered as relevant and aggregation is not required. The dataset was curated by two research scholars with good domain knowledge. We report the statistics of our dataset in Figures 2 and 3. In figure 2 we can observe the amount of redundancy and irrelevance prevalent in the extracted sentence-level information. In figure 3, we observe that although a number of argument roles in a document constitute of a single relevant argument mention (referred to as *Singles*), a significant number of argument roles constitute of multiple number of relevant argument mentions (referred to as *Multiples*). This highlights the fact that the number of relevant arguments for a particular argument role or type can be flexible and the model should be able to accommodate that flexibility. We release the manually annotated test set along with the annotation guidelines to further research prospects in this novel task.[1]

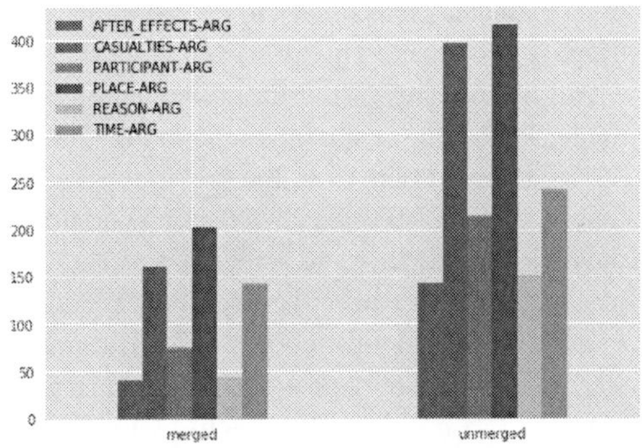

Figure 2: Distribution of sentence-level and document-level argument mentions in the annotated ArgFuse dataset. In the figure, merged refers to document-level annotations and unmerged refers to sentence-level annotations.

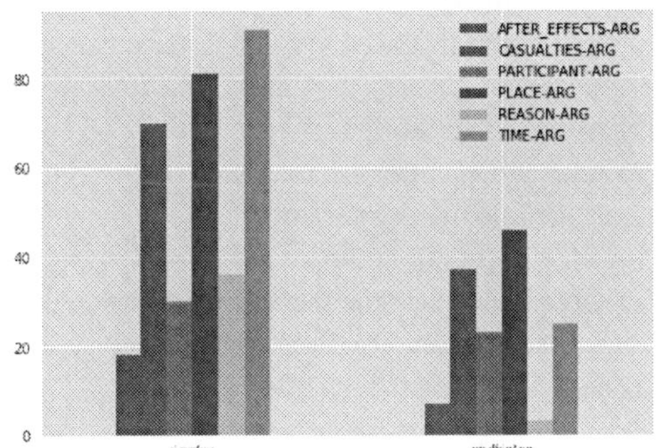

Figure 3: Distribution of single and multiple argument mentions among the document-level arguments in the annotated ArgFuse dataset. *Singles* refer to a category of argument roles which constitute of a single argument mention and *Multiples* refer to a category of argument roles which constitute of more than one relevant argument mentions at a document-level.

[1]https://github.com/DebanjanaKar/ArgFuse

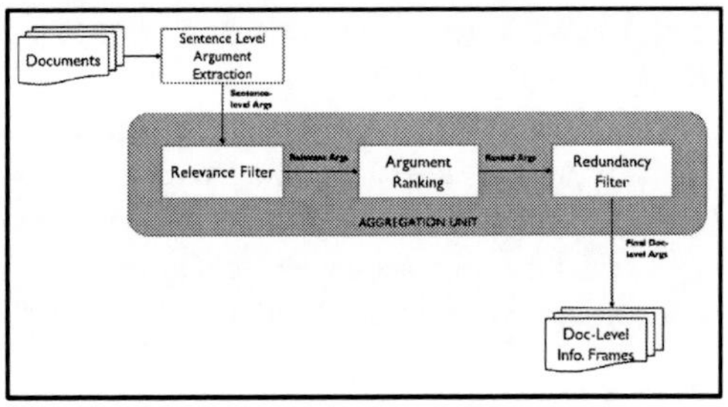

Figure 4: General overview of the complete argument aggregation framework.

4 Information Aggregation

In this section, we detail the approaches that were taken to build a weakly-supervised argument aggregation framework. The framework primarily involves two main modules: i) Sentence-level Information Extraction (IE), which extracts the sentence-level arguments along with their event type, the ii) Aggregation Unit, which renders document-level information frames. A general overview of the pipeline is illustrated in Figure 4. We explain each of these modules in detail in the sections to follow.

4.1 Event Argument Extraction

Given a document D of event type E, the objective of this sub-task is to extract the argument label sequence $(y_1, ..., y_n)$ for the corresponding word sequence $(x_1, ..., x_n)$, n being the number of tokens in D. For example, for a given document: *"The flood waters destroyed 500 homes in Assam ..."*, the corresponding label sequence would be: 'O O O AFTER_EFFECTS_ARG AFTER_EFFECTS_ARG AFTER_EFFECTS_ARG O PLACE_ARG ...'. To ensure high accuracy and low error propagation, we have adopted (Kar et al., 2021)'s approach of sentence-level event argument extraction using causal knowledge structures for this sub-task. (Kar et al., 2021)'s approach provides state-of-the-art results on the INDEE dataset (Maheshwari et al., 2020) and ensures efficient extraction of the low resource, complex causal arguments like *Reason* and *After-Effects* using the specially designed causality feature. The causality feature for each event consists of words and phrases which are used frequently in a causal context for particular event scenarios. The input document, concatenated with the feature at either extremes is encoded using a fine-tuned BERT encoder and each token is ultimately classified to one of the six argument types in the TO format (adopted from (Maheshwari et al.,

2020)). While we adopt (Kar et al., 2021)'s approach in our work, the event extraction module can be easily substituted with more suitable models in the future thus leveraging the modular nature of our algorithm. Using (Kar et al., 2021)'s approach, we extract the sentence-level event arguments for our corpus with an F1 score of 86.12%.

4.2 Aggregation

The aggregation unit is the primary module which identifies the most relevant and informative arguments from a pool of sentence-level argument mentions at a document-level scope. As illustrated in Figure 4, the aggregation unit consists of i) the Relevance Filter, which sieves the irrelevant arguments, ii) the Argument Ranking module, which ranks the arguments based on their informativeness and iii) the Redundancy Filter, which sieves the redundant arguments at a document level. The detailed architecture of the aggregation unit is illustrated in Figure 5.

4.2.1 Relevance Filter

Sentence-level IE outputs have often been observed to contain arguments that are not relevant to the document's focus. The main task of the Relevance Filter unit is to sieve such arguments. Given the extracted sentence level arguments of a particular argument type along with the context of its constituent document, the relevance filter proceeds to classify each argument mention as relevant or not. Since we did not possess labelled samples for this task, we manually annotated 500 training and 100 test instances. We observe that identifying irrelevant instances is relatively easier with explicit contextual and syntactic cues. Hence, on fine-tuning a ROBERTA-based classifier for our subtask,even with a very limited number of training instances, we obtain an F1 score of 85%. The performance metrics of the relevance filter is detailed in Table 1.

4.2.2 Redundancy Filter

Detection of redundant arguments is comparatively more challenging compared to the sub-task of relevance detection. While certain groups of argument mentions are explicitly redundant (eg. duplicate mentions, substrings), other groups of redundant argument mentions are more implicit in nature. To effectively identify redundant arguments in a low-resource setting, we employ active learning strategies. Given a pair of arguments (a_i, a_j) along with the context of it's constituent document, we train a binary classifier to maximize $P(y|a_i, a_j)$, where $y = 1$, if (a_i, a_j) are redundant else $y = 0$. To train a binary classifier for such a task, a large annotated corpus would have been effective but in the absence of such a corpus, we adopt the effective technique of active learning with 1045 manually annotated seed instances. After each epoch of active learning, 50 most uncertain samples are identified using the Monte Carlo estimation of error reduction (Roy and McCallum, 2001). These samples are then manually annotated and transferred from the pool of unannotated test samples to the list of annotated training instances. This process is repeated until we do not see any further improvement in the F1 Score. Based on the findings reported in (Hu et al., 2018), to avoid bias from the previous epoch, we fine-tune the pre-trained BERT-based classifier on the entire annotated dataset for every run of active learning. Once we have the necessary annotations derived from the multi-epoch active learning session, we train our binary classifier using all the annotated samples for 15 epochs. Our relevance filter is evaluated in Table 1.

4.3 Inference

The steps followed during inference are illustrated in Figure 5. The process starts by employing the trained Relevance filter to segregate relevant argument mentions from irrelevant ones. The relevant argument mentions are then ranked based on their informativeness. Given a list of argument-mentions $(arg_1, arg_2, ..., arg_m)$; m being the total number of mentions in the list of type t, our objective is to rank the mentions based on which argument instance imparts greater knowledge about the document's event. To compare the informativeness of the arguments, we rank the arguments using the unsupervised Biased TextRank (Kazemi et al., 2020). Biased TextRank is formally defined as:

$$R(V_i) = BiasWeight * (1 - d) + d * R^{'}(V_i)$$
$$R^{'}(V_i) = \sum_{V_j \in In(V_i)} \frac{w_{ij}}{\sum_{V_k \in Out(V_j)} w_{jk}} * R(V_j)$$

where, $R(V_i)$ is the score assigned to the vertex V_i, $In(V_i)$ denotes the incoming and $Out(V_i)$ denotes the outgoing edges from the vertex V_i. The damping factor d is set to 0.85. In our task, each of the arguments in the list correspond to a vertex and the vertices are connected by a weighted edge. The weight of each edge is determined

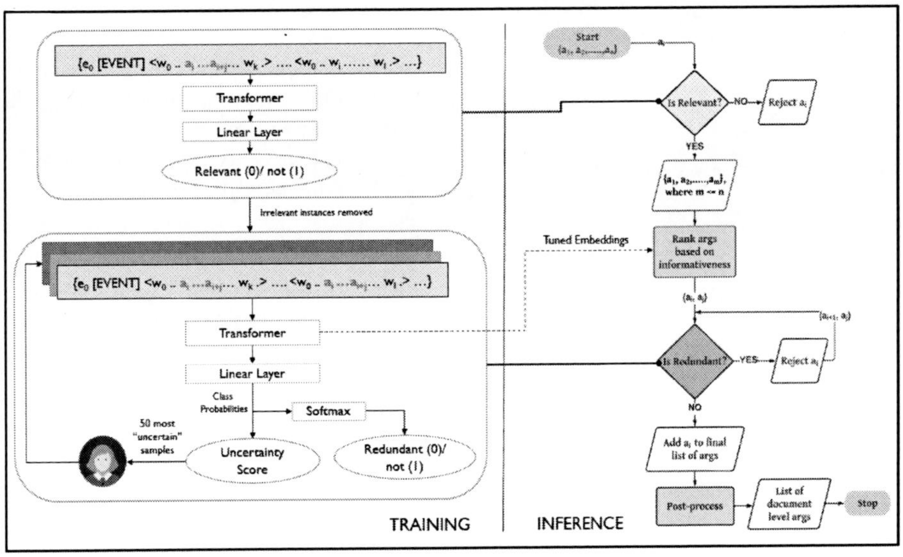

Figure 5: Detailed illustration of ArgFuse. This figure depicts the flow of control during inference with ArgFuse. The spans $(a_i..a_i + j)$ in the relevance and redundancy filters refer to argument mention spans within sentences in the input document.

by the cosine similarity between two arguments (arg_i, arg_j). The bias weight is determined by calculating the cosine similarity between the bias text and the argument text. The bias texts comprise of short text snippets defined for each argument type along with the document and it's event type. Each of the arguments and the bias texts are encoded using the tuned embeddings from the redundancy filter. Higher the score of the argument (or vertex), more informative is the argument. The ranked list contains the arguments sorted in a non-decreasing order based on their obtained Biased TextRank scores.

Each argument from the ranked list of argument mentions is compared sequentially with the other arguments using the Redundancy filter. If any pair of arguments are classified redundant, the argument with lower score is discarded and the process is continued. To reduce loss of information further, we adopt the following rules:

1. If an argument type contains a single argument mention extracted at the sentence level, the argument is added to the document-level information frame directly.

2. If all the mentions in a list of arguments of argument type t are classified irrelevant or redundant rendering a null set, we add the argument with the highest score from the list to the document-level information frame.

Once all the sentence-level arguments of a document have been processed through the above described modules, a precise document-level information frame is rendered.

5 Experiments & Results

In this section we shall detail the execution details of the experiments and analyse the results obtained.

5.1 Experiments

We have experimented with different encodings and classifiers in our work. For the Sentence Level Event-Argument Extraction task we have encoded the text using Huggingface's (Wolf et al., 2020) bert-base-multilingual-cased model pre-trained on 104 languages[2] (Devlin et al., 2019). For encoding text in the relevance filter, the pretrained roberta-base- model[3](Liu et al., 2019) was used while for the redundancy filter, the pretrained bert-base-model[4] was used. The ROBERTA-based relevance filter was trained for 3 epochs on 500 training samples while the redundancy filter was trained for 15 epochs after retrieving required annotations from 5 epochs of active learning. The batch size for our experiments was 8. All our experiments were performed on a Tesla K40-C server.

[2]https://huggingface.co/bert-base-multilingual-cased
[3]https://huggingface.co/roberta-base
[4]https://huggingface.co/bert-base-cased

Modules	Macro			Micro
	P	R	F1	F1
Relevance Filter	81	85	83	85
Redundancy Filter	69	71	70	70

Table 1: Module-wise performance measure using F1-scores (in %). Macro & Micro denote the averaging scheme adopted for these metrics.

Models	**P**	**R**	**F1**
GiveMe5W1H	25.13	25.17	25.15
TextRank @ k = 1	65.63	50.33	56.97
TextRank @ k = 2	66.59	51.18	57.87
Biased TRank @ k = 1	**70.48**	56.73	62.86
Biased TRank @ k = 2	60.48	**68.91**	64.42
ArgFuse	67.98	64.90	**66.40**

Table 2: Comparison of our models with the defined baselines. We can observe that our model reports the best performance compared to the other solutions.

5.2 Metrics

To analyse the generated document-level information frames and report the performance of the designed framework, we have adopted Precision, Recall and F1-Score as the metrics of our choice. To calculate the above mentioned metrics we count TP, FP and FN as follows:

- *True Positive (TP):* When the detected argument exists in the true argument list.
- *False Positive (FP):* When detected argument does not exist in the true argument list.
- *False Negative (FN):* When argument from true argument list is not among the detected arguments.

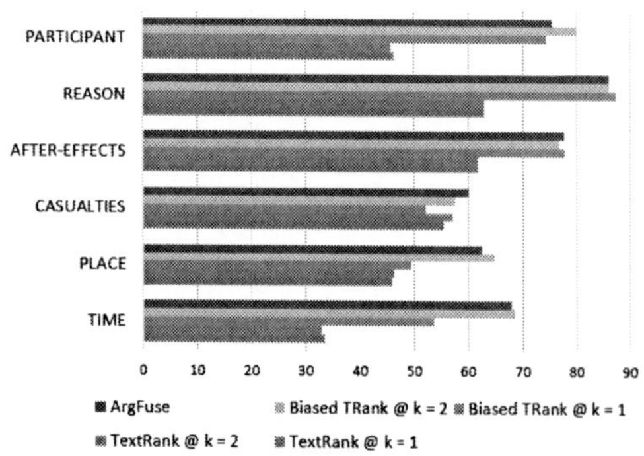

Figure 6: Comparison of Argument-Wise F1-Scores.

5.3 Results

We present our findings and results for each module in Table 1. For evaluating the results of our complete framework, we first prepare our reference text to which the machine output will be compared. Each of the manually curated information frames are presented as a sentence in the reference text in a newline. The presented sentence contains the aggregated arguments for each argument type separated by the comma delimiter. We compare our final framework with three baseline models:

- GiveMe5W1H (Hamborg et al., 2019): is an unsupervised approach for extracting document level phrases related to the six 5W1H questions (what, where, when, who, why, and how) from English News Articles. We map the six questions to our argument types so that we could run the system on our dataset and evaluate.
- TextRank (Mihalcea and Tarau, 2004): We use the graph based ranking algorithm to rank the sentence-level argument phrases for each argument type in a document extracted using (Kar et al., 2021)'s model. We select the top-k arguments as the representative arguments for that argument type from the document.
- Biased TRank: Similar to the above described baseline, but instead of TextRank we have used Biased TextRank (Kazemi et al., 2020) to rank the extracted sentence level arguments directly.

The final results are reported in Table 2.

6 Analysis

In this section, we present a thorough analysis of our findings and the novel task that we introduce. We investigate the contributions as well as the pitfalls of our framework and attempt to provide directions for improvement. In the sections to follow, we analyse our framework both quantitatively and qualitatively.

6.1 Quantitative Analysis

In this section we shall scrutinize the performance of each module in our framework as well as analyze the overall performance. The module wise performance is reported in Table 1. The final results are reported in Table 2. We can observe that while the completely unsupervised method (GiveMe5W1H)

	Sentence-Level (machine)	Document-Level (machine)	Document-Level (manual)
1.	**Document Excerpt**: 1 dead 18 hurt in explosion at natural gas plant. An explosion on Tuesday at a natural gas facility near Austria's border with Slovakia left one person dead authorities said. A further 18 people were injured in the morning blast at the plant in Baumgarten an der March east of Vienna regional Red Cross official Sonja Kellner said. (...)		
	Tuesday, in the morning, natural gas plant., natural gas facility near Austria's border with Slovakia, plant in Baumgarten an der March east of Vienna, plant, 1 dead 18 hurt, one person dead, 18 people were injured, fire	Tuesday, in the morning, natural gas facility near Austria's border with Slovakia, 18 people were injured, fire	Tuesday in the morning, plant in Baumgarten an der March east of Vienna, 1 dead 18 hurt, fire
2.	**Document Excerpt**: 3-year-old playing with stove may have started deadly New York fire. A child playing with a stove may have caused the fire in a New York City apartment building that killed 12 people including four children Mayor Bill de Blasio said on Friday. (....)		
	7 pm EST midnight GMT on Thursday, 1990, 2007, New York, New York City apartment building, first floor of a brick building and quickly spread upstairs, Bronx nightclub, Bronx building, killed 12 people including four children, killing people on multiple floors, Children ages 1 2 and 7 died along with four men and four women local media reported., An unidentified boy also died., killing 87 people, 10 immigrants from Mali including nine children died, playing with stove may have started deadly, playing with a stove may have caused, space heater, 3-year-old, A child, arsonist	7 pm EST midnight GMT on Thursday, first floor of a brick building and quickly spread upstairs, killed 12 people including four children, playing with stove may have started deadly, A child	7 pm EST midnight GMT on Thursday, New York City apartment building, first floor of a brick building and quickly spread upstairs, killed 12 people including four children, playing with a stove may have caused, 3-year-old

Figure 7: Comparison of sentence-level outputs with reduced document-level machine and human outputs. Highlighted phrases refer to the arguments that differ from the document-level gold standard. Phrases in red are the *Place* arguments while the ones in Purple and Blue are the *Casualties* and the *Participant* arguments respectively.

has a poorer extraction capacity, the other semi-supervised models exhibit a stronger performance. We also observe that the approaches processing contextual information like Biased TRank and our model ArgFuse report a much higher performance thus highlighting the importance of contextual information in this task. We find that while Biased TRank @ k = 1 reports the highest precision score, Biased TRank @ k = 2 reports the highest recall score. The stark difference between the precision and recall values of these two baseline methods is reflective of the problem of fixing a suitable 'k' value for the task of aggregation. While the higher number of argument roles with a single mention in our dataset (*singles* as illustrated in Figure 3) is favourable for a higher precision value for Biased TRank @ k = 1, allowing the inclusion of more arguments in the final document frame can be attributed to the high recall score of Biased TRank @ k = 2. However, fixing the number of argument mentions to be included in the final document frame increases the count of false negatives for k = 1 and increases the number of false positives for k = 2. Our model presents a dynamic approach of including any number of relevant and precise arguments for representing document-level information. ArgFuse reports state-of-the-art results with a an acceptable balance between the precision and recall values.

In Figure 6, the argument-wise results of the various baseline models along with that of ArgFuse is presented. We can observe that for most of the arguments, ArgFuse and Biased TRank report the highest performance, with ArgFuse reporting better or comparable performance in 4 out the 6 arguments. We find that ArgFuse reports comparatively poorer performance for arguments like *Reason* and *Participant* which constitute the argument classes with least number of samples (as depicted in Figure 2). Also, argument classes like *Reason* mostly constitute of *singles* as depicted in Figure 3 and hence reports a higher score using Biased TRank @ k = 1.

6.2 Qualitative Analysis

In this section we closely look at the failure cases for error analysis. In Figure 7, we record two examples from our dataset with both human and machine annotated information frames which are representative of the generic merits and demerits of our

Documen Excerpt: Strong quake of magnitude 6.0 rocks Jakarta: USGS. JAKARTA: Indonesias capital Jakarta was rocked on Tuesday by a strong earthquake which forced some buildings to be evacuated but there was no immediate tsunami threat or reported injuries, a government agency said. (....)

GiveMe5W1H	Biased TRank	ArgFuse	Human
the 6.0 magnitude quake, December 2016, struck at a depth 27 miles, there, Jakarta, a strong earthquake which forced **some buildings to be evacuated**	mid-December., coastal town of Cipatujah on Java island, causing damage to hundreds of houses and other buildings., **some buildings to be evacuated**, undersea earthquake	**Tuesday, Indonesias capital Jakarta**:, three people were killed, **some buildings to be evacuated**, undersea earthquake	Tuesday, Indonesias capital Jakarta, some buildings to be evacuated

Figure 8: Comparison among various baseline models and ArgFuse. The highlighted arguments are the ones that match with the gold standard output.

model. In the first example, we notice that instead of selecting "Baumgarten", the mention containing the NERs "Austria" and "Slovakia" is chosen. This is indicative of the bias of the ranking process towards more popular named entities and might not favour mentions containing rare named entities. In the second example, for the *Place* arguments, we observe that "New York, New York City apartment building" are rightly deemed redundant by our redundancy classifier, and the argument "New York" is discarded. When the arguments "New York City apartment building, first floor of a brick building and quickly spread upstairs" are evaluated, they are incorrectly classified as redundant. When the argument mentions, such as the above mentioned pair, are very similar in both their surface forms and content, the model sometimes fails to capture their exclusivity in terms of information. In case of the participant arguments, we observe in the second example that the irrelevant argument "arsonist" is correctly discarded. However, for both the *Casualty* arguments in the first example and the *Participant* arguments in the second example, the relevant arguments are again very similar in nature, and the model ranks the incorrect argument mention over the correct ones. For example, in example 1, "18 people were injured" is ranked higher than the other candidate argument mentions thus resulting in some loss of information.

In Figure 8, we present the comparison between the outputs generated by ArgFuse and some of the other baseline models. We observe that the outputs retrieved from both GiveMe5W1H and Biased TRank present with irrelevant and redundant content. The output of ArgFuse correlates the most with the gold standard output for the document. This can be regarded to the explicit relevance and redundancy checks in the ArgFuse algorithm which mines precise document level information frames effectively.

7 Conclusion

In this paper, we present an extractive approach to aggregate sentence-level argument or entity mentions to produce precise document-level information frames from lengthy text articles effectively. With a very scarce amount of work being conducted in the field of document-level IE, we develop and open-source our dataset of aggregated argument mentions. To the best of our knowledge, we present the baseline for the task of argument aggregation and open-source our work for research. We closely analyse the merits and demerits of the model and encourage scientists to build on the pitfalls discussed and enhance the aggregation capabilities at a document level. For future work, we want to analyse the model's aggregation capabilities in crosslingual and multilingual environments and extend the aggregation capabilities across document boundaries. As explored in works like (Piskorski et al., 2008; Ji and Grishman, 2008), extending *ArgFuse* to aggregate information from multiple news sources can present with a very useful and practical use case.

Acknowledgments

The work done in this paper is an outcome of the project titled "A Platform for Cross-lingual and Multi-lingual Event Monitoring in Indian Languages", supported by IMPRINT-1, MHRD, Govt. of India, and MeiTY, Govt. of India.

References

Iz Beltagy, Kyle Lo, and Arman Cohan. 2019. Scibert: A pretrained language model for scientific text.

Jacob Devlin, Ming-Wei Chang, Kenton Lee, and Kristina Toutanova. 2019. BERT: Pre-training of deep bidirectional transformers for language understanding. In *Proceedings of the 2019 Conference of the North American Chapter of the Association for Computational Linguistics: Human Language Technologies, Volume 1 (Long and Short Papers)*, pages 4171–4186, Minneapolis, Minnesota. Association for Computational Linguistics.

Seth Ebner, Patrick Xia, Ryan Culkin, Kyle Rawlins, and Benjamin Van Durme. 2020. Multi-sentence argument linking. In *Proceedings of the 58th Annual Meeting of the Association for Computational Linguistics*, pages 8057–8077, Online. Association for Computational Linguistics.

Felix Hamborg, Corinna Breitinger, and Bela Gipp. 2019. Giveme5w1h: A universal system for extracting main events from news articles. In *Proceedings of the 13th ACM Conference on Recommender Systems, 7th International Workshop on News Recommendation and Analytics (INRA 2019)*.

Peiyun Hu, Zachary C Lipton, Anima Anandkumar, and Deva Ramanan. 2018. Active learning with partial feedback. *arXiv preprint arXiv:1802.07427*.

Sarthak Jain, Madeleine van Zuylen, Hannaneh Hajishirzi, and Iz Beltagy. 2020. SciREX: A challenge dataset for document-level information extraction. In *Proceedings of the 58th Annual Meeting of the Association for Computational Linguistics*, pages 7506–7516, Online. Association for Computational Linguistics.

Heng Ji and Ralph Grishman. 2008. Refining event extraction through cross-document inference. In *Proceedings of ACL-08: HLT*, pages 254–262, Columbus, Ohio. Association for Computational Linguistics.

Debanjana Kar, Sudeshna Sarkar, and Pawan Goyal. 2021. Event argument extraction using causal knowledge structures.

Ashkan Kazemi, Verónica Pérez-Rosas, and Rada Mihalcea. 2020. Biased TextRank: Unsupervised graph-based content extraction. In *Proceedings of the 28th International Conference on Computational Linguistics*, pages 1642–1652, Barcelona, Spain (Online). International Committee on Computational Linguistics.

Yinhan Liu, Myle Ott, Naman Goyal, Jingfei Du, Mandar Joshi, Danqi Chen, Omer Levy, Mike Lewis, Luke Zettlemoyer, and Veselin Stoyanov. 2019. Roberta: A robustly optimized bert pretraining approach.

Yi Luan, Dave Wadden, Luheng He, Amy Shah, Mari Ostendorf, and Hannaneh Hajishirzi. 2019. A general framework for information extraction using dynamic span graphs. In *Proceedings of the 2019 Conference of the North American Chapter of the Association for Computational Linguistics: Human Language Technologies, Volume 1 (Long and Short Papers)*, pages 3036–3046, Minneapolis, Minnesota. Association for Computational Linguistics.

Ayush Maheshwari, Hrishikesh Patel, Nandan Rathod, Ritesh Kumar, Ganesh Ramakrishnan, and Pushpak Bhattacharyya. 2020. Tale of tails using rule augmented sequence labeling for event extraction.

Rada Mihalcea and Paul Tarau. 2004. TextRank: Bringing order into text. In *Proceedings of the 2004 Conference on Empirical Methods in Natural Language Processing*, pages 404–411, Barcelona, Spain. Association for Computational Linguistics.

Teruko Mitamura, Yukari Yamakawa, Susan Holm, Zhiyi Song, Ann Bies, Seth Kulick, and Stephanie Strassel. 2015. Event nugget annotation: Processes and issues. In *Proceedings of the The 3rd Workshop on EVENTS: Definition, Detection, Coreference, and Representation*, pages 66–76, Denver, Colorado. Association for Computational Linguistics.

Thien Huu Nguyen, Kyunghyun Cho, and Ralph Grishman. 2016. Joint event extraction via recurrent neural networks. In *Proceedings of the 2016 Conference of the North American Chapter of the Association for Computational Linguistics: Human Language Technologies*, pages 300–309.

L. Page, S. Brin, R. Motwani, and T. Winograd. 1998. The pagerank citation ranking: Bringing order to the web. In *Proceedings of the 7th International World Wide Web Conference*, pages 161–172, Brisbane, Australia.

Jakub Piskorski, Hristo Tanev, Martin Atkinson, and Erik Van Der Goot. 2008. Cluster-centric approach to news event extraction. In *Proceedings of the 2008 Conference on New Trends in Multimedia and Network Information Systems*, page 276–290, NLD. IOS Press.

Nicholas Roy and Andrew McCallum. 2001. Toward optimal active learning through monte carlo estimation of error reduction. *ICML, Williamstown*, pages 441–448.

Amir Pouran Ben Veyseh, Tuan Ngo Nguyen, and Thien Huu Nguyen. 2020. Graph transformer networks with syntactic and semantic structures for event argument extraction. In *Proceedings of the 2020 Conference on Empirical Methods in Natural Language Processing: Findings*, pages 3651–3661.

David Wadden, Ulme Wennberg, Yi Luan, and Hannaneh Hajishirzi. 2019. Entity, relation, and event extraction with contextualized span representations. *arXiv preprint arXiv:1909.03546*.

Xiaozhi Wang, Ziqi Wang, Xu Han, Zhiyuan Liu, Juanzi Li, Peng Li, Maosong Sun, Jie Zhou, and Xiang Ren. 2019. HMEAE: Hierarchical modular event argument extraction. In *Proceedings of the*

2019 Conference on Empirical Methods in Natural Language Processing and the 9th International Joint Conference on Natural Language Processing (EMNLP-IJCNLP), pages 5777–5783, Hong Kong, China. Association for Computational Linguistics.

Thomas Wolf, Lysandre Debut, Victor Sanh, Julien Chaumond, Clement Delangue, Anthony Moi, Pierric Cistac, Tim Rault, Remi Louf, Morgan Funtowicz, Joe Davison, Sam Shleifer, Patrick von Platen, Clara Ma, Yacine Jernite, Julien Plu, Canwen Xu, Teven Le Scao, Sylvain Gugger, Mariama Drame, Quentin Lhoest, and Alexander Rush. 2020. Transformers: State-of-the-art natural language processing. In *Proceedings of the 2020 Conference on Empirical Methods in Natural Language Processing: System Demonstrations*, pages 38–45, Online. Association for Computational Linguistics.

Hang Yang, Yubo Chen, Kang Liu, Yang Xiao, and Jun Zhao. 2018. DCFEE: A document-level Chinese financial event extraction system based on automatically labeled training data. In *Proceedings of ACL 2018, System Demonstrations*, pages 50–55, Melbourne, Australia. Association for Computational Linguistics.

Shun Zheng, Wei Cao, Wei Xu, and Jiang Bian. 2019. Doc2EDAG: An end-to-end document-level framework for Chinese financial event extraction. In *Proceedings of the 2019 Conference on Empirical Methods in Natural Language Processing and the 9th International Joint Conference on Natural Language Processing (EMNLP-IJCNLP)*, pages 337–346, Hong Kong, China. Association for Computational Linguistics.

Modality and Negation in Event Extraction

Sander Bijl de Vroe*, Liane Guillou*, Miloš Stanojević, Nick McKenna, Mark Steedman
School of Informatics, University of Edinburgh
{sbdv, liane.guillou, m.stanojevic, nick.mckenna}@ed.ac.uk
steedman@inf.ed.ac.uk

Abstract

Language provides speakers with a rich system of modality for expressing thoughts about events, without being committed to their actual occurrence. Modality is commonly used in the political news domain, where both actual and possible courses of events are discussed. NLP systems struggle with these semantic phenomena, often incorrectly extracting events which did not happen, which can lead to issues in downstream applications. We present an open-domain, lexicon-based event extraction system that captures various types of modality. This information is valuable for Question Answering, Knowledge Graph construction and Fact-checking tasks, and our evaluation shows that the system is sufficiently strong to be used in downstream applications.

1 Introduction

Linguistic modality is frequently used in natural language to express uncertainty with respect to events and states. Downstream NLP tasks that depend on knowing whether an event actually occurred, such as Knowledge Graph construction, Fact-checking, Question Answering and Entailment Graph construction, can benefit from understanding modality. Such information is crucial in the medical domain, for instance, where it facilitates more accurate Information Extraction and search for radiology reports (Wu et al., 2011; Peng et al., 2018). Similarly, if we pose a question in the socio-political domain, such as *Did the protesters attack the police?*, our answer will be different depending on the evidence that the system has observed: *Protesters attacked the police* [yes] or *Protesters are unlikely to have attacked the police* [uncertain][1].

These challenges are exacerbated by the prevalence of the phenomenon. In a multi-domain uncertainty corpus (Szarvas et al., 2012), sentences containing uncertainty cues are significantly more common in newswire text (18%) compared to encyclopedic text (13%). Modality is also frequently observed in editorials (Bonyadi, 2011). We show that within the news genre, modality is common in the politics and sports domains, where experts often make predictions and state their opinions on the possible outcomes of events such as elections or sports matches, and analyse alternative outcomes where situations unfold differently.

We present MoNTEE[2], an open-domain system for **Mo**dality and **N**egation **T**agging in **E**vent **E**xtraction. Tagging these phenomena allows us to distinguish between events that took place (e.g. *Protesters attacked the police*), those that did not take place (*Had protesters attacked the police...*), or are uncertain at the time that a document is written (*Protesters may have attacked the police*).

The extracted relations include a predicate and one or two arguments, for example: **Protesters**-*attack*-**police** (from the sentence *Protesters attacked the police*). The predicates are analysed according to the following semantic phenomena: negation, lexical negation, modal operators, conditionality, counterfactuality and propositional attitude. See Table 1 for examples of each category.

We contribute a lexicon of words and phrases that trigger modality, a parser that extracts and tags open-domain event relations for modality (along with an intrinsic evaluation), and a corpus study focusing on the politics domain of a large corpus of news text.

*The first two authors contributed equally to this work
[1]Assuming trustworthy source text

[2]https://gitlab.com/lianeg/montee

Proceedings of the 4th Workshop on Challenges and Applications of Automated Extraction of Socio-political Events from Text (CASE), pages 31–42
August 5–6, 2021.

Category	Example
∅	Protesters attacked the police
Negation	Protesters did **not** attack the police
Lexical negation	Protesters **refrained** from attacking the police
Modal operator	Protesters **may** have attacked the police
Conditional	**If** protesters attack the police...
Counterfactual	**Had** protesters attacked the police...
Propositional attitude	Journalists **said** that protesters attacked the police

Table 1: Modality and negation categories

2 Background

2.1 Semantic Phenomena

Modality: In this work, the focus is on any kind of modality indicating uncertainty, including modal verbs, conditionals, propositional attitudes, and negation. We see modality primarily as a signal for determining whether or not the event in question actually occurred, so that downstream applications can take this into account. We begin by discussing the typical, more specific category of modal operators.

Linguistic modality communicates a speaker's *attitude* towards the propositional content of their utterance. Formally, modality has been defined in terms of quantification over possible worlds (Kratzer, 2012). Other definitions focus on categorising the speaker's attitude, such as epistemic necessity (*That must be John.*), epistemic possibility (*It might rain tomorrow.*), deontic necessity (*You must go.*), and deontic possibility (*You may enter.*) (Van Der Auwera and Ammann, 2005). Sometimes a lexical trigger of modality is ambiguous between categories; English *may*, for example, is ambiguous between an epistemic possibility reading (*It may rain tomorrow.*) and a deontic possibility reading (*You may enter.*)

These definitions have brought about a variety of annotation schemes in practice. Prabhakaran et al. (2012) propose five classes of modality: *ability*, *effort*, *intention*, *success*, and *want*, and train a classifier on crowd-sourced annotated data. Baker et al. (2010) extend the number of modality classes to include *requirement*, *permission*, and *belief*, and combine these with negation. Peñas et al. (2011) take a coarser, epistemic approach, asking whether events are *asserted*, *negated*, or *speculated*, and Saurı et al. (2006) enrich the TimeML specification language with yet other categories (e.g. evidentiality, conditionality).

In English, modality can be expressed in a variety of ways. The modal auxiliaries (e.g. *might*, *should*, *can*) are commonly used, but modality can be lexicalised in many other trigger words. Nouns (e.g. *possibility*), adjectives (e.g. *obligatory*), adverbs (e.g. *probably*) and verbs (e.g. *presume that*) can all indicate modality. In the long tail, speakers have access to vastly productive phrases that indicate their attitude. The following examples occurred naturally in the news domain (Zhang and Weld, 2013): *That's how close they were to ..., I cannot come up with a scenario that has..., That's based on the world wide assumption that....*

Conditionality: A conditional sentence is composed of a subordinate clause (which we will refer to as the antecedent) and a main clause (the consequent). The antecedent and consequent are connected by a conditional conjunction (which in English is often the word *if*), as in the sentence *If they attack there will be war* (Dancygier, 1998). Conditional sentences can have a variety of semantic interpretations, but the most commonly studied, the *hypothetical* conditional, expresses that the consequent (*there will be war*) will hold true if the antecedent (the *attack*) is satisfied (Athanasiadou and Dirven, 1997). For our purposes, the most important part of their semantics is that neither the antecedent nor the consequent are normally entailed by the sentence, so that the speaker is not committed to their truth.

Counterfactuality: In the counterfactual construction a more complicated semantic relation is established between antecedent and consequent, as in the example: *Had they protested, they would be content.* As with modality, this has been formalised more precisely with a possible world semantics (Lewis, 1973; Kratzer, 1981). With a counterfactual, the speaker communicates that in any world similar to the current one, differing only by the proposition in the antecedent, the consequent would hold true (Lewis, 1973). In the above example, if the world is altered by the *protest* in the antecedent, *they would be content* holds true. Again, the crucial semantic information for our work is that neither the antecedent nor the consequent are entailed.

Negation is a semantic category used to change the truth value of a proposition in order to convey that an event, situation or state does not hold (Horn, 1989). It may be expressed explicitly using various means, most notably closed-class function words such as *not, no, never, neither, nor, none* and *without*, but can also be expressed lexically in open grammatical categories such as nouns (e.g. *impossibility*), verbs (e.g. *decline, prevent*), and adjectives (e.g. *unsuccessful*). It may also be expressed implicitly, such as with combinations of certain verb types and tenses (e.g. *The polls were supposed to have closed at midnight*). In this work we consider only explicit cues of negation.

Propositional Attitude and Evidentiality: Propositional attitude allows speakers to indicate the cognitive relations that entities bear to a proposition (McKay and Nelson, 2000). For example, in *Republicans think that Trump has won*, the speaker expresses that *Republicans* hold certain beliefs. In English, such reports are often made using propositional attitude verbs such as *claim, warn* or *believe*. Normally only the entity's thoughts regarding the event are entailed, not the event itself. Propositional attitudes are often used as markers of *evidentiality* in English (Biber and Finegan, 1989). These are important in Question Answering. For example when answering a question using the sentence *The Kremlin says protesters attacked the police* as evidence, mentioning the source (*The Kremlin*) might be particularly important.

2.2 Modality Taggers and Annotated Datasets

A number of approaches have been proposed for the automatic tagging of modality in text. These differ in both the granularity of the classes of modality that the model tags, and the model design.

At the lowest granularity all modality classes are collapsed into a single label. This strategy was employed in the pilot task on modality and negation detection at CLEF 2012, in which participants were asked to automatically label a set of events/states as negated, modal, neither, or both (Morante and Daelemans, 2012). The submitted systems were either purely rule-based (Lana-Serrano et al., 2012; Pakray et al., 2012), or applied rules to the output of a parser (Rosenberg et al., 2012). Modality tagging has also been cast as a supervised learning task (Prabhakaran et al., 2012). Performance of their classifier is reasonably strong on in-domain data (variable across 5 proposed modality classes), but out-of-domain data proves challenging.

Due to the lack of a large, open-domain modality training dataset, we opt for a lexicon-based approach in line with that of Baker et al. (2010). They combine a set of eight modality tags that capture *factivity* with negation, to denote whether an event/state did or did not happen. They employ two strategies for tagging modal triggers and their targets: 1) string and POS-tag matching between entries in a modality lexicon and the input sentence, 2) a structure-based method which applies rules derived from the lexicon to a flattened dependency tree, inserting tags for modality triggers and targets into the sentence.

Although there is no large, open-domain corpus in which modality is labelled, a number of small datasets exist for specific domains including biomedical text (Thompson et al., 2011), news (Thompson et al., 2017), reviews (Konstantinova et al., 2012), and web-crawled text comprising news, web pages, blogs and Wikipedia (Morante and Daelemans, 2012).

2.3 Event Extraction

Since the introduction of the Open Information Extraction (OIE) task by Banko et al. (2007), a range of open-domain information extraction systems have been proposed for the extraction of relation tuples from text. OIE systems make use of patterns, which may be hand-crafted (Fader et al., 2011; Angeli et al., 2015) or learned through methods such as bootstrapping (Wu and Weld, 2010; Mausam et al., 2012). These patterns may be applied at the sentence level, or to semantically simplified independent clauses identified during a pre-processing step (Del Corro and Gemulla, 2013; Angeli et al., 2015). The majority of systems are restricted to the extraction of binary relations (i.e. relation *triples* consisting of a predicate and two arguments), but systems have also been proposed for the extraction of n-ary relations (Akbik and Löser, 2012; Mesquita et al., 2013). Our system is a form of n-ary event extraction; we extract both binary and unary relations, and relations of higher valencies can be inferred by combining sets of binary relations. A comprehensive survey of OIE systems is provided by Niklaus et al. (2018).

3 Event Extraction System Overview

Whilst many event extraction systems have been developed, none capture the wide range of modality phenomena introduced in Section 2.1. For example, neither OpenIE nor OLLIE extract unary relations. They also fail to adequately handle all of the phenomena we are interested in, in particular counterfactuals and lexical negation. (See Sec-

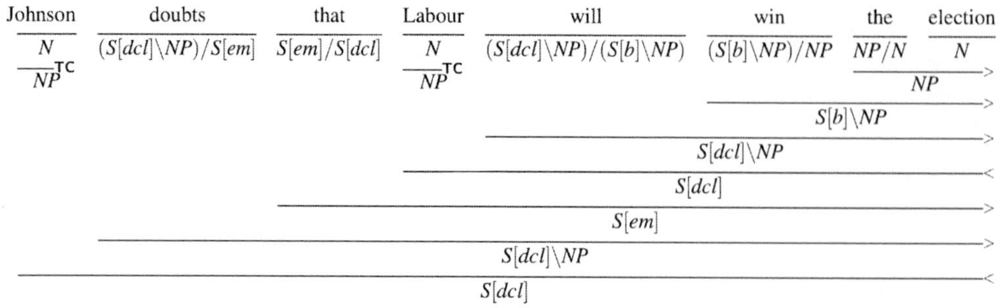

Figure 1: CCG parse tree for *Johnson doubts that Labour will win the election*

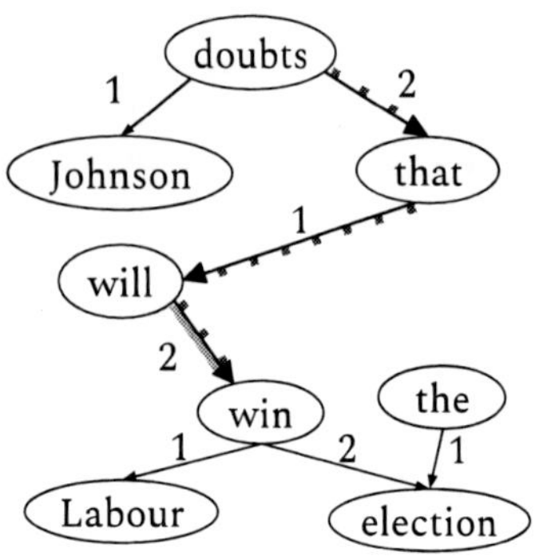

Figure 2: CCG dependency graph for *Johnson doubts that Labour will win the election*; marked paths from *doubts* (blue, dotted) and *will* (orange, solid) to *win*.

tion 6 for a comparison of our system with OpenIE and OLLIE.) We therefore construct our own event extraction system.

Our system takes as input a text document, and for each sentence outputs a set of event relations. An event relation tuple consists of a predicate and either one, or two arguments (e.g. **(The) protest**-*ended*, **Angela Merkel**-*addressed*-**NPD protesters**). We use a pipeline approach similar to that described by Hosseini et al. (2018), which allows us to extract open-domain relations.

Each sentence in the document is parsed using the *RotatingCCG* parser (Stanojević and Steedman, 2019) over which we construct a CCG dependency graph using a method similar to the one proposed by Clark et al. (2002). (See Figure 2 for an example of a dependency graph and Figure 1 for the CCG parse tree from which it was extracted.) CCG dependency graphs are more expressive than standard dependency trees because they can encode long-range dependencies, coordination and reentrancies. We traverse the dependency graph, starting from verb and preposition nodes, until an argument node is reached. The traversed nodes, which are used to form the predicate strings, may include (non-auxiliary) verbs, verb particles, adjectives, and prepositions. The CCG argument slot position, corresponding to the grammatical case of the argument (e.g. 1 for nominative, 2 for accusative), is appended to the predicate.

Our focus is on the extraction of binary and unary relations. Binary relations may be extracted from dependency paths between two entities. Extraction of unary relations, which have only one such endpoint, poses a harder challenge (Szpektor and Dagan, 2008) – we must decide whether they are truly a unary relation, or form part of a binary relation. Therefore linguistic knowledge must be carefully applied to extract meaningful unary relations. We extract unary relations for the following cases: verbs with a single argument including intransitives (*bombs exploded*) and passivised transitives (*protests were held*), and copular constructions (*Greta Thunberg is a climate activist*).

In addition to binary and unary relations we also extract n-ary relations which combine two binary relations via prepositional attachment. These are of the form: **arg1**-*predicate-arg2-preposition*-**arg3**, and are constructed by combining the two binary relations **arg1**-*predicate*-**arg2** and **arg2**-*preposition*-**arg3**. For example **Protesters**-*marched on*-**Parliament Square** and **Parliament Square**-*in*-**London** combine to form the new relation **Protesters**-*marched on Parliament Square in*-**London** (from the sentence: *Protesters marched on Parliament Square in London*).

Passive predicates are mapped to active ones. Modifiers such as *managed to* as in the example *Boris Johnson managed to secure a Brexit deal* are also included in the predicate. As these may be rather sparse, we provide the option to also extract the relation without the modifier.

Lemma	Category	POS-tag	Strength
succeed	MOD	VB	4
shall	MOD	MD	3
conceivably	MOD	RB	2
impossible	MOD	JJ	0
as long as	COND	RB	2
concede	ATT_SAY	VB	4
reckon	ATT_THINK	VB	2

Table 2: Example lexicon entries

Arguments are classified as either a Named Entity (extracted by the CoreNLP (Manning et al., 2014) Named Entity recogniser), or a general entity (all other nouns and noun phrases). Arguments are mapped to types by linking to their Freebase (Bollacker et al., 2008) IDs using AIDA-Light (Nguyen et al., 2014), and subsequently mapping these IDs to their fine-grained FIGER types (Ling and Weld, 2012). For example, *Angela Merkel* would be mapped to *person/politician* and *NPD* (Nationaldemokratische Partei Deutschland) to *government/political_party*. The type system may be leveraged to identify events belonging to specific domains, for example, to identify and track political events such as elections, debates, protests etc. and the entities involved.

4 Lexicon

Since many of the phenomena we capture involve lexical trigger items, we opt for a lexicon-based approach. Triggers identified using the lexicon can then be linked to event nodes in the CCG dependency graph. Entries in the lexicon cover modality, lexical negation, propositional attitude, and conditionality, with counterfactuality handled separately. Each entry contains the lemma, the categories that it covers, the POS-tag and an estimate of the epistemic strength that the word would normally indicate. A few examples are included in Table 2.

Our lexicon is constructed by pooling together various lexical resources. The majority of the entries derive from the modality lexicon presented by Baker et al. (2010), who use it for a similar rule-based tagging approach. Their lexicon contains just under a thousand instances, but includes multiple forms for each verb inflection. Using only infinitival forms, we add approximately 200 of the modal entries to our own lexicon.

For modelling propositional attitude, we include a list of reporting verbs found in Fay (1990). This added roughly another 120 phrases to the resource.

Algorithm 1 Tagging Modal Events

```
procedure TagModalEvents(sentence s, events e, lexicon l)
    G, event_nodes ← CCG_dep_parse(s, e)
    trigger_nodes ← [ ]
    for n in G do
        if check_lexicon(n,l) or check_cf(n,G) then
            trigger_nodes.add(n)
        end if
    end for
    for e_n in event_nodes do
        for t_n in trigger_nodes do
            if path_between(e_n, t_n) then
                e_n ← update(e_n,t_n.tag)
            end if
        end for
        e_n.tag ← tag_precedence(e_n)
        event_nodes.update(e_n)
    end for
    return event_nodes
end procedure
```

The new entries were separated by attitudes expressed through speech (tag ATT_SAY, e.g. *say, state*) and attitudes of thought (tag ATT_THINK, e.g. *suspect, assume*).

More phrases expressing uncertainty are found in a data set of news domain sentences describing conflicting events, such as a *win* and a *loss* (Guillou et al., 2020). Such sentences often contained descriptions of events that didn't actually happen. Yet more related words were found by generating each entry's WordNet synonyms and antonyms (Miller, 1995). We filtered and annotated these manually to obtain just under another 200 phrases, and added these to the lexicon. We also took inspiration from Somasundaran et al. (2007), especially for conditionals. In aggregate, this work resulted in a resource of 530 phrases.

We also annotated each phrase with a modal category. Our lexicon contains the categories *deontic*, *intention* and *desire*, and for the remaining phrases lists a indication of epistemic strength, with values 4 (*definitely*), 3 (*probably*), 2 (*possibly*), 1 (*probably not*) and 0 (*definitely not*). The latter correspond to lexical negation. The epistemic strength values were manually annotated by the authors, and are proposed as a means to collect subsets of events, such as all events marked as *probable* or higher. This phenomenon deserves more attention in future research however, as it is highly contextualised. For example, *could win the lottery* should deserve a different annotation to *could have breakfast*.

5 Modality Parser

We use the CCG-based event extraction system (Section 3) and the expanded modality lexicon (Section 4) in tandem to assign modal categories to events. The procedure is described in Algorithm 1. The focus of the tagger is to identify the bulk of uncertain events: we prioritise recall over precision, so that we can expect events without a tag to have actually happened.

The event extractor produces a CCG dependency graph $\mathcal{G}$ that contains a node n for each word in the sentence (line 2 of the algorithm). We then decide which of these nodes is a trigger (lines 4-7). For modality, negation, lexical negation, propositional attitude and conditionals, we tag these nodes if the node's lemma is present in the lexicon (*check_lexicon* function, line 5). The loop in the algorithm covers the simple case of single token modal triggers (such as *possible*), and can be extended to multi token triggers (e.g. *shoot for*)[3].

Counterfactual nodes are identified separately. The *check_cf* function (line 5) finds instances of the token "had" that are assigned one of two indicative CCG supertags: $(((S\backslash NP)\backslash(S\backslash NP))/(S[pt]\backslash NP))/NP$ or $((S/S)/(S[pt]\backslash NP))/NP$. For example in the sentence *The protesters would have been arrested, had they attacked the police*, the token "had" would be assigned the CCG supertag $(((S\backslash NP)\backslash(S\backslash NP))/(S[pt]\backslash NP))/NP$ and is therefore recognised as an instance of counterfactual had. Additionally, any instance of "if" that governs an instance of "had", is labelled as counterfactual. Upon realising that even this common counterfactual pattern was rare in the corpus, we decided not to engineer further counterfactual patterns.

We can then decide whether an event node should be tagged, by checking whether there is a path in the dependency graph from the trigger nodes to the event node (lines 9-12). Figure 2 illustrates the intuition behind walking the dependency graph. The graph shows a path from both *doubt* and *will* to *win*. This works because the existence of a path between a trigger node and an event node corresponds to the trigger node taking syntactic scope over the event node. The semantic phenomena we handle all rely heavily on this syntactic process (for example negation, see McKenna and Steedman (2020)).

[3]We implement this as a recursive loop over a Trie data structure.

A single event node may be connected to multiple triggers, so we choose the final tag on line 15. Since our primary concern is whether the event happened, we do not combine tags and instead assign a single tag based on the following order of precedence: MOD, ATT_SAY, ATT_THINK, COND, COUNT, LNEG, NEG. The negation categories need to be ordered last because an event that is negated and modal is still uncertain (e.g. *might not play* shouldn't result in NEG_play), but the ordering is otherwise arbitrary.

6 Comparison with Existing Event Extraction Systems

We highlight the capabilities of our system on five example sentences, comparing with two existing event extraction systems: OpenIE (Angeli et al., 2015) and OLLIE (Mausam et al., 2012). Note that this is not intended as a conclusive evaluation of systems, but rather as a high-level overview of the phenomena captured by each of the systems. See Table 3 for a comparison of the relations extracted by MoNTEE, OpenIE and OLLIE. The examples are all naturally occurring sentences from the news domain, obtained by a web search targeted to the modality categories discussed in this paper. To enable a fair comparison, we focus on the extraction of binary relations, as neither OpenIE nor OLLIE was designed to extract unary relations.

Whilst Stanford OpenIE (Angeli et al., 2015), OLLIE (Mausam et al., 2012), and OLLIE's predecessor ReVerb (Fader et al., 2011) may be used to extract binary relations for events, they do not explicitly mark events for modality or negation. Stanford OpenIE (Angeli et al., 2015) typically includes modals as part of the predicate (for example: (Protesters; may have attacked; police)), but ignores the other categories of linguistic modality described in Section 5. In particular it does not extract relations for sentences involving negation or propositional attitude, omits lexical negations, and is easily confused by sentences involving conditionals or counterfactuals.

OLLIE (Mausam et al., 2012) handles the phenomena in more detail. It identifies conditionals by detecting markers such as "if" and "when", and labels the *enabling condition* for extracted relations that are governed by a conditional[4]. It typically includes modals and negation as part of the predicate,

[4]The labelling of *conditional* is not applied in the first example in Table 3 as no relation is extracted for the consequent.

MoNTEE	OpenIE	OLLIE
The guerrillas are ready to talk with the Soviets, if Moscow is willing.		
MOD_(guerrillas; talk; Soviets)	(guerrillas; are; ready)	(Moscow; is; willing)
COND_(Moscow; be willing)	(guerrillas; talk with; Soviets)	
	(guerrillas; talk; if Moscow is willing)	
	(guerrillas; talk; willing)	
	(Moscow; is; if Moscow is willing)	
	(Moscow; is; willing)	
Had Trump won the election, Cummings would still be in Downing Street.		
COUNT_(Trump; win; election)	(Trump; Had Trump won; election)	(Trump; Had won; the election)
MOD_(Cummings; be in; D.St.)	(Cummings; would; would still be in D.St.)	(Cummings; would still be in; D.St.)
Protesters did not attack the Police.		
NEG_(Protesters; attack; police)	∅	(Protesters; did not attack; the police)
Parliament failed to investigate the Kremlin.		
(Parliament; failed to investigate; Kremlin)	(Parliament; investigate; Kremlin)	(Parliament; failed to investigate; the Kremlin)
LNEG_(Parliament.; investigate; Kremlin)		(Parliament; to investigate; the Kremlin)
Ed Miliband says the government betrayed Yorkshire.		
ATT_SAY_(government; betray; Yorkshire)	∅	(the government; betrayed; Yorkshire)
(Ed-Miliband; say)		[attrib=Ed Miliband says]

Table 3: Comparison of MoNTEE with OpenIE and OLLIE

and captures propositional attitude in its handling of attribution (e.g. *Ed Miliband says...*). Like OpenIE, OLLIE is not designed to handle counterfactuals. In terms of lexical negations, OLLIE extracts the predicate both with and without the negation cue, which is undesirable if the downstream NLP application needs to be able to distinguish between events that took place and those that did not.

7 Evaluating System Performance

In the absence of a pre-existing open-domain evaluation dataset that closely matches the task we are interested in, we conduct an intrinsic evaluation of our modality-aware event extraction system. We measure performance on a set of 100 extracted event relations with manually annotated labels denoting the degree of certainty (happened, didn't happen, uncertain). An event relation consists of a predicate plus argument pair (e.g. (Protesters; attack; police)). Note that we exclude both OLLIE and OpenIE from this evaluation as neither system is designed to handle the complete set of modality or negation phenomena we are interested in (c.f. Section 6).

We filtered the articles in the NewsSpike corpus (Zhang and Weld, 2013) to obtain those where at least 20% of the event relations are tagged (to guarantee a reasonably dense distribution of modality). We then randomly selected five articles and processed them using our system to extract event relations. From these articles we selected 100 event relations[5]. At the sentence-level we ensured that we include only one event relation for each predicate node in the dependency graph, since all event relations with the same predicate node will be assigned the same modality.

The set of 100 event relations was manually annotated by two of the authors of this paper, one native English speaker and one fluent speaker. For each event relation, we asked the annotators to answer the question *Does the text entail that the event definitely happens?* using the following labels: the event happened (2), is uncertain (1), didn't happen (0). Inter-annotator agreement over the set of 100 event relations was measured using Cohen's Kappa (Cohen, 1960). The agreement score was 0.77, indicating *substantial agreement*, and the annotations differed for only 16 examples. Following the initial annotation task, the two annotators resolved the disagreements, which resulted in the gold standard test set.

To evaluate our system, we mapped system-assigned modal and negation tags to the set of certainty labels, with LNEG and NEG tags mapped to 0 (didn't happen), empty tags mapped to 2 (happened), and all other tags mapped to 1 (uncertain). In Table 4 we report the micro- and macro-averaged precision, recall and F1 scores. As the number of event relations per modality tag category is too small for a meaningful error analysis over types,

[5]We excluded those event relations for which the predicate contains only a preposition as these have little meaning unless they form part of a high-order n-ary relation.

	Precision	Recall	F1
Micro-average	0.81	0.81	0.81
Macro-average	0.72	0.88	0.76

Table 4: Intrinsic evaluation results

we provide aggregated scores. The distribution of certainty labels is also uneven, with few negations marked in the gold standard. We therefore take the micro-averaged F1 score of 0.81 to be the definitive result.

We performed an error analysis of the 17 errors made by our system on the test set of 100 event relations. Parsing was a common issue, with five errors attributed to general parsing mistakes, and five errors due to missing dependency links between reporting verbs and events in quoted text (e.g. *"Police were attacked", they said*). Two mistakes were due to human error, as the annotators also missed these reporting verbs in longer sentences. Then, three errors arose from issues with the lexicon. Two of these stemmed from lack of coverage: our lexicon does not handle temporal displacement, as in *We won't act **until** the white house gives more information*. The other was caused by incorrect application of a lexical entry, which would need to be disambiguated using context. Finally, two errors could also have been avoided by handling linguistic *aspect*, as in *they began the process to...*. Future research could thus focus on expanding the lexicon by these final categories of displacement, and taking context into account when linking a word to the lexicon.

8 Corpus Analysis

We conducted a corpus analysis of extracted relations over the NewsSpike corpus (Zhang and Weld, 2013). NewsSpike contains approximately 540K multi-source news articles (approximately 20M sentences) collected over a period of six weeks. We report on the distributions of tagged phenomena over the set of binary relations[6] extracted from news articles in the complete corpus (general domain), and for the subsets of articles related to the politics and sports domains.

The NewsSpike corpus does not include topic or domain information in the article-level metadata. Therefore to identify articles belonging to the politics and sports domains we leveraged the named

[6]The corpus study of unary relations is left for future work

	General	Politics	Sports
Articles	532,651	58,521	196,098
Sentences	20,683,584	2,280,312	8,056,704
Relations	96,774,467	11,265,585	37,936,677
Distribution of tags (percentage of all relations)			
∅	77.83	74.78	78.75
Tag	22.17	25.22	21.25
Distribution of *types* of tag (percentage of tagged relations)			
Modal	64.59	66.04	65.10
ATT_say	21.54	21.28	19.94
ATT_think	2.22	1.72	2.32
Conditional	4.03	4.09	3.99
Counterfactual	0.17	0.19	0.19
Negation	6.86	6.00	7.79
Lexical Negation	0.58	0.67	0.67

Table 5: Relation tagging summary by news domain

entity linker AIDA-Light (Nguyen et al., 2014) and the FIGER type system (Ling and Weld, 2012). We first identified the set of fine-grained FIGER types related to each sub-domain, and then obtained the set of entities belonging to each type. Next we used the output of AIDA-Light to identify the set of articles for which more than 40% of the entities found by the linker belonged to the politics domain, with at least two political entities. We repeated this process for the sports domain, with a lowered threshold of 25%, as the sports topic is less likely to overlap with other topics.

The distribution of relation tags over the general, politics, and sports domains is shown in Table 5. For the politics domain just over 25% of the extracted relations are tagged by the modality parser, which is more than for the sports or general domains. In particular, modals are more prevalent. This suggests that whilst it is important to identify modality in the general news domain, it is particularly important in the politics domain.

The top ten most frequent trigger words found in the general domain are: the propositional attitude trigger *say*, the modal triggers *will*, *would*, *can*, *could*, *may*, *should*, *want* and *have to*, and the conditional trigger *if*. The same top ten are also observed for the politics domain (with different frequencies), and for the sports domain the propositional attitude trigger *think* replaces *want*. The similarity of these lists is perhaps not surprising as all three domains belong to the news genre.

9 Future Work

An obvious limitation of our approach is that it does not take into account the context in which events and trigger words occur. Modality is a context-dependent phenomenon, so using the sentential context would improve accuracy. For example, the word *unbelievable* is ambiguous between an *unlikely* and an *amazing, and happened* reading. Relatedly, our concept of epistemic strength is highly context-sensitive, and requires further development. A promising avenue is to develop a pre-training procedure for a modality-aware contextualised language model (Devlin et al., 2019; Zhou et al., 2020). We plan to use our modal lexicon to identify sentences with modality triggers. We will then gather human annotations of the certainty that each event happened, and use this annotated data to train a modality-aware language model able to classify event uncertainty. Such a system might eventually even tackle the long-tail of modal examples mentioned in Section 2.1.

We will also investigate the application of zero shot and few shot learning to the problem of detecting modality and negation. This could provide a way to leverage a large pre-trained language model together with a small annotated corpus.

Our system was developed for English, but work is already underway to develop event extraction systems for other languages including German and Chinese. Extending to other languages would allow us to apply our methods to multilingual and cross-lingual NLP tasks. Finally, most CCG parsers, including the one used in this work, are trained on English CCGbank (Hockenmaier and Steedman, 2007). This makes them perform well on news text, but accuracy suffers on out-of-domain sentences, primarily those involving questions. The results could be improved by retraining the parser on the CCG annotated questions dataset (Rimell and Clark, 2008; Yoshikawa et al., 2019), allowing us to apply our system to the task of open-domain Question Answering in an extrinsic evaluation.

10 Conclusion

We have presented MoNTEE, a modality-aware event extraction system that can distinguish between events that took place, did not take place, and for which there is a degree of uncertainty. Being able to make such distinctions is crucial for many downstream NLP applications, including Knowledge Graph construction and Question Answering. Our parser performs strongly on an intrinsic evaluation of examples from the politics domain and our corpus analysis supports our claim that modality is an important phenomenon to handle in this domain.

Acknowledgments

This work was funded by the ERC H2020 Advanced Fellowship GA 742137 SEMANTAX and a grant from The University of Edinburgh and Huawei Technologies.

The authors would like to thank Mark Johnson, Ian Wood, and Mohammad Javad Hosseini for helpful discussions, and the reviewers for their valuable feedback.

References

Alan Akbik and Alexander Löser. 2012. KrakeN: N-ary facts in open information extraction. In *Proceedings of the Joint Workshop on Automatic Knowledge Base Construction and Web-scale Knowledge Extraction (AKBC-WEKEX)*, pages 52–56, Montréal, Canada. Association for Computational Linguistics.

Gabor Angeli, Melvin Jose Johnson Premkumar, and Christopher D. Manning. 2015. Leveraging linguistic structure for open domain information extraction. In *Proceedings of the 53rd Annual Meeting of the Association for Computational Linguistics and the 7th International Joint Conference on Natural Language Processing (Volume 1: Long Papers)*, pages 344–354, Beijing, China. Association for Computational Linguistics.

Angeliki Athanasiadou and René Dirven. 1997. Conditionality, hypotheticality, counterfactuality. *Amsterdam Studies in the Theory and History of Linguistic Science Series 4*, pages 61–96.

Kathryn Baker, Michael Bloodgood, Bonnie Dorr, Nathaniel W. Filardo, Lori Levin, and Christine Piatko. 2010. A modality lexicon and its use in automatic tagging. In *Proceedings of the Seventh International Conference on Language Resources and Evaluation (LREC'10)*, Valletta, Malta. European Language Resources Association (ELRA).

Michele Banko, Michael J. Cafarella, Stephen Soderland, Matt Broadhead, and Oren Etzioni. 2007. Open information extraction from the web. In *Proceedings of the 20th International Joint Conference on Artifical Intelligence*, IJCAI'07, page 2670–2676, San Francisco, CA, USA. Morgan Kaufmann Publishers Inc.

Douglas Biber and Edward Finegan. 1989. Styles of stance in english: Lexical and grammatical marking of evidentiality and affect. *Text-interdisciplinary journal for the study of discourse*, 9(1):93–124.

Kurt Bollacker, Colin Evans, Praveen Paritosh, Tim Sturge, and Jamie Taylor. 2008. Freebase: A collaboratively created graph database for structuring human knowledge. In *Proceedings of the 2008 ACM SIGMOD International Conference on Management of Data*, SIGMOD '08, page 1247–1250, New York, NY, USA. Association for Computing Machinery.

Alireza Bonyadi. 2011. Linguistic manifestations of modality in newspaper. *International Journal of Linguistics*, 3(1):E30.

Stephen Clark, Julia Hockenmaier, and Mark Steedman. 2002. Building deep dependency structures using a wide-coverage CCG parser. In *Proceedings of the 40th Annual Meeting of the Association for Computational Linguistics*, pages 327–334, Philadelphia, Pennsylvania, USA. Association for Computational Linguistics.

Jacob Cohen. 1960. A coefficient of agreement for nominal scales. *Educational and Psychological Measurement*, 20(1):37–46.

Barbara Dancygier. 1998. *Conditionals and Prediction: Time, Knowledge and Causation in Conditional Constructions*, volume 87 of *Cambridge Studies in Linguistics*. Cambridge University Press.

Luciano Del Corro and Rainer Gemulla. 2013. Clausie: Clause-based open information extraction. In *Proceedings of the 22nd International Conference on World Wide Web*, WWW '13, page 355–366, New York, NY, USA. Association for Computing Machinery.

Jacob Devlin, Ming-Wei Chang, Kenton Lee, and Kristina Toutanova. 2019. BERT: Pre-training of deep bidirectional transformers for language understanding. In *Proceedings of the 2019 Conference of the North American Chapter of the Association for Computational Linguistics: Human Language Technologies, Volume 1 (Long and Short Papers)*, pages 4171–4186, Minneapolis, Minnesota. Association for Computational Linguistics.

Anthony Fader, Stephen Soderland, and Oren Etzioni. 2011. Identifying relations for open information extraction. In *Proceedings of the 2011 Conference on Empirical Methods in Natural Language Processing*, pages 1535–1545, Edinburgh, Scotland, UK. Association for Computational Linguistics.

Richard Fay, editor. 1990. *Collins Cobuild English Grammar*. Collins, United Kingdom.

Liane Guillou, Sander Bijl de Vroe, Mohammad Javad Hosseini, Mark Johnson, and Mark Steedman. 2020. Incorporating temporal information in entailment graph mining. In *Proceedings of the Graph-based Methods for Natural Language Processing (TextGraphs)*, pages 60–71.

Julia Hockenmaier and Mark Steedman. 2007. CCG-bank: A corpus of CCG derivations and dependency structures extracted from the Penn Treebank. *Computational Linguistics*, 33(3):355–396.

Laurence Horn. 1989. *A Natural History of Negation*. University of Chicago Press.

Mohammad Javad Hosseini, Nathanael Chambers, Siva Reddy, Xavier R. Holt, Shay B. Cohen, Mark Johnson, and Mark Steedman. 2018. Learning typed entailment graphs with global soft constraints. *Transactions of the Association for Computational Linguistics*, 6:703–717.

Natalia Konstantinova, Sheila C.M. de Sousa, Noa P. Cruz, Manuel J. Maña, Maite Taboada, and Ruslan Mitkov. 2012. A review corpus annotated for negation, speculation and their scope. In *Proceedings of the Eighth International Conference on Language Resources and Evaluation (LREC'12)*, pages 3190–3195, Istanbul, Turkey. European Language Resources Association (ELRA).

Angelika Kratzer. 1981. Partition and revision: The semantics of counterfactuals. *Journal of Philosophical Logic*, 10(2):201–216.

Angelika Kratzer. 2012. *Modals and conditionals: New and revised perspectives*, volume 36. Oxford University Press.

Sara Lana-Serrano, Daniel Sánchez-Cisneros, Paloma Martínez Fernández, Antonio Moreno-Sandoval, and Leonardo Campillos Llanos. 2012. An approach for detecting modality and negation in texts by using rule-based techniques. In *CLEF 2012 Evaluation Labs and Workshop, Online Working Notes, Rome, Italy, September 17-20, 2012*, volume 1178 of *CEUR Workshop Proceedings*. CEUR-WS.org.

David Lewis. 1973. Counterfactuals and comparative possibility. *Journal of Philosophical Logic*, pages 418–446.

Xiao Ling and Daniel S. Weld. 2012. Fine-grained entity recognition. In *Proceedings of the Twenty-Sixth AAAI Conference on Artificial Intelligence*, AAAI'12, page 94–100. AAAI Press.

Christopher Manning, Mihai Surdeanu, John Bauer, Jenny Finkel, Steven Bethard, and David McClosky. 2014. The Stanford CoreNLP natural language processing toolkit. In *Proceedings of 52nd Annual Meeting of the Association for Computational Linguistics: System Demonstrations*, pages 55–60, Baltimore, Maryland. Association for Computational Linguistics.

Mausam, Michael Schmitz, Stephen Soderland, Robert Bart, and Oren Etzioni. 2012. Open language learning for information extraction. In *Proceedings of the 2012 Joint Conference on Empirical Methods in Natural Language Processing and Computational Natural Language Learning*, pages 523–534, Jeju Island, Korea. Association for Computational Linguistics.

Thomas McKay and Michael Nelson. 2000. Propositional attitude reports.

Nick McKenna and Mark Steedman. 2020. Learning negation scope from syntactic structure. In *Proceedings of the Ninth Joint Conference on Lexical and Computational Semantics*, pages 137–142.

Filipe Mesquita, Jordan Schmidek, and Denilson Barbosa. 2013. Effectiveness and efficiency of open relation extraction. In *Proceedings of the 2013 Conference on Empirical Methods in Natural Language Processing*, pages 447–457, Seattle, Washington, USA. Association for Computational Linguistics.

George A Miller. 1995. Wordnet: a lexical database for english. *Communications of the ACM*, 38(11):39–41.

Roser Morante and Walter Daelemans. 2012. Annotating modality and negation for a machine reading evaluation. In *CLEF 2012 Evaluation Labs and Workshop, Online Working Notes, Rome, Italy, September 17-20, 2012*, volume 1178 of *CEUR Workshop Proceedings*. CEUR-WS.org.

Dat Ba Nguyen, Johannes Hoffart, Martin Theobald, and Gerhard Weikum. 2014. Aida-light: High-throughput named-entity disambiguation. *Workshop on Linked Data on the Web*, 1184:1–10.

Christina Niklaus, Matthias Cetto, André Freitas, and Siegfried Handschuh. 2018. A survey on open information extraction. In *Proceedings of the 27th International Conference on Computational Linguistics*, pages 3866–3878, Santa Fe, New Mexico, USA. Association for Computational Linguistics.

Partha Pakray, Pinaki Bhaskar, Somnath Banerjee, Sivaji Bandyopadhyay, and Alexander F. Gelbukh. 2012. An automatic system for modality and negation detection. In *CLEF 2012 Evaluation Labs and Workshop, Online Working Notes, Rome, Italy, September 17-20, 2012*, volume 1178 of *CEUR Workshop Proceedings*. CEUR-WS.org.

Anselmo Peñas, Eduard H Hovy, Pamela Forner, Álvaro Rodrigo, Richard FE Sutcliffe, Corina Forascu, and Caroline Sporleder. 2011. Overview of qa4mre at clef 2011: Question answering for machine reading evaluation. In *CLEF (Notebook Papers/Labs/Workshop)*, pages 1–20. Citeseer.

Yifan Peng, Xiaosong Wang, Le Lu, Mohammadhadi Bagheri, Ronald Summers, and Zhiyong Lu. 2018. Negbio: a high-performance tool for negation and uncertainty detection in radiology reports. *AMIA Summits on Translational Science Proceedings*, 2018:188.

Vinodkumar Prabhakaran, Michael Bloodgood, Mona Diab, Bonnie Dorr, Lori Levin, Christine D. Piatko, Owen Rambow, and Benjamin Van Durme. 2012. Statistical modality tagging from rule-based annotations and crowdsourcing. In *Proceedings of the Workshop on Extra-Propositional Aspects of Meaning in Computational Linguistics*, pages 57–64, Jeju, Republic of Korea. Association for Computational Linguistics.

Laura Rimell and Stephen Clark. 2008. Adapting a lexicalized-grammar parser to contrasting domains. In *Proceedings of the 2008 Conference on Empirical Methods in Natural Language Processing*, pages 475–484, Honolulu, Hawaii. Association for Computational Linguistics.

Sabine Rosenberg, Halil Kilicoglu, and Sabine Bergler. 2012. CLaC Labs: Processing modality and negation. working notes for QA4MRE pilot task at CLEF 2012. In *CLEF (Online Working Notes/Labs/Workshop)*, volume 1178 of *CEUR Workshop Proceedings*. CEUR-WS.org.

Roser Saurı, Marc Verhagen, and James Pustejovsky. 2006. Annotating and recognizing event modality in text. In *Proceedings of 19th International FLAIRS Conference*.

Swapna Somasundaran, Josef Ruppenhofer, and Janyce Wiebe. 2007. Detecting arguing and sentiment in meetings. In *Proceedings of the 8th SIGdial Workshop on Discourse and Dialogue*, pages 26–34.

Miloš Stanojević and Mark Steedman. 2019. CCG parsing algorithm with incremental tree rotation. In *Proceedings of the 2019 Conference of the North American Chapter of the Association for Computational Linguistics: Human Language Technologies, Volume 1 (Long and Short Papers)*, pages 228–239, Minneapolis, Minnesota. Association for Computational Linguistics.

György Szarvas, Veronika Vincze, Richárd Farkas, György Móra, and Iryna Gurevych. 2012. Cross-genre and cross-domain detection of semantic uncertainty. *Computational Linguistics*, 38(2):335–367.

Idan Szpektor and Ido Dagan. 2008. Learning entailment rules for unary templates. In *Proceedings of the 22nd International Conference on Computational Linguistics (Coling 2008)*, pages 849–856, Manchester, UK. Coling 2008 Organizing Committee.

P. Thompson, R. Nawaz, J. McNaught, and S. Ananiadou. 2011. Enriching a biomedical event corpus with meta-knowledge annotation. *BMC Bioinformatics*, 12:393.

Paul Thompson, Raheel Nawaz, John Mcnaught, and Sophia Ananiadou. 2017. Enriching news events with meta-knowledge information. *Language Resources and Evaluation*, 51(2):409–438.

Johan Van Der Auwera and Andreas Ammann. 2005. Overlap between situational and epistemic modal marking. *World atlas of language structures*, pages 310–313.

Andrew S Wu, Bao H Do, Jinsuh Kim, and Daniel L Rubin. 2011. Evaluation of negation and uncertainty detection and its impact on precision and recall in search. *Journal of digital imaging*, 24(2):234–242.

Fei Wu and Daniel S. Weld. 2010. Open information extraction using Wikipedia. In *Proceedings of the 48th Annual Meeting of the Association for Computational Linguistics*, pages 118–127, Uppsala, Sweden. Association for Computational Linguistics.

Masashi Yoshikawa, Hiroshi Noji, Koji Mineshima, and Daisuke Bekki. 2019. Automatic generation of high quality CCGbanks for parser domain adaptation. In *Proceedings of the 57th Annual Meeting of the Association for Computational Linguistics*, pages 129–139, Florence, Italy. Association for Computational Linguistics.

Congle Zhang and Daniel S Weld. 2013. Harvesting parallel news streams to generate paraphrases of event relations. In *Proceedings of the 2013 Conference on Empirical Methods in Natural Language Processing*, pages 1776–1786.

Ben Zhou, Qiang Ning, Daniel Khashabi, and Dan Roth. 2020. Temporal common sense acquisition with minimal supervision. In *Proceedings of the 58th Annual Meeting of the Association for Computational Linguistics*, pages 7579–7589, Online. Association for Computational Linguistics.

Characterizing News Portrayal of Civil Unrest in Hong Kong, 1998–2020

James A. Scharf, Arya D. McCarthy, Giovanna Maria Dora Dore
Johns Hopkins University
jscharf8@jhu.edu

Abstract

We apply statistical techniques from natural language processing to a collection of Western and Hong Kong–based English-language newspaper articles spanning the years 1998–2020, studying the difference and evolution of its portrayal. We observe that both content and attitudes differ between Western and Hong Kong–based sources. ANOVA on keyword frequencies reveals that Hong Kong–based papers discuss protests and democracy less often. Topic modeling detects salient aspects of protests and shows that Hong Kong–based papers made fewer references to police violence during the Anti-Extradition Law Amendment Bill Movement. Diachronic shifts in word embedding neighborhoods reveal a shift in the characterization of salient keywords once the Movement emerged. Together these raise questions about the existence of anodyne reporting from Hong Kong–based media. Likewise, they illustrate the importance of sample selection for protest event analysis.

1 Introduction

In an era where movements against entrenched power structures are both widespread and well documented, we can conduct computational analyses of language to guide, support, and challenge hypotheses about unrest and its discussion in mainstream written media sources. We direct these tools to analyze portrayals of protest and unrest in Hong Kong over a period of 22 years.

Public protests in Hong Kong date back to British colonial rule and have evolved from the bloody riots of the 1960s to the protests of 2019–2020, when up to two million people took to the streets over an extradition bill. They feared it would make the Hong Kong inhabitants subject to China's legal system in violation of the Basic Law[1], which

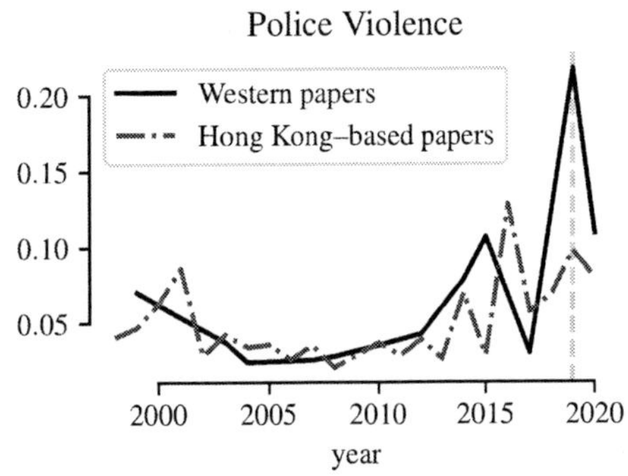

Figure 1: Words related to the topic of police violence in Hong Kong sharply rose in prominence in 2019, but only in Western news sources. The corresponding increase in Hong Kong–based news was muted.

guarantees that Hong Kong's capitalist system, judicial independence, and existing civil and political liberties would remain unchanged until 2047. Hong Kong protests captured the world's attention with defiant crowds commemorating the 1989 Tiananmen Square incidents, the July 1, 1997 transfer of sovereignty from the UK to China, and students blockading roads in the Admiralty district while doing their homework during the pro-democracy Umbrella Movement in 2014 (Weiss and Aspinall, 2012). Over time, the instability created by the protests has become a threat to the credibility of Hong Kong as a financial hub and the possibility of applying the principles of *one country, two systems* beyond Hong Kong and Macau (Overholt, 2021).

We apply a host of techniques from natural language processing to mark inconsistencies in event characterizations, analyzing news articles related to episodes of civil unrest between 1998 and 2020, in both western- and Hong Kong–based English-language newspapers. In the volatile context of Hong Kong politics, newspapers' tendency to re-

[1] https://www.basiclaw.gov.hk/en/basiclaw

Proceedings of the 4th Workshop on Challenges and Applications of Automated Extraction of Socio-political Events from Text (CASE), pages 43–52
August 5–6, 2021, ©2021 Association for Computational Linguistics

port more dramatic than ordinary events may encourage reporting bias that either emphasizes or undermines the legitimacy of the protests or the legitimacy of the regime against which the protests are directed (Snyder and Kelly (1977); Earl et al. (2004); Schrodt et al.).

Our contributions are manifold. Foremost, our work is novel amongst work on protests and natural language due to the expanse of our time horizon. Second, we characterize crucial differences in Western- and Hong Kong–based portrayals of protest: statistically significant differences in protest-related lexical choice (§5.1), reinforced by differences in treatment of democracy and police violence (§5.2), though with no major differences in sentiment (§5.4). Third, we find several key points where coverage differs (§5.2), including a major shift in the notion of "confrontation".

2 Related Work

Content analysis (Berelson, 1952), in general, is a set of non-invasive techniques for studying communication artifacts such as documents, photographs, and recordings. Computational methods have supercharged content analysis by complementing subject matter expertise with the potential for massive scale. Lucy et al. (2020) consider the content of United States history textbooks in Texas, using word embedding similarity, topic models, and dependency parsing to generate clues toward differing portrayals of race and gender. Field et al. (2018) relate the content of Russian state-run news articles to the nation's economic performance, finding an agenda of distraction through the framework of Granger causality (Granger, 1988). Other attempts at content analysis and stylometry consider authorship (Mosteller and Wallace, 1984; Bergsma et al., 2012), native language identification (Koppel et al., 2005; Bergsma et al., 2012), and deceptive communication in reviews (Ott et al., 2013).

With the advent of fast-paced 'social' media, recent work (De Silva and Riloff, 2014; Alsaedi et al., 2017; Sech et al., 2020) has aimed to characterize unrest through Tweets, short communiques on the platform Twitter.

Within the specific focus of protests, the closest work to ours in longitudinal scope is Papanikolaou and Papageorgiou (2020), whose 541 thousand news articles (albeit not all about protest) reflect Greece from 1996 to 2014; other similarly broad-scale work is rare. Wueest et al. (2013) apply topic models and named entity recognition to protest event analysis. The CLEF 2019 ProtestNews shared task asked participants to perform event extraction, even in news articles about a country outside of the training set. The organizers report consistent drops in performance after this shift. Inverting this, our work calls into question different views on protest in the same location.

3 Data

We collected a corpus of news articles collected from six Western-based English language newspapers: *The New York Times*, *The Wall Street Journal*, *The Washington Post*, *The Financial Times*, *The Guardian*, and *The Times*; and two Hong Kong–based English language newspapers: *The China Daily* and *The South China Morning Post*, covering multiple incidents of protests that took place between January 1998 and June 2020. The newspapers were purposefully selected because they are English-language newspapers; the selection ensures newspaper diversity within western- and Hong Kong–based newspapers to allow for insights into differences across cultures.

The articles were collected through keyword-based searches in ProQuest Newspapers for the western English language newspapers, and Newsbank Access World News Research Collection for the English language Hong Kong newspapers. Keywords used in the search "Hong Kong" + "protests", "Hong Kong" + "rallies", "Hong Kong" + "marches", and "Hong Kong" + "riots". We used the East Coast editions for *The New York Times* and *The Wall Street Journal*; the UK editions for *Financial Times*, *The Guardian*, and *The Times*, and the overseas edition for *China Daily* (which is run and printed in Hong Kong). To be eligible for collection, articles had to be at least 300 words long.

We manually screened the collected articles to eliminate irrelevant items such as duplicates within each publication, readers' letters, and articles that included any of the research chosen keywords but whose content was not about the protest incidents.

Following the manual screening, we retained 4676 articles, with a mean length of 782 tokens. The *South China Morning Post* and *The New York Times* published the largest number of articles about protests in Hong Kong between 1998 and 2020. The *South China Morning Post* published the most articles on Hong Kong protests among all newspapers, and *The New York Times* published the most among western-based newspapers.

4 Method

We aim to contrast the treatment of civil unrest in Hong Kong, both across news sources and over time. Here we outline four techniques to suit this purpose: analysis of word choice with ANOVA, analysis of word clusters with latent Dirichlet allocation, analysis of word usage with embedded neighborhood shifts, and analysis above the word level with sentiment analysis.

4.1 Comparing lexical frequency

Word frequency exposes obvious discrepancies in word choice and word usage. A lack of event-related keywords in contemporaneous articles from different newspapers may signal the omission of events in some of them.

Each source will have some degree of variation in keyword counts. An author's voice accounts for some mismatch in frequency, but not all. It is therefore challenging to determine whether the distribution of keyword counts is due to pure chance or something more meaningful. Analysis of Variance (ANOVA) is a sampling theory–based method for comparing the means of a quantitative response variable, when the explanatory variable is categorical (Agresti, 2017). A statistically significant p-value supports that the means of both populations are different. According to Agresti (2017), ANOVA is analogous to regression with a continuous response variable and a categorical explanatory variable.

We apply ANOVA to our corpus to determine important differences in frequencies. We first select 19 keywords of interest related to Hong Kong protests.[2] Then, for one keyword at a time, we 1) split the corpus in two by some categorical attribute, 2) obtain the keyword's frequency in each article of both corpora, and then 3) apply ANOVA to establish whether our categorical variable is associated with a variation in frequency. In this work, we use the location of the article's publisher as the categorical variable.

This statistical analysis cannot, however, reveal the *motive* for a difference in lexical choice. It merely raises the question to subject matter experts. It then befalls those experts to determine whether the difference arises due to intentional omission, niceties of a newspaper's style guide, or some other feature.

ANOVA uses the F-test to check equality of the word frequencies in each group. We set a significance level of $\alpha = 0.05$ and employ the Bonferroni correction (Dunn, 1961).

We also attempted to identify discrepancies between the words used by different subsets of articles using a weighted log-odds ratio (Monroe et al., 2017) with an informative Dirichlet prior (following Jurafsky et al., 2014; Field et al., 2018; Lucy et al., 2020), to mixed results. We omit this from later discussion.

4.2 Topic modeling

Topic modeling characterizes documents by the topics they contain, automatically identifying the topics from corpora. We use latent Dirichlet allocation (LDA; Blei et al., 2003) for our topic models. It is a probabilistic generative model that maintains distributions over the words within each topic and the topics with each article, representing each article in the traditional vector space model (Salton et al., 1975). With LDA, we capture and convey the prevalence of various topics, so that we can contrast these across news sources and over time.

We perform topic modeling with MALLET (McCallum, 2002). To preprocess the articles, we lemmatize all tokens with WordNet's `morphy` feature (Miller, 1995). We also extract common bigrams. The resulting unigrams and bigrams were converted to term–document matrices and provided as inputs to MALLET. We created models, setting the number of topics from $k = 10$ to 60, and evaluated the coherence of the resultant topics according to Mimno et al. (2011). We found that using 13 topics produced the highest coherence score. We then identified each of these topics with an identifying label (see Table 2).

Our topic model represents each article as a mixture of topics. More prevalent topics have higher mixture weight, and the weights sum to 1 for each article. (In LDA, these can be interpreted as samples from a k-dimensional Dirichlet distribution.) We can estimate a topic's prevalence in a news source or year by averaging the topic's weight across the articles from that source or year.

[2] *confront, confrontation, crackdown, democracy, freedom, freedom_of_speech, independence, occupation, protest, protests, resistance, rights, riot, rule_of_law, severe, tension, terrorism, terrorist, unrest.*

4.3 Comparing lexical usage

Complementary to the previous methods which consider *which* words are used, we would like to investigate the evolution of *how* words are used differently, both in the Western/non-Western split and over time.

Diachronic shifts in word usage are often identified with changes in words' neighborhoods in an embedding space (Hamilton et al., 2016; Gonen et al., 2020). For instance, (Hamilton et al., 2016) used these to find a shift in the word "broadcast" from agricultural to television contexts between the 1850s and 1900s. A word embedding model seeks to assign similar vectors (measured by dot product) to words in similar contexts, and different vectors to words in different contexts. If the usage of a word changes, then this should be reflected in changes to the word's context and consequent changes in the word's embedding.

We re-implement and extend the difference-in-usage model of Gonen et al. (2020), which measures how the contexts of words differ.

1. Partition the corpus $\mathcal{C}$ into $\mathcal{C}_a$ and $\mathcal{C}_{\overline{a}}$ based on the attribute of interest a.

2. Fit separate word embedding models for each partition: $\mathcal{M}_a$ and $\mathcal{M}_{\overline{a}}$.

3. Select a keyword w of interest.

4. Obtain the set of nearest neighbors $\mathrm{NN}_a(w)$ and $\mathrm{NN}_{\overline{a}}(w)$ of w according to each of $\mathcal{M}_a$ and $\mathcal{M}_{\overline{a}}$.[3]

5. Score the usage-change of w as the size of the intersection, $|\,\mathrm{NN}_a(w) \cap \mathrm{NN}_{\overline{a}}(w)|$.

After this process, if w is used differently based on the presence or absence of the attribute, we expect its score to be quite small. Words whose usage does not depend on the attribute will have similar neighborhoods in each split.

To extend the work of Gonen et al. (2020), we contextualize the similarity score of a given word against a reference set. Considering all words that occur at least 100 times, in which percentile does w's similarity score fall? We find this to be more meaningful than the raw similarity score.

We focus on three splits, but apply the same methods of analysis to each split. For the first split, we divide the corpus by the location of the source. For the second split, we consider whether the 2019-2020 mark a turning point in media coverage of protests, whereas for the third split, we investigate whether June and July, high points in the 2019-2020 protests, mark any shifts in media coverage. For all splits, we calculate the scores of words that appear at least 100 times in both sub-corpora. Then, we use those scores to calculate the percentile of a given keyword's score. This makes it clearer to compare these relative scores.

4.4 Sentiment analysis

Sentiment analysis measures the attitude of an author from the tone and connotations of their document. While it may be performed based on hand-crafted sentiment (valency) lexica (Mohammad, 2018), we select a technique that is robust to the specific words that are chosen. We select a BERT-based model to classify a given sentence as positive or negative because of its near state-of-the-art sentiment classification abilities.

We treat sentiment as a binary attribute[4] $(+, -)$ and use a probabilistic classifier trained on the Stanford Sentiment Treebank (SST-2; Socher et al., 2013). The model uses DistilBERT (Sanh et al., 2019) for feature extraction from text; DistilBERT has previously been used for sentiment analysis of product reviews (Büyüköz et al., 2020). We split each article into sentences, then classify each sentence. An article's sentiment is taken as the average sentiment over all of its sentences.

While this sentiment score obscures the reason for the author's attitude (*Were they opposed to the protests, or opposed to the police response?*), it still provides coarse-grained evidence of stylometric differences between news sources.

5 Results and Discussion

In this section, we analyze and give historical context for the results of the four techniques from §4.

5.1 Comparing lexical frequency

The ANOVA results in Table 1 show that 15 of our 19 selected keywords have statistically significant differences in frequency. The top five keywords with the highest F-statistics, in descending order, are "democracy", "protest", "protests", "freedom", and "occupation".

[3]Following the recommendation of Wendlandt et al. (2018) and Gonen et al. (2020), we use 1000 nearest neighbors.

[4]There is merit to including a third 'it's complicated' class (Kenyon-Dean et al., 2018).

Keyword	p-value	F-statistic
democracy	**7.4e-103**	490.5
protest	**5.3e-76**	354.6
protests	**4.2e-65**	300.6
freedom	**3.2e-31**	137.2
occupation	**1.9e-27**	119.4
crackdown	**5.8e-17**	70.6
confrontation	**1.4e-15**	64.1
tension	**1.5e-15**	64.0
resistance	**3.8e-12**	48.4
confront	**3.4e-08**	30.5
riot	**1.9e-07**	27.2
unrest	**7.3e-06**	20.1
rights	**2.6e-05**	17.6
freedom_of_speech	**6.8e-04**	11.5
independence	**7.2e-04**	11.4
severe	1.3e-02	6.1
rule_of_law	2.3e-01	1.4
terrorist	4.9e-01	0.4
terrorism	5.2e-01	0.4

Table 1: ANOVA of 19 selected keywords' frequency between Western-based and Hong Kong–based articles. Kewords are sorted by F-statistic; significant differences after Bonferroni correction are **bolded**.

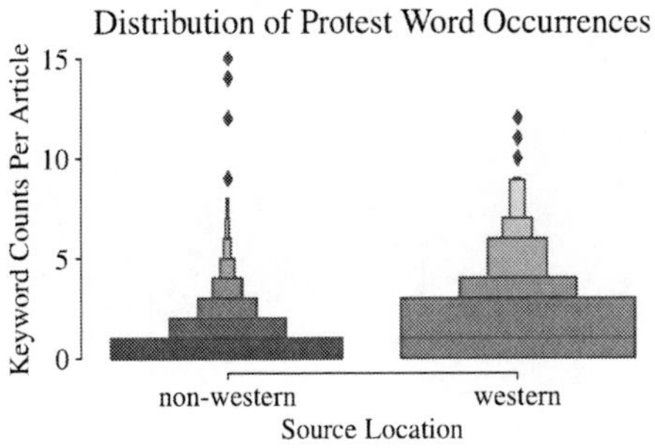

Figure 2: Quantile plot of "Protest" Counts Per Source Location

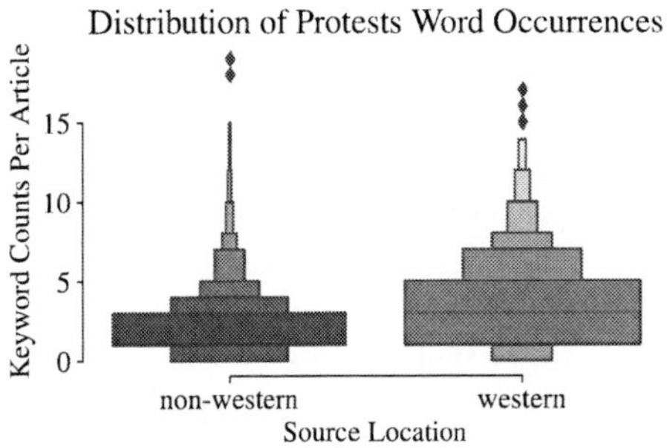

Figure 3: Quantile plot of "Protests" Counts Per Source Location

We find consistent suppression of discussion of protests in Hong Kong–based sources. The high F-statistic of "protest" and "protests" implies a disparity in the coverage of protests. Figure 2 shows how the median number of times "protest" is lower in Hong Kong–based media sources than Western-based sources.

In conjunction with the following subsection's findings of the prevalence of the "democracy movements" topic, the high F-statistics of "democracy" and "freedom" suggest that discourse about democracy is much more common in Western-based sources than in Hong Kong–based sources.

5.2 Topic modeling

Table 2 shows the most prominent words for the 13 topics we identified in §4.2.

Figure 5 shows the evolution of topics over time, revealing that at several key points in Hong Kong's history, Western-based and Hong Kong–based sources wrote about different topics. This is not entirely unexpected for a number of reasons, including a media organization's possible desire to appeal to their own readership and therefore maintain loyal readers. Furthermore, the local nature of Hong Kong–based media might encourage them to include more domestic events and details. This might be shown by the pervasiveness of the Marches/Rallies topic and the Bill topic in Hong Kong-based media when compared to the presence of the same topic in Western-based media. Hong Kong-based newspapers may have reported any marches or rallies that took place between 1998 and 2020, whereas Western-based newspapers may have focused only on landmark ones such as those organized around the anniversaries of the July 1 Handover or the June 4 Tiananmen Square incidents. As for the Bill topic, Hong Kong-based media coverage peaks in 2010, when the Legislature debated a number of legal initiatives, whereas the western-based coverage of the same topic remain relatively stable and much lower overtime."

The topics reflect known events in Hong Kong's history; spikes in the students/schools topic track the Scholarist movement and its resurgence in 2014 in the Umbrella Revolution. Several spikes emerge around discussions of the election process for Hong Kong's chief executive. However, at key points

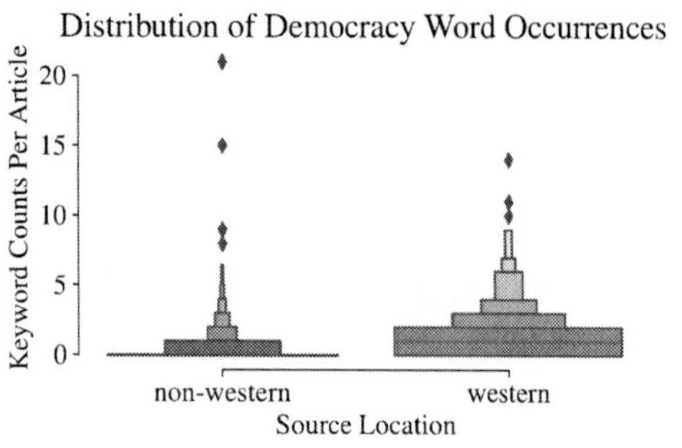

Figure 4: Quantile plot of "Democracy" Counts Per Source Location

in Hong Kong's history of social unrest Western-based media and Hong Kong–based media the topics diverge completely. For example, in July 2019 Western-based newspapers reported police violence to a far greater extent than Hong Kong–based media.

5.3 Comparing lexical usage

The methods from §4.3 reveal semantic divergence in certain keywords between Western-based and non-Western-based news sources. We also find that June–July is a turning point, after which the meaning of several keywords shifts for at least the remainder of 2019.

Western-based vs. Hong Kong–based sources We divide the data by the location of each article's publisher. Corpus $\mathcal{C}_{\text{West}}$ is composed of all 711 articles published by Western-based sources. Corpus $\mathcal{C}_{\overline{\text{West}}}$ is composed of all 3464 articles published by Hong Kong–based sources.

We then trained Word2Vec models on both corpora. Despite the relatively small size of corpus W, a visual inspection of the resulting Word2Vec model shows sound performance. We then scored each keyword in Table 1 and compared each models' nearest neighbors.

We observe noticeable semantic differentiation between the two models for several keywords. For example, "resistance" has an unexpectedly low score. In comparison to the scores of all words that appear more than 100 times in both corpora, the score of "resistance" is only in the 17th percentile.

A visual inspection of the term's nearest neighbors in the Western-based model suggests an association with the feelings of protesters (ex. "frustration", "anxiety"). In contrast, the nearest neighbors of "resistance" in the Hong Kong–based model relate to adversarial behavior. This is evidence of the dichotomous framing of anti-government demonstrators.

Authors commonly employ the the words "tension" and "severe" to describe protest events and confrontations. "Tension" and "severe" both had low similarity scores, with the score of the former in the 1st percentile and the score of the latter in the 7th percentile. This is evidence of high semantic divergence between Western and non-Western news sources in their usage of polarizing framing.

Curiously, "protest" scored only in the 91st percentile. We attribute this finding to be a function of low prevalence of the word in Hong Kong–based protests, which may also betray self-censorship. Additionally, we interpret the finding to mean that the context in which "protest" occurs is not dissimilar in our two corpora.

Before vs. after July 2019 Here, we sought to quantify the degree to which the introduction of the Fugitive Offenders amendment bill acted as a pivotal moment in the style of newspapers' portrayal of the Hong Kong protesters.

We again obtain the scores of words with a frequency higher than 100 in both corpora to contextualize our keywords' scores. We find that "resistance" again has a low score, and therefore high semantic shift. We inspected its nearest neighbors in each model and saw that the term became associated with dissent in the months after July 2019.

We note a similar trend for "confront" (9th percentile) and "confrontation" (11th percentile). After July 1, confrontations became associated with "provocative", "battles", and "mayhem". These changes may be suggestive of how English-language Hong Kong-based newspapers intended to shape the international understanding of what was happening in Hong Kong, favoring the inclusion of strong and negative terms to portray the 2019 street protests.

5.4 Sentiment analysis

We find a consistent pessimism across news sources: all display positive sentiment in only 30% to 40% of their content. While no clear-cut relationship can be established between whether an article is from a western source from its sentiment, Hong Kong-based sources are more negative. There is, however, internal variation. The *China Daily* with

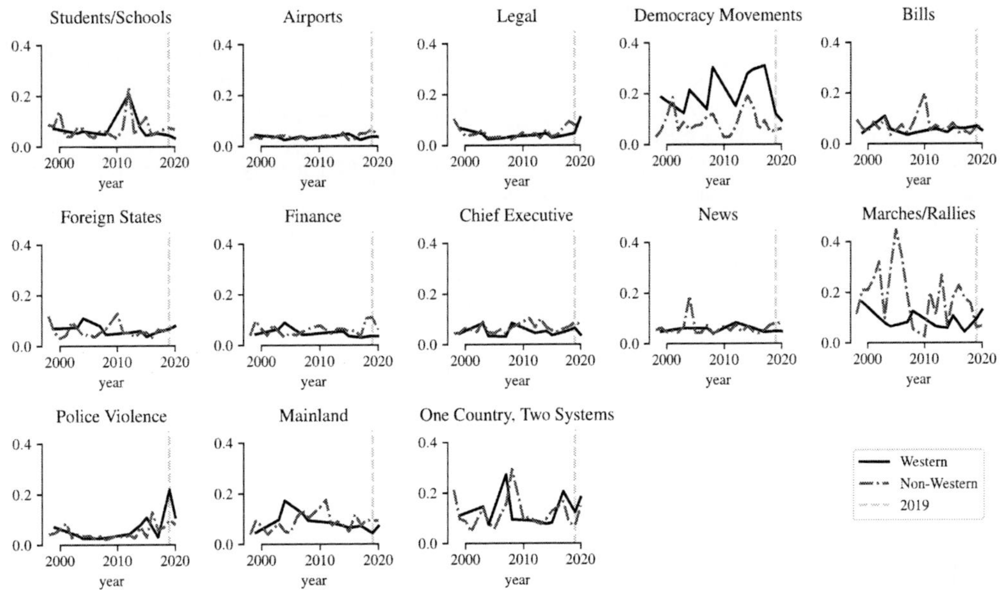

Figure 5: Mean topic representation (out of 1) over time, for Western and Hong Kong–based sources. 2019 is highlighted in dashed grey.

a share of 37.9 positive articles is the second most positive in sentiment, following the *Wall Street Journal*, whereas the *South China Morning Post*, with a share of 30.5, displayed the least positive sentiment across articles

6 Conclusion

We show that techniques from natural language processing can guide, answer, and suggest questions in social science. While past work focuses on single movements or eras, we characterize the portrayal of civil unrest in Hong Kong over a period of 22 years. Using a curated and manually filtered corpus of 4512 articles from Western-based and Hong Kong–based newspapers, we identified clear differences in framing both across time and between Western-based and Hong Kong–based newspapers.

Our approaches shed light on the ways in which Western and Hong Kong–based portrayals have evolved over time. For instance, while both discussed the Scholarist movement's rise to prominence in 2012 in roughly equal proportions, the discussion of police violence was much more prominent in Western sources than in Hong Kong–based sources. Similarly, Western-based sources are far more likely to discuss protests than Hong Kong–based sources. This has implications for the extraction of protest-related events from corpora with politically opposed sources such as ours. Further, July 1, 2019 marked a turning point across Western and non-Western sources in the characteristics of usage for confrontation-related vocabulary.

The efficacy of event extraction models presupposes that the event in question is discussed in the considered collection of documents. In characterizing significant differences in portrayal across news sources, we implore that a critical eye be applied to the data *selection* process. We are working to quantify the degree to which event extraction systems are stymied by content and framing differences.

Finally, we have binned our articles at the granularity of years for much of our analysis. This blends news coverage leading up to unrest and portrayals of it afterward. Is it possible that language in news media causes (or at least, Granger-causes) protest sizes? Future work will more precisely measure differences in news content and framing around flashpoints of civil unrest.

References

Alan Agresti. 2017. *Statistical methods for the social sciences*. Pearson.

Nasser Alsaedi, Pete Burnap, and Omer Rana. 2017. Can we predict a riot? disruptive event detection using twitter. *ACM Trans. Internet Technol.*, 17(2).

Topic	Top 10 words
Students/schools	student, university, school, young, education, campus, class, group, family, child
Airports	station, mtr, airport, staff, service, yesterday, sha, cathay, day, airline
Legal	court, law, case, chan, legal, yesterday, wong, justice, mask, charge
Democracy movements	mr, democracy, leader, chinese, movement, pro, party, street, occupy, pro_democracy
Bills	bill, pro, council, extradition, lawmaker, election, party, legislative, mainland, camp
Foreign states	state, foreign, chinese, united, president, united_state, country, trump, international
Finance	cent, per_cent, hk, market, property, billion, company, million, price, sale
Chief executive	lam, bill, executive, chief_executive, carrie, carrie_lam, extradition, cheng, extradition_bill, demand
News	chinese, medium, mainland, taiwan, news, social, state, post, company, social_medium
Marches/rallies	march, rally, group, july, civil, june, yesterday, front, day, organiser
Police violence	officer, force, violence, gas, tear, tear_gas, attack, riot, police_officer, arrested
Mainland	mainland, world, event, number, day, tourist, local, ha_been, place, unrest
One country, two systems	law, system, national, country, security, central, one_country, rule_of_law, two_system, tung

Table 2: The 13 topics found and used in our topic modeling analysis.

Western	Hong Kong–based
conflict	dissent
beyond	approaches
frustration	pragmatism
cited	insurrectionists
helps	odds
anxiety	adversaries
meant	outpouring
word	nerve
stark	inflict
uprisings	craft

Table 3: "Resistance" nearest neighbors of Western-based model vs. Hong Kong–based sources model

Western	Hong Kong–based
demonstrating	worsening
careful	disputes
saw	tensions
cars	continues
treated	controversies
eyes	risks
walked	crises
watched	turmoil
bus	conflict
deleted	divisions

Table 4: "Tension" nearest neighbors of Western-based model vs. Hong Kong–based sources model

Western-Based	Hong Kong–based
streets	rallies
violent	rally
umbrella	campaign
movement	non-cooperation
thousands	demonstrators
demonstrations	demonstrations
march	movement
clashes	citywide
hundreds	demonstration
marched	strike

Table 5: "Protest" nearest neighbors of Western-based model vs. Hong Kong–based sources model

Bernard Berelson. 1952. *Content analysis in communication research.* Free press.

Shane Bergsma, Matt Post, and David Yarowsky. 2012. Stylometric analysis of scientific articles. In *HLT-NAACL*, pages 327–337.

David M. Blei, Andrew Y. Ng, and Michael I. Jordan. 2003. Latent Dirichlet Allocation. *J. Mach. Learn. Res.*, 3(null):993–1022.

Berfu Büyüköz, Ali Hürriyetoğlu, and Arzucan Özgür. 2020. Analyzing ELMo and DistilBERT on socio-political news classification. In *Proceedings of the Workshop on Automated Extraction of Socio-political Events from News 2020*, pages 9–18, Marseille, France. European Language Resources Association (ELRA).

Lalindra De Silva and Ellen Riloff. 2014. User type classification of tweets with implications for event

Pre-July 2019	Post-July 2019
canada	uprising
global	eroding
influence	humane
governments	dissent
deep	sow
reverse	advocating
woman	define
initial	anthems
relationship	authoritarianism
growing	labelling

Table 6: "Resistance" nearest neighbors associated with provocations after July 1

Pre-July 2019	Post-July 2019
yan	alike
station	innocent
glass	resorting
chat	motivated
minutes	letting
wore	provoke
yuen	endangering
lines	deny
walls	treat
throwing	insulting

Table 7: "Confront" nearest neighbors associated with provocation after July 1

Pre-July 2019	Post-July 2019
chance	scenes
break	confrontations
procedural	mayhem
letting	battles
leave	chaotic
circumstances	tense
refusing	respite
agreed	frequent
rational	clashes
based	stand-offs

Table 8: "Confrontation" nearest neighbors associated with provocations after July 1

recognition. In *Proceedings of the Joint Workshop on Social Dynamics and Personal Attributes in Social Media*, pages 98–108, Baltimore, Maryland. Association for Computational Linguistics.

Olive Jean Dunn. 1961. Multiple comparisons among means. *Journal of the American Statistical Association*, 56(293):52–64.

Jennifer Earl, Andrew Martin, John D. McCarthy, and Sarah A. Soule. 2004. The use of newspaper data in the study of collective action. *Annual Review of Sociology*, 30(1):65–80.

Anjalie Field, Doron Kliger, Shuly Wintner, Jennifer Pan, Dan Jurafsky, and Yulia Tsvetkov. 2018. Framing and agenda-setting in Russian news: a computational analysis of intricate political strategies. In *Proceedings of the 2018 Conference on Empirical Methods in Natural Language Processing*, pages 3570–3580, Brussels, Belgium. Association for Computational Linguistics.

Hila Gonen, Ganesh Jawahar, Djamé Seddah, and Yoav Goldberg. 2020. Simple, interpretable and stable method for detecting words with usage change across corpora. In *Proceedings of the 58th Annual Meeting of the Association for Computational Linguistics*, pages 538–555, Online. Association for Computational Linguistics.

C.W.J. Granger. 1988. Some recent development in a concept of causality. *Journal of Econometrics*, 39(1):199–211.

William L. Hamilton, Jure Leskovec, and Dan Jurafsky. 2016. Diachronic word embeddings reveal statistical laws of semantic change. In *Proceedings of the 54th Annual Meeting of the Association for Computational Linguistics (Volume 1: Long Papers)*, pages 1489–1501, Berlin, Germany. Association for Computational Linguistics.

Dan Jurafsky, Victor Chahuneau, Bryan R. Routledge, and Noah A. Smith. 2014. Narrative framing of consumer sentiment in online restaurant reviews. *First Monday*, 19.

Kian Kenyon-Dean, Eisha Ahmed, Scott Fujimoto, Jeremy Georges-Filteau, Christopher Glasz, Barleen Kaur, Auguste Lalande, Shruti Bhanderi, Robert Belfer, Nirmal Kanagasabai, Roman Sarrazingendron, Rohit Verma, and Derek Ruths. 2018. Sentiment analysis: It's complicated! In *Proceedings of the 2018 Conference of the North American Chapter of the Association for Computational Linguistics: Human Language Technologies, Volume 1 (Long Papers)*, pages 1886–1895, New Orleans, Louisiana. Association for Computational Linguistics.

Moshe Koppel, Jonathan Schler, and Kfir Zigdon. 2005. Determining an author's native language by mining a text for errors. In *Proceedings of the Eleventh ACM SIGKDD International Conference on Knowledge Discovery in Data Mining*, KDD '05, page 624–628, New York, NY, USA. Association for Computing Machinery.

Li Lucy, Dorottya Demszky, Patricia Bromley, and Dan Jurafsky. 2020. Content analysis of textbooks via natural language processing: Findings on gender, race, and ethnicity in texas u.s. history textbooks. *AERA Open*, 6(3):2332858420940312.

Andrew Kachites McCallum. 2002. Mallet: A machine learning for language toolkit. Http://mallet.cs.umass.edu.

George A. Miller. 1995. WordNet: A lexical database for English. *Commun. ACM*, 38(11):39–41.

David Mimno, Hanna Wallach, Edmund Talley, Miriam Leenders, and Andrew McCallum. 2011. Optimizing semantic coherence in topic models. In *Proceedings of the 2011 Conference on Empirical Methods in Natural Language Processing*, pages 262–272, Edinburgh, Scotland, UK. Association for Computational Linguistics.

Saif Mohammad. 2018. Obtaining reliable human ratings of valence, arousal, and dominance for 20,000 English words. In *Proceedings of the 56th Annual Meeting of the Association for Computational Linguistics (Volume 1: Long Papers)*, pages 174–184, Melbourne, Australia. Association for Computational Linguistics.

Burt L. Monroe, Michael P. Colaresi, and Kevin M. Quinn. 2017. Fightin' words: Lexical feature selection and evaluation for identifying the content of political conflict. *Political Analysis*, 16(4):372–403.

Frederick Mosteller and David L Wallace. 1984. *Applied Bayesian and classical inference: the case of the federalist papers*. Springer.

Myle Ott, Claire Cardie, and Jeffrey T. Hancock. 2013. Negative deceptive opinion spam. In *Proceedings of the 2013 Conference of the North American Chapter of the Association for Computational Linguistics: Human Language Technologies*, pages 497–501, Atlanta, Georgia. Association for Computational Linguistics.

William H. Overholt. 2021. Hong kong: The rise and fall of "one country, two systems".

Konstantina Papanikolaou and Haris Papageorgiou. 2020. Protest event analysis: A longitudinal analysis for Greece. In *Proceedings of the Workshop on Automated Extraction of Socio-political Events from News 2020*, pages 57–62, Marseille, France. European Language Resources Association (ELRA).

G. Salton, A. Wong, and C. S. Yang. 1975. A vector space model for automatic indexing. *Commun. ACM*, 18(11):613–620.

Victor Sanh, Lysandre Debut, Julien Chaumond, and Thomas Wolf. 2019. Distilbert, a distilled version of BERT: smaller, faster, cheaper and lighter. *CoRR*, abs/1910.01108.

Philip A. Schrodt, Erin M. Simpson, and Deborah J. Gerner. Monitoring conflict using automated coding of newswire reports: A comparison of five geographical regions.

Justin Sech, Alexandra DeLucia, Anna L. Buczak, and Mark Dredze. 2020. Civil unrest on Twitter (CUT): A dataset of tweets to support research on civil unrest. In *Proceedings of the Sixth Workshop on Noisy User-generated Text (W-NUT 2020)*, pages 215–221, Online. Association for Computational Linguistics.

David Snyder and William R. Kelly. 1977. Conflict intensity, media sensitivity and the validity of newspaper data. *American Sociological Review*, 42(1):105–123.

Richard Socher, Alex Perelygin, Jean Wu, Jason Chuang, Christopher D. Manning, Andrew Ng, and Christopher Potts. 2013. Recursive deep models for semantic compositionality over a sentiment treebank. In *Proceedings of the 2013 Conference on Empirical Methods in Natural Language Processing*, pages 1631–1642, Seattle, Washington, USA. Association for Computational Linguistics.

Meredith Leigh Weiss and Edward Aspinall. 2012. *Student activism in Asia: Between protest and powerlessness*. U of Minnesota Press.

Laura Wendlandt, Jonathan K. Kummerfeld, and Rada Mihalcea. 2018. Factors influencing the surprising instability of word embeddings. In *Proceedings of the 2018 Conference of the North American Chapter of the Association for Computational Linguistics: Human Language Technologies, Volume 1 (Long Papers)*, pages 2092–2102, New Orleans, Louisiana. Association for Computational Linguistics.

Bruno Wueest, Klaus Rothenhäusler, and Swen Hutter. 2013. Using computational linguistics to enhance protest event analysis.

Regressing Location on Text for Probabilistic Geocoding

Benjamin J. Radford
University of North Carolina at Charlotte
benjamin.radford@uncc.edu

Abstract

Text data are an important source of detailed information about social and political events. Automated systems parse large volumes of text data to infer or extract structured information that describes actors, actions, dates, times, and locations. One of these sub-tasks is geocoding: predicting the geographic coordinates associated with events or locations described by a given text. We present an end-to-end probabilistic model for geocoding text data. Additionally, we collect a novel data set for evaluating the performance of geocoding systems. We compare the model-based solution, called ELECTRo-map, to the current state-of-the-art open source system for geocoding texts for event data. Finally, we discuss the benefits of end-to-end model-based geocoding, including principled uncertainty estimation and the ability of these models to leverage contextual information.

1 Introduction

Text data are an important source of information about social and political events. We introduce a novel method for predicting the latitude and longitude of locations mentioned or described in natural language texts ("geocoding"). This neural network-based method offers several advantages over existing rule-based techniques for geocoding: (1) it produces a probability distribution over predicted latitudes and longitudes thereby allowing users to report the certainty of their estimates; (2) it does not require the identification of place names in the text prior to geocoding; (3) it naturally leverages contextual clues to improve predictions and disambiguate location names.

This paper proceeds by first providing a brief overview of related work in geocoding and language modeling. We then introduce a probabilistic model for geocoding texts and identify a dataset with which to train and evaluate the model. We compare our results to existing methods and conclude with suggestions for future research.

1.1 Geocoding Text

Lee et al. (2019) describe a geolocation pipeline for producing political event data that includes three steps: (1) named entity recognition (NER) identifies character strings of named places; (2) "geoparsing" software matches named locations to geographical locations; (3) events from the source text are linked to their respective locations.

Mordecai is an open source tool for Steps 1 and 2 (Halterman, 2017). Mordecai uses a pretrained named entity recognition model and word2vec (Mikolov et al., 2013) to match location names identified within an unstructured text document to known locations within the GeoNames Gazetteer (GeoNames).

Kulkarni et al. (2020) present a model-based geocoding solution. Their convolutional neural network model predicts geographic grid cell membership for each input text; it does not predict latitude and longitude values directly. This complicates comparison with the model presented here which directly regresses latitude and longitude on text. For example, the evaluation metrics the authors chose for their model are largely based on classification accuracy rather than continuous measures of nearness, as would be the case in a regression setting.[1]

1.2 Transformer Language Models

The foundation of the model described in this paper is a very large neural network language model

[1] Specifically, the authors report the area under the receiver operating characteristic curve (AUC) and classification accuracy. This classification framing contrasts with the model presented here which directly predicts latitude and longitude values and therefore is evaluated via mean absolute error in kilometers.

Proceedings of the 4th Workshop on Challenges and Applications of Automated Extraction of Socio-political Events from Text (CASE), pages 53–57
August 5–6, 2021, ©2021 Association for Computational Linguistics

called a transformer network, a "transformer." Typically, a transformer is trained on a large corpus with a self-supervised objective: either next sentence prediction and/or masked language prediction. This initial training is called "pretraining." However, these models have been shown to generalize very well to tasks for which they were not explicitly pretrained. With subsequent "fine-tuning," transformers can acquire the ability to accomplish new tasks with substantially fewer training examples than those with which they were pretrained. Vaswani et al. (2017) introduced the first transformer language model; the particular model used here is called DistilRoBERTa (Sanh et al., 2019; Liu et al., 2019).

2 Model

We introduce a model that is capable of performing Steps 1 through 3 (§ 1.1) end-to-end. That is, given training data exemplary of the desired mapping from text inputs, **X**, to geographic coordinates, **Y**, this model is fine-tuned such that it learns a function $f(\mathbf{x}_i; \mathbf{W}) \rightarrow \hat{\mathbf{y}}_i$, where **W** is the set of model parameters. This is a non-linear multivariate regression of latitude and longitude on text. We modify a pretrained DistilRoBERTa model by adding three fully-connected dense layers with sigmoid activation, an output ("head") layer, and a custom loss function. We use this model to minimize the negative log likelihood of a five component mixture of von Mises-Fisher (vMF) distributions conditional on the input text.

The von Mises distribution is an approximation of a univariate Gaussian distribution on the circumference of a circle. The vMF distribution generalizes the von Mises distribution beyond two dimensions to the surfaces of spheres and hyperspheres; when $p = 2$, the vMF distribution is equivalent to the the von Mises distribution.

Because the vMF distribution has support over the surface of the unit $p-1$ sphere in p Euclidean space, we must transform our geodetic coordinates (latitude and longitude) to Cartesian coordinates on this sphere. The formulae to do so, assuming a spherical Earth, are given by Equations 1–3.

$$x_i = \cos(\text{rad}_i^{lat}) \times \cos(\text{rad}_i^{lon}) \quad (1)$$

$$y_i = \cos(\text{rad}_i^{lat}) \times \sin(\text{rad}_i^{lon}) \quad (2)$$

$$z_i = \sin(\text{rad}_i^{lat}) \quad (3)$$

The vMF probability density function is given by Equation 4. μ, the mean direction, is a point in p space that falls on the unit $p-1$ sphere. A point x in p space can be projected onto this sphere by $L2$ normalization: $x/||x||$. The concentration parameter, κ, controls the dispersion of the distribution across the surface of the sphere. $\kappa = 0$ corresponds to a uniform distribution over the entire sphere while $\kappa = \infty$ corresponds to a point mass at μ. $I_{p/2-1}$ is the modified Bessel function of the first kind at order $p/2 - 1$.

$$f_{vmf}(x; \mu, \kappa) = \frac{\kappa^{p/2-1}}{(2\pi)^{p/2} I_{p/2-1}(\kappa)} e^{(\kappa \mu^T x)} \quad (4)$$

A probabilistic neural network model with a single vMF component is optimized by minimizing the negative log likelihood given in Equation 5.

$$-L(\mathbf{W}) = -\sum_i \ln(f_{vmf}(\mathbf{y}_i; \hat{\mu}_i, \hat{\kappa}_i)) \quad (5)$$

$$\hat{\mu}_i = f_\mu(\mathbf{x}_i; \mathbf{W})$$

$$\hat{\kappa}_i = f_\kappa(\mathbf{x}_i; \mathbf{W})$$

The outputs of the neural network, given an input text $\mathbf{x}_i$, are the parameters of a vMF distribution. Therefore, the model estimates a distribution over possible coordinates for a given input text. While the parameters of the neural network itself (**W**) are deterministic, predicting a probability distribution for each input text allows us to capture aleatoric uncertainty. Aleatoric uncertainty is the uncertainty inherent in the data themselves. In the case of geocoding text, this uncertainty may result from texts that do not distinguish between Springfield, IL and Springfield, GA, or from texts that refer to multiple locations (assuming that the model in question is unable to represent a multimodal distribution).

This uncertainty is unlikely to be homoskedastic; some texts will more precisely specify relevant locations than others. We allow for heteroskedastic uncertainty by estimating both the central tendency ($\hat{\mu}_i$) and the dispersion ($\hat{\kappa}_i$) of a target distribution.

Building on the negative vMF log likelihood loss described above, we optimize a neural network model to predict a mixture of vMF distributions.[2] For every input text, the model predicts parameters for five vMF distributions in addition to a set of mixing probabilities. The mixing probabilities describe the weights associated with each of the five vMF components. In this way, the model can fit

[2]We use the Adam optimizer with a learning rate of 5×10^{-5} and train for five epochs (Kingma and Ba, 2015). The network is difficult to train and a single-component vMF model failed to converge.

Model	n	*highProb* Mean	*highProb* Median	*best* Mean	*best* Median	*random* Mean	*random* Median
Mordecai	12,864	1101.3	161.9	348.8	14.3	1213.7	140.6
		(24.1)	(2.9)	(13.5)	(0.4)	(24.0)	(3.5)
Mordecai Complete Cases	12,585	946.0	154.5	177.0	**13.4**	**1076.7**	**134.0**
		(22.0)	(3.1)	(8.3)	(0.3)	(25.0)	(4.2)
ELECTRo-map	12,864	**108.1**	**44.1**	**96.8**	44.0	6380.8	4814.5
		(4.1)	(0.4)	(2.5)	(0.4)	(54.1)	(96.1)

Table 1: Test set (out-of-sample) geocoding performance. Reported values are measured in kilometers. Bootstrap estimated standard errors in parentheses.

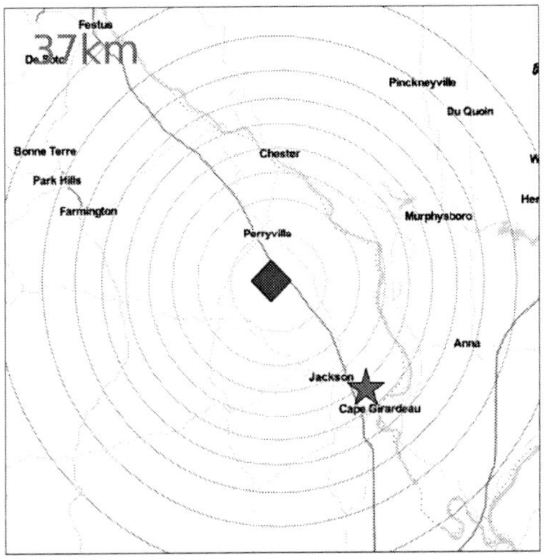

(a) "Hanover Lutheran Church is a Lutheran congregation in Cape Girardeau, Missouri, that is a member of the Lutheran Church–Missouri Synod..."

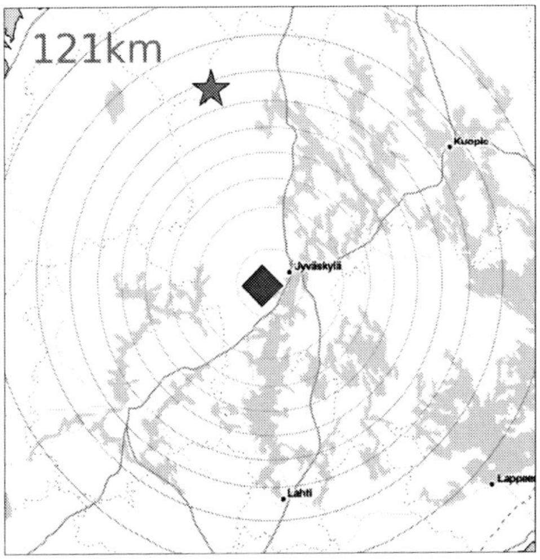

(b) "Salamanperä Strict Nature Reserve (Salamanperän luonnonpuisto) is home to Wolverine and Finnish Forest Reindeer (R. tarandus fennicus), and it is said..."

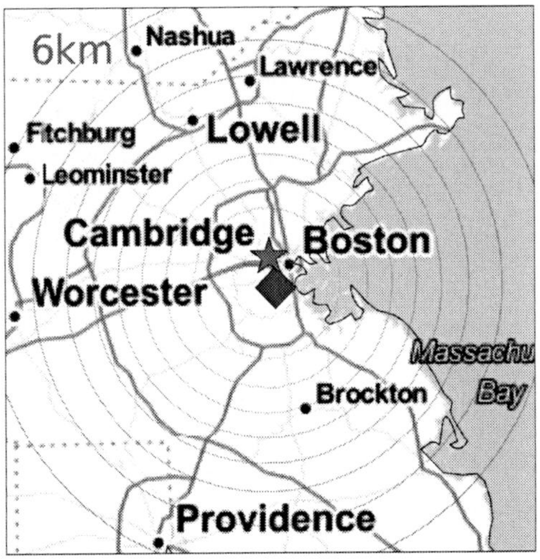

(c) "Houghton Library, on the south side of Harvard Yard adjacent to Widener Library, is Harvard University's primary repository for rare books and manuscripts..."

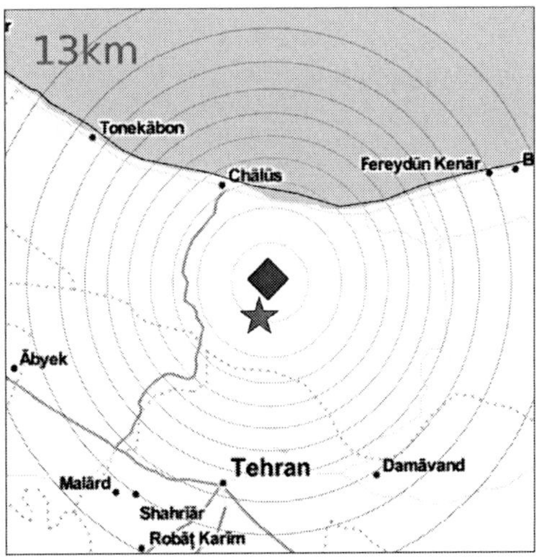

(d) "Pil (Persian –; also Romanized as Pīl; also known as Pel) is a village in Owzrud Rural District, Baladeh District, Nur County, Mazandaran Province, Iran..."

Figure 1: Predicted (diamond) and actual (star) coordinates. Contours represents 10% of the vMF mixture probability density. Approximately 95% of the probability density for each vMF mixture is shown in Figures 1a–1d.

a more flexible distributional shape than it would otherwise be able to with a single vMF component. Indexing the mixing components, ρ, by k, the revised loss function is given in Equation 6. We refer to this model as ELECTRo-map: End-to-end Location Estimation with Confidence via Transformer Regression.[3]

$$-L(\mathbf{W}) = -\sum_{k=1}^{5} \rho_k \sum_i \ln(f_{vmf}(\mathbf{y}_i; \hat{\mu}_{ik}, \hat{\kappa}_{ik})) \tag{6}$$

3 Data

To evaluate ELECTRo-map, we collect data from all Wikipedia articles with coordinates linked to Wikidata.org.[4] These data include the primary latitude and longitude associated with an article, globe, title, language, and extract attributes. The data were collected via the official Wikipedia API by iterating over the set of Wikipedia pages linked to Wikidata geographic entries.[5] Together, the data comprise the introductory sections of 1,286,475 English language articles. Most of the excerpts are between one sentence and a couple paragraphs in length. Many of these texts contain references to multiple geographic locations, but each one only has one "correct" latitude and longitude pair that describes the precise location of the article's referent. These are partitioned into a training set (1,260,746 articles), a validation set (12,864 articles) and a test set (12,865 articles).[6]

4 Evaluation

We compare the performance of ELECTRo-map against Mordecai. Because Mordecai and ELECTRo-map can both return multiple results per text, we offer three solutions for aggregating results to a single latitude and longitude prediction per observation. The first is to take the single highest probability prediction (*highProb*).[7] The second is to take the best prediction from the mixture (*best*).[8] The third is to take a random prediction from the mixture (*random*). Mordecai occasionally returns null results. In these cases, we impute a latitude and longitude pair of (0.0, 0.0). We also provide results for a complete cases analysis of Mordecai, omitting all 279 observations for which Mordecai failed to produce a geolocation.

Results are shown in Table 1. In the best case scenario, that in which the location of interest is known a priori, Mordecai clearly outperforms ELECTRo-map. Mordecai's median error is only 13.4km. However, in the more likely scenario that a single geolocation is desired for a text and no a priori knowledge of the preferred prediction is available, ELECTRo-map outperforms Mordecai. Mean and median errors for ELECTRo-map are 108.1km and 44.1km, respectively, compared to 946km and 154.5km for Mordecai. These numbers also compare favorably to the Kulkarni et al. (2020) model; in addition to classification-based metrics, the authors report the mean distance between predicted grid cell centroids and target locations. They report mean errors of between 174km and 180km.[9]

Four examples drawn from the test set are depicted in Figure 1. Predicted and actual locations are given as well as contours denoting the probability density associated with the predicted distribution. Each contour represents one decile. Each subfigure represents roughly 95% of the probability density. Captions give abridged excerpts of the associated input texts.

5 Conclusion

When humans perform geocoding manually, they often rely on contextual clues for assistance. Those clues may or may not come from the text itself. For instance, the presence of other named entities, like sports teams, may help human coders to distinguish between Washington state and Washington D.C. Automated processes for geocoding should also make use of contextual clues.

Model-based geocoding offers a natural method for both incorporating contextual clues and for dealing with the uncertainties that arise while geocoding. ELECTRo-map, for instance, quantifies uncertainty by estimating a mixture of probability distributions over likely geographic coordinates. Furthermore, model-based geocoding offers the ability to fine-tune for specific tasks: researchers

[3] https://tfwiki.net/wiki/Electro_map

[4] Found at https://www.wikidata.org/wiki/Q15181105

[5] https://en.wikipedia.org/w/api.php

[6] Test set size is kept small due to hardware limitations and the speed of Mordecai.

[7] While ELECTRo-map produces proper probabilities for each component, Mordecai only produces a country-level confidence score.

[8] Note that this rule requires knowledge of the target latitude and longitude. It therefore represents an unrealistic ideal scenario.

[9] Note that the data sets in these two papers, while both based on Wikipedia, are distinct.

may be interested in geocoding certain parts of texts and not others (e.g. birth and death places). To the extent that the model is unable to distinguish between multiple location types in the source text, this ambiguity should be reflected in the model's reported uncertainty. Model-based and gazetteer-based methods (like Mordecai) are not exclusive, though. It may be possible to derive better results by, for example, first identifying a distribution over likely locations via a statistical model and then "snapping to" a most likely location within that distribution using a gazetteer.

Finally, the success of multilingual transformers suggests that ELECTRo-map or related techniques may generalize across languages (K et al., 2020). Future efforts on model-based geocoding should seek to evaluate cross-lingual performance and measure the importance of context on location disambiguation.

Acknowledgments

We thank Dr. Yaoyao Dai of UNC Charlotte and three anonymous reviewers for their helpful feedback and suggestions.

References

GeoNames. Geonames gazetteer. Retr. February 12, 2021.

Andrew Halterman. 2017. Mordecai: Full text geoparsing and event geocoding. *Journal of Open Source Software*, 2(9):91.

Karthikeyan K, Zihan Wang, Stephen Mayhew, and Dan Roth. 2020. Cross-lingual ability of multilingual bert: An empirical study. In *International Conference on Learning Representations*.

Diederik P. Kingma and Jimmy Ba. 2015. Adam: A method for stochastic optimization. In *3rd International Conference on Learning Representations, ICLR 2015, San Diego, CA, USA, May 7-9, 2015, Conference Track Proceedings*.

Sayali Kulkarni, Shailee Jain, Mohammad Javad Hosseini, Jason Baldridge, Eugene Ie, and Li Zhang. 2020. Spatial language representation with multi-level geocoding.

Sophie J. Lee, Howard Liu, and Michael D. Ward. 2019. Lost in space: Geolocation in event data. *Political Science Research and Methods*, 7(4):871–888.

Yinhan Liu, Myle Ott, Naman Goyal, Jingfei Du, Mandar Joshi, Danqi Chen, Omer Levy, Mike Lewis, Luke Zettlemoyer, and Veselin Stoyanov. 2019. RoBERTa: A Robustly Optimized BERT Pretraining Approach. *arXiv e-prints*, page arXiv:1907.11692.

Tomas Mikolov, Ilya Sutskever, Kai Chen, Greg S Corrado, and Jeff Dean. 2013. Distributed representations of words and phrases and their compositionality. In *Advances in Neural Information Processing Systems*, volume 26. Curran Associates, Inc.

Victor Sanh, Lysandre Debut, Julien Chaumond, and Thomas Wolf. 2019. Distilbert, a distilled version of bert: smaller, faster, cheaper and lighter. *ArXiv*, abs/1910.01108.

Ashish Vaswani, Noam Shazeer, Niki Parmar, Jakob Uszkoreit, Llion Jones, Aidan N Gomez, Ł ukasz Kaiser, and Illia Polosukhin. 2017. Attention is all you need. In *Advances in Neural Information Processing Systems*, volume 30. Curran Associates, Inc.

Extracting Events from Industrial Incident Reports

Nitin Ramrakhiyani Swapnil Hingmire Sangameshwar Patil
Alok Kumar Girish K. Palshikar
{nitin.ramrakhiyani, swapnil.hingmire, sangameshwar.patil}@tcs.com
{k.alok9@tcs.com,gk.palshikar}@tcs.com
TCS Research, India

Abstract

Incidents in industries have huge social and political impact and minimizing the consequent damage has been a high priority. However, automated analysis of repositories of incident reports has remained a challenge. In this paper, we focus on automatically extracting events from incident reports. Due to absence of event annotated datasets for industrial incidents we employ a transfer learning based approach which is shown to outperform several baselines. We further provide detailed analysis regarding effect of increase in pre-training data and provide explainability of why pre-training improves the performance.

1 Introduction

The industrial revolution[1] has had a profound effect on the socio-political fabric of the world. Economic progress of societies has been highly correlated with their degree of industrialization. However, one of the flip sides of this progress has been the cost of large industrial accidents in terms of injuries to workers, damage to material and property as well as the irreparable loss of innocent human lives. Such major industrial incidents have had large social and political impacts and have prompted policy makers to devise multiple regulations towards prevention of such incidents. As an instance, the huge social uproar after the Bhopal Gas Leakage tragedy[2] had many political ramifications and resulted in creation of many new acts, rules and institutions in India and internationally.

Governmental agencies in-charge of industrial safety (OSHA; MINERVA) as well as the industrial enterprises themselves try and minimize the possibility of recurrence of industrial incidents. For this purpose, they carry out detailed investigations of incidents that have previously occurred to identify root causes and suggest preventive actions. In most cases, reports summarizing the incidents as well as their investigation are maintained in incident document repositories[3]. For example, Table 1 shows a sample incident report summary in the construction domain.

On February 1, 2014, at approximately 11:37 a.m., a 340 ft.-high guyed telecommunication tower, suddenly **collapsed** during **upgrading activities**. Four employees were **working** on the tower **removing** its diagonals. In the process, no temporary supports were installed. As a result of the tower 's **collapse** , two employees were **killed** and two others were badly **injured**.

Table 1: Sample Incident Report summary from Construction Domain

However, most of these investigative studies are carried out manually. There is little work towards automated processing of repositories of incident reports. Automated processing of incident reports requires us to solve multiple sub-problems such as identification of domain-specific entities, events, different states or conditions, relations between the events, resolving coreferences etc. As an example, we show the entities, events and states marked in red, blue and green respectively in Table 1. In this paper, we focus on an important stage from the above pipeline - extraction of events from incident reports. Event identification is central to the automated processing of incident reports because they pithily capture what exactly happened during an incident. Identification of events is also an important task required for down the line applications such as narrative understanding and visualization through knowledge representations such as Message Se-

[1] https://en.wikipedia.org/wiki/Industrial_Revolution

[2] https://en.wikipedia.org/wiki/Bhopal_disaster

[3] https://www.osha.gov/data

Proceedings of the 4th Workshop on Challenges and Applications of Automated Extraction of Socio-political Events from Text (CASE), pages 58–67
August 5–6, 2021, ©2021 Association for Computational Linguistics

quence Charts (MSC)(Palshikar et al., 2019; Hingmire et al., 2020) and event timelines(Bedi et al., 2017). Further, most of the work in event detection has focused on events in general domain such as ACE (Linguistic Data Consortium, 2005) and ECB (Bejan and Harabagiu, 2010). Little attention has been paid in the literature towards automated event extraction and analysis from industrial incident reports. To the best of our knowledge, there is no dataset of incident reports comprising of annotations for event identification (spans and attributes). This motivates us to experiment with unsupervised or weakly supervised approaches. In addition to experimenting with unsupervised baselines, we propose a transfer learning approach to extract events which first learns the nature of events in general domain through pre-training and then requires post-training with minimal training data in the domain of incidents.

We consider incident reports from two industries - civil aviation and construction and focus on identifying events involving risk-prone machinery or vehicles, common causes, human injuries and casualties and remedial measures, if any. We show that on both domains, the proposed transfer learning based approach outperforms several unsupervised and weakly supervised baselines. We further supplement the results with detailed analysis regarding effect of increase in pre-training data and explainability of pre-training through a novel clustering based approach.

We discuss relevant related work in Section 2. In Section 3, we cover the event extraction process detailing the annotation guidelines and proposed approach. In Section 4, we explain the experimental setup, evaluation and analysis. We finally conclude in Section 5.

2 Related Work

This section discusses important related work on two important aspects - automated analysis of textual incident reports/descriptions and unsupervised or weakly supervised event extraction approaches. As per the best of our knowledge, this is the first work on labelling and predicting events (a token level object) from incident report text. However, there are multiple papers which analyze incident reports at the document or sentence level for various tasks such as classification, cause-effect extraction and incident similarity. Tanguy et al.(2016) use NLP techniques to analyze aviation safety reports. The authors focus on classification of reports into different categories as well as use probabilistic topic models to analyze different aspects of incidents. The authors also propose the *timePlot* system to identify similar incident reports. Similar to (Tanguy et al., 2016), (Pence et al., 2020) perform text classification of event reports in nuclear power plants. However, both (Tanguy et al., 2016) and (Pence et al., 2020) do not focus on extraction of specific events from incident reports. Dasgupta et al. (2018) use neural network techniques to extract occupational health and safety related information from News articles related to industrial incidents. Specifically, they focus on extraction of target organization, safety issues, geographical location of the incident and penalty mentioned in the article.

In the context of event extraction approaches, multiple state-of-the-art supervised approaches have been proposed in the literature recently. However, the complex neural network architectures demand significant amounts of training data which is not available in the current scenario of event extraction in incident reports. Hence, we discuss two event extraction approaches which are weakly supervised in nature. In (Palshikar et al., 2019), the authors propose a rule based approach which considers all past tense verbs as events with a WordNet based filter retaining only "action" or "communication" events. There is no support for extraction of nominal events proposed by the authors. (Araki and Mitamura, 2018) propose an Open Domain Event Extraction approach which uses linguistic resources like WordNet and Wikipedia to generate training data in a distantly supervised manner and then train a BiLSTM based supervised event detection model using this data. Wang et al.(2019) propose a weakly supervised approach for event detection. The authors first construct a large-scale event-related candidate set and then use an adversarial training mechanism to identify events. We use the first two approaches - (Palshikar et al., 2019) and (Araki and Mitamura, 2018) as our baselines and discuss them in detail in Section 4. The third approach (Wang et al., 2019) based on adversarial training is evaluated on closed-domain datasets and hence it would be difficult to tune it and use it as a baseline for an open-domain event extraction task like ours.

3 Event Extraction in Incident Reports

Events are specific occurrences that appear in the text to denote happenings or changes in states of the involved participants. Multiple guidelines defining events and their extents in text are proposed in the literature (Linguistic Data Consortium, 2005; Mitamura et al., 2017). It is important to note that no event annotated data is available for any incident text dataset and this compels us to consider event extraction approaches which are either unsupervised or involve minimal training data. We make a two fold contribution in this regard. Firstly, we annotate a moderately sized incident text dataset[4] for evaluation and weak supervision. Secondly, we propose a transfer learning approach based on the standard BiLSTM sequence labelling architecture and compare with three baselines from literature.

3.1 Describing and Annotating Events in Incidents Reports

For incident reports, we define events to be specific verbs and nouns which describe pre-incident, incident and post-incident happenings. Though the semantics of the events are specific to this domain, the nature and function of verbs and nouns representing events in standard domains is preserved. In this paper, we focus on extraction of event triggers i.e. the primary verb/noun token indicative of an event, as against an event phrase spanning multiple tokens. Identification of the event triggers is pivotal to the event extraction problem and once an event trigger is identified it is straightforward to construct an event span by collecting specific dependency children of the trigger. We present a set of examples of sentences and their event triggers we focus on extracting in Table 2.

The pilot <EVENT>**pulled**</EVENT> the collective to <EVENT>**control**</EVENT> the <EVENT>**descent**</EVENT>.
The helicopter <EVENT>**crashed**</EVENT> in the field and <EVENT>**sustained**</EVENT> substantial <EVENT>**damage**</EVENT>.

Table 2: Examples of event triggers

Keeping in mind the domain specific semantics of the events, we choose the Open Event extraction guidelines proposed by (Araki, 2018). We differ with these guidelines at a few places and suitably modify them before guiding our annotators for the task. The details of the differences are described as follows:

- (Araki, 2018) suggests labelling of individual adjectives and adverbs as events. Based on our observations of incident text data, we rarely find adjectives or adverbs being "eventive". Hence, we restrict our events to be either verbs (verb-based) or nouns (nominal).
- (Araki, 2018) suggests labelling of states and conditions as events. In the current work, we only focus on extraction of instantaneous events and do not extract events describing long-going state-like situations or general factual information. For example, we do not extract `had` in the sentence `The plane had three occupants` as an event as it only gives information about the plane but we extract all events such as `crashed` in the sentence `The plane crashed in the sea.`
- (Araki, 2018) suggests considering light verb constructions (such as "make a turn") as a single combined event. However, we saw a need to consider more such combined verb formulations. As an example, consider the events `scheduled` and `operate` in the sentence `The plane was scheduled to operate a sight seeing flight.` To better capture the complete event semantics, we do not consider these words as separate events but as a single combined event `scheduled to operate.`

[4]the dataset can be obtained through an email request to the authors

3.2 Proposed Transfer Learning approach

Event extraction can be posed as a supervised sequence labelling problem and a standard BiLSTM-CRF based sequence labeller (Lample et al., 2016) can be employed. However, we reiterate that, as a large event annotated dataset specific to the domain of incident reports is not available, it would be difficult to train such a sequence labeller with high accuracy. We hypothesize that pre-training the BiLSTM-CRF sequence labeller with event labelled data from the general domain would help the network know about the general nature of verb-based and nominal events ("eventiveness"). Later as part of a transfer learning procedure (Yang et al., 2017), post-training of the network on a small event labelled dataset in incidents will provide us with an enriched incident event labeller. The proposed approach is based on this hypothesis and the transfer learnt model is then used to predict event triggers while testing.

	#Reports	#Events
Training subset		
AVIATION	10	182
CONSTRUCTION	15	107
Test subset		
AVIATION	30	560
CONSTRUCTION	30	224

Table 3: Annotated Dataset Statistics

4 Experimentation and Evaluation

4.1 Dataset

We base our experimentation on incidents from two domains - AVIATION and CONSTRUCTION. To develop the AVIATION dataset, we crawled all the 54 reports about civil aviation incidents[5] recorded in India between 2003 and 2011. For the CONSTRUCTION dataset, we crawled 67 incident report summaries[6] of some major construction incidents in New York (May 1990 to July 2019). We annotate 40 incident reports from AVIATION and 45 from the CONSTRUCTION dataset for both events and event temporal ordering. We treat 10 reports in AVATION and 15 in CONSTRUCTION as a small labelled training dataset. The annotated dataset statistics are presented in Table 3.

4.2 Baselines

As the first baseline (B1), we consider the approach proposed in (Palshikar et al., 2019). The authors extract Message Sequence Charts (MSC) from textual narratives which depict messages being passing between actors (entities) in the narrative. Their message extraction approach forms the basis for this event extraction baseline. The approach first identifies past tense verbs and then considers flowing the past tense to its children present tense verbs. It then classifies all identified verbs as either an "action" or "communication" using WordNet hypernyms of the verb itself or its nominal forms and ignores all verbs which are neither actions nor communications (mental events such as `thought`, `envisioned`). The approach doesn't extract nominal events, so we supplement this baseline with a simple nominal event extraction technique. We first consider a NomBank (Meyers et al., 2004) based approach which checks each noun for its presence in the NomBank and if found marks it as a nominal event. We also consider another approach based on the deverbal technique proposed by Gurevich et al. (Gurevich et al., 2008), which checks if a candidate noun is the deverbal of any verb in the VerbNet (Palmer et al.). It tags the noun as a nominal event, if such a verb is found. We take a union of the output of the two approaches and filter it using the WordNet to remove obvious false positives (such as entities, etc.) and obtain a final set of nominal events from the given incident report.

As the second baseline (B2), we consider on Open Domain Event Extraction technique proposed in (Araki and Mitamura, 2018). Most prior work on extraction of events is restricted to (i) closed domains such as ACE 2005 event ontology and (ii) limited syntactic types. In this paper, the authors highlight a need for open-domain event extraction where events are not restricted to a domain or a syntactic type and hence this becomes a suitable baseline. The authors propose a distant supervision method to identify events. The method comprises of two steps: (i) training data generation, and (ii) event detection. In the first step of distantly supervised data creation, candidate events are identified and filtered using WordNet to disambiguate for their eventiveness. Further, Wikipedia is used to identify events mentioned using proper nouns such as "Hurricane Katrina". Both these steps help to generate lots of good quality (but not gold) training data. In the second step, BiLSTM based supervised event detection model is trained on this distantly generated training data. The experimental results show that the distant supervision improves event detection performance in various domains, without any need for manual annotation of events.

As the third baseline (B3), we use the standard BiLSTM based sequence labelling neural network (Lample et al., 2016) employed frequently in information extraction tasks such as Named Entity Recognition (NER). We use the small labelled training dataset to train this BiLSTM based sequence labeller for event identification and use it to extract events while testing.

4.3 Experimentation Details

4.3.1 Word Embeddings

For representing the text tokens as input in the proposed neural network approaches, we experiment with the standard static embeddings (GloVe (Pennington et al., 2014)) and the more recent con-

[5]`https://dgca.gov.in/digigov-portal/?page=IncidentReports`

[6]`https://www.osha.gov/construction/engineering`

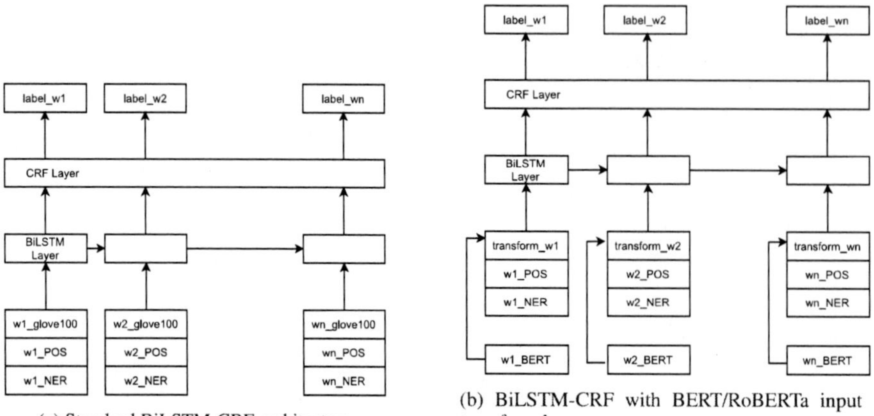

(a) Standard BiLSTM-CRF architecture

(b) BiLSTM-CRF with BERT/RoBERTa input transform layer

Figure 1: BiLSTM-CRF network models

textual embeddings (BERT (Devlin et al., 2018) and RoBERTa (Liu et al., 2019)). We consider 100-dimensional GloVe embeddings and 768-dimensional contextual BERT and RoBERTa representations for the experiments.

4.3.2 Neural Network Design and Tuning

The neural network architecture we use for baseline B3 and the proposed transfer learning approach is based on the BiLSTM-CRF architecture proposed by (Lample et al., 2016) for sequence labelling. It is shown in the Figure 1a. As part of the input we concatenate the word embeddings by 20 dimensional learnable POS and NER embeddings. We store these learnt embeddings alongwith the model and reload them during inference.

An important aspect to note is that large amount of training data is not available and hence the number of parameters which the network needs to learn should be as minimum as possible to avoid high bias. In particular the connection between the input layer which is 140 dimensional (in case of GloVe embeddings, $100 + 20\ POS + 20\ NER$) and the BiLSTM layer (with hidden units 140) is $140 \times 140 \times 2$. In case of 768-dimensional BERT/RoBERTa based representations it blows up about 6 times to $768 \times 768 \times 2$, assuming the LSTM hidden units are also 768. The network fails to learn while training using the limited data in case of 768-dimensional embeddings. So we devise a small change to the input layer to support learning in this case. We introduce a dense layer just after the 768-dimensional BERT/RoBERTa input with a linear activation function to map the 768-dimensional input into a smaller dimensional space, as shown in Figure 1b. Due to the linear activation, this layer behaves like a linear transformation of a high dimensional input vector to a lower dimensional input vector. Additionally, we concatenate the previously mentioned POS and NER learnable embeddings to the transformed input embeddings as the final input to the network.

We employ 5-fold cross-validation on the small training dataset for tuning the hyperparameters of the neural network separately for both domains and embedding types. We found minimal difference in hyperparameter values across both Aviation and Construction datasets and hence, we use similar parameters in both cases. The tuned hyperparameters with their values are shown in Table 4.

Hyperparameter	**GloVe based model (Fig. 1a)**	**BERT/ RoBERTa based model (Fig. 1b)**
input_word_embedding_dimension	100	768
input_word_transform_dimension	NA	200
input_pos_embedding_dimension	20	20
input_ner_embedding_dimension	20	20
bilstm_hidden_units	140	240
bilstm_recurrent_dropout	0.3	0.3
crf_input_dimension	70	120
optimizer	adam	adam
epochs	20	30
batch_size	8	16
pre-training_epochs	20	20
pre-training_batch_size	16	16

Table 4: Tuned Hyperparameters

4.3.3 Implementation

Baseline B1 is unsupervised and is implemented and used directly. Code for baseline B2 is made available by the authors[7] and we install and use it without any change. The BiLSTM-CRF sequence labelling networks, used for baseline (B3) and the transfer learning approach, is implemented using keras in python 3. These approaches are trained on the small training data shown in Table 3. To handle randomness in neural network weight initialization and to ensure robustness of the results, we run every neural network experiment (both hyperparameter tuning as well as final test experiments) five times and report an average of the five runs. We were able to observe standard deviation in the precision, recall and F1 of these runs to be as low as 1-2%. With respect to the pre-training data for the transfer learning approach, we use the event annotations from the ECB dataset (Bejan and Harabagiu, 2010). It is a dataset for Event Coreference tasks and has comprehensive event annotations (about 8.8K labelled events in about 9.7K sentences).

4.4 Evaluation and Analysis

As we can observe in Table 5, the proposed transfer learning approach (TL) outperforms the other baselines (B1, B2 and B3) in performance irrespective of static or contextual embeddings. Further, as expected the BiLSTM based baseline B3 shows lower recall than the transfer learning approach in which we see significantly improved recall particularly for the Construction dataset for all embedding types. We observe a similar boost in recall particularly for BERT representations on the Aviation dataset. An important point to note here is that the amount of pre-training data, leading to best results, varies between 40% to 60% for combinations of dataset and embedding type. In Table 5, we report the performance for best amount of pre-training data and present a detailed analysis on effect on increasing pre-training data in Section 4.4.1.

As part of the analysis, we first measure the effect of increase in the amount of pre-training data in the transfer learning approach and find out what amount of pre-training leads to the best results. Secondly, we try to explain why the pre-training works through a novel clustering methodology over the BiLSTM learnt context representations of the input embeddings. And thirdly, we present an ensemble approach considering a practical standpoint of using these systems in real-life use cases.

	AVIATION			CONSTRUCTION		
	P	R	F1	P	R	F1
B1	0.67	0.83	0.74	0.63	0.8	0.7
B2	0.71	0.89	0.79	0.64	0.95	0.77
$B3_{GloVe100}$	0.83	0.83	0.83	0.87	0.69	0.77
$TL_{GloVe100}$	0.86	0.84	0.85	0.91	0.75	0.82
$B3_{BERT}$	0.84	0.79	0.82	0.84	0.63	0.72
TL_{BERT}	0.87	0.83	0.85	0.9	0.73	0.81
$B3_{RoBERTa}$	0.87	0.83	0.85	0.8	0.63	0.71
$TL_{RoBERTa}$	0.86	0.85	0.86	0.85	0.79	0.82
ENS	0.90	0.83	0.86	0.95	0.75	0.84

Table 5: Evaluation - Event Extraction

4.4.1 Amount of pre-training data

As an important part of the analysis, we measure what is the effect of increase in pre-training data in the transfer learning approach. We hypothesize that the performance would rise till a certain point with increasing pre-training data and would then stabilize and change minimally. This is based on the notion that pre-training positions the network weights in a better space from where the training on domain specific data should begin. However, beyond a certain amount of pre-training the initialization may not lead to any better initial values for the weights.

To check the validity of this hypothesis, we pre-trained the network with varied amounts of pre-training data (1%, 5%, 10%, 20%, 30%, ..., 100%) and checked the performance on test data. Figure 2 and Figure 3 show the obtained F1 curves for these pre-training settings for Aviation and Construction datasets respectively. As with other experiments, each point in the graphs is an average of performance for 5 runs of training and testing.

It can be seen that with increasing pre-training data, the performance improves and reaches a peak between 30% to 70% of pre-training data available, varying for different input embedding types. We observe a small dip in performance when amounts near complete pre-training data are used. Interestingly, BERT based representations start showing promise with even 1% of pre-training data for the Aviation dataset.

4.4.2 Explanability of Pre-training

To explain why the pre-training is helping, we need to have an understanding of what the network is learning about the input embeddings of the tokens and their context from the bidirectional LSTM. It would be helpful if one could analyze the token-

[7]https://bitbucket.org/junaraki/coling2018-event

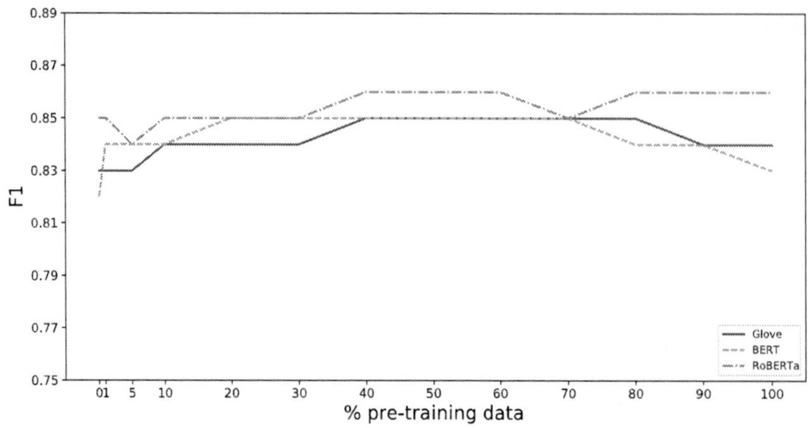

Figure 2: Increase in Pre-training Data - Aviation

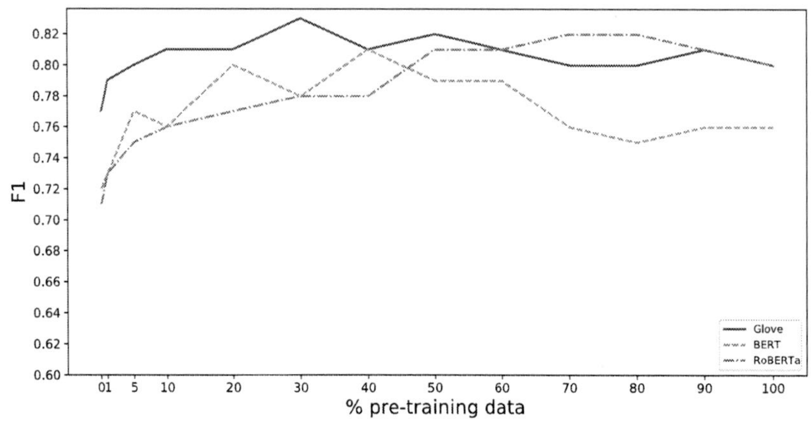

Figure 3: Increase in Pre-training Data - Construction

wise output of the BiLSTM layer, which incorporates both the input embeddings and the context information and feeds these representations to the CRF layer as features for sequence learning/inference (See Figure 1a). However, internal representations in a neural network are a set of numbers not comprehensible in a straightforward manner and would require an indirect observation to decipher what is captured by them. One such indirect analysis of these internal representations involves performing their clustering and observing if representations with similar semantics cluster together and rarely cluster with dissimilar representations. In this case, the desired semantics would mean capture of the "eventiveness" property in event tokens. We perform such a clustering based analysis on extractions in the Construction dataset.

We consider all tokens which are marked as events in the gold and are also correctly predicted as events by the transfer learnt model (TL) such as tokens t1 and t2 in Table 6. We obtain the BiLSTM output representations for these tokens by passing their sentences through the TL model truncated till the input of the CRF layer and collect these representations (r_{TL}^{t1} and r_{TL}^{t2}) in a set R_{TL}. As observed from the results, the baseline model B3 has a lower recall than the TL model and for tokens such as t1 and t2, we can categorize the predictions of the B3 model into either 'correctly predicted as

Token	Gold Label	TL Prediction	B3 Prediction
t1	EVENT	EVENT	EVENT
t2	EVENT	EVENT	O
t3	EVENT	O	O
t4	O	O	O

Table 6: Example Tokens and Predictions

events' or 'missed and marked as non-events'. We divide these tokens into the correct and incorrect sets as per their baseline model predictions. We obtain the BiLSTM output representations for these tokens from the B3 model in the similar way as earlier and respectively collect these representations (r^{t1}_{B3} and r^{t2}_{B3}) in two sets R_{B3C} (B3 corrects) and R_{B3I} (B3 incorrects). We hypothesize that all the representations which lead to a correct event prediction should belong to a subspace of "eventive" representations and should be far from the representations which lead to an incorrect prediction. Hence, representations in the set R_{TL} and R_{B3C} should cluster differently from the representations in the set R_{B3I}. So, in the context of the example tokens of Table 6, representations r^{t1}_{TL}, r^{t2}_{TL} and r^{t1}_{B3} should cluster differently from r^{t2}_{B3}.

On performing agglomerative clustering on the above representations with a maximum distance of 0.3 (standard similarity of 0.7), we find that the representations R_{TL} and R_{B3C} belong to multiple clusters which are highly separate from clusters housing the representations in R_{B3I}. This validates our hypothesis and highlights positioning of R_{TL} and R_{B3C} representations closer to the required "eventiveness" subspace and far from the R_{B3I} representation which lead to incorrect predictions. We further strengthen the claim by computing purity (Manning et al., 2008) of the representation clusters. The purity of a clustering gives a measure of the extent to which clusters contains instances of a single class. In case of predictions based on GloVe embeddings models, we observe a purity of 0.9781 and in case of BERT embeddings models, we observe a purity of 0.9832.

4.4.3 Practical standpoint

We also performed a detailed analysis with regard to the errors in verb-based and nominal event predictions. It was observed that the deep learning approaches miss important verb-based events leading to low recall particularly for the verb-based events, but identify nominal events correctly in most cases. The rule based baseline B1, captures all the verb-based events mostly as it designates most past tense verbs as events. However, the rule based approach fails to identify nominal events correctly as it doesn't observe the context of a noun while deciding its event nature. This observation prompted us to perform a novel ensemble where we create a union of all verb-based event predictions of the rule based approach and all nominal event predictions of the transfer learning based approach using glove embeddings. We believe this ensemble approach holds value from a practical standpoint in two ways. Firstly, using GloVe embeddings eases compute and maintenance requirements in deployment environments, which are higher for handling BERT/RoBERTa based contextual models. Further, as seen from the results in Table 5, GloVe embeddings perform at par with contextual representations. Secondly, when showing a user predictions of events from an incident report, she might get perturbed more because of incorrect nominal events than some extra verbal events. As seen in Table 5, this ensemble approach (row marked as ENS) shows a respectable increase in precision over the Transfer learning approach in both datasets and may be useful to employ in real life incident event identification systems.

5 Conclusion and Future Work

In this paper we focused on extracting events from reports on incidents in Aviation and Construction domains. As there is no dataset of incident reports comprising of annotations for event extraction, we contributed by proposing modifications to a set of existing event guidelines and accordingly preparing a small annotated dataset. Keeping in mind the limited data settings, we proposed a transfer learning approach over the existing BiLSTM-CRF based sequence labelling approach and experimented with different static and contextual embeddings. We observed that pretraining improves performance of event extraction for all combinations of domains and embeddings. As part of the analysis, we showed the impact of employing varying amounts of pretraining data. We also performed a novel clustering based analysis to explain why pretraining improves performance of event extraction. We also propose a novel ensemble approach motivated from a practical viewpoint.

As future work, we plan to pursue other important stages of the incident report analysis pipeline such as (i) entity/actor identification which involves finding the important participants in an incident, (ii) event argument identification which involves finding participants which are agents or experiencers of the event, (iii) state/condition identification which involve finding expressions describing long-running state-like conditions and (iv) event-event relation identification which involves establishing of relation links between events.

References

Jun Araki. 2018. *Extraction of Event Structures from Text*. Ph.D. thesis, Carnegie Mellon University.

Jun Araki and Teruko Mitamura. 2018. Open-Domain Event Detection using Distant Supervision. In *Proceedings of the 27th International Conference on Computational Linguistics (COLING)*, pages 878–891, Santa Fe, NM, USA.

Harsimran Bedi, Sangameshwar Patil, Swapnil Hingmire, and Girish Palshikar. 2017. Event timeline generation from history textbooks. In *Proceedings of the 4th Workshop on Natural Language Processing Techniques for Educational Applications (NLPTEA 2017)*, pages 69–77.

Cosmin Bejan and Sanda Harabagiu. 2010. Unsupervised event coreference resolution with rich linguistic features. In *Proceedings of the 48th Annual Meeting of the Association for Computational Linguistics*, pages 1412–1422, Uppsala, Sweden. Association for Computational Linguistics.

Tirthankar Dasgupta, Abir Naskar, Rupsa Saha, and Lipika Dey. 2018. Extraction and visualization of occupational health and safety related information from open web. In *2018 IEEE/WIC/ACM International Conference on Web Intelligence, WI 2018, Santiago, Chile, December 3-6, 2018*, pages 434–439. IEEE Computer Society.

Jacob Devlin, Ming-Wei Chang, Kenton Lee, and Kristina Toutanova. 2018. BERT: Pre-training of Deep Bidirectional Transformers for Language Understanding. *arXiv preprint arXiv:1810.04805*.

Olga Gurevich, Richard Crouch, Tracy Holloway King, and Valeria De Paiva. 2008. Deverbal nouns in knowledge representation. *Journal of Logic and Computation*, 18(3):385–404.

Swapnil Hingmire, Nitin Ramrakhiyani, Avinash Kumar Singh, Sangameshwar Patil, Girish Keshav Palshikar, Pushpak Bhattacharyya, and Vasudeva Varma. 2020. Extracting Message Sequence Charts from Hindi Narrative Text. In *Proceedings of the First Joint Workshop on Narrative Understanding, Storylines, and Events, NUSE@ACL 2020, Online, July 9, 2020*, pages 87–96. Association for Computational Linguistics.

Guillaume Lample, Miguel Ballesteros, Sandeep Subramanian, Kazuya Kawakami, and Chris Dyer. 2016. Neural architectures for named entity recognition. In *Proceedings of the 2016 Conference of the North American Chapter of the Association for Computational Linguistics: Human Language Technologies*, pages 260–270, San Diego, California. Association for Computational Linguistics.

Linguistic Data Consortium. 2005. ACE (Automatic Content Extraction) English Annotation Guidelines for Events.

Yinhan Liu, Myle Ott, Naman Goyal, Jingfei Du, Mandar Joshi, Danqi Chen, Omer Levy, Mike Lewis, Luke Zettlemoyer, and Veselin Stoyanov. 2019. RoBERTa: A Robustly Optimized BERT Pretraining Approach. *arXiv preprint arXiv:1907.11692*.

Christopher D. Manning, Prabhakar Raghavan, and Hinrich Schütze. 2008. *Introduction to Information Retrieval*. Cambridge University Press, USA.

A. Meyers, R. Reeves, C. Macleod, R. Szekely, V. Zielinska, B. Young, and R. Grishman. 2004. The NomBank Project: An Interim Report. In *HLT-NAACL 2004 Workshop: Frontiers in Corpus Annotation*, pages 24–31, Boston, Massachusetts, USA. Association for Computational Linguistics.

MINERVA. The MINERVA Portal of European Commission. `https://minerva.jrc.ec.europa.eu/en/minerva/about`. [Online; accessed 26-Apr-2021].

Teruko Mitamura, Zhengzhong Liu, and Eduard H. Hovy. 2017. Events detection, coreference and sequencing: What's next? overview of the TAC KBP 2017 event track. In *Proceedings of the 2017 Text Analysis Conference, TAC 2017, Gaithersburg, Maryland, USA, November 13-14, 2017*. NIST.

OSHA. Occupational Safety and Health Administration. `https://www.osha.gov/Publications/3439at-a-glance.pdf`. [Online; accessed 26-Apr-2021].

Martha Palmer, Claire Bonial, and Jena Hwang. Verbnet. In *The Oxford Handbook of Cognitive Science*.

Girish Palshikar, Sachin Pawar, Sangameshwar Patil, Swapnil Hingmire, Nitin Ramrakhiyani, Harsimran Bedi, Pushpak Bhattacharyya, and Vasudeva Varma. 2019. Extraction of message sequence charts from narrative history text. In *Proceedings of the First Workshop on Narrative Understanding*, pages 28–36, Minneapolis, Minnesota. Association for Computational Linguistics.

Justin Pence, Pegah Farshadmanesh, Jinmo Kim, Cathy Blake, and Zahra Mohaghegh. 2020. Data-theoretic approach for socio-technical risk analysis: Text mining licensee event reports of u.s. nuclear power plants. *Safety Science*, 124:104574.

Jeffrey Pennington, Richard Socher, and Christopher D Manning. 2014. GloVe: Global Vectors for Word Representation. In *Proceedings of the 2014 conference on empirical methods in natural language processing (EMNLP)*, pages 1532–1543.

Ludovic Tanguy, Nikola Tulechki, Assaf Urieli, Eric Hermann, and Cline Raynal. 2016. Natural language processing for aviation safety reports: From classification to interactive analysis. *Computers in Industry*, 78:80–95. Natural Language Processing and Text Analytics in Industry.

Xiaozhi Wang, Xu Han, Zhiyuan Liu, Maosong Sun, and Peng Li. 2019. Adversarial training for weakly supervised event detection. In *Proceedings of the 2019 Conference of the North American Chapter of the Association for Computational Linguistics: Human Language Technologies, Volume 1 (Long and Short Papers)*, pages 998–1008, Minneapolis, Minnesota. Association for Computational Linguistics.

Zhilin Yang, Ruslan Salakhutdinov, and William W Cohen. 2017. Transfer learning for sequence tagging with hierarchical recurrent networks. *arXiv preprint arXiv:1703.06345*.

Automatic Fake News Detection in Political Platforms – A Transformer-based Approach

Shaina Raza
Department of Computer Science, Ryerson University
shaina.raza@ryerson.ca

Abstract

The dynamics and influence of fake news on Twitter during the 2020 US presidential election remains to be clarified. Here, we use a dataset related to 2020 U.S Election that consists of news articles and tweets on those articles. Therefore, it is extremely important to stop the spread of fake news before it reaches a mass level, which is a big challenge. We propose a novel fake news detection framework that can address this challenge. Our proposed framework exploits the information from news articles and social contexts to detect fake news. The proposed model is based on a Transformer architecture, which can learn useful representations from fake news data and predicts the probability of a news as being fake or real. Experimental results on real-world data show that our model can detect fake news with higher accuracy and much earlier, compared to the baselines.

1 Introduction

Fake news refers to false or misleading information that appears as real news (Zhou & Zafarani, 2020). Fake news can be broadly categorized as either misinformation (unintentional false information) or disinformation (deliberate false information). Recent social and political events, such as 2020 United States presidential election, have seen an increase in fake news (E. Chen et al., 2021). According to a report by First Draft News [1], America's current disinformation crisis is the result of more than two decades of corruption in country's information ecosystem. There are many factors to blame for this social and political misinformation. For example, the role of social media that is unregulated, lack of investment in public media, downfall of local news outlets, and emergence of hyper-partisan online outlets.

An information (news) ecosystem consists of publishers (news media that publish the news article), information (news content) and users (Anderson, 2016). Initially, the news comes from the publishers. Then, it goes to the news websites, from where it goes to the users who share news on different platforms (blogs, social media, etc.). If the news is fake, some users may find it more sensational and interesting to comment on and share over their networks. The existence of the bots in social media makes it even worse, who spread misinformation through multiple channels to urge people believe the fake news. Therefore, it becomes crucial to stop the fake news before it reaches to a broad audience. In this paper, we aim to effectively detect the fake news.

Generally, the content of fake news is vague and misleading (C. Liu et al., 2019). According to a research (Horne & Adalı, 2017), the content of fake news consists of certain patterns, such as excessive use of capital letters, punctuations, or emotion-bearing words, which gives us clues about a news being fake or real. However, if the content of news is not sufficient, then the social contexts may be useful to assess the veracity (truthfulness) of news. The social contexts (Shu et al., 2019) refers to users' interactions, such as, comments, shares, likes, followers-followees relations etc., that are helpful to determine if a news fake or real. Sometimes, even the verified accounts in social media are involved in the propagation of fake news

[1] https://firstdraftnews.org/latest/fake-news-complicated/

Proceedings of the 4th Workshop on Challenges and Applications of Automated Extraction of Socio-political Events from Text (CASE), pages 68–78
August 5–6, 2021, ©2021 Association for Computational Linguistics

(Shahi et al., 2021). In this work, we plan to consider both news content and social contexts to detect fake news.

Generally, a news item is represented by a news ID or news title, which is not sufficient to capture the patterns of fake news. There are many important pieces of information that may be more useful. For example, a news body or news source could be (at times) more convincing in persuading readers to believe something, so, we need to pay closer attention to such information. We refer to such auxiliary information as side (metadata) information. The side information associated with a news article can be news body, source, time of publication, topics etc. In this work, we plan to consider different side information related to news. We also consider embedded tweets on news articles, which provide us additional information to determine the veracity of news.

According to a research, the fake news spreads within minutes once planted (Vosoughi et al., 2018). For example, the fake news that Elon Musk's Tesla team is inviting people to give any amount ranging from 0.1 to 20 bitcoins in exchange for double the amount, resulted in a loss of millions of dollars within the first few minutes[2]. So, it is critical to detect fake news early on before it spreads. In this work, we plan to early detect the fake news within few minutes after its propagation.

In recent years, the Transformer-based models (Vaswani et al., 2017) have gained significant popularity in different NLP tasks, such as text classification, detection methods. These models usually input whole lexical data as one piece of information or document, without considering any side information (Wu et al., 2020). In addition, the temporal information is not considered (by default) in these models. To better utilize the strengths of Transformer-based models for fake news detection, it is important to include heterogenous information (main, side and temporal information) to build a classification model. In this work, we build a novel Transformer model that considers heterogenous information for the task of fake news detection. Throughout this paper, we refer to the main information as the news headline, and we refer to side information as consisting of news-related features, social contexts (tweets), and temporal information.

We summarize our contributions as:

- We propose a novel Transformer model that considers news content and associated side information for the fake news detection task.
- We incorporate heterogenous side information in our model. In addition to only lexical data (as in typical Transformers), we also consider the non-lexical (numeric, categorical) data. We use the multi-head attention mechanism to attend to different parts of such information.
- We propose to detect fake new early within few minutes after it is planted. For that, we utilize the position encoding (Devlin et al., 2018) in the Transformer model that helps us to achieve our goal of early detection. The position encoding represents the words' order in a model, i.e., the value of a word (content) and its temporal position in a sentence.

We evaluate our system by running experiments on real-world data, which consists of news articles from various sources and social contexts from Twitter. Using an ablation study, we find that including both news content and social contexts is beneficial in detecting fake news patterns. The inclusion of more side information proves very useful as indicated in the results. We also show that our proposed model can detect fake news earlier and with greater accuracy than baselines.

The rest of the paper is organized as follows. Section 2 is about Methodology. Section 3 is for Experiment, and Section 4 is for Experimental Results and Analysis. The Related Work is covered in Section 5. Section 6 is the Conclusion and recommendations for the future work.

2 Methodology

Problem Definition: Given news and associated side information (news-related, social contexts and temporal information), the task is to determine if a news item is fake or real.

We consider the fake news detection task as a binary classification problem (news as fake or real). We also consider a multiclass classification (news as fake, real or mixed) in the experiments.

Proposed Model: In our work, we modify the structure of pre-trained Bidirectional Encoder Representations from Transformers (BERT) (Devlin et al., 2018) to add side information (in addition to main information). The same methodology can also be applied on other Transformers (RobertA, XLNet, BART, T5 etc.).

[2] https://www.bbc.com/news/technology-56402378

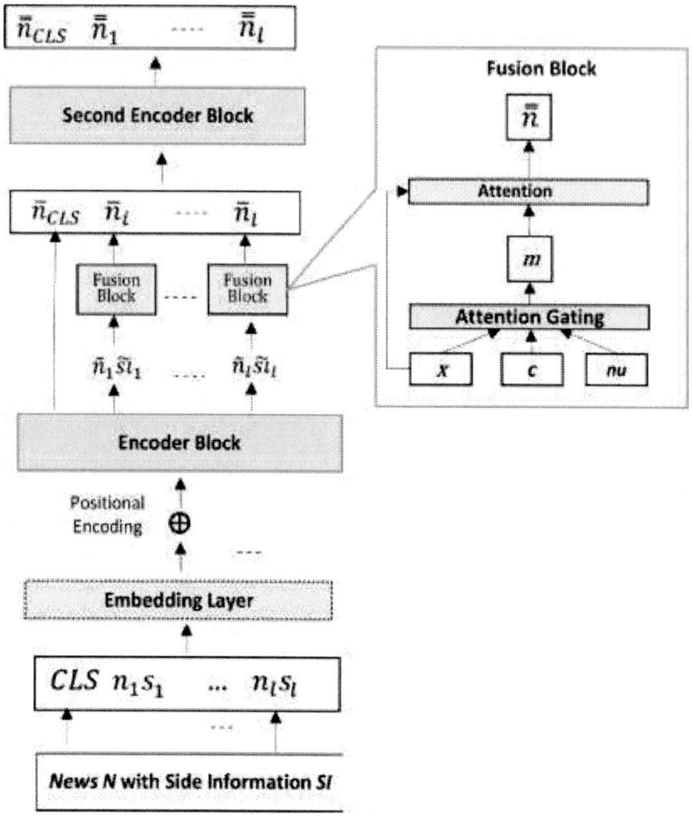

Figure 1: Proposed Model Faker

We represent each news item N by its title (main information) and side information. (Temporal, news-related, and social contexts). We believe that having more information is always beneficial. For instance, the author and source provide us with partisan information (political party as belonging to right or left wing). The temporal information is useful for determining whether a fake news is already spread or just released. Similarly, social contexts (tweets) give us additional information about users' reactions on news.

We present a novel Transformer-based model, **Faker**, as shown in Figure 1. The input to model is news items and associated side information. Each news item N has a sequence of words, i.e., $N = \{n_1, n_2, ..., n_l\}$ where l is length. For each news, we have the accompanying side information, i.e., $SI = \{si_1, si_2, ..., si_l\}$. In our work, we consider different types (lexical and non-lexical) of side information, whereas our main information is textual. We use 'word' as a general term to represent any word from N or feature from SI.

The first layer in Faker is the embedding layer. The input to the embedding layer is the sequence of words from each input N or SI. The [CLS] token is added at the start of the sequence and is later used for the class label prediction. We utilize the token and segment embedding from the BERT model to represent the syntax and semantics of each word.

Similar to (Q. Chen et al., 2019), we also assume that temporal order exists in sequences. So, we use position encoding (Vaswani et al., 2017) to capture the chronological information in the sequences. In our case, the position value of each word is decided by the timestamp of news publication.

The output from the embedding layer is then fed into the next twelve layers in the first Encoder block. After the encoding process, we get the output vector for each word from news. The contextualized representation after the first Encoder block is $\tilde{N} = \{\tilde{n}_1, \tilde{n}_2 ..., \tilde{n}_l\}$ for the news and $\widetilde{SI} = \{\tilde{si}_1, \tilde{si}_2, ..., \tilde{si}_l\}$ for the side information ($\tilde{si}$ comes from si, the dot above i under $\tilde{si}$ is hidden under the tilde ~). Each word vector from $\widetilde{N}$ and $\widetilde{SI}$ is then passed to a **F**usion **B**lock.

Fusion Block: Inside the Fusion Block, we represent each piece of information (lexical or non-lexical) from $\widetilde{N}$ and $\widetilde{SI}$ with a token (word). The x is a textual word, nu is numeric word (feature) and c is a categorical word.

Inspired by the gating mechanism introduced in (Wang et al., 2018), we first take each feature from the non-lexical data (nu and c) and combine them using a gating mechanism to produce a new non-lexical vector h, as shown in Equation (1):

$$h = g_c \odot (W_c c) + g_{nu} \odot (W_{nu} nu) + b_h \quad (1)$$

where c is categorical feature, nu is numerical feature, W denotes a weight matrix, b denotes a scalar bias, and g_c and g_{nu} are the gating vector for c and nu respectively. We may refer to g_i as a gating vector for a non-lexical feature i. The g_i is fused with x using an activation function R. Then it goes into h. The g_i is defined in Equation (2):

$$g_i = R\left(W_{g_i}[i \,||\, x] + b_i\right) \quad (2)$$

Once, we get the h, we use a weighted summation between the lexical vector x and the combined non-lexical vector h to produce a fused sequence m, as shown in Equation (3):

$$m = x + \alpha h \quad (3)$$

where x is text feature, α is a normalizing factor to dampen the magnitude of h representation within a range. The α is shown in Equation (4):

$$\alpha = \min\left(\frac{||x||_2}{||h||_2} * \beta, 1\right) \quad (4)$$

where the $||x||_2$ and $||h||_2$ denote the l_2-norms of x and h, and hyperparameter β is selected during the validation process. Subsequently, an attention is applied over the lexical and non-lexical vectors to produce the final fused representation $\bar{n}$. The output from each Fusion Block is $\bar{n}_i$ and is calculated for each word from the input sequence. The new sequence $\bar{N} = \{\bar{n}_{CLS}, \bar{n}_1, \bar{n}_2, \dots, \bar{n}_l\}$ is then fed as input to the next Encoder block. We apply the Encoder layers of our model on this sequence $\bar{n}$. At the end of the second Encoder block, we get the sequence $\bar{\bar{n}} = \{\bar{\bar{n}}_{CLS}, \bar{\bar{n}}_1, \bar{\bar{n}}_2, \dots, \bar{\bar{n}}_l\}$. The first element in $\bar{\bar{n}}$ is the [CLS] token that has the necessary information to predict the class {real, fake} label. Therefore, the $\bar{\bar{n}}_{CLS}$ goes through a final transformation to produce a value which can be used to predict a class label.

Feature	Description	Format
Article ID*	Article identifier	Integer
News title	Headline of news	Text
News source *	News Source (e.g., CNN, theonion)	Categorical
News content *	News Body	Text
Author *	Author of article	Categorical
URL *	URL of the article	Text
Publication timestamp*	Publication time as unix timestamp	Integer
Tweet ID *	ID of tweet	Integer
Embedded tweet*	Raw data from tweets (on news)	Text

Table 1: Dataset features, * is side information

3 Experiment

Fake news data: We use the NELA-GT-2020 dataset (Horne, Benjamin; Gruppi, 2021), which covers a broad set of events, including the COVID-19 pandemic and the 2020 U.S. Presidential Election. In this work, we only consider the 2020 U.S. Election event-based data, which consists of 294,504 related news articles across 403 sources between January 1st, 2020 and December 31st, 2020. The source-level ground truth labels are collected from the Media Bias/Fact Check (MBFC)[3] website.

The dataset also includes over 400,000 embedded Tweets found in news articles, which we also employ in our research. Table 1 shows the features of US Elections data that we use.

We use article IDs to create sequences based on available features (in Table 1). The embedded tweet text is also included in the sequence. Each sequence record is grouped by article ID and is sorted according to publication timestamp. The actual news articles are not labeled.

The dataset only provides us the ground truth labels (0- reliable, 1- mixed, 2- unreliable) at source-level. These source-level labels are obtained from MBFC, which considers the dimensions of veracity based on a factuality (credibility) and on conspiracy sources. We use the distant supervision (Mintz et al., 2009) to assign a label to each news story. In that, first we take the distant (weak) labels provided to each news source and use a weighted scheme to label each news article. The intuition of distant labeling is that the training labels at source-level may be imprecise and partial but can be used to create a strong

3 https://mediabiasfactcheck.com/

predictive model. This approach is also suggested in the NELA-GT-18 paper (Nørregaard et al., 2019) and has shown promising results in a recent work (Horne et al., 2019).

After doing the labeling, we get around 37k labels as 'fake', 12.5k labels as 'real' and 32k labels as 'mixed'. To handle the data imbalance problem in in the dataset, we use the under-sampling technique (Drummond et al., 2003), in which the majority class is made closer to the minority class, by removing records from the majority class. Initially, we tried the SMOTE technique, in which the distribution of minority class is increased by replicating some records, but due to limited memory, we opt for under-sampling.

Evaluation Metrics: To assess model perform, we use accuracy **ACC**, precision **Prec**, recall **Rec** and F1-score **F1**, and area under curve **AUC**. Compared to ACC, AUC is usually better at ranking predictions because AUC evaluates model performance across all possible thresholds. We treat the fake news detection as a binary classification problem using labels {'Real', 'Fake'}, and as multiclass classification using labels {'Real', Fake' and 'Mixed'}.

Comparison Methods: For the baselines, we use:

Fake-news detection methods

- TriFN (Shu et al., 2019): A matrix factorization methods that exploits user, news and publisher relationships for fake news detection.
- Declare (Popat et al., 2020): A neural network that assesses the credibility of claims on news.
- Grover (Zellers et al., 2019): a neural framework to detect fake news.

Transformer-based methods

- BERT (Devlin et al., 2018): Bidirectional Encoder Representations from Transformers.
- GPT-2 (Radford et al., 2019): Generative Pre-trained Transformer model.
- VGCN-BERT (Lu et al., 2020): Transformer-based model that uses BERT with Graph Convolutional Network for text classification

Other methods

- SVM (Chang & Lin, 2011): Support Vector Machine model for text classification.
- DeepWalk (Perozzi et al., 2014): Embedding-based deep neural model for text classification.

Experimental Settings and Hyperparameters: All the experiments are conducted on the GPUs provided by Google Colab Pro. We implemented our model using TensorFlow. The sequences are created in a chronological order of a news publication timestamp. We temporally split the time-ordered data (by timestamps) for model training. We use the last 15% of the chronologically sorted data as the test set, the second to last 15% of the data as the validation set and the initial 75% of the data as the train set. The known labels are used as the ground truth for model training and evaluation.

In the final settings, we choose the following hyperparameters: the news stories and tweets are on average 500 words, so we choose a sequence length of 500 token. We use padding if the length is shorter and truncation if it is greater. The dimensionality is set to be 768. Larger batch sizes did not work at our end due to memory limitation. So, we choose the batch size to be 8. The dropout rate is set be 0.25, epochs 10, learning rate 1e-3 and Adam optimizer is chosen for optimization.

4 Experimental Results and Analysis

We present the results of binary and multiclass classification using ACC, F1-score (harmonic mean precision and recall) and AUC in Table 2.

4.1 Binary Classification Results

According to the results shown in Table 2, our proposed method Faker consistently outperforms all other methods in inferring binary classification labels (for the evaluation metrics ACC, F1-score, and AUC). For example, our proposed model Faker's accuracy score in inferring news articles is 20-30% higher than that of the state-of-the-art fake news detection models (TriFN, Declare, and Grover), as well as Transformer-based models (BERT, GPT-2, and VGCN-BERT), and other methods (SVM and DeepWalk).

TriFN outperforms other fake news detection baselines (Declare, Grover) in terms of overall performance. This is most likely because when we use both social contexts and news content, we get better patterns for detecting fake news.

Among the Transformer based models, the general performance of BERT and VGCN-BERT is better than GPT-2. The BERT model is more suited to generative (text generation) tasks, whereas the GPT-2 model is better suited to autoregressive (time-series) tasks. The fake news and Transformer-based baselines have outperformed the simple machine learning (SVM) and neural baseline (DeepWalk).

Model/ Metric	TriFN	Grover	Declare	BERT	VGCN-BERT	GPT2	SVM	Deep Walk	Faker
Binary Classification									
ACC	0.695	0.602	0.579	0.690	0.652	0.602	0.459	0.620	**0.824**
F1	0.660	0.598	0.552	0.612	0.635	0.609	0.468	0.610	**0.768**
AUC	0.698	0.678	0.577	0.619	0.632	0.648	0.430	0.542	**0.804**
Multiclass Classification									
ACC	0.675	0.582	0.559	0.660	0.650	0.582	0.400	0.519	**0.810**
F1	0.640	0.580	0.540	0.591	0.605	0.589	0.456	0.598	**0.750**
AUC	0.680	0.660	0.563	0.601	0.632	0.636	0.420	0.529	**0.780**

Table 2: Results of all models using Binary and Multiclass classification

4.2 Multi-label Classification Results

In addition to the simplified binary classification, we infer instance labels using the original 3-class label space, as shown in Table 2.

The results show that our proposed model Faker consistently outperforms all the models on multiclass classification on the quality metrics: ACC, F1-score and AUC. Similar to the results of binary classification, the general performance of TriFN is better than other fake news baselines. The BERT-based models (in general) performs better than GPT-2, which outperform simple baselines.

In terms of efficiency, the benefits of Faker are far more pronounced in the binary classification setting. This is most likely due to the fact that when the 'mixed' label is removed, the models are better able to identify the instances as real or false.

4.3 Sampling Ratio

We sample the training set, which is controlled by a sampling ratio parameter $\theta \in \{0.2, 0.4, 0.6, 0.8, 1.0\}$. Here, $\theta = 0.2$ denotes 20% and $\theta = 1.0$ means 100% of training instances used. We have shown the results with sample ratio of 1.0 in Table 2. For the other ratios, we show results in Appendices.

The results in Figure 4 in Appendix A show that our proposed model Faker consistently outperforms baselines in inferring binary labels by 5-30%. Figure 5 in Appendix B results also show that Faker's scores during multiclass classification is consistently higher than other baselines for all values of θ. Overall, the F1-score and AUC of Faker is significantly higher in the multi-label classification compared to other approaches.

4.4 Precision-Recall of Binary Classification

We also test model perform on a small subset of 4000 instances for binary classification in Table 3.

	Actual Fake	Actual Real
Predicted Fake	2008	110
Predicted Real	37	1845

Table 3: Confusion Matrix of Sample data

The results in Table 3 show that Faker accuracy is 96.3%. We get the precision 94.8%, which means that we have a few false positives (news is real but predicted as fake) and we can correctly predict a large portion of true positives (i.e., news is fake and predicted as fake). We also get the recall value of 98.81%, which shows that we have much more true positives than false negatives. Generally, a false negative (news is fake but predicted as real) is a worse error than a false positive in fake news detection. In our experiment, we get less false negatives than the false positives (which are also fewer). Our F1-score is 96.46%, which is also high.

4.5 Effectiveness of Early Detection

In this experiment, we compare the performance of our model and baselines on early fake news detection. We follow the methodology of Liu and Wu (Y. Liu & Wu, 2018) to define a propagation path for each news story. The idea is that any observation data after the detection deadline cannot be used for training. According to the research in fake news detection, the fake news usually takes less than an hour to spread. Therefore, we choose minutes as the unit for the detection deadlines.

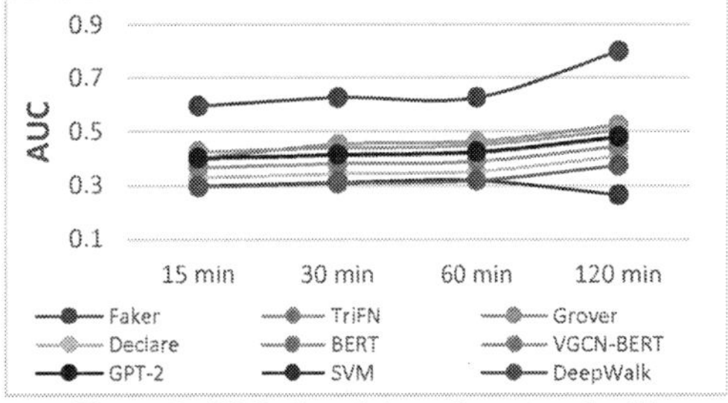

Figure 2: AUC of models on detection deadlines

The results in Figure 2 shows that, in general, the models perform better when the detection deadline delayed. This is shown with the overall better performance of those methods in later detection deadlines (except for SVM). This probably shows that more data obviously helps us to better classify the truth. Our proposed Faker model consistently achieves the best AUC for all the detection deadlines. Faker also achieve good performance even in the early stage after the news is released.

The ability of Faker to detect early is attributed to its position-aware mechanism, which learns the hidden patterns from the sequences of news data and tweets, and then classify the news articles. Using position encoding, the ranking position of each data point in a time-ordered sequence is considered. The model, then, pays more attention to those data points that reflect the truthfulness of the news article with respect to a temporal pattern. For example, the ranking position of a data point might give us an important clue as to whether a concerned news article is fake in the recent time.

4.6 Ablation Study

In ablation study, we remove a key feature component from a model one a time and investigate its impact on performance. Due to limited space, we just show the AUC performance of reduced variants with binary classification. In our experiments, we tested many variants of Faker but mention the important ones below:

Faker: Original model with news, tweets and side information.

Faker(n): Faker with only news-related information - removing social contexts (tweets).

Faker(s) Faker with only social contexts.

Faker(h-): Original Faker with headline removed from news content

Faker(b-): Original Faker with body removed

Faker(so-): Faker with news source removed.

The results are shown as in Figure 3:

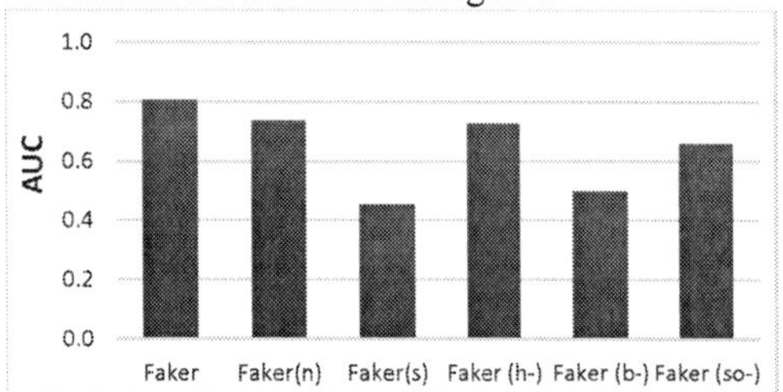

Figure 3: AUC of Faker's variants

From the results in Figure 3, we see that when we remove the social contexts as in Faker(n), the model performance is impacted but the model performance is impacted more when we remove the news content as in Faker (s). This probably shows that news related information is very important to learn the patterns of fake news. However, together both news and social contexts gives us more accurate results, as demonstrated by highest AUC of Faker. The Faker(n) variant also appears to indicate that the body text is not entirely responsible for the overall performance, but it is pretty close to the default system with all features.

The results also show that model performance is impacted more when we remove the news body, compared to the removal of the headline or the source of the news. This is seen with the lower accuracy of Faker(b-) compared to both the Faker(h-) and Faker(so-). This shows that headline and source are important, but news body alone carries more information. Between source and headline, the source seems to be more informative, this is perhaps related to the partisan information.

We also test different setting, for example, number of layers, dropout rate, number of heads, batch size, and removing certain embedding, such as positional embeddings. With all these experiments, we find that our current setup is the best for achieving our goals.

5 Related Work

Following the 2016 election, Google, Twitter, and Facebook all took steps to combat fake news. Facebook and Twitter also allow users to mark news stories as fake. A marked news story usually then goes through a manual fact-checking process. Manual fact-checking is inefficient for detecting fake news early because it is a time-consuming process, and it is also not scalable to handle a large volume of fake news online. In this paper, we look at automated methods for detecting fake news.

The automatic fake news detection methods can be broadly categorized as: content-based and social contexts-based methods. Most of the existing content-based detection methods (Horne & Adalı, 2017; Przybyla, 2020; Zellers et al., 2019) use style-based features (e.g., sentence segmentation, tokenization, bag-of-words, latent topics, and POS tagging) or linguistic features (e.g., frequencies of words, case schemes, context-free grammar and syntax etc.,) from news articles to detect fake news.

One challenge of content-based techniques is that fake news style, platform, and topics are changing constantly. Models trained on one dataset may perform poorly on a new dataset with a different content, style, or language. Furthermore, because the target variables in fake news change over time, certain labels become obsolete, while others must be re-labeled. These algorithms also necessitate a massive amount of training data to detect fake news. By the time these methods gather enough data, fake news has spread far enough.

To solve the issues of content-based methods, the researchers begin focusing on social contexts to detect fake news. The existing social contexts-based approaches are categorized into two types: (i) stance-based methods, and (ii) propagation-based methods. The stance-based approaches exploit the users' viewpoints from social media posts to determine the truth (De Maio et al., 2020; Y. Liu & Wu, 2020; Nakamura et al., 2020; Shu et al., 2019). The propagation-based methods (Huang et al., 2020; Jiang et al., 2019; Y. Liu & Wu, 2018; Qian et al., 2018) utilize the information related to the dissemination of fake news, e.g., how users spread it. These methods use techniques such as graphs and multi-dimensional points for fake news detection (Huang et al., 2020; Y. Liu & Wu, 2018).

While social context methods are useful when there is a lack of news content, they also introduce additional challenges. Gathering social contexts, for example, is a broad topic. The data for social contexts is not only large, but also incomplete, noisy, and unstructured, which may render existing detection algorithms ineffective.

Fake news detection is a subtask of text classification (C. Liu et al., 2019), which is solved by various machine learning and deep learning methods. Some work (Y. Liu & Wu, 2018) uses RNN and CNN networks to build propagation paths for detecting the fake news. Some other work (Shu et al., 2019) uses matrix factorization methods to detect fake news. A few works (Zellers et al., 2019) use LSTM networks on users' comments to explain if a news is real or fake. A few works (Nguyen et al., 2020) also uses graph networks to propose an explainable fake news detection system.

In recent years, there has been a greater focus in NLP research using the Transformer models, such as BERT (Devlin et al., 2018). BERT is used in some fake news detection models (Jwa et al., 2019; C. Liu et al., 2019; Vijjali et al., 2020) to classify the news as real or fake. Despite the robust design proposed in these models, a few limitations are noted. First, these models do not consider a richer set of features from the news items and social contexts. Second, the focus in these methods is not on early fake news detection.

The inclusion of temporal information is important to early detect fake news (Y. Liu & Wu, 2020). Also the inclusion of side (meta-data) information related to news or social contexts is important to understand the nature of fake news data (Shu et al., 2019). Recently, an exploratory study (Shahi et al., 2021) on fake news gives us more new insights about the timeline of misinformation. In our work, we consider both the temporal and side information to detect fake news.

The existing works on fake news focus either on news content or social contexts to detect fake news, we consider both in our work. Compared to some previous works (Nguyen et al., 2020; Popat et al., 2020; Shu et al., 2019) that consider both these aspects, we include a wider set of news-related as well as social context (tweets). A few works (Y. Liu & Wu, 2020; Shu et al., 2019) propose early detection of fake news. Compared to these methods, we can detect fake detect the fake news much earlier (i.e., after a few minutes of news propagation). Compared to the previous works, we consider the latest state-of-the-art neural architectures (Transformers).

6 Conclusion and Recommendations

In our work, we propose a Transformer-based architecture for fake news detection. We utilize the news content and social contexts to detect the patterns of fake news. We also early detect the fake news through a position-aware encoding. We achieve higher performance compared to the baselines, which shows the usefulness of our proposed approach. In addition to fake news detection, this model can also serve for general classification tasks.

To further improve the proposed method, a recommendation is to consider more social contexts, such as friends' networks, propagation paths and implicit users' feedbacks. It would also be very useful to consider malicious social media users' profiles and their activities. Another recommendation is to combat data and concept drifts. It would also be very useful to understand the tactics of fake news producers in real-time scenarios. Furthermore, data labelling scheme can be investigated because of the possibility of incorrectly labelled data, which may lead to data biases (Kishore Shahi, 2020). A possible extension of this work is to mitigate those biases. We also want to break filter bubbles and burst echo chambers created due to the spread of fake news.

References

Anderson, C. W. (2016). News ecosystems. *The SAGE Handbook of Digital Journalism*, 410–423.

Chang, C.-C., & Lin, C.-J. (2011). LIBSVM: a library for support vector machines. *ACM Transactions on Intelligent Systems and Technology (TIST)*, *2*(3), 1–27.

Chen, E., Chang, H., Rao, A., Lerman, K., Cowan, G., & Ferrara, E. (2021). COVID-19 misinformation and the 2020 US presidential election. *The Harvard Kennedy School Misinformation Review*.

Chen, Q., Zhao, H., Li, W., Huang, P., & Ou, W. (2019). Behavior sequence transformer for E-commerce recommendation in Alibaba. *Proceedings of the ACM SIGKDD International Conference on Knowledge Discovery and Data Mining*.

De Maio, C., Fenza, G., Gallo, M., Loia, V., & Volpe, A. (2020). Cross-relating heterogeneous Text Streams for Credibility Assessment. *IEEE Conference on Evolving and Adaptive Intelligent Systems, 2020-May*.

Devlin, J., Chang, M. W., Lee, K., & Toutanova, K. (2018). BERT: Pre-training of deep bidirectional transformers for language understanding. *ArXiv Preprint ArXiv:1810.04805*.

Drummond, C., Holte, R. C., & others. (2003). C4. 5, class imbalance, and cost sensitivity: why under-sampling beats over-sampling. *Workshop on Learning from Imbalanced Datasets II*, *11*, 1–8.

Horne, Benjamin; Gruppi, M. (2021). NELA-GT-2020: A Large Multi-Labelled News Dataset for The Study of Misinformation in News Articles. *ArXiv Preprint ArXiv:2102.04567*.

Horne, B. D., & Adalı, S. (2017). This just in: Fake news packs a lot in title, uses simpler, repetitive content in text body, more similar to satire than real news. *ArXiv Preprint ArXiv:*1703.09398

Horne, B. D., NØrregaard, J., & Adali, S. (2019). Robust fake news detection over time and attack. *ACM Transactions on Intelligent Systems and Technology*, *11*(1).

Huang, Q., Zhou, C., Wu, J., Liu, L., & Wang, B. (2020). Deep spatial–temporal structure learning for rumor detection on Twitter. *Neural Computing and Applications, August*.

Jiang, S., Chen, X., Zhang, L., Chen, S., & Liu, H. (2019). User-characteristic enhanced model for fake news detection in social media. *CCF International Conference on Natural Language Processing and Chinese Computing*, 634–646.

Jwa, H., Oh, D., Park, K., Kang, J. M., & Lim, H. (2019). exBAKE: Automatic fake news detection model based on Bidirectional Encoder Representations from Transformers (BERT). *Applied Sciences (Switzerland)*, *9*(19), 4062.

Kaliyar, R. K., Goswami, A., Narang, P., & Sinha, S. (2020). FNDNet – A deep convolutional neural network for fake news detection. *Cognitive Systems Research*, *61*, 32–44.

Kishore Shahi, G. (2020). *AMUSED:* An Annotation Framework of Multi-modal Social Media Data. *arXiv preprint arXiv:2010.00502.*

Liu, C., Wu, X., Yu, M., Li, G., Jiang, J., Huang, W., & Lu, X. (2019). A Two-Stage Model Based on BERT for Short Fake News Detection. *Lecture Notes in Computer Science (Including Subseries Lecture Notes in Artificial Intelligence and Lecture Notes in Bioinformatics)*, 172–183.

Liu, Y., & Wu, Y. F. B. (2018). Early detection of fake news on social media through propagation path classification with recurrent and convolutional networks. *32nd AAAI Conference on Artificial Intelligence, AAAI 2018*, 354–361.

Liu, Y., & Wu, Y. F. B. (2020). FNED: A Deep Network for Fake News Early Detection on Social Media. *ACM Transactions on Information Systems*, *38*(3).

Lu, Z., Du, P., & Nie, J. Y. (2020). VGCN-BERT: Augmenting BERT with Graph Embedding for Text Classification. In *Lecture Notes in Computer Science (including subseries Lecture Notes in Artificial Intelligence and Lecture Notes in Bioinformatics): Vol. 12035 LNCS*.

Mintz, M., Bills, S., Snow, R., & Jurafsky, D. (2009). Distant supervision for relation extraction without labeled data. *Proceedings of the Joint Conference of the 47th Annual Meeting of the ACL and the 4th International Joint Conference on Natural Language Processing of the AFNLP*, 1003–1011.

Mohammadrezaei, M., Shiri, M. E., & Rahmani, A. M. (2018). Identifying Fake Accounts on Social Networks Based on Graph Analysis and Classification Algorithms. *Security and Communication Networks, 2018*.

Nakamura, K., Levy, S., & Wang, W. Y. (2020). r/Fakeddit: A new multimodal benchmark dataset for fine-grained fake news detection. In *LREC 2020 - 12th International Conference on Language Resources and Evaluation, Conference Proceedings*.

Nguyen, V.-H., Nakov, P., & Kan, M.-Y. (2020). FANG: Leveraging Social Context for Fake News Detection Using Graph Representation. *Proceedings of the 29th ACM International*

Conference on Information & Knowledge Management, 1165-1174

Nørregaard, J., Horne, B. D., & Adalı, S. (2019). NELA-GT-2018: A large multi-labelled news dataset for the study of misinformation in news articles. *Proceedings of the 13th International Conference on Web and Social Media, ICWSM 2019, Icwsm*, 630–638.

Perozzi, B., Al-Rfou, R., & Skiena, S. (2014). Deepwalk: Online learning of social representations. *Proceedings of the 20th ACM SIGKDD International Conference on Knowledge Discovery and Data Mining*, 701–710.

Popat, K., Mukherjee, S., Yates, A., & Weikum, G. (2020). Declare: Debunking fake news and false claims using evidence-aware deep learning. In *Proceedings of the 2018 Conference on Empirical Methods in Natural Language Processing, EMNLP 2018*.

Przybyla, P. (2020). Capturing the Style of Fake News. *Proceedings of the AAAI Conference on Artificial Intelligence*, *34*(01), 490–497.

Qian, F., Gong, C., Sharma, K., & Liu, Y. (2018). Neural user response generator: Fake news detection with collective user intelligence. *IJCAI International Joint Conference on Artificial Intelligence*, *2018-July*, 3834–3840.

Radford, A., Wu, J., Child, R., Luan, D., Amodei, D., & Sutskever, I. (2019). Language models are unsupervised multitask learners. *OpenAI Blog*, *1*(8), 9.

Shahi, G. K., Dirkson, A., & Majchrzak, T. A. (2021). An exploratory study of COVID-19 misinformation on Twitter. *Online Social Networks and Media*, 100104

Shu, K., Wang, S., & Liu, H. (2019). Beyond news contents: The role of social context for fake news detection. *WSDM 2019 - Proceedings of the 12th ACM International Conference on Web Search and Data Mining*, *9*, 312–320.

Vaswani, A., Shazeer, N., Parmar, N., Uszkoreit, J., Jones, L., Gomez, A. N., Kaiser, Ł., & Polosukhin, I. (2017). Attention is all you need. *Advances in Neural Information Processing Systems*, 5998–6008.

Vijjali, R., Potluri, P., Kumar, S., & Teki, S. (2020). Two stage transformer model for covid-19 fake news detection and fact checking. *ArXiv Preprint ArXiv:2011.13253*.

Vosoughi, S., Roy, D., & Aral, S. (2018). The spread of true and false news online. *Science*, *359*(6380), 1146–1151.

Wang, Y., Shen, Y., Liu, Z., Liang, P. P., Zadeh, A., & Morency, L. P. (2018). Words Can Shift: Dynamically Adjusting Word Representations Using Nonverbal Behaviors. *In Proceedings of the AAAI Conference on Artificial Intelligence*, 7216-7223.

Wu, F., Qiao, Y., Chen, J.-H., Wu, C., Qi, T., Lian, J., Liu, D., Xie, X., Gao, J., Wu, W., & Zhou, M. (2020). MIND: A Large-scale Dataset for News Recommendation. *Proceedings of the 58th Annual Meeting of the Association for Computational Linguistics*, 3597–3606.

Yang, S., Shu, K., Wang, S., Gu, R., Wu, F., & Liu, H. (2019). Unsupervised fake news detection on social media: A generative approach. *Proceedings of the AAAI Conference on Artificial Intelligence*, *33*(01), 5644–5651.

Zellers, R., Holtzman, A., Rashkin, H., Bisk, Y., Farhadi, A., Roesner, F., & Choi, Y. (2019). Defending against neural fake news. In *arXiv*preprint arXiv:1905.12616.

Zhou, X., & Zafarani, R. (2020). A Survey of Fake News: Fundamental Theories, Detection Methods, and Opportunities. *ACM Computing Surveys*, *53*(5).

Appendix A. Binary Classification Sampling Ratios

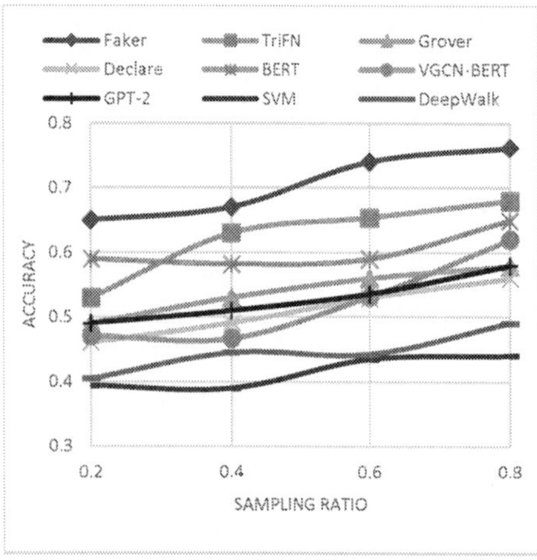

Figure 4 (a): Binary Classification Accuracy

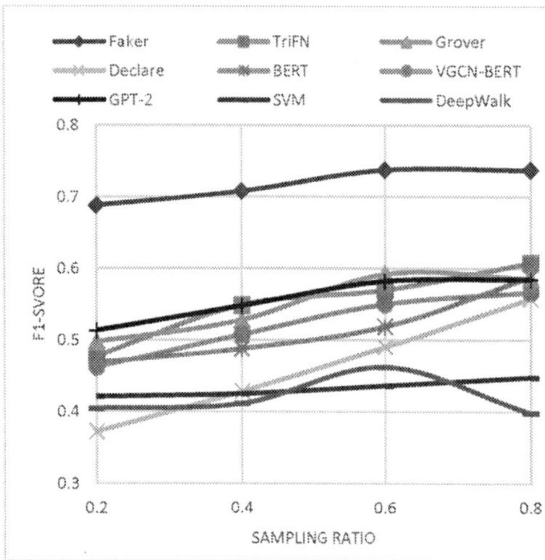

Figure 4 (b): Binary Classification F1-score

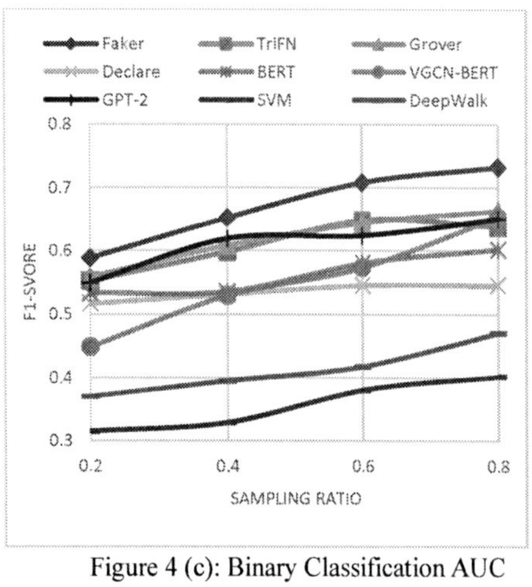

Figure 4 (c): Binary Classification AUC

Appendix B. Multiclass Classification Sampling Ratios

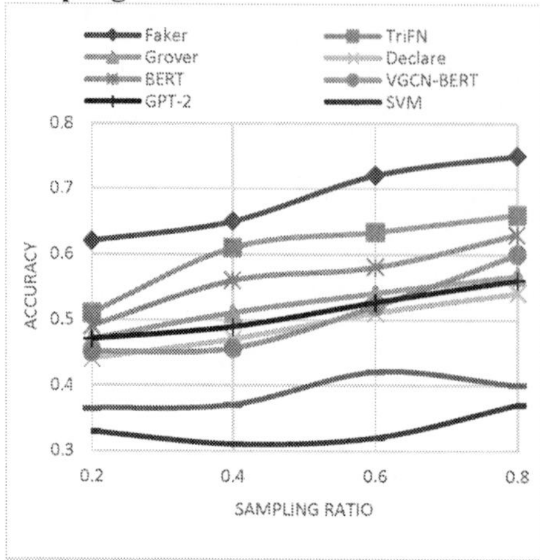

Figure 5(a): Multiclass Classification ACC

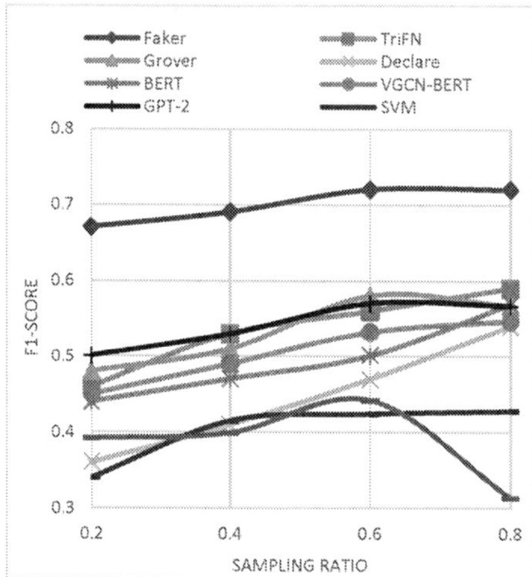

Figure 5(b): Binary Classification F1-score

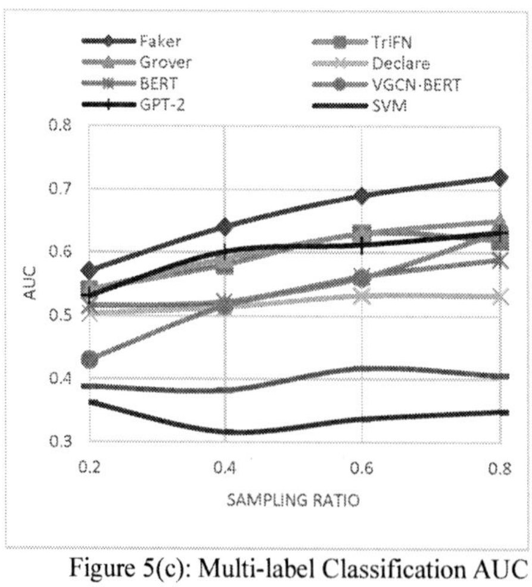

Figure 5(c): Multi-label Classification AUC

Multilingual Protest News Detection - Shared Task 1, CASE 2021

Ali Hürriyetoğlu[⋆], Osman Mutlu[⋆], Erdem Yörük[⋆], Farhana Ferdousi Liza[†], Ritesh Kumar[◇], Shyam Ratan[◇]

[⋆]Koç University [†]University of Essex [◇]Dr. Bhimrao Ambedkar University, Agra

{ahurriyetoglu,omutlu,eryoruk}@ku.edu.tr

farhana.ferdousi.liza@essex.ac.uk

ritesh78_llh@jnu.ac.in, shyamratan2907@gmail.com

Abstract

Benchmarking state-of-the-art text classification and information extraction systems in multilingual, cross-lingual, few-shot, and zero-shot settings for socio-political event information collection is achieved in the scope of the shared task Socio-political and Crisis Events Detection at the workshop CASE @ ACL-IJCNLP 2021. Socio-political event data is utilized for national and international policy- and decision-making. Therefore, the reliability and validity of such datasets are of utmost importance. We split the shared task into three parts to address the three aspects of data collection (Task 1), fine-grained semantic classification (Task 2), and evaluation (Task 3). Task 1, which is the focus of this report, is on multilingual protest news detection and comprises four subtasks that are document classification (subtask 1), sentence classification (subtask 2), event sentence coreference identification (subtask 3), and event extraction (subtask 4). All subtasks have English, Portuguese, and Spanish for both training and evaluation data. Data in Hindi language is available only for the evaluation of subtask 1. The majority of the submissions, which are 238 in total, are created using multi- and cross-lingual approaches. Best scores are between 77.27 and 84.55 F1-macro for subtask 1, between 85.32 and 88.61 F1-macro for subtask 2, between 84.23 and 93.03 CoNLL 2012 average score for subtask 3, and between 66.20 and 78.11 F1-macro for subtask 4 in all evaluation settings. The performance of the best system for subtask 4 is above 66.20 F1 for all available languages. Although there is still a significant room for improvement in cross-lingual and zero-shot settings, the best submissions for each evaluation scenario yield remarkable results. Monolingual models outperformed the multilingual models in a few evaluation scenarios, in which there is relatively much training data.

1 Introduction

Every day across the globe, hundreds of different socio-political protest events against various decisions taken by the respective governments or authorities take place. These events are of interest to political scientists, policy makers, democracy watchdogs and other stakeholders for multiple reasons including analysing the nature, scope and extent of such events, forming public opinion about various causes, gauging the state of freedom and democracy across different nations and others. However, manually keeping track of such events at a national level itself is a very challenging task and it is more so if we are trying to get a sense of these events across the globe. Given this, automated methods of collecting and, possibly, processing protest news events from multiple countries and locations gain great significance. But the automated identification and collection of such events in multiple languages also comes with its own set of significant challenges. This task was designed to address some of these challenges..

The task of event information detection, in general, could be divided into multiple subsequent steps and the efficiency at each of these steps could drastically affect the quality of the resultant event database. Thus, we believe one must consider a complete pipeline including the following steps i) classification of documents and sentences as relevant or not (in the sense that whether they describe an event or not - in this specific case event is a protest event); ii) identification of the sentences that provide information about the same event; and iii) extraction of event information. Finally the resultant database of the events should be tested against a manually created list of events to evaluate the performance of the state-of-the-art systems on this task. We have formulated these different steps into three inter-dependent tasks - Task 1 is a Multilingual Protest News Detection task, Task 2 complements the first task with fine-grained semantic event classification (Haneczok et al., 2021) using data reported by Piskorski et al. (2020) and Task 3 evaluates the performance of the systems developed for Task 1 on a real-world scenario, in this it specifically evaluates the system for the task

Proceedings of the 4th Workshop on Challenges and Applications of Automated Extraction of Socio-political Events from Text (CASE), pages 79–91
August 5–6, 2021, ©2021 Association for Computational Linguistics

of identifying the events surrounding Black Lives Matter movement, using data from Twitter and New York Times (Giorgi et al., 2021).

In order to benchmark the state-of-the-art in these three tasks, we organized the shared task Socio-political and Crisis Events Detection[1]. The shared task is held in the scope of the workshop Challenges and Applications of Automated Extraction of Socio-political Events from Text (CASE 2021)[2] (Hürriyetoğlu et al., 2021) that is held at the Joint Conference of the 59th Annual Meeting of the Association for Computational Linguistics and the 11th International Joint Conference on Natural Language Processing (ACL-IJCNLP 2021).[3] We report results of the Task 1 that is Multilingual Protest News Detection in this report.

Task 1 follows Extracting Protests from News (ProtestNews) and Event Sentence Coreference Identification (ESCI) tasks that were organized at Conference and Labs of the Evaluation Forum (CLEF 2019) (Hürriyetoğlu et al., 2019a,b) and Automated Extraction of Socio-political Events from News (AESPEN 2020) at Language Resources and Evaluation Conference (LREC) (Hürriyetoğlu et al., 2020) respectively. The ProtestNews and ESCI were monolingual tasks comprising only English data from various countries and evaluated for cross-context generalization of automated text processing systems across texts collected from different countries. This edition of the shared task series focuses on language generalization of the event information collection systems in four languages viz. English, Hindi, Portuguese, and Spanish. The Task 1 we present in this report follows all the steps we find essential for event information collection in a multilingual setting. It is divided into the following subtasks.

Subtask 1; Document classification:
The first subtask aims to identify if a news article contains information about a past or ongoing socio-political event.

Subtask 2; Sentence classification:
The second subtask asks the question if a sentence contains information about a past or ongoing event.

Subtask 3; Event sentence coreference identification:
The third sub-task is about identifying which event sentences (per definition provided in subtasks 1 and 2) are about the same event. The event sentences in question are from the same document.

Subtask 4; Event Extraction:
The final subtask is the extraction of event entity spans such as triggers and event arguments.

We particularly focus on events that are in the scope of contentious politics and characterized by riots and social movements, i.e., the repertoire of contention (Giugni, 1998; Tarrow, 1994). We utilize an extended version of the GLOCON Gold standard dataset that is created based on this definition in this task (Hürriyetoğlu et al., 2021). The languages in scope for all of the subtasks are English, Spanish, and Portuguese. The subtask 1 comprises test data in Hindi as well. This setting creates a total of 13 evaluation scenarios such as subtask 1 English, Subtask 4 Portuguese, etc. Participants had access to training data for all the subtasks and in all languages. There is no training data in Hindi language and its test data is available only for subtask 1. Moreover, training data in Spanish and Portuguese are relatively small in comparison to data in English.

This report discusses relevant work in Section 2, annotation of the data set utilized in the benchmark in Section 3, task and data descriptions in Sections 4 and 5. We provide results of baseline systems we developed for subtasks 1 and 2 and participant submissions in sections 7 and 8. We conclude the report in section 9.

2 Related Work

Automated socio-political event information collection has a long history (Hutter, 2014; Schrodt and Yonamine, 2013). Many event ontologies such as IDEA (Bond et al., 2003), CAMEO (Gerner et al., 2002), ACLED (Raleigh et al., 2010), and PLOVER[4] have been proposed in this domain. These ontologies facilitated development of automated event information collection tools such as MPEDS (Hanna, 2017), PETRARCH (Norris et al., 2017), TABARI, and BBN Accent, EMBERS (Saraf and Ramakrishnan, 2016). The databases that are created using automated methods at various levels are GDELT (Leetaru and Schrodt, 2013), ICEWS (O'Brien, 2010), MMAD (Weidmann and Rød, 2019), PHOENIX, POLDEM (Kriesi et al., 2019), SPEED (Nardulli

[1] `https://github.com/emerging-welfare/case-2021-shared-task`, accessed on May 26, 2021. The repository contains sample data, evalution scripts, and samples of submission files.

[2] `https://emw.ku.edu.tr/case-2021/`, accessed on May 26, 2021.

[3] `https://2021.aclweb.org/`, accessed on May 26, 2021.

[4] `https://github.com/openeventdata/PLOVER`, accessed on May 30, 2021.

et al., 2015), TERRIER (Liang et al., 2018), and UCDP (Sundberg et al., 2012). Although majority of this work is on western countries and English language, there are considerable number of similar studies on collecting socio-political event information from text originated from countries other than western countries and in languages other than English (Sönmez et al., 2016; Danilova, 2015). The main data source of the event information has been text of news articles. But the use of social media posts has gradually increased in recent times (Zhang and Pan, 2019; Sech et al., 2020).

The application of state-of-the-art automation using machine learning and computational linguistics techniques requires gold standard annotated corpora that can be utilized for the task and benchmarks that facilitate comparison of the proposed methods for protest event information collection (Wang et al., 2016; Lorenzini et al., 2016). However, there are only a few corpora shared for research purposes in this domain (Makarov et al., 2016; Sönmez et al., 2016; Sech et al., 2020) and to the best of our knowledge, there is no benchmark available. Our efforts via this task establishes a common ground for comparison and benchmarking in a multilingual setting.

The multilingual text processing has become a critical target in computational linguistics and machine learning. Tackling this task enables us to collect information about global events that are reported and to trace occurrence of similar events in many languages. Moreover, this technology facilitates event information collection from local sources, which provide detailed information about events. New benchmark data sets such as XTREME (Hu et al., 2020) and system proposals such as mBERT (Devlin et al., 2019a), XLM (Lample and Conneau, 2019), mBART (Liu et al., 2020), and XLM-R (Conneau et al., 2020) have demonstrated promising results on various tasks (Hakala and Pyysalo, 2019). Multilingual embedding creation is the other major research line, in which the approaches such as LASER (Artetxe and Schwenk, 2019a) and LaBSE (Feng et al., 2020) have been proposed. These methodological advancements extend the exploration space for detecting event information. Consequently, this technology contributes to the resolution of the popularity or ideological bias of the sources toward popular and mainstream events both at global and local levels.

In general, it is not an optimum decision to work with a single language due to biases, absence of event information in a single source or international sources etc. We must invest in generalizability and multilinguality of the event information collection systems and therefore in the current task we incorporate these aspects as well. By design, zero- or few-shot learning is required to tackle some subtask and language combinations (Pires et al., 2019) in this task since the released data set contained relatively small training data in Spanish and Portuguese and no training data in Hindi. Thus the final evaluation provides some insights into these approaches for contentious socio-political event data collection and classification task.

3 Annotation

The multilingual version of the corpus GLOCON Gold (Hürriyetoğlu et al., 2021), which was reported as containing data only in English, is utilized in this task. This corpus is created by random sampling from news archives and double annotation (Yörük et al., 2021) for the data in English, Spanish, and Portuguese. There are document, sentence, and token level annotations that are performed on the whole news articles. The quality of the annotations are ensured by a detailed annotation manual[5], adjudications, spot-checks, and semi-automated quality checks before the next level of annotation starts. A cascaded annotation workflow is applied. For instance, quality of the document level annotations is ensured before the sentence level annotation starts. The inter-annotator aggrements (IAA) that are measured using Krippendorf's alpha (Krippendorff et al., 2016) are .75 and .65 in average for document- and sentence-level annotations. The token level IAA is between .35 and .60 for the information types in scope. All disaggrements are resolved by the annotation supervisor. Moreover, spot-checks and semi-automated error corrections have fixed 10% of the annotation errors in total (Hürriyetoğlu et al., 2021). The document and sentence level annotations yielded the data for subtasks 1 and 2 respectively. The token level annotations produced the data for subtasks 3 and 4.

The data in Hindi is prepared applying a slightly different methodology but using the same annotation manual. A native graduate student from India has annotated these articles at the document level. Twenty Hindi newspapers and periodicals available on the web are used as sources for this data set. This data set contains all possible articles and editorials related to ongoing farmer protest in India against the three farm bills (1.Bill on agri market, 2.Bill on contract farming, and 3.Bill relating to commodities) passed by the government of India in August, 2020. [6] The current annotated data set cov-

[5] https://github.com/emerging-welfare/general_info/tree/master/annotation-manuals, accessed on May 29, 2021.

[6] https://en.wikipedia.org/wiki/2020%

ers equal proportion of articles from each source, which are twenty except the periodical Panchjanya, which has only 19 articles. All articles are searched and collected manually from web pages of each newspaper and periodical with the metadata date, date of article retrieval, URL, location of incident, and location of newspaper.

Overall, the news articles used in this task are obtained from China and South Africa in English, from Brazil in Portuguese, from Argentine in Spanish, and from India in English and Hindi. The annotation team consists of graduate students in social and political sciences. Students from Turkey, Brazil, and India have annotated text in English, Spanish and Portuguese, and Hindi respectively. These students are trained on contentious politics of their target country and annotation methodology before they started the annotation. News reports that are not related to a target country are excluded from the token level annotations in order to improve precision of the annotations.

4 Task Description

Task 1 consists of four subtasks that are at document, sentence, and token levels. The subtasks are as follows.

Subtask 1 aims at classifying news articles. If the document reports an event that has happened or is ongoing, it should be labelled as relevant. Scheduled events, speculations, and anything else should be marked as irrelevant. Subtask 1 is a binary classification problem.

Subtask 2 has the same aim as subtask 1 but for sentences of a document. [7] A sentence should have some token(s) that qualify as event trigger or a reference to an event trigger in another sentence.

Subtask 3 is about determining event sentences that provide information about the same event. All event sentences in a document are clustered according to the events they report.

Subtask 4 marks all tokens in an event sentence based on the information they hold[7]. The event trigger and its arguments such as participant, place, target, organizer, time, and facility name are annotated. The event trigger can be a coreferent of a trigger in another sentence.

The subtasks are multilingual by means of comprising data in English, Portuguese, and Spanish languages both for training and evaluation of the automated text processing systems. Moreover, the tasks are a few-shot scenario since Portuguese and Spanish training data is significantly less than English data. Finally, the subtask 1 includes a zero-shot setting in which participants do not have access to data in Hindi language, but they should predict documents in Hindi language.

Hürriyetoğlu et al. (2021) have showed that, although, event information collection could be performed utilizing systems developed only for subtask 4 with potential contribution of the systems developed for subtask 3 in principle, this setting is not possible in practice due to challenge of reliable annotation of event information at token level for development and evaluation of event extraction systems. Document and sentence annotation significantly facilitates reliable annotation of event information at token level. Moreover, authors have demonstrated a considerable increase in F1 in case document and sentence classification systems are applied before token level event extraction. Thus, we consider application of these subtasks in this order indispensable for reliable collection of event information.

5 Data Description

We share text data in English, Spanish and Portuguese for training and evaluation. Also, there is data in Hindi language for evaluation of the subtask 1. Finally, participants are free to use any additional data they may think that will help to improve their systems.

This section provides details on the format, size, and preparation of the data shared with the participants. Moreover, we describe how data across subtasks depend on each other and how we deal with copyright issues in the subsection on the data preparation.

5.1 Data Format

Listing 1: A training sample from subtask 1.

```
{
 "id":100187,
 "text":"Hall of fame\nResults -
    Pyeongchang 2018 Winter
    Olympic Games\nSee the full
    results from th",
 "label":0
}
```

All of our data is shared in JSON files except for subtask 4 which is shared as plain text files. The subtasks 1 and 2 are both text classification tasks, so their format, which can be seen in Listing 1, are the same, differing only in JSON field names. The "label" is the correct label assigned to the article/sentence and "text" is the article/sentence's text.

E2%80%932021_Indian_farmers%27_protest, accessed on June 9, 2021.

[7]The annotators see the whole document during the annotation

"text" field is named "sentence" for subtask 2 data. The "label" field is not shared for test data.

Listing 2: A training sample from subtask 3.

```
{
 "id":55471,
  "sentences": [
    "Lt-Col Andre Traut said the
       teenager laid the
       complaint at the Robertson
        police station following
       a farmworkers' protest in
       the area.",
    "Table grape harvesters
       started protesting about
       their working conditions
       in De Doorns last month.",
    "The protests spread to 15
       other towns and resulted
       in two deaths and the
       destruction of property.",
    "The farmworkers' strike
       resumed on Tuesday when
       their demands were not met
       ."
  ],
  "sentence_no":[2,5,7,8],
  "event_clusters":[[5,7,8],[2]]
}
```

As shown in Listing 2, fields for subtask 3 consist of positive sentences of an article ("sentences"), the ordering of these sentences in the article ("sentence_no") and correct clustering of these sentences ("event_clusters"). The "event_clusters" field is not shared for test data. Finally, for subtask 4, we share text files in BIO format, which is the standard for information extraction tasks (Ramshaw and Marcus, 1995). Below in b we provide a sample in BIO format.[8] The sample in human readable format is demonstrated in a. The bold face indicates the event trigger and the underlined tokens specify the arguments of the event trigger.

a. The <u>recruits</u>, <u>at Valluvar Kottam</u> **shouted slogans** including, "<u>HCL</u> lend us your ears, give us back our two years" while undertaking the day-long **fast**.

b. The$_{\text{O}}$ recruits$_{\text{B-participant}}$,$_{\text{O}}$ at$_{\text{B-fname}}$ Valluvar$_{\text{I-fname}}$ Kottam$_{\text{I-fname}}$ shouted$_{\text{B-trigger}}$ slogans$_{\text{I-trigger}}$ including$_{\text{O}}$,$_{\text{O}}$ "$_{\text{O}}$ HCL$_{\text{B-target}}$ lend$_{\text{O}}$ us$_{\text{O}}$ your$_{\text{O}}$ ears$_{\text{O}}$,$_{\text{O}}$ give$_{\text{O}}$ us$_{\text{O}}$ back$_{\text{O}}$ our$_{\text{O}}$ two$_{\text{O}}$ years$_{\text{O}}$ "$_{\text{O}}$ while$_{\text{O}}$ undertaking$_{\text{O}}$ the$_{\text{O}}$ day-long$_{\text{O}}$ fast$_{\text{B-trigger}}$.$_{\text{O}}$

[8]The participants receive this in vertical format.

5.2 Data Size

Total size[9] of the shared data for all languages and subtasks can be seen at Table *1*. The distribution of labels for training data for each subtask are as follows:

- Positive sample ratio for subtask 1 is .21, .13 and .13 for English, Portuguese and Spanish respectively.
- Positive sample ratio for subtask 2 is .19, .24 and .16 for English, Portuguese and Spanish respectively.
- For subtask 3, number of clusters in a sample in percentages can be found at Table 2
- The number of spans/entities for subtask 4 are shown in Table 3.

The sample size should be the same for the subtasks 3 and 4 in principle since they both are annotated when a news article is positive. However, it can be observed in Table 1 that subtask 3 has significantly less data than subtask 4. This is due to the exclusion of the articles with single positive sentence from subtask 3, as they only have one possible clustering solution.

		Subtask 1	Subtask 2	Subtask3	Subtask 4
English	Train	9,324	22,825	596	808
	Test	2,971	1,290	100	179
Portuguese	Train	1,487	1,182	21	33
	Test	372	1,445	40	50
Spanish	Train	1,000	2,741	11	30
	Test	250	686	40	50
Hindi	Train	-	-	-	-
	Test	268	-	-	-

Table 1: Sample[9] counts for all subtasks in all languages.

	1	2	3	4+
English	.62	.27	.06	.05
Portuguese	.57	.33	.05	.05
Spanish	.73	.27	.0	.0

Table 2: Number of clusters (events) in a sample in percentages in subtask 3 in all languages.

5.3 Data Preparation

Before preparing the data we had to consider the data shared in previous editions of the shared task, copyright issues and possible inference between data of separate subtasks.

Some portion of the data in English was shared with academic community in previous shared

[9]A sample is denoted as an article for subtasks 1, 3 and 4, and a sentence for subtask 2.

	English	Portuguese	Spanish
trigger	4,595	122	157
participant	2,663	73	88
place	1,570	61	15
target	1,470	32	64
organizer	1,261	19	25
etime	1,209	41	40
fname	1,201	48	49

Table 3: Number of spans in subtask 4 training data in all languages.

tasks (Hürriyetoğlu et al., 2019b, 2020) and publications as sample data (Hürriyetoğlu et al., 2021). On the one hand, a sample previously shared in training data should not be placed in test data since its correct answer is known. On the other hand, a sample previously shared in test data should not be shared in training data since that would make previous shared task obsolete.

We respect the copyright of the news sources. We never share the whole text of a news article. To further prevent possible copyright issues, we share only one third of the text starting from the beginning of the document in subtask 1, scramble the sentences in subtask 2, and use only positively labeled sentences in subtasks 3 and 4.

The final data preparation step is about avoiding inference of the labels of the data for a subtask from data of the other subtasks. As it is described in Section 3, our annotation process happens in a cascaded manner: sentence level depending on document level, token and sentence coreference depending on sentence and document levels. These dependencies between levels create the possibility to infer an upper level's label using a lower level's data (upmost level being document level). For example, for a sample in document level test data, one can easily confirm this sample is positive by checking to see if any of its sentences are shared in sentence level data. So when we prepare our data, we make sure there are no overlaps between levels that have these dependencies. This exclusion applies in the following cases:

- From our subtask 3 and 4 data, we exclude samples whose sentence(s) are in subtask 1's test data.
- From our subtask 3 and 4 data, we exclude samples that are in subtask 1's test data.
- From our subtask 2 data, we exclude sentences that belong to articles that are in subtask 1's test data.

As these cases show, the overlaps are handled in a top-down manner. Handling them in bottom-up manner, meaning excluding samples from upper levels (moving samples from test to training data), would disrupt the positive sample ratio and possibly create a bias in the data. Since sentence coreference and token level data are not dependent on each other, this process of sampling and exclusion is not carried out in this case. Data for these subtasks is derived from the same documents by respecting the training and evaluation splits.

6 Evaluation

Although the subtasks form a coherent flow, task participants can focus on one or more of them. Therefore, participants can choose the tasks or subtask(s) they would like to participate in. Participants have access to all of the data for all tasks and subtasks. Any combination of these resources to achieve high performance for any of the tasks is allowed. For instance, Task 1 data could be used to potentially improve the performance on Task 2 and vice versa.

Participants had access to the test data for a week and could submit up to five submissions for each subtask and language combination. The best score of each team is reflected to the leaderboard.[10] Additional submissions are allowed (after the competition ended) on a separate Codalab page[11] in case participating teams would like to run additional experiments or create multiple submissions of the same system for measuring standard deviation of their systems. However, the additional submission page allows only one submission for each language and subtask combination per day.

F1-macro is calculated on the predictions on the test data for the subtasks 1 and 2. We use a python implementation[12] of the original[13] conlleval evaluation script for subtask 4. The subtask 3 is evaluated using scorch - a python implementation of CoNLL-2012 average score for the test data (Pradhan et al., 2014). [14]. We carry out separate evaluation for each subtask using the test data for each language separately.

7 Baseline Systems

We created baseline models for the subtasks 1 and 2 in English, Portuguese, and Spanish. Document

[10] `https://competitions.codalab.org/competitions/31247#results`, accessed on June 9, 2021.

[11] `https://competitions.codalab.org/competitions/31639`, accessed on June 9, 2021.

[12] `https://github.com/sighsmile/conlleval`, accessed on June 6, 2021.

[13] `www.cnts.ua.ac.be/conll2000/chunking/conlleval.txt`, accessed on June 11, 2021.

[14] `https://github.com/LoicGrobol/scorch`, accessed on June 6, 2021.

classification is a challenging task. For simplicity, we have done document classification on the summaries of documents, which are the most important sentence in the document generated using the LexRank extractive summarization method (Erkan and Radev, 2004). Thus document summarization task was converted into an important part of the sentence classification task pipeline. As such, the input text for the document classification is a sentence rather than a set of sentences.

We have used an Attention (i.e. Transformer) (Devlin et al., 2019b) based Neural Network model for feature representation (Minaee et al., 2021) and multilingual sentence representations (Reimers and Gurevych, 2020) for the subtasks 1 and 2 with three languages — English, Spanish and Portuguese. Among available approaches (Schwenk and Douze, 2017; Artetxe and Schwenk, 2019b; Reimers and Gurevych, 2020), Reimers and Gurevych (2020) provide efficient representation for sentences for 50+ languages from various language families. The main motivation of using the multilingual approach is to learn efficient representation for the low resource (Non-English) languages. Specifically, we have used 'distiluse-base-multilingual-cased' for learning sentence representation of the three languages. We have also used language-specific sentence representation (Reimers and Gurevych, 2019) for the English language. Specifically, for the experiment, we used 'paraphrase-distilroberta-base-v1', which is a 'DistilBERT-base-uncased' model fine-tuned on a large dataset of paraphrase sentences. We apply a Linear Support Vector Machine (SVM) classifier trained on these features. The multilingual representation yields competitive results in our experiments for the language-specific representation in English language classification.

We have used 70% of the training data to train the model and 30% of the data to validate the models for subtasks 1 and 2. For the document classification task, the validation scores are 74.85 for the English language, 49.27 for the Spanish language, and 56.67 for the Portuguese language. The test scores are 76.78, 64.45, 64.13 for English, Portuguese and Spanish respectively. For the sentence classification task (subtask 2) the F1-macro on the validation data is 79.67 with the language-specific representation of the English language. With multilingual representation, the validation F1-macro is 76.90 for the English language, 73.93 for the Portuguese, and 73.42 for the Spanish language. The score on the test data is 67.08, 67.42 , and 66.75, for English, Portuguese and Spanish respectively.

8 Results

43 people that form around 30 teams were registered for Task 1. In total 238 submissions are prepared for the different subtasks and language combinations by 13 teams. The scores of the submissions are calculated on a Codalab page.[15] The teams that have participated are ALEM (Gürel and Emin, 2021), AMU-EuraNova (Bouscarrat et al., 2021), DAAI (Hettiarachchi et al., 2021), DaDeFrTi (Re et al., 2021), FKIE_itf_2021 (Becker and Krumbiegel, 2021), Handshakes AI Research (HSAIR) (Kalyan et al., 2021b), IBM MNLP IE (Awasthy et al., 2021), SU-NLP (Çelik et al., 2021), NoConflict (Hu and Stoehr, 2021) II-ITT (Kalyan et al., 2021a), and NUS-IDS (Tan et al., 2021). Two participants that has the user names Jitin, and jiawei1998 on the Codalab page of the task did not write any description paper. [16]

We provide details of the results and submissions of the participating teams for each subtask in the following subsections.

Team	English	Hindi	Portuguese	Spanish
ALEM	80.82_4	N/A	72.98_5	46.47_7
AMU-EuraNova	53.46_9	29.66_7	46.47_8	46.47_7
DAAI	84.55_1	77.07_3	82.43_2	69.31_4
DaDeFrTi	80.69_5	78.77_1	77.22_4	73.01_2
FKIE_itf_2021	73.90_7	54.24_6	62.39_6	68.20_5
HSAIR	77.58_6	59.55_5	81.21_3	69.84_3
IBM MNLP IE	83.93_2	78.53_2	84.00_1	77.27_1
SU-NLP	81.75_3	N/A	N/A	N/A
NoConflict	51.94_{10}	N/A	N/A	N/A
jitin	67.39_8	70.49_4	52.23_7	62.05_6

Table 4: The performance of the submissions in terms of F1-macro and their ranks as a subscript for each language and each team participating in subtask 1.

8.1 Subtask 1

Subtask 1 results are provided in Table 4. The team "DAAI" has submitted the best results for English test data using a Big-Bird-RoBERTa. Team "DaDeFrTi" obtained the best score on Hindi data, which is a zero-shot cross-lingual setting by training a multilingual XLM-RoBERTa (XLM-R) based classification model with additional data either acquired from external data sets, collected from the web or translated from the original data. Finally, the "IBM MNLP IE" has ranked first for

[15] `https://competitions.codalab.org/competitions/31247#results`, accessed on May 26, 2021.

[16] The mapping between the team names and the Codalab user names is as follows: ALEM: alaeddin, AMU-EuraNova: lbouscarrat, DAAI: hansih, DaDeFrTi: davegh, FKIE_itf_2021: skent, Handshakes AI Research (HSAIR): vivekkalyanHS, IBM MNLP IE: kjbarker, SU-NLP:fcelik, NoConflict: pitehu, IIITT: AdeepH, and NUS-IDS: tanfiona

Team	English	Portuguese	Spanish
ALEM	79.67_5	42.79_{10}	45.30_{10}
AMU-EuraNova	75.64_9	81.61_6	76.39_6
DaDeFrTi	79.28_6	86.62_3	85.17_2
FKIE_itf_2021	64.96_{11}	75.81_8	70.49_9
HSAIR	78.50_7	85.06_4	83.25_3
IBM MNLP IE	84.56_2	88.47_1	88.61_1
IIITT	82.91_4	79.51_7	75.78_7
SU-NLP	83.05_3	N/A	N/A
NoConflict	85.32_1	87.00_2	79.97_5
jiawei1998	76.14_8	84.67_5	83.05_4
jitin	66.96_{10}	69.02_9	72.94_8

Table 5: The performance of the submissions in terms of F1-macro and their ranks as a subscript for each language and each team participating in subtask 2.

	Scores		
Team	English	Portuguese	Spanish
DAAI	80.40_3	90.23_5	81.83_5
FKIE_itf_2021	77.05_6	91.33_3	82.52_3
Handshakes AI Research	79.01_4	90.61_4	81.95_4
IBM MNLP IE	84.44_1	92.84_2	84.23_1
NUS-IDS	81.20_2	93.03_1	83.15_2
SU-NLP	78.67_5	N/A	N/A

Table 6: The performance of the submissions in terms of CoNLL-2012 average score Pradhan et al. (2014) and their ranks as a subscript for each language and each team participating in subtask 3.

	Scores		
Team	English	Portuguese	Spanish
AMU-EuraNova	69.96_3	61.87_4	56.64_4
Handshakes AI Research	73.53_2	68.15_2	62.21_2
IBM MNLP IE	78.11_1	73.24_1	66.20_1
SU-NLP	2.58_5	N/A	N/A
jitin	66.43_4	64.19_3	58.35_3

Table 7: The performance of the submissions in terms of F1 score based on CoNLL 2003 (Tjong Kim Sang and De Meulder, 2003) and their ranks as a subscript for each language and each team participating in subtask 4.

Portuguese and Spanish. The team trains three XLM-R based classification models that consist of ensemble of multiple models with various configurations.

Team "ALEM" compares mono-lingual and multilingual BERT based models, opting for mono-lingual models for English and Portuguese, and multilingual model for Spanish test data. Team "AMU-EuraNova" divides the given text into chunks with small overlaps and generates a prediction for each chunk in order to solve the length issue that multilingual BERT faces, but it receives a poor score due to the way they reduce multiple chunks' predictions into a final one. Team "FKIE_itf_2021" uses frozen multilingual BERT embeddings to train 100 small neural nets and ensemble them via majority voting. Team "Handshakes AI Research" trains a classification model with LaBSE embeddings. Team "SU-NLP" makes use of vanilla RoBERTa. Team "NoConflict" uses the same model they trained for subtask 2 to test for subtask 1 English data.

8.2 Subtask 2

Subtask 2 results are demonstrated in Table 5. Team "NoConflict" does extra pre-training of English only RoBERTa model on political news articles before finetuning on English training data to achieve first place for English test data. The best scores for Portuguese and Spanish were submitted by "IBM MNLP IE" by applying the same approach, which is multilingual training, they followed for subtask 1.

Team "DaDeFrTi" trains a multilingual XLM-R based classification model with additional data either acquired from external data sets, collected from the web or translated from the original data. Team "ALEM" compares mono-lingual and multilingual BERT based models, opting for mono-lingual models for all languages. Team "AMU-EuraNova" uses the same model as their subtask 1 solution, but it achieves reasonable scores this time due to majority of samples being smaller than their chunking size. Team "FKIE_itf_2021" uses frozen multilingual BERT embeddings to train a single small MLP. Team "Handshakes AI Research" trains a multilingual XLM-R based classification model. Team "SU-NLP" uses an ensemble of vanilla RoBERTa and a CNN model that's fed stemmed text as an extra channel. Team "IIITT" uses an ensemble of 3 classification models based on multilingual BERT, multilingual Distill BERT and English-only RoBERTa.

8.3 Subtask 3

The results of subtask 3 are reported in Table 6. The Team "IBM MNLP IE" submitted the best results for the test data in English and Spanish. This team applies agglomerative clustering with scores of pairs of sentences obtained by a XLM-R based model. Team "NUS-IDS" uses the clustering algorithm employed by Örs et al. (2020) with scores of pairs of sentences obtained by BERT based LSTM model with extra semantic features. Their multilingual model achieves first place for Portuguese and second place for Spanish test data. Their English-only model achieved second place for English test data.

Team "DAAI" uses different sentence transformers as a pairwise scorer and applies hierarchical clustering algorithm, fine-tuning or training them from scratch. Team "FKIE_itf_2021" uses frozen multilingual BERT embeddings to train a pairwise scorer and applies a greedy clustering algorithm. Team "Handshakes AI Research" uses multilingual BERT embeddings to train a pairwise scorer and applies a greedy clustering algorithm. Moreover, they use extra data for English, and translations from English for Portuguese and Spanish data. Team "SU-NLP" uses an ensemble of 3 transformer based models as a pairwise scorer and applies the clustering algorithm proposed by Örs et al. (2020).

8.4 Subtask 4

We provide the results of the subtask 4 in Table 7. Results of the team "IBM MNLP IE" are by far the best for all languages. This team approaches this subtask as sequence labelling problem and fine-tunes a pre-trained language model (XLM-R large) with the data provided. The model they created using the training data for all languages ranked first for the test data in Portuguese and in Spanish. Their ensemble model that comprises five different English-only models performed the best for the test data in English.

Team "Handshakes AI Research" also considers subtask 4 as a sequence labelling problem and fine-tunes XLM-R multilingual using the Viterbi algorithm for the final classification. They use a previously defined technique to produce translations from English data to the rest of the languages, trying to mitigate the issue of smaller data size for Portuguese and Spanish. They achieved second place for English, Portuguese and Spanish test sets with this model. Team "AMU-EuraNova" uses the same chunking method with mBERT as their subtask 1 solution, but with extra stability experiments and behavioural fine-tuning with additional named entity data sets. Team "SU-NLP" trains a bidirectional LSTM on top of RoBERTa's contextualized word embeddings with conditional random fields.

9 Conclusion and Future Work

This shared task shows that multilingual and cross-lingual approaches perform surprisingly well for subtasks of protest event information collection. We observed that merging the training data from multiple languages improves the performance. Moreover, the performance of the first and second submissions, which are prepared by two different teams, for the cross-lingual zero-shot setting for subtask 1 in Hindi language are 78.77 and 78.53 in terms of F1-macro, thereby demonstrating the promising suitability of the approach for zero-shot multilingual setting. Another significant outcome is that "IBM MNLP IE" has outperformed all other teams by more than 4 points of F1-macro in all languages in subtask 4, which is the most challenging subtask.

Monolingual models outperforms multilingual models in case sufficient training data (Subtask 1, English) or additional further pre-training data is available (Subtask 2, English). These conditions are satisfied mostly for evaluation scenarios pertaining to English language. Although, multilingual models yield best performance in some scenarios, the monolingual models ranked second or third place.

Automated event information collection approaches are prone to major issues like bias toward majority class and popular content and limited generalizability that affect reliability and validity of them (Leins et al., 2020; Bhatia et al., 2020; Chang et al., 2019; Wang et al., 2016; Eck, 2021; Lorenzini et al., 2016; Schrodt, 2020; Raleigh, 2020; Boschee, 2021). We consider this benchmark as the first step to obtain comparable results across various automated approaches in a multilingual setting. We form a basis for increasing variety of the data that can be utilized for developing and evaluating event information collection systems by extending the language data that has various levels of availability such as few-shot and zero-shot settings. Furthermore, this benchmark allows determination of the most suitable text processing approaches for this task by identifying the performance levels that can be achieved applying recent technology. Last but not least, the random sampling of the corpus utilized in the shared task enables realistic recall quantification that has been challenging to measure to date (Hürriyetoğlu et al., 2021; Yörük et al., 2021).

We will be extending available training data and include additional data in different languages in the future iterations of this benchmark.

Acknowledgments

The authors from Koc University are funded by the European Research Council (ERC) Starting Grant 714868 awarded to Dr. Erdem Yörük for his project Emerging Welfare. Farhana Ferdousi Liza would like to acknowledge the support of the Business and Local Government Data Research Centre (ES/S007156/1) funded by the Economic and Social Research Council (ESRC) for undertaking this work.

References

Mikel Artetxe and Holger Schwenk. 2019a. Massively Multilingual Sentence Embeddings for Zero-Shot Cross-Lingual Transfer and Beyond. *Transac-*

tions of the Association for Computational Linguistics, 7:597–610.

Mikel Artetxe and Holger Schwenk. 2019b. Massively Multilingual Sentence Embeddings for Zero-Shot Cross-Lingual Transfer and Beyond. *Transactions of the Association for Computational Linguistics*, 7:597–610.

Parul Awasthy, Jian Ni, Ken Barker, and Radu Florian. 2021. IBM MNLP IE at CASE 2021 task 1: Multi-granular and multilingual event detection on protest news. In *Proceedings of the 4th Workshop on Challenges and Applications of Automated Extraction of Socio-political Events from Text (CASE 2021)*, online. Association for Computational Linguistics (ACL).

Nils Becker and Theresa Krumbiegel. 2021. FKIE_itf_2021 at CASE 2021 Task 1: Using Small Densely Fully Connected Neural Nets for Event Detection and Clustering. In *Proceedings of the 4th Workshop on Challenges and Applications of Automated Extraction of Socio-political Events from Text (CASE 2021)*, online. Association for Computational Linguistics (ACL).

Shraey Bhatia, Jey Han Lau, and Timothy Baldwin. 2020. You are right. i am alarmed–but by climate change counter movement. *arXiv preprint arXiv:2004.14907*.

Doug Bond, Joe Bond, Churl Oh, J. Craig Jenkins, and Charles Lewis Taylor. 2003. Integrated data for events analysis (idea): An event typology for automated events data development. *Journal of Peace Research*, 40(6):733–745.

Elizabeth Boschee. 2021. Keynote Abstract: Events on a Global Scale: Towards Language-Agnostic Event Extraction. In *Proceedings of the 4th Workshop on Challenges and Applications of Automated Extraction of Socio-political Events from Text (CASE 2021)*, online. Association for Computational Linguistics (ACL).

Lo Bouscarrat, Antoine Bonnefoy, Ccile Capponi, and Carlos Ramisch. 2021. AMU-EURANOVA at CASE 2021 Task 1: Assessing the stability of multilingual BERT. In *Proceedings of the 4th Workshop on Challenges and Applications of Automated Extraction of Socio-political Events from Text (CASE 2021)*, online. Association for Computational Linguistics (ACL).

Furkan Çelik, Tuğberk Dalkılıç, Fatih Beyhan, and Reyyan Yeniterzi. 2021. SU-NLP at CASE 2021 Task 1: Protest News Detection for English. In *Proceedings of the 4th Workshop on Challenges and Applications of Automated Extraction of Socio-political Events from Text (CASE 2021)*, online. Association for Computational Linguistics (ACL).

Kai-Wei Chang, Vinod Prabhakaran, and Vicente Ordonez. 2019. Bias and fairness in natural language processing. In *Proceedings of the 2019 Conference on Empirical Methods in Natural Language Processing and the 9th International Joint Conference on Natural Language Processing (EMNLP-IJCNLP): Tutorial Abstracts*, Hong Kong, China. Association for Computational Linguistics.

Alexis Conneau, Kartikay Khandelwal, Naman Goyal, Vishrav Chaudhary, Guillaume Wenzek, Francisco Guzmán, Edouard Grave, Myle Ott, Luke Zettlemoyer, and Veselin Stoyanov. 2020. Unsupervised cross-lingual representation learning at scale. In *Proceedings of the 58th Annual Meeting of the Association for Computational Linguistics*, pages 8440–8451, Online. Association for Computational Linguistics.

Vera Danilova. 2015. A pipeline for multilingual protest event selection and annotation. In *2015 26th International Workshop on Database and Expert Systems Applications (DEXA)*, pages 309–313.

Jacob Devlin, Ming-Wei Chang, Kenton Lee, and Kristina Toutanova. 2019a. BERT: Pre-training of deep bidirectional transformers for language understanding. In *Proceedings of the 2019 Conference of the North American Chapter of the Association for Computational Linguistics: Human Language Technologies, Volume 1 (Long and Short Papers)*, pages 4171–4186, Minneapolis, Minnesota. Association for Computational Linguistics.

Jacob Devlin, Ming-Wei Chang, Kenton Lee, and Kristina Toutanova. 2019b. Bert: Pre-training of deep bidirectional transformers for language understanding. In *NAACL-HLT (1)*.

Kristine Eck. 2021. Keynote Abstract: Machine Learning in Conflict Studies: Reflections on Ethics, Collaboration, and Ongoing Challenges. In *Proceedings of the 4th Workshop on Challenges and Applications of Automated Extraction of Socio-political Events from Text (CASE 2021)*, online. Association for Computational Linguistics (ACL).

Günes Erkan and Dragomir R. Radev. 2004. Lexrank: Graph-based lexical centrality as salience in text summarization. *J. Artif. Int. Res.*, 22(1):457479.

Fangxiaoyu Feng, Yinfei Yang, Daniel Cer, Naveen Arivazhagan, and Wei Wang. 2020. Language-agnostic bert sentence embedding. *arXiv preprint arXiv:2007.01852*.

Deborah J Gerner, Philip A Schrodt, Omür Yilmaz, and Rajaa Abu-Jabr. 2002. Conflict and mediation event observations (cameo): A new event data framework for the analysis of foreign policy interactions. *International Studies Association, New Orleans*.

Salvatore Giorgi, Vanni Zavarella, Hristo Tanev, Nicolas Stefanovitch, Sy Hwang, Hansi Hettiarachchi, Tharindu Ranasinghe, Vivek Kalyan, Paul Tan, Shaun Tan, Martin Andrews, Hu Tiancheng, Niklas Stoehr, Francesco Ignazio Re, Daniel Vegh, Dennis Atzenhofer, Brenda Curtis, and Ali Hürriyetoğlu.

2021. Discovering Black Lives Matter events in the United States - Shared Task 3, CASE 2021. In *Proceedings of the 4th Workshop on Challenges and Applications of Automated Extraction of Socio-political Events from Text (CASE 2021)*, online. Association for Computational Linguistics (ACL).

Marco G. Giugni. 1998. Was It Worth the Effort? The Outcomes and Consequences of Social Movements. *Annual Review of Sociology*, 24:371–393.

Alaeddin Gürel and Emre Emin. 2021. ALEM at CASE 2021 Task 1: Multilingual Text Classification on News Articles. In *Proceedings of the 4th Workshop on Challenges and Applications of Automated Extraction of Socio-political Events from Text (CASE 2021)*, online. Association for Computational Linguistics (ACL).

Kai Hakala and Sampo Pyysalo. 2019. Biomedical named entity recognition with multilingual BERT. In *Proceedings of The 5th Workshop on BioNLP Open Shared Tasks*, pages 56–61, Hong Kong, China. Association for Computational Linguistics.

Jacek Haneczok, Guillaume Jacquet, Jakub Piskorski, and Nicolas Stefanovitch. 2021. Fine-grained event classification in news-like text snippets shared task 2, CASE 2021. In *Proceedings of the 4th Workshop on Challenges and Applications of Automated Extraction of Socio-political Events from Text (CASE 2021)*, online. Association for Computational Linguistics (ACL).

Alex Hanna. 2017. MPEDS: Automating the Generation of Protest Event Data.

Hansi Hettiarachchi, Mariam Adedoyin-Olowe, Jagdev Bhogal, and Mohamed Gaber. 2021. DAAI at CASE 2021 Task 1: Transformer-based Multilingual Socio-political and Crisis Event Detection. In *Proceedings of the 4th Workshop on Challenges and Applications of Automated Extraction of Socio-political Events from Text (CASE 2021)*, online. Association for Computational Linguistics (ACL).

Junjie Hu, Sebastian Ruder, Aditya Siddhant, Graham Neubig, Orhan Firat, and Melvin Johnson. 2020. XTREME: A massively multilingual multi-task benchmark for evaluating cross-lingual generalisation. In *Proceedings of the 37th International Conference on Machine Learning*, volume 119 of *Proceedings of Machine Learning Research*, pages 4411–4421. PMLR.

Tiancheng Hu and Niklas Stoehr. 2021. Team "NoConflict" at CASE 2021 Task 1:Pretraining for Sentence-Level Protest Event Detection. In *Proceedings of the 4th Workshop on Challenges and Applications of Automated Extraction of Socio-political Events from Text (CASE 2021)*, online. Association for Computational Linguistics (ACL).

Ali Hürriyetoğlu, Hristo Tanev, Vanni Zavarella, Jakub Piskorski, Reyyan Yeniterzi, Erdem Yörük, Osman Mutlu, Deniz Yüret, and Aline Villavicencio. 2021. Challenges and Applications of Automated Extraction of Socio-political Events from Text (CASE 2021): Workshop and Shared Task Report. In *Proceedings of the 4th Workshop on Challenges and Applications of Automated Extraction of Socio-political Events from Text (CASE 2021)*, online. Association for Computational Linguistics (ACL).

Ali Hürriyetoğlu, Erdem Yörük, Deniz Yüret, Çağrı Yoltar, Burak Gürel, Fırat Duruşan, and Osman Mutlu. 2019a. A task set proposal for automatic protest information collection across multiple countries. In *Advances in Information Retrieval*, pages 316–323, Cham. Springer International Publishing.

Ali Hürriyetoğlu, Erdem Yörük, Deniz Yüret, Çağrı Yoltar, Burak Gürel, Fırat Duruşan, Osman Mutlu, and Arda Akdemir. 2019b. Overview of CLEF 2019 Lab ProtestNews: Extracting Protests from News in a Cross-Context Setting. In *Experimental IR Meets Multilinguality, Multimodality, and Interaction*, pages 425–432, Cham. Springer International Publishing.

Ali Hürriyetoğlu, Vanni Zavarella, Hristo Tanev, Erdem Yörük, Ali Safaya, and Osman Mutlu. 2020. Automated extraction of socio-political events from news (AESPEN): Workshop and shared task report. In *Proceedings of the Workshop on Automated Extraction of Socio-political Events from News 2020*, pages 1–6, Marseille, France. European Language Resources Association (ELRA).

Ali Hürriyetoğlu, Erdem Yörük, Osman Mutlu, Fırat Duruşan, Çağrı Yoltar, Deniz Yüret, and Burak Gürel. 2021. Cross-Context News Corpus for Protest Event-Related Knowledge Base Construction. *Data Intelligence*, 3(2):308–335.

Swen Hutter. 2014. Protest event analysis and its offspring. In Donatella della Porta, editor, *Methodological Practices in Social Movement Research*, pages 335–367. Oxford: Oxford University Press, Oxford.

Pawan Kalyan, Duddukunta Reddy, Adeep Hande, Ruba Priyadharshini, Ratnasingam Sakuntharaj, and Bharathi Raja Chakravarthi. 2021a. IIITT at CASE 2021 Task 1: Leveraging Pretrained Language Models for Multilingual Protest Detection. In *Proceedings of the 4th Workshop on Challenges and Applications of Automated Extraction of Socio-political Events from Text (CASE 2021)*, online. Association for Computational Linguistics (ACL).

Sureshkumar Vivek Kalyan, Tan Paul, Tan Shaun, and Martin Andrews. 2021b. Shared Task 1 System Description : Exploring different approaches for multilingual tasks. In *Proceedings of the 4th Workshop on Challenges and Applications of Automated Extraction of Socio-political Events from Text (CASE 2021)*, online. Association for Computational Linguistics (ACL).

Hanspeter Kriesi, Bruno Wüest, Jasmine Lorenzini, Peter Makarov, Matthias Enggist, Klaus Rothenhäusler,

Thomas Kurer, Silja Häusermann, and Altiparmakis Patrice Wangen. 2019. Poldem–protest event dataset 30.

Klaus Krippendorff, Yann Mathet, Stéphane Bouvry, and Antoine Widlöcher. 2016. On the reliability of unitizing textual continua: Further developments. *Quality and quantity*, 50(6):2347–2364.

Guillaume Lample and Alexis Conneau. 2019. Cross-lingual language model pretraining. *Advances in Neural Information Processing Systems (NeurIPS)*.

Kalev Leetaru and Philip A Schrodt. 2013. GDELT: Global data on events, location, and tone, 1979–2012. In *ISA annual convention*, volume 2, pages 1–49. Citeseer.

Kobi Leins, Jey Han Lau, and Timothy Baldwin. 2020. Give me convenience and give her death: Who should decide what uses of NLP are appropriate, and on what basis? In *Proceedings of the 58th Annual Meeting of the Association for Computational Linguistics*, pages 2908–2913, Online. Association for Computational Linguistics.

Yan Liang, Khaled Jabr, Christan Grant, Jill Irvine, and Andrew Halterman. 2018. New techniques for coding political events across languages. In *2018 IEEE International Conference on Information Reuse and Integration (IRI)*, pages 88–93.

Yinhan Liu, Jiatao Gu, Naman Goyal, Xian Li, Sergey Edunov, Marjan Ghazvininejad, Mike Lewis, and Luke Zettlemoyer. 2020. Multilingual Denoising Pre-training for Neural Machine Translation. *Transactions of the Association for Computational Linguistics*, 8:726–742.

Jasmine Lorenzini, Peter Makarov, Hanspeter Kriesi, and Bruno Wueest. 2016. Towards a Dataset of Automatically Coded Protest Events from English-language Newswire Documents. In *Paper presented at the Amsterdam Text Analysis Conference*.

Peter Makarov, Jasmine Lorenzini, and Hanspeter Kriesi. 2016. Constructing an annotated corpus for protest event mining. In *Proceedings of the First Workshop on NLP and Computational Social Science*, pages 102–107, Austin, Texas. Association for Computational Linguistics.

Shervin Minaee, Nal Kalchbrenner, Erik Cambria, Narjes Nikzad, Meysam Chenaghlu, and Jianfeng Gao. 2021. Deep learning–based text classification: A comprehensive review. *ACM Comput. Surv.*, 54(3).

Peter F. Nardulli, Scott L. Althaus, and Matthew Hayes. 2015. A Progressive Supervised-learning Approach to Generating Rich Civil Strife Data. *Sociological Methodology*, 45(1):148–183.

Clayton Norris, Philip Schrodt, and John Beieler. 2017. PETRARCH2: Another event coding program. *The Journal of Open Source Software*, 2(9).

Sean P. O'Brien. 2010. Crisis Early Warning and Decision Support: Contemporary Approaches and Thoughts on Future Research. *International Studies Review*, 12(1):87–104.

Faik Kerem Örs, Süveyda Yeniterzi, and Reyyan Yeniterzi. 2020. Event clustering within news articles. In *Proceedings of the Workshop on Automated Extraction of Socio-political Events from News 2020*, pages 63–68, Marseille, France. European Language Resources Association (ELRA).

Telmo Pires, Eva Schlinger, and Dan Garrette. 2019. How multilingual is multilingual BERT? In *Proceedings of the 57th Annual Meeting of the Association for Computational Linguistics*, pages 4996–5001, Florence, Italy. Association for Computational Linguistics.

Jakub Piskorski, Jacek Haneczok, and Guillaume Jacquet. 2020. New benchmark corpus and models for fine-grained event classification: To BERT or not to BERT? In *Proceedings of the 28th International Conference on Computational Linguistics*, pages 6663–6678, Barcelona, Spain (Online). International Committee on Computational Linguistics.

Sameer Pradhan, Xiaoqiang Luo, Marta Recasens, Eduard Hovy, Vincent Ng, and Michael Strube. 2014. Scoring coreference partitions of predicted mentions: A reference implementation. In *Proceedings of the 52nd Annual Meeting of the Association for Computational Linguistics (Volume 2: Short Papers)*, pages 30–35, Baltimore, Maryland. Association for Computational Linguistics.

Clionadh Raleigh. 2020. Keynote abstract: Too soon? the limitations of AI for event data. In *Proceedings of the Workshop on Automated Extraction of Socio-political Events from News 2020*, page 7, Marseille, France. European Language Resources Association (ELRA).

Clionadh Raleigh, Andrew Linke, Håvard Hegre, and Joakim Karlsen. 2010. Introducing acled: an armed conflict location and event dataset: special data feature. *Journal of peace research*, 47(5):651–660.

Lance Ramshaw and Mitch Marcus. 1995. Text chunking using transformation-based learning. In *Third Workshop on Very Large Corpora*.

Francesco Re, Daniel Vegh, Dennis Atzenhofer, and Niklas Stoehr. 2021. Team "DaDeFrNi" at CASE 2021 Task 1: Document and Sentence Classification for Protest Event Detection. In *Proceedings of the 4th Workshop on Challenges and Applications of Automated Extraction of Socio-political Events from Text (CASE 2021)*, online. Association for Computational Linguistics (ACL).

Nils Reimers and Iryna Gurevych. 2019. Sentence-bert: Sentence embeddings using siamese bert-networks. In *Proceedings of the 2019 Conference on Empirical Methods in Natural Language Processing*. Association for Computational Linguistics.

Nils Reimers and Iryna Gurevych. 2020. Making monolingual sentence embeddings multilingual using knowledge distillation. In *Proceedings of the 2020 Conference on Empirical Methods in Natural Language Processing (EMNLP)*, pages 4512–4525.

Parang Saraf and Naren Ramakrishnan. 2016. Embers autogsr: Automated coding of civil unrest events. In *Proceedings of the 22nd ACM SIGKDD International Conference on Knowledge Discovery and Data Mining*, KDD '16, page 599608, New York, NY, USA. Association for Computing Machinery.

Philip Schrodt and f Jay Yonamine. 2013. A guide to event data: Past, present, and future. *All Azimuth: A Journal of Foreign Policy and Peace*, 2:5 – 22.

Philip A. Schrodt. 2020. Keynote abstract: Current open questions for operational event data. In *Proceedings of the Workshop on Automated Extraction of Socio-political Events from News 2020*, page 8, Marseille, France. European Language Resources Association (ELRA).

Holger Schwenk and Matthijs Douze. 2017. Learning joint multilingual sentence representations with neural machine translation. In *Proceedings of the 2nd Workshop on Representation Learning for NLP*, pages 157–167, Vancouver, Canada. Association for Computational Linguistics.

Justin Sech, Alexandra DeLucia, Anna L. Buczak, and Mark Dredze. 2020. Civil unrest on Twitter (CUT): A dataset of tweets to support research on civil unrest. In *Proceedings of the Sixth Workshop on Noisy User-generated Text (W-NUT 2020)*, pages 215–221, Online. Association for Computational Linguistics.

Çağıl Sönmez, Arzucan Özgür, and Erdem Yörük. 2016. Towards building a political protest database to explain changes in the welfare state. In *Proceedings of the 10th SIGHUM Workshop on Language Technology for Cultural Heritage, Social Sciences, and Humanities*, pages 106–110. Association for Computational Linguistics.

Ralph Sundberg, Kristine Eck, and Joakim Kreutz. 2012. Introducing the ucdp non-state conflict dataset. *Journal of Peace Research*, 49(2):351–362.

Fiona An Ting Tan, Sujatha Das Gollapalli, and See-Kiong Ng. 2021. NUS-IDS at CASE 2021 Task 1: Improving Multilingual Event Sentence Coreference Identification With Linguistic Information. In *Proceedings of the 4th Workshop on Challenges and Applications of Automated Extraction of Socio-political Events from Text (CASE 2021)*, online. Association for Computational Linguistics (ACL).

S. Tarrow. 1994. *Power in Movement: Social Movements, Collective Action and Politics*. Cambridge Studies in Comparative Politics. Cambridge University Press.

Erik F. Tjong Kim Sang and Fien De Meulder. 2003. Introduction to the conll-2003 shared task: Language-independent named entity recognition. In *Proceedings of the Seventh Conference on Natural Language Learning at HLT-NAACL 2003 - Volume 4*, CONLL 03, page 142147, USA. Association for Computational Linguistics.

Wei Wang, Ryan Kennedy, David Lazer, and Naren Ramakrishnan. 2016. Growing pains for global monitoring of societal events. *Science*, 353(6307):1502–1503.

Nils B. Weidmann and Espen Geelmuyden Rød. 2019. *The Internet and Political Protest in Autocracies*, chapter Coding Protest Events in Autocracies. Oxford Studies in Digital Politics, Oxford.

Erdem Yörük, Ali Hürriyetoğlu, Çağrı Yoltar, and Fırat Duruşan. 2021. Random Sampling in Corpus Design: Cross-Context Generalizability in Automated Multicountry Protest Event Collection. *American Behavioral Scientist*, 0(0):00027642211021630.

Han Zhang and Jennifer Pan. 2019. Casm: A deep-learning approach for identifying collective action events with text and image data from social media. *Sociological Methodology*, 49(1):1–57.

Handshakes AI Research at CASE 2021 Task 1: Exploring different approaches for multilingual tasks

Vivek Kalyan* **Paul Tan*** **Shaun Tan*** **Martin Andrews**

Handshakes, Singapore

{first.last}@handshakes.com.sg

Abstract

The aim of the CASE 2021 Shared Task 1 (Hürriyetoğlu et al., 2021) was to detect and classify socio-political and crisis event information at document, sentence, cross-sentence, and token levels in a multilingual setting, with each of these subtasks being evaluated separately in each test language. Our submission contained entries in all of the subtasks, and the scores obtained validated our research finding: That the multilingual aspect of the tasks should be embraced, so that modeling and training regimes use the multilingual nature of the tasks to their mutual benefit, rather than trying to tackle the different languages separately. Our code is available at https://github.com/HandshakesByDC/case2021/

1 Introduction

The CASE Shared Task 1 concerned news events that are in the scope of contentious politics and characterized by riots and social movements, denoted "GLOCON Gold" (Hürriyetoğlu et al., 2020). The aim of the shared task was to detect and classify socio-political and crisis event information at document, sentence, cross-sentence, and token levels in a multilingual setting:

- Subtask 1 : Document classification: Does a news article contain information about a past or ongoing event?
- Subtask 2 : Sentence classification: Does a sentence contain information about a past or ongoing event?
- Subtask 3 : Event sentence coreference identification: Which event sentences (from Subtask 2) are about the same event?
- Subtask 4 : Event extraction: What is the event trigger and its arguments?

The detailed description of the subtasks can be found in Hürriyetoğlu et al. (2019) and Hürriyetoğlu et al. (2021).

2 Team Organisation

In order to efficiently allocate resources, separate, parallel research efforts were initially made towards each subtask, with periodic knowledge sharing taking place between subtasks.

Data issues with Subtask 1 (whereby, due to copyright reasons, a significant number of the news articles were severely truncated in the dataset provided), our original approach to this subtask was abandoned, and the approach from Subtask 2 was quickly redeployed towards Subtask 1 in the late stages of the Shared Task test phase - hence the ordering herein of system descriptions.

3 Methods

All subtask teams used off-the-shelf pre-trained models, and training was conducted only on the training data provided through the Shared Task (except as noted in Subtask 3, where some additional public data was used).

The key language models used for the subtasks were pre-trained models sourced from the Hugging Face library[1]:

- DistilBERT, Multilingual ('m-distilBERT') (Sanh et al., 2019)
- BERT-Base, Multilingual Cased ('m-BERT') (Devlin et al., 2019)
- 'XLM-RoBERTa' (multilingually trained, -base version) (Conneau et al., 2020)

For generating embeddings for sentences, and as part of the word-at-a-time translation technique

*Equal contributions

[1] https://huggingface.co/models

Proceedings of the 4th Workshop on Challenges and Applications of Automated Extraction of Socio-political Events from Text (CASE), pages 92–97
August 5–6, 2021, ©2021 Association for Computational Linguistics

used in Subtask 4, we used the following publicly available pre-trained models:

- 'LASER' (Language-Agnostic SEntence Representations) (Artetxe and Schwenk, 2019)
- Language-agnostic BERT Sentence Embedding ('LaBSE') (Feng et al., 2020)
- Multilingual Universal Sentence Encoder ('M-USE') (Yang et al., 2020)
- Multilingual Unsupervised and Supervised Embeddings ('MUSE') (Lample et al., 2017)

Due to the use of pre-trained models, the computational resources required no more than single-GPU workstations.

4 Subtask System Descriptions

4.1 Subtask 2 - Sentence Classification

Does a sentence contain information about a past (or ongoing) event, or not? (Binary classification)

4.1.1 Experimental Approach

The sentence classification subtask had a relatively high quantity of training data with all test languages having corresponding training data. Our approach was to find the best combined training dataset to train the largest multilingual model available.

To create internal classification baselines, we initially used a linear classifier over LASER embeddings and then progressed to m-distilBERT. Then, using the efficient pipeline created, we performed ablation tests to select the best training dataset across all models, from among the training datasets that we constructed.

The remaining time was spent fine-tuning the largest multilingual model available, XLM-RoBERTa. Based on our experimental results, we decided to train a single model to generate the final submission on all languages.

4.1.2 Model and Data Architecture

Our final training dataset used the training data from all languages into a single combined dataset. This dataset was split 80/20 for training and internal validation sets.

Our final model was a pre-trained XLM-RoBERTa model, fine-tuned on the article data from Subtask 1 and Subtask 2, with a 'classification head' (i.e. a single linear layer on top of the pooled output from the transformer layers) trained on the Subtask 2-specific training data. For the classification component, we selected the model that maximised validation F_1 scores, and our component scores are listed in Table 1.

4.1.3 Experimental Results

We found that the best performing training dataset was made by combining all 3 datasets provided in their original language into a single all-encompassing dataset : The multilingual model benefiting from seeing all of the data as one coherent set.

Dataset	English	Spanish	Portuguese
Validation	0.7610	0.6950	0.6670
Competition	0.7750	0.8325	0.8506
Final Placing	7/11	3/10	4/10

Table 1: Averaged Model Performance for Subtask 2

Performance on Spanish and Portuguese showed good improvements by training on all data instead of only its own language, whereas there was little-to-no improvement for English likely due to the relatively large amount of training data.

4.2 Subtask 1 - Document Classification

Does a news article contain information about a past (or ongoing) event? (Binary classification)

4.2.1 Experimental Approach

The document classification subtask had the unique challenge of testing on Hindi - a language not present in the training data. Therefore, we aimed to create a classifier that would perform the classification task across seen and unseen languages.

Similar to Subtask 2, we achieved this by using pre-trained multilingual embedding models that have proven capabilities in using semantic similarity across languages. On top of these models, we then trained a classifier capable of performing on other languages due to consistent embeddings.

Time constraints prevented the training of larger models such as XML-RoBERTa-large, which we believe could have lead to better results (based on our experience in other work).

4.2.2 Model and Data Architecture

Our final model was a 4-layer MLP classifier on top of 768-dimensional LaBSE embeddings, trained and validated on a dataset that directly combined all 3 languages in the training set (split 80/20 as internal training and validation sets).

4.2.3 Experimental Results

Due to time constraints, we were unable to perform any ablation tests on the Subtask 1 data. Thus, we assumed that training with all languages (as in Subtask 2) would yield good performance and may generalize better to unseen languages. A single model was used for the final submission, and the results are given in Table 2.

Dataset	[en]	[es]	[pt]	Hindi
Val.	0.7060	0.5710	0.6510	-
Comp.	0.7758	0.6984	0.8121	0.5955
Placing	6/10	3/8	3/8	5/7

Table 2: Averaged Model Performance for Subtask 1

4.2.4 Subtask 1 Discussion

Performance on Spanish and Portuguese showed the benefits of training on all data instead of only individual languages. For the unseen language Hindi, it is possible that the model over-fitted to the provided languages during training - though it is impressive that the simple technique used is capable of domain-transfer 'out-of-the-box'.

4.3 Subtask 3 - Event Coreference Identification

Which event sentences (from Subtask 2) are about the same event? (All-vs-all linking)

4.3.1 Experimental Approach

Subtask 3 had significantly less training data for Spanish (11 documents) and Portuguese (21 documents) compared to English (596 documents) (collectively, "ACL-St3"). To take advantage of the larger quantity of English data, we made Spanish and Portuguese translations of the English training portion to investigate whether models improved in performance when trained on translations.

Additionally, we used an external English dataset (Choubey and Huang, 2021) to obtain a balanced set of $8,030$ coreferential and non-coreferential sentence pairs ("EACL-2021") to investigate whether the models improve when also trained on more data.

Our final architecture was a two-stage process where we (i) first predict whether each sentence pair in a document is co-referential (binary classification), followed by (ii) a greedy clustering of sentences predicted to be co-referential.

For the first stage, we made use of a pre-trained m-BERT fine-tuned as a sentence pair coreference classifier (this returned a confidence score that any two given sentences are coreferential). The second stage formed clusters based upon whether the coreference classification estimate exceeded 0.5, greedily expanding the clusters in the process.

The training data was prepared by extracting unique sentence pairs from each document, labelling only sentence pairs in the same cluster as "coreferential" and the others as "non-coreferential".

4.3.2 Model and Data Architecture

Our best-performing solution comprised training m-BERT model trained once for each individual target language, fine-tuned as a sentence-pair coreference classifier (maximising $F_{0.6}$ on the validation set when trained/validated on a $90/10$ split of each specific dataset).

The individual language datasets were treated separately (and these combinations were found to give the best performance):

- English: ACL-St3 and EACL-2021 combined
- Portuguese / Spanish: For each language, we combined their respective portion of the ACL-St3 dataset, and translations of the English ACL-St3 dataset into that language (using output from the Google translate API, unmodified).

4.3.3 Experimental Results

The performance of the English language model was marginally better (an uplift of around 1% in absolute score) when the model was trained with EACL-2021 than without.

We found better model performance on Spanish and Portuguese when models were trained on Spanish and Portuguese translations of the English training data than without.

The results of our best-performing model for each language, scored using CoNLL-2012 average (Pradhan et al., 2014), are given in Table 3.

Dataset	[en]	[es]	[pt]
Validation	0.8990	0.9330	0.8220
Competition	0.7901	0.8195	0.9061
Final Placing	4/6	4/5	4/5

Table 3: Averaged Model Performance for Subtask 3

4.4 Subtask 4 - Event Extraction

For a given event sentence, what is the event trigger and its arguments? (BIO sentence annotation)

4.4.1 Experimental Approach

For Subtask 4, we use a pre-trained XLM-RoBERTa with a Token Classification head and fine-tuned it on GLOCON dataset.

As stated in our overall approach, we aimed to maximise our multilingual capabilities while not requiring labour intensive data collection for each new language. To that end, we make a distinction between our primary language (English) which we expect to have more data for, and our secondary languages (Spanish, Portuguese) where there is less data. Our goal is to be able to add new secondary language capabilities with as little data requirements as possible.

Following Xie et al. (2018) and Wu et al. (2020), we apply techniques from Lample et al. (2017) to translate our primary language training data word-by-word into our secondary languages, and directly copy the entity label of each primary language word to its corresponding translated word. Using embeddings from Bojanowski et al. (2017), we learn a mapping, using the MUSE library, from the primary to the secondary language making use of identical character strings between the two languages. To produce the word-to-word translations, we use the learned mapping to map the primary language word into the secondary language embedding space, and find its nearest neighbour as the corresponding translated word. Additionally, as described in Conneau et al. (2018), we mitigated the "hubness" problem by using cross-domain similarity local scaling (CSLS) to measure the distance between the mapped embedding vector of the primary language word and the embedding vector of a secondary language word. For an illustrative example please see Tables 4 and 5.

Thus, we are able to train our model on new secondary languages without requiring task-specific secondary language data, but rather secondary language embeddings and bilingual primary-secondary dictionaries to create the mapping. For each language, our training sets consisted of 90% of the English training data and the translated secondary language data, and our validation set was the (entire) original secondary language training data set, plus the remaining 10% of the English training data[2].

$[en]$ KSRTC buses were attacked at ten places.
$[pt]$ Os ônibus KSRTC foram atacados em dez lugares.
$[es]$ Los autobuses KSRTC fueron atacados en diez lugares.

Table 4: Sentence-wise translations (contrast with words/grammar of Table 5)

$base[en]$	$[en] \rightarrow [pt]$	$[en] \rightarrow [es]$
KSRTC	DERSA	BIZKAIBUS
buses	ônibus	autobuses
were	foram	fueron
attacked	atacou	atacado
at	na	en
ten	dez	diez
places	lugares	lugares
.	.	.

Table 5: Word-by-Word translation example, allowing for consistent BIO tagging

The final classification is decoded using the Viterbi Algorithm (Viterbi, 1967). Instead of training transition probabilities based upon our limited training data, we instead explicitly encoded constraints (by setting selected transition probabilities to zero) to ensure that we do not violate the BIO tagging scheme.

4.4.2 Experimental Results

The results of our model for each language, are given in Table 6. There was no performance degradation between training the model on {1 primary + 1 secondary language} vs {1 primary + 2 secondary languages}, which is promising for application to other secondary languages in the future.

Dataset	[en]	[es]	[pt]
Validation	82.53	62.17	72.75
Competition	73.53	62.21	68.15
Final Placing	2/5	2/4	2/4

Table 6: F_1 Model Performance for Subtask 4

It is interesting to observe that the difference in scores between validation and test sets was approximately 5%. This might indicate that either that

[2]One dataset-specific issue : Care had to be taken to avoid translating the English validation set as it resulted in the model having access to a form of the validation set (data leakage).

Model	Viterbi	W-to-W	English F_1	Spanish F_1	Portuguese F_1	Average F_1
Baseline BERT			71.54	-	-	-
MultiLingual BERT			70.99	54.94	64.96	63.63
XLM-RoBERTa			70.81	53.46	68.14	64.14
XLM-RoBERTa	✓		72.80	54.65	70.46	65.97
XLM-RoBERTa	✓	✓	82.53	62.17	72.75	72.48

Table 7: Model ablation for Subtask 4 on validation set. 'Viterbi': The BIO tagging is cleaned using Viterbi decoding. 'W-to-W': Models are trained with word-to-word translated data.

the test set has a rather different distribution from the validation set or that we may have biased the validation set in some manner.

We also observe in Table 7 that adding translated secondary language data helped to improve the performance on our *primary* data. While we did not dig deeper into the cause, we did notice that with the translated data the model took about twice the number of epochs to converge.

5 Discussion

In Subtasks 1, 2 and 3, we found that our Competition performance was generally higher than that obtained on our own validation split of the training data. This surprising outcome is difficult to explain, though may be because:

- Low data effects : Our validation data sets were necessarily quite small, and we may have simply had a non-representative selection of harder examples in those subsets
- Test data is 'constructed' : Perhaps there are some additional statistical effects that the Shared Task organisers want to analyse, and thus the test data distribution is intentionally different (eg: split into 'easy' and 'hard' subsets) from the training data

6 Conclusions

We showed that it is possible to achieve strong performance on new languages without task specific training data in the new language, provided that there is good enough training data in another language (English in this case) to supplement the training process.

This multilingual use-case is of commercial interest within our organisation and we thank the organisers of the Shared Task for the opportunity to explore these issues using curated datasets.

Acknowledgments

We would like to thank Ethan Phan, Yuan Lik Xun, Rainer Berger and Charles Poon for their valuable input during the Shared Task, as well as Handshakes for being supportive of this research project.

References

Mikel Artetxe and Holger Schwenk. 2019. Massively multilingual sentence embeddings for zero-shot cross-lingual transfer and beyond.

Piotr Bojanowski, Edouard Grave, Armand Joulin, and Tomas Mikolov. 2017. Enriching word vectors with subword information. *Transactions of the Association for Computational Linguistics*, 5:135–146.

Prafulla Kumar Choubey and Ruihong Huang. 2021. Automatic data acquisition for event coreference resolution. In *Proceedings of the 16th Conference of the European Chapter of the Association for Computational Linguistics: Main Volume*, Online. Association for Computational Linguistics.

Alexis Conneau, Kartikay Khandelwal, Naman Goyal, Vishrav Chaudhary, Guillaume Wenzek, Francisco Guzmán, Edouard Grave, Myle Ott, Luke Zettlemoyer, and Veselin Stoyanov. 2020. Unsupervised cross-lingual representation learning at scale.

Alexis Conneau, Guillaume Lample, Marc'Aurelio Ranzato, Ludovic Denoyer, and Hervé Jégou. 2018. Word translation without parallel data.

Jacob Devlin, Ming-Wei Chang, Kenton Lee, and Kristina Toutanova. 2019. BERT: Pre-training of deep bidirectional transformers for language understanding. In *Proceedings of the 2019 Conference of the North American Chapter of the Association for Computational Linguistics: Human Language Technologies, Volume 1 (Long and Short Papers)*, pages 4171–4186, Minneapolis, Minnesota. Association for Computational Linguistics.

Fangxiaoyu Feng, Yinfei Yang, Daniel Cer, Naveen Arivazhagan, and Wei Wang. 2020. Language-agnostic bert sentence embedding.

Ali Hürriyetoğlu, Osman Mutlu, Farhana Ferdousi Liza, Erdem Yörük, Ritesh Kumar, and Shyam

Ratan. 2021. Multilingual protest news detection - shared task 1, case 2021. In *Proceedings of the 4th Workshop on Challenges and Applications of Automated Extraction of Socio-political Events from Text (CASE 2021)*, online. Association for Computational Linguistics (ACL).

Ali Hürriyetoğlu, Erdem Yörük, Deniz Yüret, Çağrı Yoltar, Burak Gürel, Fırat Duruşan, Osman Mutlu, and Arda Akdemir. 2019. Overview of clef 2019 lab protestnews: Extracting protests from news in a cross-context setting. In *Experimental IR Meets Multilinguality, Multimodality, and Interaction*, pages 425–432, Cham. Springer International Publishing.

Ali Hürriyetoğlu, Vanni Zavarella, Hristo Tanev, Erdem Yörük, Ali Safaya, and Osman Mutlu. 2020. Automated extraction of socio-political events from news (AESPEN): Workshop and shared task report. In *Proceedings of the Workshop on Automated Extraction of Socio-political Events from News 2020*, pages 1–6, Marseille, France. European Language Resources Association (ELRA).

Ali Hürriyetoğlu, Erdem Yörük, Osman Mutlu, Fırat Duruşan, Çağrı Yoltar, Deniz Yüret, and Burak Gürel. 2021. Cross-Context News Corpus for Protest Event-Related Knowledge Base Construction. *Data Intelligence*, pages 1–28.

Guillaume Lample, Alexis Conneau, Ludovic Denoyer, and Marc'Aurelio Ranzato. 2017. Unsupervised machine translation using monolingual corpora only. *arXiv preprint arXiv:1711.00043*.

Sameer Pradhan, Xiaoqiang Luo, Marta Recasens, Eduard Hovy, Vincent Ng, and Michael Strube. 2014. Scoring coreference partitions of predicted mentions: A reference implementation. In *Proceedings of the 52nd Annual Meeting of the Association for Computational Linguistics (Volume 2: Short Papers)*, pages 30–35, Baltimore, Maryland. Association for Computational Linguistics.

Victor Sanh, Lysandre Debut, Julien Chaumond, and Thomas Wolf. 2019. Distilbert, a distilled version of bert: smaller, faster, cheaper and lighter. *ArXiv*, abs/1910.01108.

A. Viterbi. 1967. Error bounds for convolutional codes and an asymptotically optimum decoding algorithm. *IEEE Transactions on Information Theory*, 13(2):260–269.

Qianhui Wu, Zijia Lin, Börje F. Karlsson, Biqing Huang, and Jian-Guang Lou. 2020. Unitrans: Unifying model transfer and data transfer for cross-lingual named entity recognition with unlabeled data.

Jiateng Xie, Zhilin Yang, Graham Neubig, Noah A. Smith, and Jaime Carbonell. 2018. Neural cross-lingual named entity recognition with minimal resources.

Yinfei Yang, Daniel Cer, Amin Ahmad, Mandy Guo, Jax Law, Noah Constant, Gustavo Hernandez Abrego, Steve Yuan, Chris Tar, Yun-hsuan Sung, Brian Strope, and Ray Kurzweil. 2020. Multilingual universal sentence encoder for semantic retrieval. In *Proceedings of the 58th Annual Meeting of the Association for Computational Linguistics: System Demonstrations*, pages 87–94, Online. Association for Computational Linguistics.

IIITT at CASE 2021 Task 1: Leveraging Pretrained Language Models for Multilingual Protest Detection

Pawan Kalyan Jada[1], **Duddukunta Sashidhar Reddy**[1], **Adeep Hande**[1],
Ruba Priyadharshini[2], **Ratnasingam Sakuntharaj**[3], **Bharathi Raja Chakravarthi**[4]
[1] Indian Institute of Information Technology Tiruchirappalli
[2] ULTRA Arts and Science College, India, [3]Eastern University, Sri Lanka
[4]Insight SFI Research Centre for Data Analytics, National University of Ireland Galway
pawankj19c@iiitt.ac.in

Abstract

In a world abounding in constant protests resulting from events like a global pandemic, climate change, religious or political conflicts, there has always been a need to detect events/protests before getting amplified by news media or social media. This paper demonstrates our work on the sentence classification subtask of multilingual protest detection in CASE@ACL-IJCNLP 2021. We approached this task by employing various multilingual pre-trained transformer models to classify if any sentence contains information about an event that has transpired or not. Furthermore, we performed soft voting over the models, achieving the best results among the models, accomplishing a macro F1-Score of 0.8291, 0.7578, and 0.7951 in English, Spanish, and Portuguese, respectively. The source codes for our systems are published[1].

1 Introduction

The recent surge in social media users has led many people to express their opinions on various global issues. These opinions travel far and wide within a matter of seconds (Hossny et al., 2018). This can influence many people and may engage public movements (Won et al., 2017a). Therefore, there is a definite need to detect these protests and analyse them to know the significant areas of disinterest.

Being a free and easy to use platform, social media has become a part of our day to day life. It incorporates people of different ages, gender, location, religions, background, and so on. The enormous number of rich and diversified users results in an enormous amount of information being generated, which is helpful in many ways (Kapoor et al., 2018). Some of this even contains private information about the users, which others could misuse. Cases were also found where certain users were being targeted and harassed by people using this platform, a common scenario in cyberbullying (Abaido, 2020).

Social media plays a crucial role in amplifying these protests and movements (Won et al., 2017b). It enables political groups and protesters to organise protest movements and share information. It acts as a platform for the people who are underrepresented by giving a voice to them. It also offers new opportunities for people to engage in activism, political resistance, and protest outside the political groups and civic institutions. Thus, it has a social impact on everyone (Pulido et al., 2018). It is to be noted that social media, similar to news media, plays a vital role in its social and political events worldwide (Holt et al., 2013). For the above reasons, we can state that social media plays a crucial role in most worldwide events.

The English language is widely regarded as the first *Lingua Franca*. Statistically, it is one of the most widely spoken languages globally, having official status in over 53 countries (Crystal, 2008). Over 400 million people speak English as their primary language and widely spoken in the United States and the United Kingdom. *BlackLivesMatter* (Dave et al., 2020), *EarthDay* (Rome, 2010) are some of the major protests that have occurred in these countries. Español commonly referred to as Spanish, is spoken by over 360 million people worldwide, with most of its speakers residing in Mexico, Argentina, Spain. *15-M Movement* (Casero-Ripollés and Feenstra, 2012) and *YoSoy132* (García and Treré, 2014) are some of the recent protests where people have been vocal about in the Spanish language. Portuguese has over 220 million native speakers. Brazil, Portugal, Angola are some of the major countries where this language is spoken. Protests like *Racism Kills, May 68* (Ross, 2008) are the recent ones that occurred in the Portuguese language.

The recent upheavals of protests are due to so-

[1]https://github.com/adeepH/CASE-2021-Task-1

Proceedings of the 4th Workshop on Challenges and Applications of Automated Extraction of Socio-political Events from Text (CASE), pages 98–104
August 5–6, 2021, ©2021 Association for Computational Linguistics

Sentence	Language	Label
Fabius ran against Royal for the presidential nomination in 2007.	English	Event
He planned to start a race war.	English	Event
Metro police intervened and the fire was put out.	English	Not-event
Pero no es ése el mayor problema.	Spanish	Event
La Argentina retrocedería un paso todos los días.	Spanish	Event
Carrió no objetó que se trató de un secuestro.	Spanish	Not-event
Os servidores do Piauí estão em greve há 17 dias.	Portuguese	Not-event
É uma nova experiência mobilizatória.	Portuguese	Event
É decidiram ir às aulas e passar o dia de saia.	Portuguese	Not-event

Table 1: Examples of the dataset indicating events of the past and not-events.

cial media, youth, exaggeration of certain events. (Basile and Caselli, 2020). Any early detection of mass protest detection through social media platforms such as Facebook, Twitter, and Instagram to help minimizing the aftermath of the protests (Wilson, 2017). This has motivated Natural Language Processing (NLP) researchers to develop NLP systems to generalize on data coming from diverse sources to leverage the NLP systems to more realistic environments (Büyüköz et al., 2020). Hence, there is a need to develop NLP systems that could be generalized to any protest/events (Peng et al., 2013), which has motivated us to participate in the shared task for multilingual protest detection (Hürriyetoğlu et al., 2019a, 2021) The objective of the task is to identify if any sentence talks about any mentions of protests or events in three languages, namely, English, Spanish, and Portuguese. Hence, we treat this as a sequence classification task.

The rest of the paper is organized as follows, Section 2 presents previous work on protest detection and analysis. Section 3 entails a comprehensive analysis of the dataset used for our cause. Next, section 4 gives a detailed description of the models used for the multilingual event detection. Finally, section 5 analyses the results obtained, and Section 6 concludes our work while discussing the potential directions for future work.

2 Related Work

The need to detect events that could lead to protests is of prime interest to sociologists and governments (Danilova et al., 2016). There are several active ongoing projects for socio-political event systems such as KEDS (Kansas Event Data System) (Schrodt and Hall, 2006), CAMEO (Conflict and Mediation Event Observation) (Gerner et al., 2002), and several other databases for protest detection systems (Danilova, 2015). These methods have focused on news data as they have traditionally been the most reliant source of events. Protest detection has been one of the major issues in the context of social and political (Ettinger et al., 2017). Papanikolaou and Papageorgiou (2020) presented a computational social science methodology to analyse protests in Greece. Hürriyetoğlu et al. (2021) constructed a corpus of protest events comprising various language sources from various countries. Several systems were submitted to the CLEF ProtestNews Track that consisted of three shared tasks, primarily aimed at identifying and extracting event information spanning to multiple countries (Hürriyetoğlu et al., 2019b, 2020).

3 Dataset

This dataset comprises 26,208 sentences in three languages, namely English, Spanish, and Portuguese. The dataset consists of two classes:

- **Event**: The sentence indicates an event of the past.
- **Not-event**: The sentence does not talk about any event.

The volume of sequences indicating *Not-event* is higher in contrast to that of the *Event* label. Therefore, the dataset distribution is quite imbalanced. We can also notice that the number of English samples exceeds that of Spanish and Portuguese ones. Refer to Table 1 for examples of sentences talking about events and not talking about events displayed in English, Spanish, and Portuguese. The dataset distribution is displayed in Table 2. For our cause, we split the training and validation set in the ratio of 80:20.

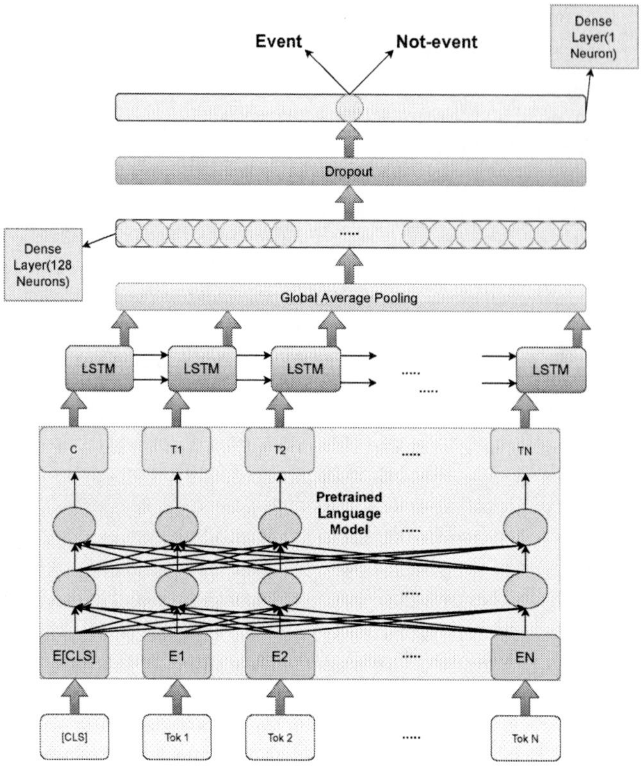

Figure 1: System Architecture based on BERT (Devlin et al., 2019)

Language	English	Spanish	Portuguese
Not-event	18,602	2,291	901
Event	4,223	450	281
Total	22,285	2,741	1,182

Table 2: Classwise distribution of the training set

4 Methodology

We used pretrained transformer-based models for identifying if a sentence talks about an event or not. The models that were used are BERT (Devlin et al., 2019), RoBERTa (Liu et al., 2019) and DistilBERT (Sanh et al., 2019). Even though there are 3 different languages, we used a single model for all three due to memory constraints and reduced training time. We fine-tuned these models for sequence classification. Soft Voting is done on all these models to produce the respective final outputs for the languages. In soft voting, each classifier predicts that a specific data point belongs to the particular target class. A weighted sum of the predictions is done based on the importance of the classifier (all models have equal weights). The overall prediction is chosen as the target with the greatest sum of the weighted probability, thus winning the vote (Beyeler, 2017; Hande et al., 2021).

4.1 BERT

Bidirectional **E**ncoder **R**epresentations from **T**ransformers (BERT) (Devlin et al., 2019) is a pretrained language model which was created with the objective that fine-tuning a pretrained model yields better performance. BERT's pretraining phase includes two tasks. Firstly, Masked Language Modeling (MLM) is where certain words are randomly masked in a sequence. About 15% of the words in a sequence is masked. The model then attempts to predict the masked words. Secondly, Next Sentence Prediction (NSP), where the model has an additional loss function, NSP loss, indicates if the second sequence follows the first one. Around 50% of the inputs are a pair, and they randomly chose the other 50. Here, we use a *bert-base-multilingual-cased* (Pires et al., 2019) trained on top of 104 languages in the largest Wikipedia corpus. This model has 12 layers, 12 Attention heads with over 179 million parameters.

	Event			Not-event			Overall			
Model	P	R	F1	P	R	F1	Acc	M(P)	M(R)	M(F1)
mBERT	0.928	0.917	0.922	0.641	0.675	0.658	0.873	0.784	0.796	0.790
DistilmBERT	0.924	0.947	0.936	0.729	0.646	0.685	0.893	0.827	0.797	0.810
RoBERTa	0.910	0.938	0.924	0.670	0.578	0.621	0.873	0.790	0.758	0.772
SoftVoting	0.937	0.939	0.938	0.720	0.713	0.717	**0.899**	**0.829**	**0.826**	**0.827**

Table 3: Precision (P), recall (R), and F1-Score of the models on the validation set; M(P), M(R), and M(F1) are the Macro averages of precision, recall, and F1-Score respectively

4.2 DistilmBERT

DistilBERT (Sanh et al., 2019) is the distilled version of BERT. DistilBERT employs a triple loss language modelling, where it integrates cosine distance loss with knowledge distillation. DistilBERT has 40% fewer parameters than BERT but still promises 97% of the latter's performance. It is also 60% faster than BERT. In this system, we used a cased multilingual DistilBERT model as they are three different languages. For our cause, we fine-tune *distilbert-base-multilingual-cased*, which is distilled from the mBERT checkpoint. The model has 6 layers, 768 dimensions, and 12 Attention heads, totalizing about 134 million parameters.

4.3 RoBERTa

Robustly Optimized BERT (RoBERTa) (Liu et al., 2019) follows the same architecture of BERT while differing in the pretraining strategy. It is pretrained with MLM as its objective where the model tries to predict the masked words. RoBERTa model is trained on the vast English Wikipedia and CC-News datasets. The NSP is not employed as a pretraining strategy, and the tokens are dynamically masked, making the model slightly different to BERT. During tokenization, RoBERTa follows byte-pair encoding (BPE) (Gallé, 2019) as opposed to WordPiece employed in BERT. We use *roberta-base*, a pretrained language model consisting of 12 layers, 768 hidden, 12 attention heads, and 125 million parameters.

4.4 System Description

For our system, we fine-tune the pretrained models discussed in Section 4.1, 4.2, and 4.3. We combine the three datasets as the number of samples for Spanish and Portuguese are quite low. After combining the models, we split the validation set accordingly, maintaining the split's ratio and tabulating the results on the concatenated dataset in Table3. The embeddings are extracted from these models to be fed as input to the LSTM layer, (Hochreiter and Schmidhuber, 1997) as shown in Figure1. The resulting output is fed into a global average pooling layer (Lin et al., 2014) and then passed into fully connected layers, followed by a sigmoid activation function to obtain the resulting probability score for the input sentences. The same parameters are used for all three models. A dropout layer (Srivastava et al., 2014) is also added in between the fully connected layers for regularization. Refer Table 4 for the parameters used in the model.

Parameters	**Values**
Number of LSTM units	128
Dropout Rate	0.2
Batch Size	16
Max Length	128
Optimizer	Adam
Learning Rate	3e-5
Activation Function	Sigmoid
Loss Function	cross-entropy

Table 4: Parameters used for training the Models

5 Results and Analysis

All pretrained language models are fine-tuned in Google Colab[2] for ten epochs. We use the Tensorflow implementation of the models[3] on the Huggingface transformers library[4]. We compare the macro F1-Scores of our fine-tuned models on the validation set, which were created by splitting the given dataset. The remaining split is the training data. The validation set contains samples from all three languages. It has 4,387 *Not-event* sequences and 963 *Event* sequences making a combined total of 5,350. The results are shown in Table3.

We fine-tuned BERT, DistilBERT, and RoBERTa models on the training set. We have combined the

[2]https://colab.research.google.com/

[3]https://huggingface.co/transformers/pretrained_models.html

[4]https://huggingface.co/

Language	Macro F1-Score
English	0.8291
Spanish	0.7578
Portuguese	0.7951

Table 5: Macro F1-Scores on the Test Set

three language corpora into a single corpus comprising of all the three languages together. The main intention towards using a multilingual model is that the representations learnt during one language's pretraining would help the other. We can observe that DistilBERT achieved a better F1-Score among the models mentioned in the previous sections. RoBERTa gave the lowest score among these. The reason could be that the RoBERTa model was not multilingual, unlike the other two; however, it still managed to get a score very close to the BERT model. It is imperative that performing soft voting on all three models has managed to increase the score. One of the reasons for the poor performance of the models is the imbalance in the distribution of the classes. In the dataset, there are 21,794 *Not-event* sentences and only 4,954 *Event* ones. The models performed very well in the majority class and poorly in the minority class. Having more *Event* samples could have certainly helped the model in distinguishing better among the classes. Based on the performance of soft voting on the validation set, we have used the same for the test set. The results for the test set are shown in Table5. The reason for relatively low scores of Spanish and Portuguese could be due to the inadequate support of the training set (2,741 and 1,182) instead of English (22,825). We also believe that our approach of combining datasets could have influenced the performance of the low support datasets.

6 Conclusion

The need to develop automated systems to detect any event is an active protest has constantly been increasing because of the escalation of social media users and several platforms to support them. In this paper, we have explored several multilingual language models to classify if a given sentence talks about an event that has happened (*Event*) or not (*Not-event*) in three languages. Our work primarily focuses on fine-tuning language models and feeding them to an architecture we created. We also observe that the problem of class imbalance has had a significant impact on the performance of the models. The soft voting approach has achieved macro F1-Scores of 0.8291, 0.7578, and 0.7951 for English, Spanish, and Portuguese, respectively. For future work, we intend to explore class weighting techniques and semi-supervised approaches to improve our performance.

References

Ghada Abaido. 2020. Cyberbullying on social media platforms among university students in the united arab emirates. *International journal of adolescence and youth*, 25:407–420.

Angelo Basile and Tommaso Caselli. 2020. Protest event detection: When task-specific models outperform an event-driven method. In *Experimental IR Meets Multilinguality, Multimodality, and Interaction*, pages 97–111, Cham. Springer International Publishing.

Michael Beyeler. 2017. *Machine Learning for OpenCV*. Packt Publishing Ltd.

Berfu Büyüköz, Ali Hürriyetoğlu, and Arzucan Özgür. 2020. Analyzing ELMo and DistilBERT on sociopolitical news classification. In *Proceedings of the Workshop on Automated Extraction of Sociopolitical Events from News 2020*, pages 9–18, Marseille, France. European Language Resources Association (ELRA).

Andreu Casero-Ripollés and Ramón Feenstra. 2012. The 15-m movement and the new media: A case study of how new themes were introduced into spanish political discourse. *Media International Australia incorporating Culture and Policy*, 144:68.

David Crystal. 2008. Two thousand million? *English Today*, 24(1):3–6.

Vera Danilova. 2015. A pipeline for multilingual protest event selection and annotation. In *2015 26th International Workshop on Database and Expert Systems Applications (DEXA)*, pages 309–313.

Vera Danilova, Svetlana Popova, and Mikhail Alexandrov. 2016. Multilingual protest event data collection with gate. In *Natural Language Processing and Information Systems*, pages 115–126, Cham. Springer International Publishing.

Dhaval M Dave, Andrew I Friedson, Kyutaro Matsuzawa, Joseph J Sabia, and Samuel Safford. 2020. Black lives matter protests and risk avoidance: The case of civil unrest during a pandemic. Working Paper 27408, National Bureau of Economic Research.

Jacob Devlin, Ming-Wei Chang, Kenton Lee, and Kristina Toutanova. 2019. BERT: Pre-training of deep bidirectional transformers for language understanding. In *Proceedings of the 2019 Conference of the North American Chapter of the Association for Computational Linguistics: Human Language Technologies, Volume 1 (Long and Short Papers)*, pages 4171–4186, Minneapolis, Minnesota. Association for Computational Linguistics.

Allyson Ettinger, Sudha Rao, Hal Daumé III, and Emily M. Bender. 2017. Towards linguistically generalizable NLP systems: A workshop and shared task. In *Proceedings of the First Workshop on Building Linguistically Generalizable NLP Systems*, pages 1–10, Copenhagen, Denmark. Association for Computational Linguistics.

Matthias Gallé. 2019. Investigating the effectiveness of BPE: The power of shorter sequences. In *Proceedings of the 2019 Conference on Empirical Methods in Natural Language Processing and the 9th International Joint Conference on Natural Language Processing (EMNLP-IJCNLP)*, pages 1375–1381, Hong Kong, China. Association for Computational Linguistics.

Rodrigo Gómez García and Emiliano Treré. 2014. The# yosoy132 movement and the struggle for media democratization in mexico. *Convergence*, 20(4):496–510.

Deborah J Gerner, Philip A Schrodt, Omur Yilmaz, and Rajaa Abu-Jabr. 2002. The creation of cameo (conflict and mediation event observations): An event data framework for a post cold war world. In *annual meeting of the American Political Science Association*, volume 29.

Adeep Hande, Karthik Puranik, Ruba Priyadharshini, and Bharathi Raja Chakravarthi. 2021. Domain identification of scientific articles using transfer learning and ensembles. In *Trends and Applications in Knowledge Discovery and Data Mining*, pages 88–97, Cham. Springer International Publishing.

Sepp Hochreiter and Jürgen Schmidhuber. 1997. Long short-term memory. *Neural Computation*, 9(8):1735–1780.

Kristoffer Holt, Adam Shehata, Jesper Strömbäck, and Elisabet Ljungberg. 2013. Age and the effects of news media attention and social media use on political interest and participation: Do social media function as leveller? *European Journal of Communication*, 28(1):19–34.

Ahmad Hany Hossny, Terry Moschuo, Grant Osborne, Lewis Mitchell, and Nick Lothian. 2018. Enhancing keyword correlation for event detection in social networks using svd and k-means: Twitter case study. *Social Network Analysis and Mining*, 8(1):1–10.

Ali Hürriyetoğlu, Osman Mutlu, Farhana Ferdousi Liza, Erdem Yörük, Ritesh Kumar, and Shyam Ratan. 2021. Multilingual protest news detection - shared task 1, case 2021. In *Proceedings of the 4th Workshop on Challenges and Applications of Automated Extraction of Socio-political Events from Text (CASE 2021)*, online. Association for Computational Linguistics (ACL).

Ali Hürriyetoğlu, Erdem Yörük, Deniz Yüret, Çağrı Yoltar, Burak Gürel, Fırat Duruşan, and Osman Mutlu. 2019a. A task set proposal for automatic protest information collection across multiple countries. In *Advances in Information Retrieval*, pages 316–323, Cham. Springer International Publishing.

Ali Hürriyetoğlu, Erdem Yörük, Deniz Yüret, Çağrı Yoltar, Burak Gürel, Fırat Duruşan, Osman Mutlu, and Arda Akdemir. 2019b. Overview of clef 2019 lab protestnews: Extracting protests from news in a cross-context setting. In *Experimental IR Meets Multilinguality, Multimodality, and Interaction*, pages 425–432, Cham. Springer International Publishing.

Ali Hürriyetoğlu, Vanni Zavarella, Hristo Tanev, Erdem Yörük, Ali Safaya, and Osman Mutlu. 2020. Automated extraction of socio-political events from news (AESPEN): Workshop and shared task report. In *Proceedings of the Workshop on Automated Extraction of Socio-political Events from News 2020*, pages 1–6, Marseille, France. European Language Resources Association (ELRA).

Ali Hürriyetoğlu, Erdem Yörük, Osman Mutlu, Fırat Duruşan, Çağrı Yoltar, Deniz Yüret, and Burak Gürel. 2021. Cross-Context News Corpus for Protest Event-Related Knowledge Base Construction. *Data Intelligence*, pages 1–28.

Kawal Kapoor, Kuttimani Tamilmani, Nripendra Rana, Pushp Patil, Yogesh Dwivedi, and Sridhar Nerur. 2018. Advances in social media research: Past, present and future. *Information Systems Frontiers*, 20.

Min Lin, Qiang Chen, and Shuicheng Yan. 2014. Network in network.

Yinhan Liu, Myle Ott, Naman Goyal, Jingfei Du, Mandar Joshi, Danqi Chen, Omer Levy, Mike Lewis, Luke Zettlemoyer, and Veselin Stoyanov. 2019. Roberta: A robustly optimized bert pretraining approach.

Konstantina Papanikolaou and Haris Papageorgiou. 2020. Protest event analysis: A longitudinal analysis for Greece. In *Proceedings of the Workshop on Automated Extraction of Socio-political Events from News 2020*, pages 57–62, Marseille, France. European Language Resources Association (ELRA).

Yifan Peng, Manabu Torii, Cathy H. Wu, and K. Vijay-Shanker. 2013. A generalizable nlp framework for fast development of pattern-based biomedical relation extraction systems. *BMC Bioinformatics*, 15.

Telmo Pires, Eva Schlinger, and Dan Garrette. 2019. How multilingual is multilingual BERT? In *Proceedings of the 57th Annual Meeting of the Association for Computational Linguistics*, pages 4996–5001, Florence, Italy. Association for Computational Linguistics.

Cristina M. Pulido, Gisela Redondo-Sama, Teresa Sordé-Martí, and Ramon Flecha. 2018. Social impact in social media: A new method to evaluate the social impact of research. *PLOS ONE*, 13(8):1–20.

Adam Rome. 2010. The genius of earth day. *Environmental History*, 15(2):194–205.

Kristin Ross. 2008. *May'68 and its Afterlives*. University of Chicago Press.

Victor Sanh, Lysandre Debut, Julien Chaumond, and Thomas Wolf. 2019. Distilbert, a distilled version of bert: smaller, faster, cheaper and lighter. *ArXiv*, abs/1910.01108.

Philip A Schrodt and Blake Hall. 2006. Twenty years of the kansas event data system project. *The political methodologist*, 14(1):2–8.

Nitish Srivastava, Geoffrey E. Hinton, Alex Krizhevsky, Ilya Sutskever, and Ruslan Salakhutdinov. 2014. Dropout: a simple way to prevent neural networks from overfitting. *Journal of Machine Learning Research*, 15(1):1929–1958.

S. Wilson. 2017. Detecting mass protest through social media. *Social media and society*, 6:5–25.

Donghyeon Won, Zachary C Steinert-Threlkeld, and Jungseock Joo. 2017a. Protest activity detection and perceived violence estimation from social media images. In *Proceedings of the 25th ACM international conference on Multimedia*, pages 786–794.

Donghyeon Won, Zachary C. Steinert-Threlkeld, and Jungseock Joo. 2017b. Protest activity detection and perceived violence estimation from social media images. *CoRR*, abs/1709.06204.

NUS-IDS at CASE 2021 Task 1: Improving Multilingual Event Sentence Coreference Identification With Linguistic Information

Fiona Anting Tan, Sujatha Das Gollapalli, See-Kiong Ng
Institute of Data Science
National University of Singapore, Singapore
tan.f@u.nus.edu, idssdg@nus.edu.sg, seekiong@nus.edu.sg

Abstract

Event Sentence Coreference Identification (ESCI) aims to cluster event sentences that refer to the same event together for information extraction. We describe our ESCI solution developed for the ACL-CASE 2021 shared tasks on the detection and classification of socio-political and crisis event information in a multilingual setting. For a given article, our proposed pipeline comprises of an accurate sentence pair classifier that identifies coreferent sentence pairs and subsequently uses these predicted probabilities to cluster sentences into groups. Sentence pair representations are constructed from fine-tuned BERT embeddings plus POS embeddings fed through a BiLSTM model, and combined with linguistic-based lexical and semantic similarities between sentences. Our best models ranked 2nd, 1st and 2nd and obtained CoNLL F_1 scores of 81.20%, 93.03%, 83.15% for the English, Portuguese and Spanish test sets respectively in the ACL-CASE 2021 competition.

1 Introduction

The ability to automatically extract sentences that refer to the same event from any given document is useful for downstream information extraction tasks like event extraction and summarization, timeline extraction or cause and effect extraction (Örs et al., 2020). Event Sentence Coreference Identification (ESCI) aims to cluster sentences with event mentions such that each cluster comprises of sentences that refer to the same specific event.

We address ESCI for news articles referring to socio-political and crisis event information in a multilingual setting, introduced as one of the ACL-CASE 2021's shared tasks (Hürriyetoğlu et al., 2021). Given that news articles comprise of multiple events spread across a few sentences, and the syntax referring to the same event differs in different contexts, ESCI for news articles is a challenging NLP problem (Hürriyetoğlu et al., 2020). Furthermore, considering the availability of news in various languages, ESCI techniques that are applicable beyond English and robust across different languages are desirable.

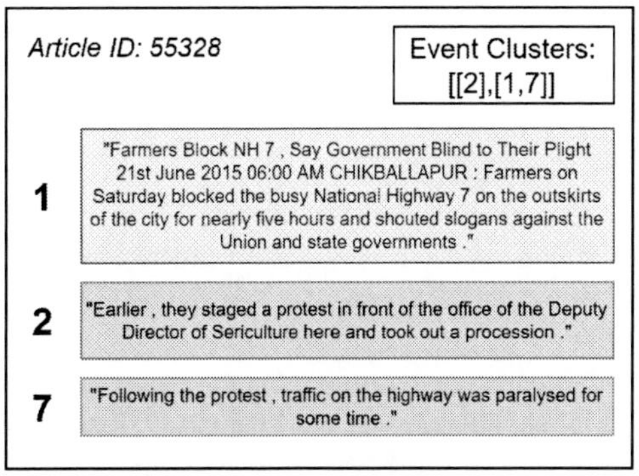

Figure 1: Example English article from training dataset from ACL-CASE 2021. The sentences $1, 2, 7$ with event mentions as well as the target clustering $\{$[2], [1,7]$\}$ are highlighted.

The ESCI task is illustrated using an example article shown in Figure 1. As shown in this figure, ESCI involves the identification of the event clusters (e.g. $\{$[2], [1,7]$\}$ in the figure) based on the content of the individual sentences.

Contributions: We propose a two-step solution for the ESCI task. In Step-1, we obtain sentence pair embeddings by fine-tuning Bidirectional Encoder Representations from Transformers (BERT) (Devlin et al., 2019) embeddings combined with parts-of-speech (POS) embeddings that are fed through a bi-directional long short-term memory (BiLSTM) model. Next, these sentence pair embeddings are combined with novel features based on lexical and semantic similarities to train a classifier that predicts if the sentence pair is coreferent.

Proceedings of the 4th Workshop on Challenges and Applications of Automated Extraction of Socio-political Events from Text (CASE), pages 105–112
August 5–6, 2021, ©2021 Association for Computational Linguistics

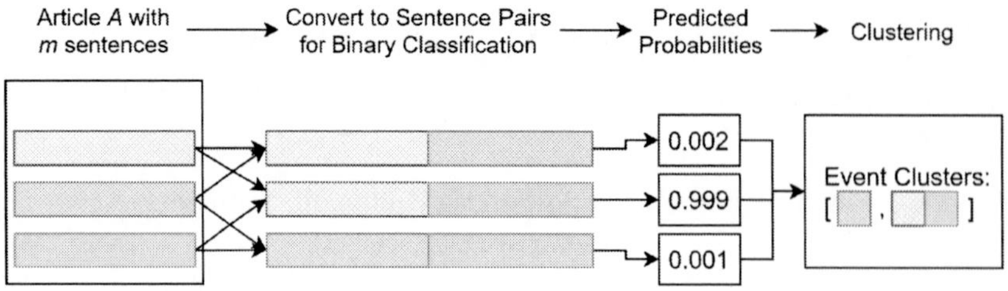

Figure 2: Overall model pipeline. *Notes.* (1) Convert article into sentence pairs for binary classification, and (2) Taking predicted probabilities to perform article level clustering of sentences.

Step-2 involves the clustering of sentences using sentence pair probabilities predicted from Step-1. We apply the clustering algorithm from Örs et al. (2020) to obtain a variable number of clusters for each article.

We illustrate the effectiveness of our proposed solution via detailed validation experiments on the training datasets from ACL-CASE 2021. We show that our features are effective on documents from all three languages studied in the competition, viz, English, Portuguese, and Spanish. Indeed, on the ACL-CASE 2021 Shared Task 1 Subtask 3, our best-performing models ranked 2nd, 1st and 2nd and obtained CoNLL F_1 scores of 81.20%, 93.03%, 83.15% for the English, Portuguese and Spanish test sets respectively.

Organization: In the next section, we present closely related work on ESCI. Subsequently, Section 3 introduces our features and classification model while Section 4 discusses our dataset, experimental setup, results, and findings. In Section 5, we conclude the paper with some future directions.

2 Related Work

Most end-to-end event coreference systems approach the task in a two-stage manner: (1) To detect the mention or event of interest, and (2) To resolve the given mentions or events and cluster if coreferent (Zhang et al., 2018). In our work, we focus only on latter task of coreference resolution and have direct access to identified event sentences.

Early works of ESCI adopted linguistic (Bejan and Harabagiu, 2010) or template-based features (Choubey and Huang, 2017). Subsequently, neural network methods to encode textual events and contexts became increasingly popular (Krause et al., 2016). The combination of the two methods have also proved to be effective in recent works (Zeng et al., 2020; Barhom et al., 2019).

In the previous run of ESCI by the same organisers (Hürriyetoğlu et al., 2019, 2020), the best-performing team (Örs et al., 2020) deconstructed the task into two steps: (1) To predict if a sentence pair is coreferent or not, and (2) Use the predictions as scores for clustering. This approach is common amongst other event coreference resolution methods too (Barhom et al., 2019). We employ this general approach and focus on enriching the feature space using linguistic-based similarity measures along with richer text embeddings based on BERT with POS embeddings.

3 Our Approach

Figure 2 summarizes our proposed pipeline. In this section, we describe our approach in detail.[1]

Let A be an article containing m sentences with event mentions $\{s_1, s_2, ..., s_m\}$. To produce a list of c clusters that group these m sentences, we adopt the approach of Örs et al. (2020) and first extract sentence pairs from A. Next, binary classification is performed to identify if a given pair is coreferent. Let (h, t) represent a sentence pair, with h and t referring to the lower and higher sentence numbers in A, respectively. The features employed for training a binary classifier that identifies coreferent sentences are described next.

3.1 Features for Sentence Pair Classification

BERT Embeddings: We utilize BERT, the bidirectional encoder transformer architecture (Devlin et al., 2019), to obtain sentence pair representations for our task. The models were pretrained with masked language modeling (MLM) and next sentence prediction (NSP) objectives. Our sentence pair input is encoded in this order: the special starting token "[CLS]", the head sentence, the separator "[SEP]" token, the tail sentence, another separator

[1]Our code and supplementary materials can be found on Github at `https://github.com/NUS-IDS/EventSentenceCoref`

token, and padding up to a fixed maximum length.

The encoded inputs, alongside attention mask and token type indexes, are fed into the BERT model. BERT acts as an encoder by producing sentence pair representations, which is later passed on to the BiLSTM model along with other features to train our classifier. As BERT is exposed to label information in the downstream layers, we are able to obtain fined-tuned representations for our task.

POS Embeddings: For each sentence, we obtain parts-of-speech (POS) tags for each word token to represent grammatical structure. To align with tokens of BERT embeddings, we similarly concatenate a starting token, POS tags of the head sentence plus a separator token, POS tags of the tail sentence plus a separator token, followed by padding. These POS tags are subsequently encoded as one-hot vectors and combined with the BERT embeddings per word before feeding them through a BiLSTM.

Lexical and Semantic Similarities: Event mentions in a sentence often correspond to specific POS and Named-Entity (NE) tags. Thus, similarity values capturing the overlap of these token types between the two sentences are indicative of whether they are coreferent. We incorporated lexical similarity based on surface-form overlap of POS and NE tags of sentences and semantic similarity based on sentence embeddings and overlap of the dependence trees of the two sentences. We represent the counts of verb, nouns, and entities occurring in both head and tail sentences using two similarity functions: raw counts and Jaccard overlap. These six features are referred to as "Basic Similarities" in our experiments.

For an "extended" set of similarities, we also computed the cosine similarity based on words of the sentences after stopword removal, and normalized dot product of vectors corresponding to words with POS tags pertaining to nouns, adjectives, verbs, and adverbs, and NER tags corresponding to tangible types such as person, organizations, products, geopolitical location. That is, named-entity tags corresponding to concepts such as money, quantities, and dates as well as POS tags corresponding to punctuation, and pronouns were ignored since they are unlikely to refer to event mentions.

For *semantic similarity* we use cosine similarity between the average word vectors from GloVE[2] for the two sentences. Ozates, et al.(2016) proposed incorporating the type information of the dependency relations for sentence similarity calculation in context of sentence summarization for better capturing the syntactic and semantic similarity between two sentences. We use similarity between two sentences computed using their proposed "Simple Bigram Approximate Kernel" as an additional feature.

Overall, the set of "Extended Similarities", correspond to a total of 27 features.

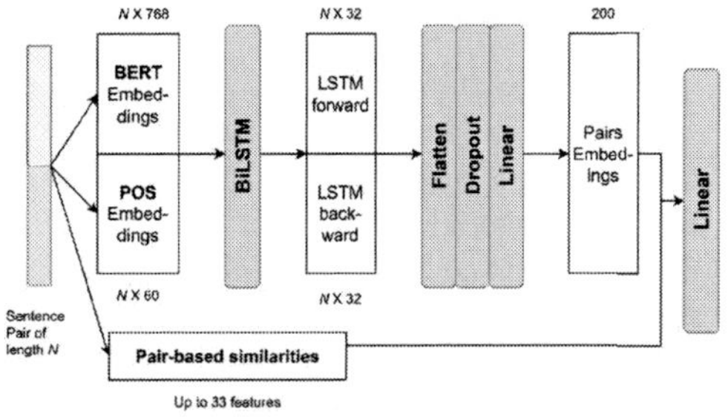

Figure 3: Overview of the sentence pair classification model. BERT embeddings, POS embeddings and similarity features are used to train a BiLSTM-based deep learning model.

3.2 Sentence Pair Classifier

Our deep learning setup for learning sentence pair classification is shown in Figure 3. We use the features described in the previous section for training our classifier. The BERT with POS embeddings are first fed into a BiLSTM layer with an output dimension of 64. Next, we flatten the $n \times 64$ matrix into a $n * 64$ vector and run it through a dropout layer with 0.3 dropout rate. Another linear layer is applied to convert the representation into a vector with length 200. From here, we concatenate our similarity features and send them through a linear layer to obtain class probabilities representing the coreferent (label = 1) and non-coreferent (label = 0) classes.

3.3 Article-level Clustering

Given labels corresponding to each pair of sentences obtained from our classification module, we employ the clustering algorithm from Örs et al. (2020) for grouping the sentences in the document. This algorithm, similar to hierarchical clustering, creates clusters in a bottom-up fashion using maximum scores instead of the minimum distance to

[2] `http://nlp.stanford.edu/data/glove.6B.zip`

Obs Unit	English	Portuguese	Spanish
	Train		
Articles	596	21	11
Sentences	2581	88	45
Pairs	6241	235	86
	Test		
Articles	100	40	40
Sentences	486	144	188
Pairs	1554	257	549

Table 1: Number of observations at different unit levels for train and test set

group two points into the same cluster. For us, score of a pair refers to the probability of the sentences being coreferent with. We refer the interested reader to Algorithm 2 in Örs et al. (2020) for the pseudo-code. In contrast, with algorithms such as k-medoids, the algorithm employed in our solution has the advantage of determining a different number of clusters for each article in a flexible manner.

4 Experiments and Results

4.1 Dataset and Evaluation

We used the data from ACL-CASE 2021 (Hürriyetoğlu et al., 2021) (Task 1 Subtask 3) for training and testing our models. The dataset comprises of news articles referring to socio-political and crisis event in three languages: English, Portuguese, and Spanish. We refer the interested reader to the overview paper (Hürriyetoğlu et al., 2021) and the task websites[3] for details of this dataset. We summarize the train and test sizes of the dataset in Table 1. For the train set, we were provided with 596 English news articles, 21 Portuguese articles, and 11 Spanish articles. For each article, only sentences with event mentions are included in the dataset instead of all sentences.

The test performance was evaluated using the CoNLL-2012 average F_1 scores obtained by averaging across MUC, B^3 and $CEAF_e$ F_1 scores (Pradhan et al., 2012) and was computed on the setup provided by the organizers on Codalab.

4.2 Experimental Setup

Training Datasets: To handle the low number of examples available with Portuguese and Spanish, we create two datasets for training our models: (1) The "Multilingual train set" is obtained by simply putting the examples from all languages together whereas (2) the "English train set" is obtained by first employing the Google Translate API[4] and translating all available non-English training examples to English and combining with the English training data. The multilingual dataset can be used directly for training language-agnostic models, for example using cross-lingual embeddings (Conneau et al., 2017) and Multilingual BERT.

Feature Extraction: We experimented with two BERT implementations from Huggingface (Wolf et al., 2020). The first model, `bert-base-cased`, was pretrained on English text and has 12 layers, 768 hidden, 12 heads and 109M parameters. We fine-tuned this model using our "English train set". Our second model, `bert-base-multilingual-cased`, was pretrained on the top 104 languages in Wikipedia and has 12 layers, 768 hidden, 12 heads and 179M parameters. We fine-tuned this model using our "Multilingual train set".

We used Stanford's `Stanza` package (Qi et al., 2020) for obtaining POS, NER, and dependency tree tags. The "Universal POS tags" (`upos` scheme) with 17 POS tags and the NER tags referring to PERSON, NORP (Nationalities/religious/political group), FAC (Facility), ORG (Organization), GPE (Countries/cities/states), LOC (Location), PRODUCT, EVENT, WORK_OF_ART, and LANGUAGE were used in experiments.[5]

When constructing the "Basic Similarities", all words are lemmatised before we compare their surface-form overlap. For entities, we use `token_sort_ratio`[6] score of more than 90% to define a positive overap occurence instead of an exact match to allow for some small discrepancy in NEs (e.g. "Sohrabuddin Sheikh" and "Sohrabuddin Sheikh 's" refer to the same entity).

Classifier Settings: To train our classifier, we used the Adam optimizer with $\beta_1 = 0.9$, $\beta_2 = 0.999$ and a learning rate of $2e-5$ with linear decay. Cross Entropy Loss was used with class weights computed from the training sample. Each

[3] https://emw.ku.edu.tr/case-2021/, https://github.com/emerging-welfare/case-2021-shared-task

[4] https://pypi.org/project/google-trans-new

[5] At present, NER models are only available for Spanish and English in Stanza.

[6] https://github.com/seatgeek/fuzzywuzzy

	CoNLL F_1	ARI		F_1	
		Macro	Micro	Macro	Micro
BERT	84.46	64.73	54.76	68.76	60.82
+ POS embeddings	83.15	56.81	48.94	60.58	54.44
+ Basic similarities	84.31	64.63	55.98	67.54	60.35
+ Extended similarities	**84.92**	**66.78**	**57.66**	**70.68**	**62.94**
Multilingual BERT	82.56	59.97	52.64	62.00	55.41
+ POS embeddings	83.98	61.79	52.89	65.59	58.33
+ Basic similarities	82.83	60.62	50.09	64.47	56.20
+ Extended similarities	81.80	57.53	48.74	61.71	54.70

Table 2: Evaluation results over validation sets from 5 folds. *Notes.* Scores are reported in percentages (%) and averaged across the folds. Best score per column is bolded.

iteration was of batch size 16 and all experiments were ran on Tesla V100 SXM2 32GB GPU device.

Five-fold cross-validation (5-CV) experiments were used for parameter tuning. We also report macro and micro Adjusted Rand Index (ARI) and F_1 scores in addition to ConLL F_1 since they were used for selecting the top-3 runs for the test set in line with the measures employed in the previous rounds of the competition (Hürriyetoğlu et al., 2019, 2020). Since the test labels were not released and evaluation is performed on the competition setup, only CoNLL F_1 scores are reported for the test data. Other details, such as hyperparameter settings and run times, are included in Appendix A.1.

4.3 Results and Analysis

Table 2 reports the average scores for our 5-CV setup across the five scoring metrics (CoNLL F_1, Macro ARI, Micro ARI, Macro F_1 and Micro F_1). Table 3 reports the CoNLL F_1 score on the test data for the winning system and our models at the ACL-CASE 2021 Shared Task 1 Subtask 3 across the three languages – English, Portuguese, and Spanish.

Based on CV experiments, our best model for all scoring measures is the English BERT model with all features included, achieving 84.92% CoNLL F_1 score. The same model also performed the best on the English test set with 81.20% CoNLL F_1 score and was ranked 2nd among fellow competitors on this shared task.

For non-English test sets, our best performing model is the Multilingual BERT model with all features excluding "Extended similarities". This model achieved 93.03% CoNLL F_1 score and ranked 1st for Portuguese. For Spanish, we obtained a CoNLL F_1 score of 83.15% and ranked 2nd among competitors.

4.3.1 BERT versus Multilingual BERT

For the English test set, the BERT model performs better than the Multilingual BERT model on average (79.19% versus 78.01%). Additionally, because the train/validation splits are predominantly comprised of English articles (596/628 = 94.90%), the fluctuations in performance on validation splits largely tally with the fluctuations in performance on the English portion of the data. Therefore, unsurprisingly, BERT (English) performs better than Multilingual BERT for English data.

For non-English test sets, we obtained best performance using the Multilingual BERT model. We hypothesize that the translation of non-English examples to English might have caused some loss of inherent signals present in other languages that are useful for the ESCI task. These signals are possibly better harnessed by retaining the language and using language-specific Stanza taggers along with Multilingual BERT.

Overall, we find that combining BERT embeddings, POS embeddings and basic similarity features achieve the best validation performance across all measures. We observe that "Extended similarities" do not show uniform improvement in performance in multilingual settings. Arguably, there is redundancy among our lexical similarity features and semantic similarities were not found to improve performance on the ESCI task. However, considering the small-scale of our working datasets, these features need further study.

5 Conclusions and Future Work

We presented a two-step solution for the ESCI task of ACL-CASE 2021. Our solution based on

	CoNLL F_1		
	English	Portuguese	Spanish
Best Score in Competition	84.44	93.03	84.23
BERT	80.54	88.85	80.18
+ POS embeddings	77.79	90.58	82.17
+ Basic similarities	77.23	90.21	80.11
+ Extended similarities	**81.20**	92.18	80.91
Multilingual BERT	77.89	87.22	76.55
+ POS embeddings	79.33	90.92	81.43
+ Basic similarities	78.13	**93.03**	**83.15**
+ Extended similarities	76.68	90.36	81.52

Table 3: Evaluation results over test sets submitted to Codalab. *Notes.* Scores are reported in percentages (%). Our best score per column is bolded.

sentence pair classification effectively harnesses BERT and POS embeddings and combines them with linguistic similarity features for accurate sentence coreference resolution across languages. Indeed, our models ranked 2nd, 1st and 2nd obtaining CoNLL F_1 scores of 81.20%, 93.03%, 83.15% for the English, Portuguese and Spanish test sets, respectively, in the competition.

In this paper, we focused on within-document coreference sentences. It is common for coreference resolution tasks to also focus on cross-document settings (i.e. identify coreferent event mentions across multiple documents) (Zeng et al., 2020) as such models can better aid downstream tasks like contradiction detection or identification of "fake news". In future, we hope to extend our models to work across documents. Additionally, multiple events might be presented in a sentence. The shared task focuses on hard clustering (i.e. each sentence can only belong to one cluster). However, we believe it is valuable to also investigate cases where the event clusters overlap.

Acknowledgments

This research is supported by the National Research Foundation, Singapore under its Industry Alignment Fund - Pre-positioning (IAF-PP) Funding Initiative. Any opinions, findings and conclusions or recommendations expressed in this material are those of the author(s) and do not reflect the views of National Research Foundation, Singapore.

References

Shany Barhom, Vered Shwartz, Alon Eirew, Michael Bugert, Nils Reimers, and Ido Dagan. 2019. Revisiting joint modeling of cross-document entity and event coreference resolution. In *Proceedings of the 57th Annual Meeting of the Association for Computational Linguistics*, pages 4179–4189, Florence, Italy. Association for Computational Linguistics.

Cosmin Bejan and Sanda Harabagiu. 2010. Unsupervised event coreference resolution with rich linguistic features. In *Proceedings of the 48th Annual Meeting of the Association for Computational Linguistics*, pages 1412–1422, Uppsala, Sweden. Association for Computational Linguistics.

Prafulla Kumar Choubey and Ruihong Huang. 2017. Event coreference resolution by iteratively unfolding inter-dependencies among events. In *Proceedings of the 2017 Conference on Empirical Methods in Natural Language Processing*, pages 2124–2133, Copenhagen, Denmark. Association for Computational Linguistics.

Alexis Conneau, Guillaume Lample, Marc'Aurelio Ranzato, Ludovic Denoyer, and Hervé Jégou. 2017. Word translation without parallel data. *CoRR*.

Jacob Devlin, Ming-Wei Chang, Kenton Lee, and Kristina Toutanova. 2019. BERT: Pre-training of deep bidirectional transformers for language understanding. In *Proceedings of the 2019 Conference of the North American Chapter of the Association for Computational Linguistics: Human Language Technologies, Volume 1 (Long and Short Papers)*, pages 4171–4186, Minneapolis, Minnesota. Association for Computational Linguistics.

Ali Hürriyetoğlu, Osman Mutlu, Farhana Ferdousi Liza, Erdem Yörük, Ritesh Kumar, and Shyam Ratan. 2021. Multilingual protest news detection - shared task 1, case 2021. In *Proceedings of the 4th Workshop on Challenges and Applications of Automated Extraction of Socio-political Events from Text*

(*CASE 2021*), online. Association for Computational Linguistics (ACL).

Ali Hürriyetoğlu, Erdem Yörük, Deniz Yüret, Çağrı Yoltar, Burak Gürel, Fırat Duruşan, and Osman Mutlu. 2019. A task set proposal for automatic protest information collection across multiple countries. In *Advances in Information Retrieval*, pages 316–323, Cham. Springer International Publishing.

Ali Hürriyetoğlu, Vanni Zavarella, Hristo Tanev, Erdem Yörük, Ali Safaya, and Osman Mutlu. 2020. Automated extraction of socio-political events from news (AESPEN): Workshop and shared task report. In *Proceedings of the Workshop on Automated Extraction of Socio-political Events from News 2020*, pages 1–6, Marseille, France. European Language Resources Association (ELRA).

Sebastian Krause, Feiyu Xu, Hans Uszkoreit, and Dirk Weissenborn. 2016. Event linking with sentential features from convolutional neural networks. In *Proceedings of The 20th SIGNLL Conference on Computational Natural Language Learning*, pages 239–249, Berlin, Germany. Association for Computational Linguistics.

Faik Kerem Örs, Süveyda Yeniterzi, and Reyyan Yeniterzi. 2020. Event clustering within news articles. In *Proceedings of the Workshop on Automated Extraction of Socio-political Events from News 2020*, pages 63–68, Marseille, France. European Language Resources Association (ELRA).

Şaziye Betül Özateş, Arzucan Özgür, and Dragomir Radev. 2016. Sentence similarity based on dependency tree kernels for multi-document summarization. In *Proceedings of the Tenth International Conference on Language Resources and Evaluation (LREC'16)*, pages 2833–2838, Portorož, Slovenia. European Language Resources Association (ELRA).

Sameer Pradhan, Alessandro Moschitti, Nianwen Xue, Olga Uryupina, and Yuchen Zhang. 2012. CoNLL-2012 shared task: Modeling multilingual unrestricted coreference in OntoNotes. In *Joint Conference on EMNLP and CoNLL - Shared Task*, pages 1–40, Jeju Island, Korea. Association for Computational Linguistics.

Peng Qi, Yuhao Zhang, Yuhui Zhang, Jason Bolton, and Christopher D. Manning. 2020. Stanza: A Python natural language processing toolkit for many human languages. In *Proceedings of the 58th Annual Meeting of the Association for Computational Linguistics: System Demonstrations*.

Thomas Wolf, Lysandre Debut, Victor Sanh, Julien Chaumond, Clement Delangue, Anthony Moi, Pierric Cistac, Tim Rault, Remi Louf, Morgan Funtowicz, Joe Davison, Sam Shleifer, Patrick von Platen, Clara Ma, Yacine Jernite, Julien Plu, Canwen Xu, Teven Le Scao, Sylvain Gugger, Mariama Drame, Quentin Lhoest, and Alexander Rush. 2020. Transformers: State-of-the-art natural language processing. In *Proceedings of the 2020 Conference on Empirical Methods in Natural Language Processing: System Demonstrations*, pages 38–45, Online. Association for Computational Linguistics.

Yutao Zeng, Xiaolong Jin, Saiping Guan, Jiafeng Guo, and Xueqi Cheng. 2020. Event coreference resolution with their paraphrases and argument-aware embeddings. In *Proceedings of the 28th International Conference on Computational Linguistics*, pages 3084–3094, Barcelona, Spain (Online). International Committee on Computational Linguistics.

Rui Zhang, Cícero Nogueira dos Santos, Michihiro Yasunaga, Bing Xiang, and Dragomir Radev. 2018. Neural coreference resolution with deep biaffine attention by joint mention detection and mention clustering. In *Proceedings of the 56th Annual Meeting of the Association for Computational Linguistics (Volume 2: Short Papers)*, pages 102–107, Melbourne, Australia. Association for Computational Linguistics.

A Appendix

A.1 Replication Checklist

- Hyperparameters: Apart from hyperparameters mentioned in Section 4.2, our BERT models take the default configuration from Huggingface (Wolf et al., 2020).

- Time taken: For 5 folds over 10 epochs each, our code takes on average $5hours : 27minutes : 48seconds$ to train, validate and predict. For a single run over 10 epochs, our code takes on average $43minutes : 49seconds$ to train and predict.

FKIE_itf_2021 at CASE 2021 Task 1: Using Small Densely Fully Connected Neural Nets for Event Detection and Clustering

Nils Becker
Fraunhofer FKIE
Fraunhoferstraße 20
53343 Wachtberg
nils.becker@
fkie.fraunhofer.de

Theresa Krumbiegel
Fraunhofer FKIE
Fraunhoferstraße 20
53343 Wachtberg
theresa.krumbiegel@
fkie.fraunhofer.de

Abstract

In this paper we present multiple approaches for event detection on document and sentence level, as well as a technique for event sentence co-reference resolution. The advantage of our co-reference resolution approach, which handles the task as a clustering problem, is that we use a single neural net to solve the task, which stands in contrast to other clustering algorithms that often are build on more complex models. This means that we can set our focus on the optimization of a *single* neural network instead of having to optimize numerous different parameters. We use small densely connected neural networks and pre-trained multilingual transformer embeddings in all subtasks. We use either document or sentence embeddings, depending on the task, and refrain from using word embeddings, so that the implementation of complicated network structures and unfolding of RNNs, which can deal with input of different sizes, is not necessary. We achieved an average macro F1 of 0.65 in subtask 1 (i.e., document level classification), and a macro F1 of 0.70 in subtask 2 (i.e., sentence level classification). For the co-reference resolution subtask, we achieved an average CoNLL-2012 score across all languages of 0.83.

1 Introduction

Gathering information about current and past events is quite important since such information can help to detect, analyze, prevent and forecast dangerous social and political situations. An accumulation of protest events in a certain region may indicate massive discrepancies between two or more parties. Such situations can escalate and result in violence. Using modern systems and data including for example news articles, violent events can be forecast (Schrodt et al., 2013). Today, caused by a globally connected world, there exists an endless stream of news and information. To conquer this flood of data, much human effort is needed. Therefore, automation of information analysis can help to reduce the workload.

One task in this area is the detection of events in texts consisting of natural language, for example newspaper articles. It is an easy task for humans to read, understand and identify such events. For computers it is more difficult to process natural language and detect event mentions.

In this paper, we present our approaches for event detection in articles and sentences based on simple densely connected neural networks as part of task 1 (Hürriyetoğlu et al., 2021) of the Shared Task on Socio-Political and Crisis Events Detection at CASE @ ACL-IJCNLP 2021. The first task is split up into four different subtasks. We participated in the first three.

For the first subtask, we used an accumulation of trained neural nets with majority voting, where each net is a densely connected net consisting of only six layers including the in- and output layer. For the second subtask, we used a single net with the same specifications as in the first subtask. The third subtask aims at co-reference resolution of event sentences. We see this subtask as a typical clustering task. Therefore, we use a comparison based algorithm, which reduces the clustering problem mainly to the optimization of a single neural net. Co-reference resolution in our case, is based on the comparison of sentence pairs and will be described later in more detail.

All code used in this paper is publicly available [1].

The paper will proceed as follows: First, related work will be introduced. After that, the subtasks the we participated in will be described. The next chapter presents our methodology, including data

[1] https://github.com/s6nlbeck/FKIE_itf_Task1.git

Proceedings of the 4th Workshop on Challenges and Applications of Automated Extraction of Socio-political Events from Text (CASE), pages 113–119
August 5–6, 2021, ©2021 Association for Computational Linguistics

preparation and system descriptions for all subtasks. Then, the results are depicted. In the end, we come to a conclusion and give an outlook for future work.

2 Related Work

Since this workshop is a follow up event of the CLEF ProtestNews 2019 and AESPEN at LREC 2020 Shared Task, many approaches were already made as mentioned by Hürriyetoğlu et al. (2019) and Hürriyetoğlu et al. (2020). Aside from these approaches, a variety of other experiments trying to solve the task of event detection can be found in the literature. In earlier years, pattern matching approaches as described by Riloff et al. (1993) were common and successful for the detection of events, but often required much human effort and domain knowledge for pattern construction. This lead to the idea propagated by Riloff and Shoen (1995) of the automatic construction of such patterns. With the rise of available and affordable computing power, these techniques were replaced by modern machine learning techniques and especially artificial neural networks. State of the art systems for event detection, see for example Cui et al. (2020), use a combination of different kinds of neural nets, like bidirectional LSTMs and modified graph convolutional networks. Other models, as presented by Nguyen and Grishman (2015), use convolutional neural networks and reduce the task to a multi class labeling problem. Event detection can also be seen as a question answering task, where one could ask if an event exists in the given text or not, as done by Liu et al. (2020).

What all of the systems have in common is that they need a representation of text that is understandable for a computer. Piskorski et al. (2020) showed that modern transformer embeddings are the best choice by comparing them to classic word embeddings and achieving superior results with them. Based on these findings, we decided to make use of them in our work too.

For subtask 3, common clustering algorithms could be used for co-reference resolution, when using suitable metrics. Co-reference resolution using mention pair models, such as those proposed by Ng (2010), Örs et al. (2020) and Radford (2020), could also be implemented.

3 Task Description

The first task of the workshop consists of four different subtasks. The different subtasks build upon each other, starting at document level (subtask 1) and go on to gradually focus on smaller instances (sentence level, word level). We provide three different models for the first three subtasks. The data for all three subtasks is provided in a JSON format.

3.1 Subtask 1

In the first subtask, the challenge is to identify if a news article contains a past or ongoing event. For training, data in three different languages, namely English, Spanish and Portuguese, was provided. Each training sample consists of an unique identifier, a news article as the text basis and a binary label which marks if the article contains an event or not. Label 0 means that no event is included, label 1 means that an event is present. In total, the dataset comprises 11811 entries and is described in detail in table 1.

	en	es	pr	total
1	1912	131	197	2240
0	7412	869	1290	9571
total	9324	1000	1487	11811
prop. 1	20.5%	13.1%	13.2%	19%

Table 1: Details of training data for subtask 1

A training instance of subtask 1 looks as follows:


```
{"id":100023,"text":"2 policemen
   suspended for torturing man\
   nHYDERABAD:The Ranga Reddy
   superintendent of police on
   Monday suspended a head
   constable and a constable for
   adopting 'heinous' methods in
   interrogating Jangaiah, an
   accused in a missing person
   case.\nTNN | Sep 3, 2001, 02.0
   8 AM IST\nhyderabad:the ranga
   reddy superintendent ","label"
   :0}
```


3.2 Subtask 2

The second subtask is quite similar to the first one, the only difference being that the event detection has to be done at sentence level. Thus, the goal is to decide for each sentence if it contains an event or not. Each entry in the training corpus contains a single sentence instead of a whole news article. The dataset is much larger than the set for subtask 1, containing 26748 instances, as shown in table 2.

	en	es	pr	total
1	4223	450	281	4954
0	18602	2291	901	21794
total	22825	2741	1182	26748
prop. 1	18.5%	16.4%	23.8%	18.5 %

Table 2: Details of training for subtask 2

In the following an example of the training data of subtask 2 is given:

{"id":66133,"label":0,"sentence": "He had also made headlines for kidnapping his 13-year-old brother and taking him to Syria."}

3.3 Subtask 3

The third subtask differs from both of the other subtasks. It aims at event sentence co-reference resolution. This means that it has to be decided which sentences are about the same event. In this case, co-reference resolution can be seen as a clustering task. Each example in the training data consist of an unique identifier, multiple sentences and their respective event cluster. An overview of the data distribution for subtask three is given in table 3.

	en	es	pr	total
instances	596	11	21	628

Table 3: Details of training data for subtask 3

An example of a shortened training instance is given below. Each instance has four fields. One field contains an array including the event sentences. The depicted example has a total of four sentences. Each sentence is further represented as a number. For example, the sentence beginning with "Around 30,000..." is represented by the number 4. The event clusters are given as arrays. Each array contains the numbers of the sentences of the respective cluster. We can see that in the given example, sentence 15 is a cluster by itself and the other three sentences, sentences 4, 5 and 11, build another cluster. The last field is the id field, which contains an unique identifier for the entry.

{"event_clusters":[[15],[4,5,11]] , "sentence_no":[4,5,11,15], " sentences":["Around 30,000..." ,"Several...", "RFEA chief ...","On Tuesday..."], "id":55 666}

4 Methodology

4.1 Subtask 1 and 2 - Data Preparation

For our experiments for subtasks 1 and 2, we use the Flair framework (Akbik et al., 2019). The utilised document embeddings are generated using the pre-trained multilingual cased Bert model. The Bert model uses bidirectional LSTMs to create context sensitive embeddings (Devlin et al., 2019). Each embedding is represented by a 768-dimensional vector. We use the Bert model to generate the embeddings without any text preprocessing. For the first subtask, each news article is transformed into one vector, whereas in the second subtask every sentence is transformed into a same sized sentence embedding.

4.2 Subtask 1 and 2 - System Description

For the first subtask we use an accumulation of one hundred separately trained densely connected neural nets with one input layer of size 768, four hidden layers with 64 neurons and one output layer with one single unit. Each net is trained for 20 epochs with the adam optimizer and a learning rate of 0.001. As an activation function, we use the sigmoid function for each neuron. Since we are dealing with a binary classification task, we use binary crossentropy as a loss function. After each epoch the training data is shuffled. For the first subtask, a majority vote is used to decide if the article contains an event or not.

During the development phase, we also tested different structures of CNNs using the data from the shared tasks of 2019. The best result was gained with a small densely residual network like structure, as proposed by Huang et al. (2017), with a macro F1 score of 0.77. On the same data, our final approach reached a score of 0.81.

For the second subtask we use a single net with the same specifications as described for subtask 1.

4.3 Subtask 3 - Data preparation

The main part of our approach for subtask 3 is based on a neural network which is able to compare two sentences and determine if they belong to the same event cluster.

For each entry in the dataset a number of training instances are generated. A training instance is a triple which includes the sentence embeddings of two different sentences and a binary label which shows if the two sentences belong to the same event cluster or not.

This means that for every instance of the dataset, first the needed embeddings are calculated in the same way as in the subtasks before. After that, the positive and negative sentence pairs are generated and the matching labels are added. The sentences in the negative sentence pairs do not belong to the same event cluster, the ones in the positive pairs do. This results in a set of triples containing all possible combinations of sentences with corresponding labels. The generated entries for each instance are merged into one big dataset.

4.4 Subtask 3 - System Description

Since the third subtask differs substantially from the other subtasks, we developed and used another model compared to subtasks 1 and 2. As modern sentence embeddings based on neural nets are quite powerful, we also considered to use neural nets for clustering. As mentioned in section 2, many different clustering algorithms are available. In the area of using neural networks for clustering, self organizing maps (Kohonen, 1990) and neural gases (Martinetz et al., 1993) can be considered. Neural techniques like these are mainly used for representing topological structures in the given data. To use them for clustering, time-consuming additional steps would be needed beforehand.

Popular clustering algorithms like DBSCAN (Ester et al., 1996) include numerous hyperparameters which have to be optimized before the models can be used sensibly. Additionally, for some models the amount of clusters must be specified in advance. An example for this is the k-Means algorithm (Hamerly and Elkan, 2004). This makes them unsuitable for our use case.

We argue that it would be desirable if one did not have to define a fixed amount of cluster or to optimize many different hyperparameters before using the model.

In the following we present a supervised clustering algorithm based on a neural network. This neural network needs to be trained in advance. The task of the trained net is to decide if two sentences belong to the same cluster or not. Our approach reduces the amount of work that has to be invested before using the model, as only the neural net needs to be optimized.

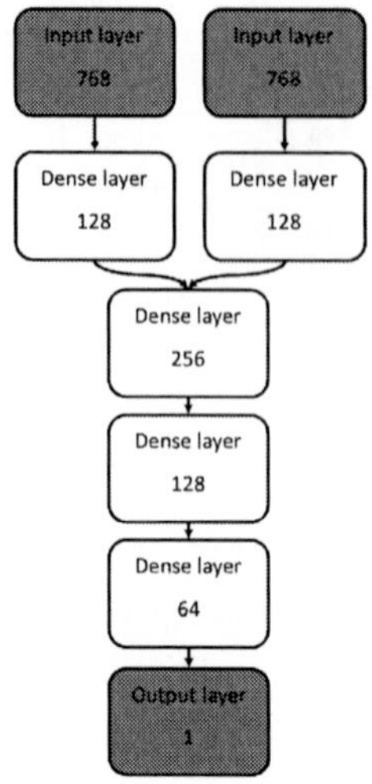

Figure 1: Structure of the used neural net.

The comparison of the event sentences is done by a neural network with two inputs and one output. Using the prepared data triples that were just mentioned, the net can be trained and optimized in a regular manner. The goal is to decide correctly for two sentences if they belong to the same event cluster. If this succeeds for all sentence pairs, we can in theory build perfect event clusters. The output generated by the neural net is needed for the final clustering which is implemented by using a graph.

The used neural network consists of two input layers with 768 neurons. To reduce the input size after both input layers, a layer of 128 neurons is used. To connect both size reduced inputs to each other, a 256 sized layer is used, followed by a 64 sized layer and an output layer with a single neuron like pictured in figure 1.

In total, the model has 238,081 trainable parameters, including the bias weights. Like in subtask 1 and 2 we use the same optimizer, loss and activation function and learning rate.

As mentioned before, the trained neural network is used as a comparison function, which determines if two sentences belong to the same event cluster or not. We use the results ot this comparison for building a graph $G = (V, E)$. The graph consists of a set of nodes $V = v_1, ..., v_n$ and a set of edges $E = \{\{v_x, v_y\} \mid v_x, v_y \in V \text{ and } v_x \neq v_y\}$. The sentences are represented by the nodes. If the network predicts that the two sentences belong to the same cluster, an edge is added in the graph between the corresponding nodes, otherwise no edge

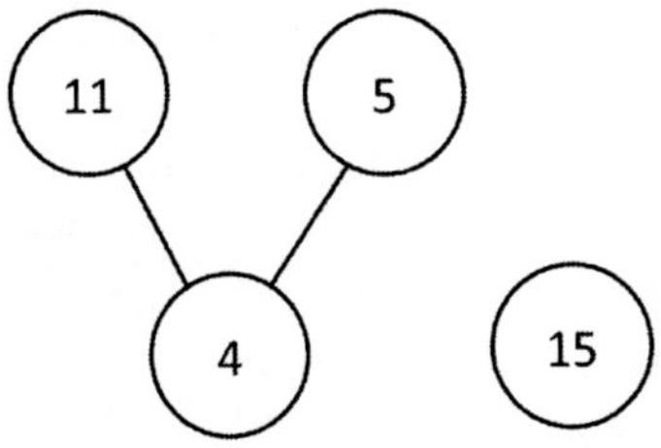

Figure 2: Example of a possible generated graph

is added. The resulting graph is analyzed with regard to disjoint subgraphs. Each individual subgraph represents an event cluster. Figure 2 shows a possible graph with two distinct clusters.

5 Results

5.1 Subtask 1

For both of the first subtasks, the macro F1 score is used for evaluation on the provided test set. In the first subtask we achieved a macro F1 score of 0.74 on the English documents, 0.68 on the Spanish documents, 0.62 on the Portuguese ones and 0.54 on the Hindi documents. Averaged over all test data, a score of 0.65 was achieved, which is slightly better in comparison to the results of a single net. Mostly, the use of multiple nets leads to a small increase in performance as can be seen in table 4. Only with regard to the Spanish data, the single net performed slightly better than the combination of multiple nets. However, this may be an outlier and requires further analysis.

	en	es	pr	hi	avg
100 nets	0.74	0.68	0.62	0.54	0.65
single net	0.72	0.70	0.60	0.50	0.63

Table 4: Result for subtask 1 using different amount of nets

We compare these results to the results that were achieved during development of the systems. For the preliminary evaluation we used 20 percent of the training set as a test set. The evaluation results for subtask 1 are shown in table 5. We reached a macro F1 score of 0.76 for English, 0.66 for Spanish and 0.68 for Portuguese. This lead to an average over all languages of 0.70.

We see that the results achieved on the self-compiled test set are similar to the ones achieved on the test set of the organizers. Only Portuguese stand out with a difference in performance of 0.06.

	en	es	pr	avg
macro F1	0.76	0.66	0.68	0.70

Table 5: Preliminary results for subtask 1

5.2 Subtask 2

Since the improvement using an accumulation of neural nets is only marginal for the classification at sentence level, we used a single net for the second subtask. We scored a macro F1 of 0.65 on the English data, 0.76 on the Spanish data and 0.70 on the Portuguese data, as specified in table 6.

	en	es	pr	avg
macro F1	0.65	0.76	0.70	0.70

Table 6: Result for subtask 2 on different languages

Considering the results of the first two subtasks, which both use very similarly constructed models, it is noticeable that in subtask 1 the best results are achieved on the English data, while in subtask 2 English constitutes the worst performing language class.

For subtask 2, a similar constructed test set as in subtask 1 was used during development. On this set we achieved an average score of 0.73 over all languages. Details for the different languages can be found in table 7. The results are slightly better than the ones for subtask 1.

	en	es	pr	avg
macro F1	0.78	0.73	0.68	0.73

Table 7: Preliminary results for subtask 2

Moreover, we find that the performance of our system declines notably with regard to English when using the test set provided by the organizers. Further analysis is needed to determine what causes this.

5.3 Subtask 3

For evaluating the system submitted for subtask 3, the CoNLL-2012 average score was used. The scores were calculated for each language separately. The amount of test data is quite low, as shown in table 8, the systems were tested on only 180 examples in total.

On the English data we achieved a score of 0.77 and on the Spanish data a score of 0.83. The best

	en	es	pr	total
instances	100	40	40	180

Table 8: Distribution of classes in test data for subtask 3

result with a score of 0.91 was reached on the Portuguese dataset. An overview is given in table 9.

	en	es	pr	avg
CoNLL-2012 avg	0.77	0.83	0.91	0.83

Table 9: Results for subtask 3 for different languages

During the development and testing phase using the training set, the overall score averaged over all three languages was 0.82. The basis for this result was a self compiled test set including 20 percent of the examples of each language included in the training set. The relatively good score for Portuguese on the final test set stands out, since very few data for training was available for this language. An analysis of the training and test data could be helpful to see if there are differences that cause this behaviour.

6 Conclusion

We presented three different approaches for the three different subtasks. The accumulation of several neural nets used in subtask 1 improved the results of the model just very slightly in comparison to a single densely connected neural net.

In general, we can see that working on word level is not mandatory. Sentence and document embeddings in combination with simple dense nets can lead to good results. This decreases the complexity of the task immensely. The results on the sentence level improve in comparison to the ones achieved on the document level, with exception of the results for the English data. The clear difference between the results obtained on the self-compiled test set and the test set of the organizers with regard to English serves as a good starting point for future work.

For subtask 3, we presented a simple solution for event sentence co-reference resolution, focusing on the optimization of a function for comparison by using a multi input neural network. Using this approach, we were able to solve the task in a way that does not require metrics, thresholds and other hyperparameters, which are often needed in clustering, and thus save time during the clustering process. For future work it would be interesting to use bidirectional LSTMs and other techniques to improve the results for co-reference resolution further.

References

Alan Akbik, Tanja Bergmann, Duncan Blythe, Kashif Rasul, Stefan Schweter, and Roland Vollgraf. 2019. Flair: An easy-to-use framework for state-of-the-art nlp. In *NAACL 2019, 2019 Annual Conference of the North American Chapter of the Association for Computational Linguistics (Demonstrations)*, pages 54–59.

Shiyao Cui, Bowen Yu, Tingwen Liu, Zhenyu Zhang, Xuebin Wang, and Jinqiao Shi. 2020. Edge-enhanced graph convolution networks for event detection with syntactic relation. In *Proceedings of the 2020 Conference on Empirical Methods in Natural Language Processing: Findings*, pages 2329–2339.

Jacob Devlin, Ming-Wei Chang, Kenton Lee, and Kristina Toutanova. 2019. BERT: Pre-training of deep bidirectional transformers for language understanding. In *Proceedings of the 2019 Conference of the North American Chapter of the Association for Computational Linguistics: Human Language Technologies, Volume 1 (Long and Short Papers)*, pages 4171–4186, Minneapolis, Minnesota. Association for Computational Linguistics.

Martin Ester, Hans-Peter Kriegel, Jörg Sander, Xiaowei Xu, et al. 1996. A density-based algorithm for discovering clusters in large spatial databases with noise. In *Kdd*, volume 96, pages 226–231.

Greg Hamerly and Charles Elkan. 2004. Learning the k in k-means. *Advances in neural information processing systems*, 16:281–288.

Gao Huang, Zhuang Liu, Laurens Van Der Maaten, and Kilian Q Weinberger. 2017. Densely connected convolutional networks. In *Proceedings of the IEEE conference on computer vision and pattern recognition*, pages 4700–4708.

Ali Hürriyetoğlu, Osman Mutlu, Farhana Ferdousi Liza, Erdem Yörük, Ritesh Kumar, and Shyam Ratan. 2021. Multilingual protest news detection - shared task 1, case 2021. In *Proceedings of the 4th Workshop on Challenges and Applications of Automated Extraction of Socio-political Events from Text (CASE 2021)*, online. Association for Computational Linguistics (ACL).

Ali Hürriyetoğlu, Erdem Yörük, Deniz Yüret, Çağrı Yoltar, Burak Gürel, Fırat Duruşan, Osman Mutlu, and Arda Akdemir. 2019. Overview of clef 2019 lab protestnews: Extracting protests from news in a cross-context setting. In *International Conference of the Cross-Language Evaluation Forum for European Languages*, pages 425–432. Springer.

Ali Hürriyetoğlu, Vanni Zavarella, Hristo Tanev, Erdem Yörük, Ali Safaya, and Osman Mutlu. 2020. Automated extraction of socio-political events from news (AESPEN): Workshop and shared task report. In *Proceedings of the Workshop on Automated Extraction of Socio-political Events from News 2020*, pages 1–6, Marseille, France. European Language Resources Association (ELRA).

Teuvo Kohonen. 1990. The self-organizing map. *Proceedings of the IEEE*, 78(9):1464–1480.

Jian Liu, Yubo Chen, Kang Liu, Wei Bi, and Xiaojiang Liu. 2020. Event extraction as machine reading comprehension. In *Proceedings of the 2020 Conference on Empirical Methods in Natural Language Processing (EMNLP)*, pages 1641–1651.

Thomas M Martinetz, Stanislav G Berkovich, and Klaus J Schulten. 1993. 'neural-gas' network for vector quantization and its application to time-series prediction. *IEEE transactions on neural networks*, 4(4):558–569.

Vincent Ng. 2010. Supervised noun phrase coreference research: The first fifteen years. In *Proceedings of the 48th annual meeting of the association for computational linguistics*, pages 1396–1411.

Thien Huu Nguyen and Ralph Grishman. 2015. Event detection and domain adaptation with convolutional neural networks. In *Proceedings of the 53rd Annual Meeting of the Association for Computational Linguistics and the 7th International Joint Conference on Natural Language Processing (Volume 2: Short Papers)*, pages 365–371.

Faik Kerem Örs, Süveyda Yeniterzi, and Reyyan Yeniterzi. 2020. Event clustering within news articles. In *Proceedings of the Workshop on Automated Extraction of Socio-political Events from News 2020*, pages 63–68.

Jakub Piskorski, Jacek Haneczok, and Guillaume Jacquet. 2020. New benchmark corpus and models for fine-grained event classification: To bert or not to bert? In *Proceedings of the 28th International Conference on Computational Linguistics*, pages 6663–6678.

Benjamin J Radford. 2020. Seeing the forest and the trees: Detection and cross-document coreference resolution of militarized interstate disputes. *arXiv preprint arXiv:2005.02966*.

Ellen Riloff and Jay Shoen. 1995. Automatically acquiring conceptual patterns without an annotated corpus. In *Third Workshop on Very Large Corpora*.

Ellen Riloff et al. 1993. Automatically constructing a dictionary for information extraction tasks. In *AAAI*, volume 1, pages 2–1. Citeseer.

Philip A Schrodt, James Yonamine, and Benjamin E Bagozzi. 2013. Data-based computational approaches to forecasting political violence. In *Handbook of computational approaches to counterterrorism*, pages 129–162. Springer.

DAAI at CASE 2021 Task 1: Transformer-based Multilingual Socio-political and Crisis Event Detection

Hansi Hettiarachchi, Mariam Adedoyin-Olowe, Jagdev Bhogal, Mohamed Medhat Gaber
School of Computing and Digital Technology, Birmingham City University, UK
hansi.hettiarachchi@mail.bcu.ac.uk
{mariam.adedoyin-olowe,jagdev.bhogal,mohamed.gaber}@bcu.ac.uk

Abstract

Automatic socio-political and crisis event detection has been a challenge for natural language processing as well as social and political science communities, due to the diversity and nuance in such events and high accuracy requirements. In this paper, we propose an approach which can handle both document and cross-sentence level event detection in a multilingual setting using pretrained transformer models. Our approach became the winning solution in document level predictions and secured the 3rd place in cross-sentence level predictions for the English language. We could also achieve competitive results for other languages to prove the effectiveness and universality of our approach.

1 Introduction

With technological advancements, today, we have access to a vast amount of data related to social and political factors. These data may contain information on a wide range of events such as political violence, environmental catastrophes and economic crises which are important to prevent or resolve conflicts, improve the quality of life and protect citizens. However, with the increasing data volume, manual efforts for event detection have become too expensive making the requirement of automated and accurate methods crucial (Hürriyetoğlu et al., 2020).

Considering this timely requirement, CASE 2021 Task 1: Multilingual protest news detection is designed (Hürriyetoğlu et al., 2021). This task is composed of four subtasks targeting different data levels. Subtask 1 is to identify documents which contain event information. Similarly, subtask 2 is to identify event described sentences. Subtask 3 targets the cross-sentence level to group sentences which describe the same event. The final subtask is to identify the event trigger and its arguments at the entity level. Since a news article can contain one or more events and a single event can be described together with some previous or relevant details, it is important to focus on different data levels to obtain more accurate and complete information.

This paper describes our approach for document and cross-sentence level event detection including an experimental study. Our approach is mainly based on pretrained transformer models. We use improved model architectures, different learning strategies and unsupervised algorithms to make effective predictions. To facilitate the effortless generalisation across the languages, we do not use any language-specific processing or additional resources. Our submissions achieved the 1st place in document level predictions and 3rd place in cross-sentence level predictions for the English language. Demonstrating the universality of our approach, we could obtain competitive results for other languages too.

The remainder of this paper is organised as follows. Section 2 describes the related work done in the field of socio-political event detection. Details of the task and datasets are provided in Section 3. Section 4 describes the proposed approaches. The experimental setup is described in Section 5 followed by results and evaluation in Section 6. Finally, Section 7 concludes the paper. Additionally, we provide our code to the community which will be freely available to everyone interested in working in this area using the same methodology[1].

2 Related Work

In early work, the majority of event detection approaches were data-driven and knowledge-driven (Hogenboom et al., 2011). Since the data-driven approaches are only based on the statistics of the

[1]The GitHub repository is publicly available on https://github.com/HHansi/EventMiner

Proceedings of the 4th Workshop on Challenges and Applications of Automated Extraction of Socio-political Events from Text (CASE), pages 120–130
August 5–6, 2021, ©2021 Association for Computational Linguistics

underlying corpus, they missed the important semantical relationships. The knowledge-driven or rule-based approaches were proposed to tackle this limitation, but they highly rely on the targeted domains or languages (Danilova and Popova, 2014).

Later, there was a more focus on traditional machine learning-based models (e.g. support vector machines, decision trees) including different feature extraction techniques (e.g. natural language parsing, word vectorisation) (Schrodt et al., 2014; Sonmez et al., 2016). Also, there was a tendency to apply deep learning-based approaches (e.g. CNN, FFNN) too following their success in many information retrieval and natural language processing (NLP) tasks (Lee et al., 2017; Ahmad et al., 2020). However, these approaches are less expandable to low-resource languages, due to the lack of training data to fine-tune the models.

Targeting this major limitation, in this paper we propose an approach which is based on pretrained transformer models. Due to the usage of general knowledge available with the pretrained models and their multilingual capabilities, our approach can easily support event detection in multiple languages including low-resource languages.

3 Subtasks and Data

CASE 2021 Task 1: Multilingual protest news detection is composed of four subtasks targeting event information at document, sentence, cross-sentence and token levels (Hürriyetoğlu et al., 2021). Mainly the socio-political and crisis events which are in the scope of contentious politics and characterised by riots and social movements are focused. Among these subtasks, we participated in subtask 1 and subtask 3 which are further described below.

Subtask 1: Document Classification Subtask 1 is designed as a document classification task. Participants need to predict a binary label of '1' if the news article contains information about a past or ongoing event and '0' otherwise. To preserve the multilinguality of the task, four different languages English, Spanish, Portuguese and Hindi have been considered for data preparation. Comparatively, a high number of training instances were provided with English than Spanish and Portuguese. No training data were provided for the Hindi language. For final evaluations, test data were provided without labels. The data split sizes in each language are summarised in Table 1.

Language	Train	Test
English (en)	9324	2971
Spanish (es)	1000	250
Portuguese (pt)	1487	372
Hindi (hi)	-	268

Table 1: Data distribution over train and test sets in subtask 1

Subtask 3: Event Sentence Coreference Identification (ESCI) Subtask 3 is targeted at the cross-sentence level with the intention to identify the coreference of sentences or sentences about the same event. Given event-related sentences, the targeted output is the clusters which represent separate events. As training data, per instance, a set of sentences and corresponding event clusters were provided as shown below:

```
{"sentence_no":[1,2,3],
"sentences":[
    "Maoist banners found 10th
       April 2011 05:14 AM
       KORAPUT : MAOIST banners
       were found near the
       District Primary Education
        Project ( DPEP ) office
       today in which the ultras
       threatened to kill Shikhya
        Sahayak candidates ,
       outsiders to the district
       , who have been selected
       to join the service here
       .",
    "Maoists , in the banners ,
       have also demanded release
        of hardcore cadre Ghasi
       who was arrested by police
        earlier this week .",
    "Similar banners were also
       found between Sunki and
       Ampavalli where Maoists
       also blocked road by
       felling trees ."],
"event_clusters":[[1,2],[3]]}
```

Listing 1: Subtask 3 training data sample

Data from three different languages: English, Spanish and Portuguese were provided. A few training data instances are available with non-English languages as summarised in Table 2. Similar to subtask 1, test datasets were provided with no labels (event clusters) to use with final evaluations.

Language	Train	Test
English (en)	596	100
Spanish (es)	11	40
Portuguese (pt)	21	40

Table 2: Data distribution over train and test sets in subtask 3

4 Methodology

The main motivation behind the proposed approaches for event document identification and event sentence coreference identification is the recent success gained by transformer-based architectures in various NLP and information retrieval tasks such as language detection (Jauhiainen et al., 2021) question answering (Yang et al., 2019) and offensive language detection (Husain and Uzuner, 2021; Ranasinghe and Zampieri, 2021). Apart from providing strong results compared to RNN based architectures, transformer models like BERT (Devlin et al., 2019) and XLM-R (Conneau et al., 2020) provide pretrained language models that support more than 100 languages which is a huge benefit when it comes to multilingual research. The available models have been trained on general tasks like language modelling and then can be fine-tuned for downstream tasks like text classification (Sun et al., 2019). Depending on the nature of the targeted subtask, we involved different transformer models along with different learning strategies to extract event information as mentioned below.

4.1 Subtask1: Document Classification

Document classification can be considered as a sequence classification problem. According to recent literature, transformer architectures have shown promising results in this area (Ranasinghe et al., 2019b; Hettiarachchi and Ranasinghe, 2020).

Transformer models take an input of a sequence and output the representations of the sequence. The input sequence could contain one or two segments separated by a special token [SEP]. In this approach, we considered a whole document or a news article as a single sequence and no [SEP] token is used. As the first token of the sequence, another special token [CLS] is used and it returns a special embedding corresponding to the whole sequence which is used for text classification tasks (Sun et al., 2019). A simple softmax classifier is added to the top of the transformer model to predict the probability of a class. The architecture of the transformer-based sequence classifier is shown in Figure 1.

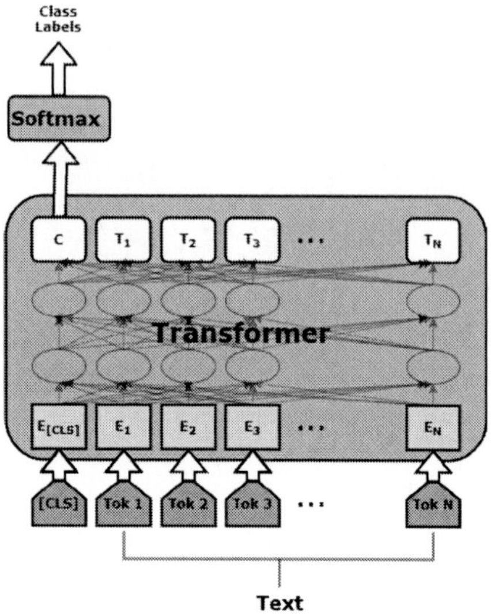

Figure 1: Text Classification Architecture

Unfortunately, the majority of transformer models such as BERT (Devlin et al., 2019) and XLM-R (Conneau et al., 2020) fails to process documents with a higher sequence length than 512. This limitation is introduced due to the self-attention operation used by these architectures which scale quadratically with the sequence length (Beltagy et al., 2020). Therefore, we specifically focused on improved transformer models targetting long documents: Longformer (Beltagy et al., 2020) and BigBird (Zaheer et al., 2020). Longformer utilises an attention mechanism that scales linearly with sequence length and BigBird utilises a sparse attention mechanism to handle long sequences.

Data Preprocessing: We applied a few preprocessing techniques to data before inserting them into the models. All the selected techniques are language-independent to support multilingual experiments. Analysing the datasets, there were documents with very low sequence length (< 5) and they were removed. Further, URLs were removed and repeating symbols more than three times (e.g. =====) were replaced by three occurrences (e.g. ===) because they are uninformative.

4.2 Subtask3: ESCI

Event Sentence Coreference Identification (ESCI) can be considered as a clustering problem. If a set of sentences are assigned to clusters based on their semantic similarity, each cluster will represent separate events. To perform clustering, each sentence needs to be mapped to an embedding which preserves its semantic details.

4.2.1 Sentence Embeddings

Different approaches were proposed to obtain sentence embeddings by previous research. Based on the word embedding models such as GloVe (Pennington et al., 2014), the average of word embeddings over a sentence was used. Later, more improved architectures like InferSent (Conneau et al., 2017) which is based on a siamese BiLSTM network with max pooling, and Universal Sentence Encoder (Cer et al., 2018) which is based on a transformer network and augmented unsupervised learning were developed. However, with the improved performance on NLP tasks by transformers, there was a tendency to input sentences into models like BERT and get the output of the first token ([CLS]) or the average of output layer as a sentence embedding (May et al., 2019; Qiao et al., 2019). These approaches were found as worse than average GloVe embeddings due to the architecture of BERT which was designed targeting classification or regression tasks (Reimers et al., 2019).

Considering these limitations and characteristics of transformer-based models, Reimers et al. (2019) proposed a new architecture named Sentence Transformer (STransformer), a modification to the transformers to derive semantically meaningful sentence embeddings. According to the experimental studies, STransformers outperformed average GloVe embeddings, specialised models like InferSent and Universal Sentence Encoder, and BERT embeddings (Reimers et al., 2019). Considering these facts, we adopt STransformers to generate sentence embeddings in our approach.

STransformer creates a siamese network using transformer models like BERT to fine-tune the model to produce effective sentence embeddings. A pooling layer is added to the top of the transformer model to generate fixed-sized embeddings for sentences. The siamese network takes a sentence pair as the input and passes them through the network to generate embeddings (Ranasinghe et al., 2019a). Then compute the similarity between embeddings using cosine similarity and compare the value with the gold score to fine-tune the network. The architecture of STransformer is shown in Figure 2.

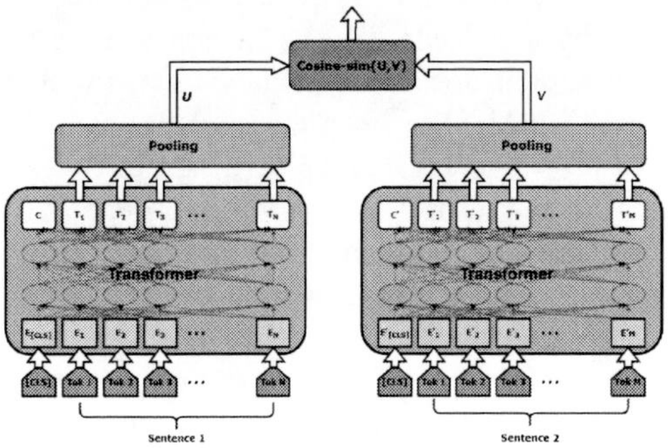

Figure 2: Siamese Sentence Transformer (STransformer) Architecture

Data Formatting: To facilitate the STransformer fine-tuning or training, we formatted given sentences into pairs and assigned the similarity of '1' if both sentences belong to the same cluster and '0' if not. During the pairing, the order of sentences is not considered. Thus, for n sentences, $(n \times (n-1))/2$ pairs were generated. For example, sentence pairs and labels generated for the data sample given in Listing 1 are shown in Table 3.

Sentence 1	Sentence 2	Label
1	2	1
1	3	0
2	3	0

Table 3: Sentence pairs and labels of data sample in Listing 1

4.2.2 Clustering

As clustering methods, we focused on hierarchical clustering and the pairwise prediction-based clustering approach proposed by Örs et al. (2020). Hierarchical clustering is widely used with event detection approaches over flat clustering because flat clustering algorithms (e.g. K-means) require the number of clusters as an input which is unpredictable (Hettiarachchi et al., 2021). Considering the availability of training data and recent successful applications, the pairwise prediction-based clustering approach is focused.

Hierarchical Clustering: For the hierarchical clustering algorithm, we used Hierarchical Agglomerative Clustering (HAC). Each sentence is converted into embeddings to input to the clustering algorithm. HAC considers all data points as separate clusters at the beginning and then merge them based on cluster distance using a linkage method. The tree-like diagram generated by this process is known as a dendrogram and a particular distance threshold is used to cut it into clusters (Manning et al., 2008). For the distance metric, cosine distance is used, because it proved to be effective for measurements in textual data (Mikolov et al., 2013; Antoniak and Mimno, 2018) and a variant of it is used with STransformer models. For the linkage method, single, complete and average schemes were considered for initial experiments and the average scheme was selected among them because it outperformed others. We picked the optimal distance threshold automatically using the training data. If training data is further split into training and validation sets to use with STransformers, only the validation set is used to pick the cluster threshold, because the rest of the data is known to the embedding generated model.

Pairwise Prediction-based Clustering: We used the pairwise prediction-based clustering algorithm proposed by Örs et al. (2020) which became the winning solution of the ESCI task in the AESPEN-2020 workshop (Hürriyetoğlu et al., 2020). Originally this algorithm used the BERT model to predict whether a certain sentence pair belongs to the same event or not. In this research, we used STransformers to make those predictions except general transformers. Since a STransformer model is designed to obtain embeddings, to derive labels (i.e. '1' if the sentence pair belong to the same event and '0' if not) from them we used cosine similarity with a threshold. The optimal value computed during the model evaluation process is used as the threshold.

5 Experimental Setup

This section describes the learning configurations, transformer models and hyper-parameters used for the experiments.

5.1 Learning Configurations

We focused on different learning configurations depending on data and model availability, and multilingual setting. Considering the availability of data and models, we used the following configurations for the experiments.

Pretrained (No Learning): Pretrained models are used without making any modifications to them to make the predictions. In this case, models pretrained using a similar objective to the target objective need to be selected.

Fine-tuning: Under fine-tuning, we retrain an available model to a downstream task or the same task model already trained. This learning allows the model to be familiar with the targeted data.

From-scratch Learning: Models are built from scratch using the targeted data. This procedure helps to mitigate the unnecessary biases made by the data used to train available models.

Language Modelling (LM): In LM, we retrain the transformer model on the targeted dataset using the model's initial training objective before fine-tuning it for the downstream task. This step helps increase the model understanding of data (Hettiarachchi and Ranasinghe, 2020).

For multilingual data, the following configurations are considered to support both high- and low-resource languages.

Monolingual Learning: In monolingual learning, we build the model from the training data only from that particular language.

Multilingual Learning: In multilingual learning, we concatenate available training data from all languages and build a single model.

Zero-shot Learning: In zero-shot learning, we use the models fine-tuned for the same task using training data from other language(s) to make the predictions. The multilingual and cross-lingual nature of the transformer models has provided the ability to do this (Ranasinghe et al., 2020; Hettiarachchi and Ranasinghe, 2021).

5.2 Transformers

We used monolingual and multilingual general transformers as well as pretrained STransformers for our experiments.

General Transformers: As monolingual models, we used transformer models built for each of the targeted languages. For English, BigBird (Zaheer et al., 2020), Longformer (Beltagy et al., 2020) and BERT English (Devlin et al., 2019) models were considered. For Spanish, BETO (Canete et al., 2020) and for Portuguese, BERTimbau (Souza

Seq. Length	Model	Macro R	Macro P	Macro F1
256	BERT-large-cased	0.8717	0.8489	0.8595
	BigBird-roberta-large	0.8790	0.9119	**0.8941**‡
	Longformer-base	0.8800	0.8868	0.8833
512	BERT-large-cased	0.8697	0.8683	0.8690
	BigBird-roberta-base	0.8763	0.9018	0.8882‡
	Longformer-base	0.8608	0.9100	0.8824‡
700	BigBird-roberta-base	0.8770	0.8807	0.8788
	Longformer-base	0.8748	0.8846	0.8796

Table 4: Results: Macro Recall (R), Precision (P) and F1 of document classification experiments for English using different sequence lengths and models. Best is in Bold and submitted systems are marked with ‡.

	Model	Training Data	Macro R	Macro P	Macro F1
English	BERT-multilingual-cased	en+es+pt	0.8505	0.8567	0.8536
	XLM-R-base	en+es+pt	0.8280	0.8727	0.8476
Spanish	BETO-cased	es	0.6944	0.8681	0.7475‡
	BERT-multilingual-cased	es	NT	NT	NT
	BERT-multilingual-cased	en+es+pt	0.7831	0.8111	0.7962‡
	XLM-R-base	es	NT	NT	NT
	XLM-R-base	en+es+pt	0.7888	0.8530	**0.8167**‡
Portuguese	BERTimbau-large	pt	0.7672	0.8900	0.8126‡
	BERT-multilingual-cased	pt	0.7595	0.8331	0.7896
	BERT-multilingual-cased	en+es+pt	0.8384	0.8890	**0.8611**‡
	XLM-R-base	pt	NT	NT	NT
	XLM-R-base	en+es+pt	0.7845	0.8449	0.8104‡

Table 5: Results of multilingual document classification experiments. Training Data column summarises the language(s) of used datasets to train models. Due to training data limitations, a few models were found to be not trainable and they are indicated with NT. Best is in Bold and submitted systems are marked with ‡.

et al., 2020) models which are variants of the BERT model were considered. As multilingual models, BERT multilingual version and XLM-R (Conneau et al., 2020) models were used. Among these models, a higher sequence length than 512 is only supported by BigBird and Longformer models available for English. We used HuggingFace's Transformers library (Wolf et al., 2020) to obtain the models.

Sentence Transformers: STransformers provide pretrained models for different tasks[2]. Among them, we selected the best-performed models trained for semantic textual similarity (STS) and duplicate question identification, because these areas are related to the same event prediction.

5.3 Hyper-parameter Configurations

We used a Nvidia Tesla K80 GPU to train the models. Each input dataset is divided into a training set and a validation set using a 0.9:0.1 split. We predominantly fine-tuned the learning rate and the number of epochs of the model manually to obtain the best results for the validation set. For document classification, we obtained $1e^{-}5$ as the best value for the learning rate and 3 as the best value for the number of epochs. The same learning rate was found as the best value for STransformers with epochs of 5. For the sequence length, different values have experimented with document classification and they are further discussed in Section 6.1. A fixed sequence length of 136 was used for ESCI considering its data.

To improve the performance of document classification, we used the majority-class self-ensemble approach mentioned in (Hettiarachchi and Ranasinghe, 2020). During the training, we trained three models with different random seeds and considered the majority-class returned by the models as the final prediction.

To train STransformers, we selected the online contrastive loss, an improved version of the con-

[2]Sentence Transformer pretrained models are available on `https://www.sbert.net/docs/pretrained_models.html`

	Model	Training Data	Seq. Length	Macro F1
English	Best System			0.8455
	BigBird-roberta-large	en	256	
	BigBird-roberta-base	en	512	0.8220
Spanish	Best System			0.7727
	XLM-R-base	en+es+pt	512	0.6931
	BERT-multilingual-cased	en+es+pt	512	0.6886
Portuguese	Best System			0.8400
	XLM-R-base	en+es+pt	512	0.8243
	BERT-multilingual-cased	en+es+pt	512	0.7982
Hindi	Best System			0.7877
	XLM-R-base	en+es+pt	512	0.7707
	BERT-multilingual-cased	en+es+pt	512	0.4647

Table 6: Document classification results for test data

trastive loss function. The contrastive loss function learns the parameters by reducing the distance between neighbours or semantically similar embeddings and increasing the distance between non-neighbours or semantically dissimilar embeddings (Hadsell et al., 2006). The online version automatically detects the hard cases (i.e. negative pairs with a low distance than the largest distance of positive pairs and positive pairs with a high distance than the lowest distance of negative pairs) in a batch and calculates the loss only for them.

6 Results and Evaluation

In this section, we report the conducted experiments and their results.

6.1 Subtask1: Document Classification

Task organisers used Macro F1 as the evaluation metric for subtask 1. Since only the training data were released, we separated a dev set from each training dataset to evaluate our approach. Depending on the data size, 20% from English and 10% from other-language training data were separated as dev data.

Initially, we analysed the performance of fine-tuned document classifiers for English using BERT and improved transformer models for long documents, along with varying sequence length. Considering the sequence length distribution in data, we picked the lengths of 256, 512 and 700 for these experiments. The obtained results are summarised in Table 4. Even though we targeted *large* versions of the models (e.g. BigBird-roberta-large), due to the resource limitations, we had to use *base* versions (e.g. BigBird-roberta-base) for some experiments. According to the results, BERT models improve the F1 when we increase the sequence length. In contrast to it, both BigBird and Longformer models have higher F1 with low sequence lengths.

For predictions in Spanish and Portuguese documents, we fine-tuned the models using both monolingual and multilingual learning approaches. Since transformers with the maximum sequence length of 512 are used, we fixed the sequence length to 512 based on the findings in English experiments. The obtained results and training configurations are summarised in Table 5. For the high-resource language (i.e. English), multilingual learning returns a low F1 than monolingual learning. However, low-resource languages show a clear improvement in F1 with multilingual learning. Since there were no training data for the Hindi language, the best multilingual models were picked to apply the zero-shot learning approach.

We report the results we obtained for test data in Table 6. According to the results, our approach which used the BigBird model became the best system for the English language. For other languages, multilingual learning performed best. Among models, XLM-R outperformed the BERT-multilingual model. Compared to the best systems submitted, our approach has very competitive results for these languages too.

6.2 Subtask3: ESCI

To evaluate subtask 3 responses, organisers used CoNLL-2012 average score[3] (Pradhan et al., 2014). Similar to subtask 1, for evaluation purpose, we separated 20% from the English training dataset as dev data. There were no sufficient data in other

[3]The implementation of the scorer is available on `https://github.com/LoicGrobol/scorch`

	Base Model	STransformer	Clustering	CoNLL Average Score
Pretrained	DistilBERT-base-uncased	quora-distilbert-base	HAC	0.8360
	MPNet-base	stsb-mpnet-base-v2	HAC	0.8360
Fine-tune	DistilBERT-base-uncased	quora-distilbert-base	HAC	0.8392
	DistilBERT-base-uncased	quora-distilbert-base	(Örs et al., 2020)	0.8376
	MPNet-base	stsb-mpnet-base-v2	HAC	0.8370
	MPNet-base	stsb-mpnet-base-v2	(Örs et al., 2020)	0.8264
From-scratch	BERT-large-cased	-	HAC	**0.8688**‡
	BERT-large-cased	-	(Örs et al., 2020)	0.8656‡
LM + From-scratch	BERT-large-cased	-	HAC	0.8543‡
	BERT-large-cased	-	(Örs et al., 2020)	0.8328

Table 7: Results of ESCI for English along with different strategies experimented. Best is in Bold and submitted systems are marked with ‡.

	Base Model	STransformer	Clustering	CoNLL Average Score
Pretrained	DistilBERT-base-uncased	quora-distilbert-multilingual	HAC	0.8360
Fine-tune	DistilBERT-base-uncased	quora-distilbert-multilingual	HAC	0.8423‡
	DistilBERT-base-uncased	quora-distilbert-multilingual	(Örs et al., 2020)	0.8362
From-scratch	BERT-multilingual-cased	-	HAC	**0.8464**‡
	BERT-multilingual-cased	-	(Örs et al., 2020)	0.8414
	XLM-R-large	-	HAC	0.8360
	XLM-R-large	-	(Örs et al., 2020)	0.8350

Table 8: Results of ESCI for English using multilingual models. Best is in Bold and submitted systems are marked with ‡.

languages for further splits.

For the English language, we experimented with the clustering approaches using the embeddings generated by different STransformer models. Initially, we focused on pretrained models and their fine-tuned versions on task data. Later we built STransformers from scratch using general transformer models and further integrated LM too. The obtained results and corresponding model details are summarised in Table 7. According to the results, STransformers build from scratch outperformed the pretrained and fine-tuned models. LM did not improve the results and it is possible when data is not enough for modelling. Among the clustering algorithms, HAC showed the best results.

We could not train any STransformer for other languages because the organisers provided a limited number of labelled instances for those languages. We used pretrained multilingual models and adhering to zero-shot learning, fine-tuned them using English data. Further English data were used to build STransformers from scratch too. All the evaluations were also done on English data and best-performing systems were chosen to make predictions for other languages. The obtained results are summarised in Table 8. Similar to the English monolingual scenario, from-scratch multilingual models performed best.

We report the results for test data in Table 9. According to the results, for all languages, we could obtain competitive results compared to the results of the best-submitted system. Since our approach can be easily extended to different languages with very few training instances, we believe the results are at a satisfactory level.

7 Conclusions

In this paper, we presented our approach for document and cross-sentence level subtasks of CASE 2021 Task 1: Multilingual protest news detection. We mainly used pretrained transformer models including their improved architectures for long document processing and sentence embedding generation. Further, different learning strategies: monolingual, multilingual and zero-shot and, classification and clustering approaches were involved. For document level predictions, our approach achieved the 1st place for the English language while being within the top 4 solutions for other languages. For cross-sentence level predictions, we secured the

	Model	Clustering	CoNLL Average Score
English	Best System		0.8444
	BERT-large-cased$_{from-scratch}$	HAC	0.8040
	BERT-large-cased$_{from-scratch}$	(Örs et al., 2020)	0.7951
Spanish	Best system		0.8423
	quora-distilbert-multilingual$_{fine-tune(en)}$	HAC	0.8183
	BERT-multilingual-cased$_{from-scratch(en)}$	HAC	0.8167
Portuguese	Best System		0.9303
	quora-distilbert-multilingual$_{fine-tune(en)}$	HAC	0.9023
	BERT-multilingual-cased$_{from-scratch(en)}$	HAC	0.9023

Table 9: ESCI results for test data

3rd place for the English language with competitive results for other languages. Despite that, our approach can support multiple languages with low or no training resources.

As future work, we hope to further improve semantically meaningful sentence embedding generation using improved architectures, learning strategies and ensemble methods. Also, we would like to analyse the impact of different clustering approaches on cross-sentence level predictions.

References

Faizan Ahmad, Ahmed Abbasi, Brent Kitchens, Donald A Adjeroh, and Daniel Zeng. 2020. Deep learning for adverse event detection from web search. *IEEE Transactions on Knowledge and Data Engineering*.

Maria Antoniak and David Mimno. 2018. Evaluating the stability of embedding-based word similarities. *Transactions of the Association for Computational Linguistics*, 6:107–119.

Iz Beltagy, Matthew E Peters, and Arman Cohan. 2020. Longformer: The long-document transformer. *arXiv preprint arXiv:2004.05150*.

José Canete, Gabriel Chaperon, Rodrigo Fuentes, and Jorge Pérez. 2020. Spanish pre-trained bert model and evaluation data. *PML4DC at ICLR*, 2020.

Daniel Cer, Yinfei Yang, Sheng-yi Kong, Nan Hua, Nicole Limtiaco, Rhomni St John, Noah Constant, Mario Guajardo-Céspedes, Steve Yuan, Chris Tar, et al. 2018. Universal sentence encoder. *arXiv preprint arXiv:1803.11175*.

Alexis Conneau, Kartikay Khandelwal, Naman Goyal, Vishrav Chaudhary, Guillaume Wenzek, Francisco Guzmán, Edouard Grave, Myle Ott, Luke Zettlemoyer, and Veselin Stoyanov. 2020. Unsupervised cross-lingual representation learning at scale. In *Proceedings of the 58th Annual Meeting of the Association for Computational Linguistics*, pages 8440–8451, Online. Association for Computational Linguistics.

Alexis Conneau, Douwe Kiela, Holger Schwenk, Loïc Barrault, and Antoine Bordes. 2017. Supervised learning of universal sentence representations from natural language inference data. In *Proceedings of the 2017 Conference on Empirical Methods in Natural Language Processing*, pages 670–680, Copenhagen, Denmark. Association for Computational Linguistics.

Vera Danilova and Svetlana Popova. 2014. Socio-political event extraction using a rule-based approach. In *OTM Confederated International Conferences" On the Move to Meaningful Internet Systems"*, pages 537–546. Springer.

Jacob Devlin, Ming-Wei Chang, Kenton Lee, and Kristina Toutanova. 2019. BERT: Pre-training of deep bidirectional transformers for language understanding. In *Proceedings of the 2019 Conference of the North American Chapter of the Association for Computational Linguistics: Human Language Technologies, Volume 1 (Long and Short Papers)*, pages 4171–4186, Minneapolis, Minnesota. Association for Computational Linguistics.

Raia Hadsell, Sumit Chopra, and Yann LeCun. 2006. Dimensionality reduction by learning an invariant mapping. In *2006 IEEE Computer Society Conference on Computer Vision and Pattern Recognition (CVPR'06)*, volume 2, pages 1735–1742. IEEE.

Hansi Hettiarachchi, Mariam Adedoyin-Olowe, Jagdev Bhogal, and Mohamed Medhat Gaber. 2021. Embed2detect: Temporally clustered embedded words for event detection in social media. *Machine Learning*, pages 1–39.

Hansi Hettiarachchi and Tharindu Ranasinghe. 2020. InfoMiner at WNUT-2020 task 2: Transformer-based covid-19 informative tweet extraction. In *Proceedings of the Sixth Workshop on Noisy User-generated Text (W-NUT 2020)*, pages 359–365, Online. Association for Computational Linguistics.

Hansi Hettiarachchi and Tharindu Ranasinghe. 2021. TransWiC at SemEval-2021 Task 2: Transformer-based Multilingual and Cross-lingual Word-in-Context Disambiguation. In *Proceedings of SemEval*.

Frederik Hogenboom, Flavius Frasincar, Uzay Kaymak, and Franciska De Jong. 2011. An overview of event extraction from text. In *DeRiVE@ ISWC*, pages 48–57. Citeseer.

Ali Hürriyetoğlu, Osman Mutlu, Farhana Ferdousi Liza, Erdem Yörük, Ritesh Kumar, and Shyam Ratan. 2021. Multilingual protest news detection - shared task 1, case 2021. In *Proceedings of the 4th Workshop on Challenges and Applications of Automated Extraction of Socio-political Events from Text (CASE 2021)*, online. Association for Computational Linguistics (ACL).

Ali Hürriyetoğlu, Vanni Zavarella, Hristo Tanev, Erdem Yörük, Ali Safaya, and Osman Mutlu. 2020. Automated extraction of socio-political events from news (aespen): Workshop and shared task report. In *Proceedings of the Workshop on Automated Extraction of Socio-political Events from News 2020*, pages 1–6.

Fatemah Husain and Ozlem Uzuner. 2021. Leveraging offensive language for sarcasm and sentiment detection in arabic. In *Proceedings of the Sixth Arabic Natural Language Processing Workshop*, pages 364–369.

Tommi Jauhiainen, Tharindu Ranasinghe, and Marcos Zampieri. 2021. Comparing approaches to dravidian language identification. In *Proceedings of the 7th Workshop on NLP for Similar Languages, Varieties and Dialects*.

Kathy Lee, Ashequl Qadir, Sadid A Hasan, Vivek Datla, Aaditya Prakash, Joey Liu, and Oladimeji Farri. 2017. Adverse drug event detection in tweets with semi-supervised convolutional neural networks. In *Proceedings of the 26th international conference on world wide web*, pages 705–714.

Christopher D Manning, Prabhakar Raghavan, and Hinrich Schütze. 2008. *Introduction to information retrieval*. Cambridge university press.

Chandler May, Alex Wang, Shikha Bordia, Samuel Bowman, and Rachel Rudinger. 2019. On measuring social biases in sentence encoders. In *Proceedings of the 2019 Conference of the North American Chapter of the Association for Computational Linguistics: Human Language Technologies, Volume 1 (Long and Short Papers)*, pages 622–628.

Tomas Mikolov, Ilya Sutskever, Kai Chen, Greg S Corrado, and Jeff Dean. 2013. Distributed representations of words and phrases and their compositionality. In *Advances in neural information processing systems*, pages 3111–3119.

Faik Kerem Örs, Süveyda Yeniterzi, and Reyyan Yeniterzi. 2020. Event clustering within news articles. In *Proceedings of the Workshop on Automated Extraction of Socio-political Events from News 2020*, pages 63–68.

Jeffrey Pennington, Richard Socher, and Christopher Manning. 2014. Glove: Global vectors for word representation. In *Proceedings of the 2014 conference on empirical methods in natural language processing (EMNLP)*, pages 1532–1543.

Sameer Pradhan, Xiaoqiang Luo, Marta Recasens, Eduard Hovy, Vincent Ng, and Michael Strube. 2014. Scoring coreference partitions of predicted mentions: A reference implementation. In *Proceedings of the 52nd Annual Meeting of the Association for Computational Linguistics (Volume 2: Short Papers)*, pages 30–35, Baltimore, Maryland. Association for Computational Linguistics.

Yifan Qiao, Chenyan Xiong, Zhenghao Liu, and Zhiyuan Liu. 2019. Understanding the behaviors of bert in ranking. *arXiv preprint arXiv:1904.07531*.

Tharindu Ranasinghe, Constantin Orasan, and Ruslan Mitkov. 2019a. Semantic textual similarity with Siamese neural networks. In *Proceedings of the International Conference on Recent Advances in Natural Language Processing (RANLP 2019)*, pages 1004–1011, Varna, Bulgaria. INCOMA Ltd.

Tharindu Ranasinghe, Constantin Orasan, and Ruslan Mitkov. 2020. TransQuest: Translation quality estimation with cross-lingual transformers. In *Proceedings of the 28th International Conference on Computational Linguistics*, pages 5070–5081, Barcelona, Spain (Online). International Committee on Computational Linguistics.

Tharindu Ranasinghe and Marcos Zampieri. 2021. MUDES: Multilingual detection of offensive spans. In *Proceedings of the 2021 Conference of the North American Chapter of the Association for Computational Linguistics: Human Language Technologies: Demonstrations*, pages 144–152, Online. Association for Computational Linguistics.

Tharindu Ranasinghe, Marcos Zampieri, and Hansi Hettiarachchi. 2019b. BRUMS at HASOC 2019: Deep learning models for multilingual hate speech and offensive language identification. In *In Proceedings of the 11th annual meeting of the Forum for Information Retrieval Evaluation*.

Nils Reimers, Iryna Gurevych, Nils Reimers, Iryna Gurevych, Nandan Thakur, Nils Reimers, Johannes Daxenberger, and Iryna Gurevych. 2019. Sentence-bert: Sentence embeddings using siamese bert-networks. In *Proceedings of the 2019 Conference on Empirical Methods in Natural Language Processing*. Association for Computational Linguistics.

Philip A Schrodt, John Beieler, and Muhammed Idris. 2014. Three'sa charm?: Open event data coding with el: Diablo, petrarch, and the open event data alliance. In *ISA Annual Convention*. Citeseer.

Cagil Sonmez, Arzucan Özgür, and Erdem Yörük. 2016. Towards building a political protest database to explain changes in the welfare state. In *Proceedings of the 10th SIGHUM Workshop on Language*

Technology for Cultural Heritage, Social Sciences, and Humanities, pages 106–110.

Fábio Souza, Rodrigo Nogueira, and Roberto Lotufo. 2020. BERTimbau: pretrained BERT models for Brazilian Portuguese. In *9th Brazilian Conference on Intelligent Systems, BRACIS, Rio Grande do Sul, Brazil, October 20-23 (to appear)*.

Chi Sun, Xipeng Qiu, Yige Xu, and Xuanjing Huang. 2019. How to fine-tune bert for text classification? In *Chinese Computational Linguistics*, pages 194–206, Cham. Springer International Publishing.

Thomas Wolf, Lysandre Debut, Victor Sanh, Julien Chaumond, Clement Delangue, Anthony Moi, Pierric Cistac, Tim Rault, Remi Louf, Morgan Funtowicz, Joe Davison, Sam Shleifer, Patrick von Platen, Clara Ma, Yacine Jernite, Julien Plu, Canwen Xu, Teven Le Scao, Sylvain Gugger, Mariama Drame, Quentin Lhoest, and Alexander Rush. 2020. Transformers: State-of-the-art natural language processing. In *Proceedings of the 2020 Conference on Empirical Methods in Natural Language Processing: System Demonstrations*, pages 38–45, Online. Association for Computational Linguistics.

Wei Yang, Yuqing Xie, Aileen Lin, Xingyu Li, Luchen Tan, Kun Xiong, Ming Li, and Jimmy Lin. 2019. End-to-end open-domain question answering with BERTserini. In *Proceedings of the 2019 Conference of the North American Chapter of the Association for Computational Linguistics (Demonstrations)*, pages 72–77, Minneapolis, Minnesota. Association for Computational Linguistics.

Manzil Zaheer, Guru Guruganesh, Avinava Dubey, Joshua Ainslie, Chris Alberti, Santiago Ontanon, Philip Pham, Anirudh Ravula, Qifan Wang, Li Yang, et al. 2020. Big bird: Transformers for longer sequences. *arXiv preprint arXiv:2007.14062*.

SU-NLP at CASE 2021 Task 1: Protest News Detection for English

Furkan Çelik, Tuğberk Dalkılıç, Fatih Beyhan, Reyyan Yeniterzi
Sabancı University
İstanbul, Turkey
{fcelik, tdalkilic, fatihbeyhan, reyyan}@sabanciuniv.edu

Abstract

This paper summarizes our group's efforts in the multilingual protest news detection shared task, which is organized as a part of the Challenges and Applications of Automated Extraction of Socio-political Events from Text (CASE) Workshop. We participated in all four subtasks in English. Especially in the identification of event containing sentences task, our proposed ensemble approach using RoBERTa and multichannel CNN-LexStem model yields higher performance. Similarly in the event extraction task, our transformer-LSTM-CRF architecture outperforms regular transformers significantly.

1 Introduction

Identifying events and extracting event related information from text is an important language understanding task which has been studied for quite some time. This challenging task has been studied in several steps or divided into some sub-tasks. The first step is identifying whether a document or a sentence contains an event or not. If it contains then the event co-reference resolution task analyses whether the context around it (such as other sentences) refer to the same event or not. Event related information such as the event trigger and its arguments are also extracted, which can be later on used to create event taxonomies.

These steps either alone or together have been studied for English extensively, similar to many other Natural Language Processing tasks. This year as part of the Challenges and Applications of Automated Extraction of Socio-political Events from Text (CASE) Workshop, a shared task covering some of these sub-tasks has been organized not only for English but also for Portuguese, Spanish and Hindi (Hürriyetoğlu et al., 2021). The common theme was the identification of protest events from news articles.

The organizers specifically focus on the four subtasks. In the first and second sub-task, the aim is to predict whether a given document (subtask 1) or sentence (subtask 2) contains information about an event (either past or ongoing). The third subtask focuses on event sentence coreference and the participants are asked to predict whether the sentences containing an event are referring to the same event or not. In subtask 4, the goal is to identify event triggers and related arguments from sentences.

It is hard to choose among these interesting subtasks, therefore we participate in all four of them. Due to time constraints we only work on English and leave the rest of the languages as future work.

The first and the second subtask focus on predicting whether a content contains an event or not. For these tasks in addition to trying standard transformer based models, we explore ensemble models which combine the strengths of different models. Furthermore, the effect of stemming the context is also explored in these subtasks. The third subtask is related to the event coreference task. For this task, we explore the rescoring and clustering approach proposed by (Örs et al., 2020). Finally, the goal of subtask 4 is to extract event information from context. For this task, we exploit the transformer-LSTM-CRF architecture which has shown success in several NER tasks.

The rest of the paper is organized as following: Section 2 describes our proposed approach for identifying whether a content contains an event or not, and details our submissions for subtasks 1 and 2. Section 3 explains our submission to the event coreference resolution subtask. Section 4 presents the experimental results for event extraction subtask and finally Section 5 concludes the paper with future work.

2 Subtask 1 & 2: Event or Not

The goal of the first two subtasks is to predict whether the provided input context contains an

Proceedings of the 4th Workshop on Challenges and Applications of Automated Extraction of Socio-political Events from Text (CASE), pages 131–137
August 5–6, 2021, ©2021 Association for Computational Linguistics

event (either past or ongoing) or not. Therefore, the task is a binary classification task. In these two subtasks the only difference is the input context. In subtask 1 the input is the whole news article while in subtask 2, it is only a sentence. The main difference between these two tasks is the length of the input. In subtask 1's dataset, even though most documents contain around 3 sentences, the maximum length in the data is almost 10 times larger than the maximum length in subtask 2 data. This makes subtask 1 slightly more challenging. One expects documents as longer input, to contain more clues about an event if there is; therefore more useful. However, there is also the risk of unrelated content causing mixed signals.

Even though this difference between the tasks, we mostly apply same approaches to both. For this binary classification problem, we use some simple neural network architectures as baselines and also investigate fine-tuning several pretrained transformer based models. The models applied are listed as follows:

- CNN: A single convolutional layer connected to a fully connected dense layer.
- LSTM: A unidirectional long short term memory model.
- GRU: A unidirectional gated recurrent unit model.
- BERT (Devlin et al., 2019): Uses bidirectional transformer architecture for language modeling. We fine-tune the BERT-base-cased [1] model.
- Albert (Lan et al., 2019): An efficient (A Lite BERT) version of BERT which outperformed BERT in several benchmark data sets. We fine-tune the Albert-base-v2 model [2] in this paper.
- RoBERTa (Liu et al., 2019): A robustly optimized version of BERT which outperformed BERT in GLUE benchmark. We fine-tune the RoBERTa-base model [3] in our experiments.

For neural networks like CNN and RNN, several pretrained word embeddings, like Google News Word2Vec[4] (Mikolov et al., 2013), NNLM (Bengio et al., 2003) model trained on Google News dataset [5] and GloVe (Pennington et al., 2014) 6B Wikipedia embeddings [6], have been tried. Since the ratio of out-of-vocabulary words were very small, character-based embeddings have not been explored. We have seen that using different embeddings resulted in minor changes, and rather fine-tuning the embedding layer or not, does not have any significant effect on the performance of models in terms of overfitting resistance or achieved scores.

NNLM and GloVe return slightly better performance compared to Word2Vec, when used in standalone CNN or RNN models. However, as we try ensembling approaches (to be described in the upcoming sections), NNLM outperforms GloVe with its high Precision score. Therefore, NNLM embedding is used in all reported experiments in this section.

2.1 Baseline Experiments

In all these subtasks, the data collections were gathered from news articles about socio-political and crisis conflicts. For the document classification task, we are provided with an imbalance training data of 9324 news articles with 7407 of them without any events and the rest as containing event. Similarly in subtask 2, among the provided 22825 sentences, only 4210 of them contain an event while the rest of them do not.

For both tasks, 20% of the provided data is used for validation purposes and rest for model training. During the training process, several balancing approaches were applied to decrease any possible negative effects caused by the imbalance data problem. But overall they did not provide any significant improvements in F1 score; therefore data is used in its original ratio without any balancing.

The experimental results of the baseline approaches are displayed in Tables 1 and 2. In subtask 1, except for RNNs, all methods listed above were tested. RNNs were not tested due to limited time and prioritization of computational resources for other more advance models. Only a single layer CNN is used in the experiments, since adding more

[1] https://huggingface.co/bert-base-cased

[2] https://huggingface.co/albert-base-v2

[3] https://huggingface.co/roberta-base

[4] https://radimrehurek.com/gensim/auto_examples/howtos/run_downloader_api.html

[5] https://tfhub.dev/google/nnlm-en-dim128/2

[6] https://nlp.stanford.edu/projects/glove/

layers caused over-fitting.

Model	Validation Set	Test Set
CNN	0.82	0.77
BERT	0.84	0.80
Albert	0.84	0.81
RoBERTa	0.86	0.81

Table 1: Subtask 1 Baseline Approaches F1 Scores

Model	Validation Set	Test Set
CNN	0.80	0.70
LSTM	0.82	0.68
GRU	0.83	0.64
BERT	0.87	0.81
Albert	0.86	0.81
RoBERTa	0.88	0.82

Table 2: Subtask 2 Baseline Approaches F1 Scores

Based on the results, transformer based approaches outperform classical neural network based approaches in both tasks. In traditional neural network based models, RNN based ones, both LSTM and GRU, suffer from serious overfitting even though all the efforts of regularization and dropout. Regarding the transformer-based models, in both subtasks, RoBERTa outperforms both BERT and Albert with close margin.

2.2 LexStem Model

In the task definition, it is mentioned that the labeled events can be either from past or continuous. This suggests various types of tense use in the context. This variety may cause model to miss some events. In order to deal with this variety, in addition to the lexical forms of the words, their stemmed versions are also included to CNN model as additional channel in the network. WordNetLemmatizer [7] is used as the stemmer. In this proposed model, which is named as *LexStem* model, one channel is used for the original form of the sentence and another channel for the stemmed version.

In order to make a fair comparison of the LexStem model, additional CNN multi-channel models are trained as well.

- CNN-LexLex: A two channels model with original form of the words are used in both channels. This one is developed to see the effect of two channels compared to one.
- CNN-StemStem: A two channels model with stemmed version of the words are used in both channels. This one is developed to see the individual effect of stem information.
- CNN-LexStem: The proposed two channel model with one channel for lexical form of the word and the other for stemmed version.

The experimental results of these models are displayed in Table 3. In the table, the first two rows are from subtask 1 and the rest of them are from subtask 2. The proposed LexStem model does not provide any significant improvements in subtask 1, therefore other multi-channel models are not tested with this task.

ST	Model	#CH	Val.	Test
1	CNN	1	0.82	0.77
1	CNN-LexStem	2	0.82	0.78
2	CNN	1	0.80	0.70
2	CNN-LexLex	2	0.82	0.69
2	CNN-StemStem	2	0.83	0.68
2	CNN-LexStem	2	0.85	0.71

Table 3: Subtask 1 & 2 Stemming Experiments F1 Scores. ST: Subtask and CH: Channel

Unlike subtask 1, for subtask 2 the LexStem model provides drastic improvements with validation data, but only slight improvement on test data. A similar improvement on test set is also observed at subtask 1. Using multi-channel architecture and therefore using more parameters probably increases model's likelihood of overfitting. This is more observable with CNN-LexLex and CNN-StemStem models. Even though with this increased overfitting possibility, CNN-LexStem model returns small yet consistent increase on test set. The possible reasons of this improvement will be explored more in the future.

2.3 Ensemble Models

RoBERTa model outperforms all other models, therefore we specifically analyze its performance and its confidence of its predictions on the validation set. Figure 1 displays how the average F1 score changes with respect to model's confidence values. In the figure, 0.05-0.95 means RoBERTa's predictions which are lower than 0.05 or higher than 0.95.

According to the Figure 1, confidence scores lower than 10% and higher than 90% achieve the

[7] https://www.nltk.org/_modules/nltk/stem/wordnet.html

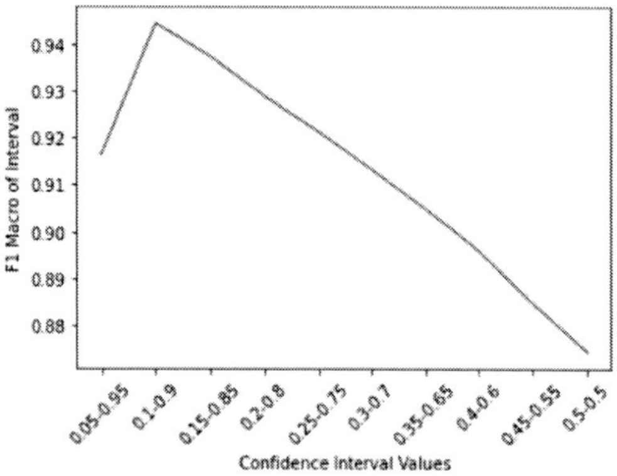

Figure 1: Subtask 2: Confidence Intervals and Their Respective Macro F1 Scores Calculated over Validation Set

Model	Validation	Test
LSTM	0.82	0.68
GRU	0.83	0.64
CNN-LexStem	0.85	0.71
RoBERTa	0.88	0.82
RoBERTa+RNN	0.89	0.83
RoBERTa+LexStem	0.88	0.84

Table 4: Subtask 2 - Ensemble Models F1 Macro Scores

highest Macro F1 score of 94% and after this, as confidence values go below 90% or above 10%, the F1 score consistently decreases. This means that as RoBERTa gets more unsure of its predictions, it is making more mistakes as expected. In order to prevent these errors, ensemble models are explored.

A weighted ensemble model is applied for any case in which RoBERTa is not confident. After trying several threshold values, 0.1 and 0.9 is chosen. Cases where RoBERTa's output are higher than 0.9 or lower than 0.1, are accepted as they are. For anything in between, an ensemble model is used. In order to find the right models to ensemble, a grid search is applied. RoBERTa is assumed to be the permanent model in this ensemble. Therefore, the search is performed over other models as either individual or in groups of two. The following models and weights return the highest performance for subtask 2:

- RoBERTa-RNN: 0.4 RoBERTa + 0.15 LSTM + 0.45 GRU
- RoBERTa-LexStem: 0.45 RoBERTa + 0.55 CNN-LexStem

The performance of these ensembles together with individual model performances are presented in Table 4. The ensemble model is only applied for subtask 2. As for subtask 1, we don't have any RNN model to ensemble or the CNN-LexStem did not provide any improvement on the validation set.

According to Table 4, both ensembles outperform RoBERTa both in the validation and test sets. This indicates that different types of neural networks have different powers, and in case when a model is not confident; using a weighted voting and combining these powers can be useful.

In conclusion, for subtask 1 RoBERTa is the top performing model based on the validation set and it is ranked the 3rd place in the public leaderboard. For subtask 2, our ensemble models receive the 3rd rank in the leaderboard.

3 Subtask 3: Event Sentence Coreference Identification

In event sentence coreference task, event containing sentences in a document are analyzed to see whether they refer to the same event or not. This task is slightly different than other ones as it does not only consist of a classification step, but also requires clustering afterwards. This two step procedure is known as the Mention-Pair model (Ng, 2010) in coreference resolution tasks. The first step includes a binary classification model to classify pairs of mentions and the second step uses these predictions to determine the coreference relations by clustering them (Ng, 2010). In this paper, we also use the two step approach, and first perform pairwise classification of sentences and then cluster them.

3.1 Two-Step Approach

For the classification part, similar to previous subtasks, base models of BERT, ALBERT and RoBERTa are fine-tuned. Additionally, an ensemble model which is a probabilistic average of these three models, is developed. In all these four binary classification models, instead of using the regular 0.5 boundary, 0.6 boundary is used to identify the positive labels, since 0.6 threshold returned better performance in our experiments.

For the clustering step, (Örs et al., 2020)'s clustering approach together with their proposed rescoring algorithm is used. Their rescoring algorithm calculates an updated score for a pair of sentences by using how sentences within the pair interact with other sentences in the document. For instance, the following pair of sentences, s_1 and s_2, has positive label predicted. If the predicted label between s_1 and s_3 is same as the prediction between s_2 and s_3, then a reward is given to s_1 and s_2 pair. But if the labels are different, then a penalty is applied. After the scores are updated, a greedy agglomerative algorithm is applied to construct the clusters (Örs et al., 2020). The same rescoring and clustering approach is used in this paper as well.

3.2 Experimental Setting

The main evaluation metric for this subtask is different than the other three. CoNLL metric, which is widely used on event/entity coreference tasks, is used in this task for the final system rankings. CoNLL is the average of MUC score (Vilain et al., 1995), B^3 score (Bagga and Baldwin, 1998) and $CEAF_e$ score (Luo, 2005).

The provided English dataset consists of 596 documents with their event containing sentences and gold clusters. This dataset is divided into training (80%) and validation (20%) sets. Unlike other tasks, this data split is performed more carefully to make sure that various types of clusters are observed in both training and validation sets. While creating these splits, two ratios are calculated and observed. The first one is the *single cluster ratio* which is calculated by dividing the number of documents with only one cluster to the total number of documents. The second one is referred to as *positive class ratio* which is calculated by dividing the number of sentence pairs with positive labels into total number of sentence pairs.

Having training and validation splits with very different *single cluster ratio* may affect the performance of clustering step. Similarly having a different *positive class ratio* may affect the classification performance. Hence, we tried different seeds for random splitting to find the splits which are similar to each other in terms of both of these ratios. The statistics of the constructed splits are presented in Table 5.

In addition to the provided training data, we also explore an external dataset from a similar shared task which was organized in 2020. AESPEN'20[8] shared task also focused on event sentence coreference identification and publicly shared a training data of 404 English news articles with their gold-

	Train	Validation
# Documents	476	120
# Sentences	2041	538
# Sentence Pairs	4918	1323
Positive Class Ratio	68%	69%
Single Clusters Ratio	61%	64%

Table 5: Statistics of the Training and Validation Sets

standard labels. We explore the effects of using this dataset as an extension to the existing one. In our experiments this year's provided dataset is referred to as *RAW*, and the extended version which contains data from both CASE and AESPEN is called *EXT*.

3.3 Experiments

Classification results of our models on validation set can be seen in Table 6. As expected, all models perform much better with the extended dataset. In general, BERT performs slightly better than the others. The Ensemble model cannot outperform BERT, but it is the second best, therefore we keep using it.

Model	RAW Data	EXT Data
BERT	86.98	92.42
ALBERT	85.74	91.57
RoBERTa	86.68	90.13
Ensemble	86.49	92.14

Table 6: Subtask 3: F1 Macro Scores of Classification Step over Validation Set

Errors of the classification step will unfortunately propagate to the next step, which is clustering. Since some of the pairwise sentences' labels are wrong, the constructed clusters will likely be wrong as well. In order to decrease the effect of this error propagation, we use the best two models from the classification step in this clustering part. The results of the BERT and the Ensemble models are summarized in Table 7.

Model	Data	Validation	Test
BERT	RAW	77.70	74.83
Ensemble	RAW	79.01	74.27
BERT	EXT	80.54	78.45
Ensemble	EXT	80.03	78.66

Table 7: Subtask 3: CONLL Scores after Clustering

As expected, models trained on the extended

[8] https://emw.ku.edu.tr/aespen-2020/

(larger) dataset return consistently higher scores. Between the BERT and the Ensemble model, there isn't a clear winner. However, in test set the highest score is retrieved with the Ensemble model which is ranked the 5th in the public leaderboard.

4 Subtask 4: Event Extraction

The goal of the final subtask is to identify the event triggers and its arguments from the sentence. The training dataset consists of 808 sentences which contain IOB type token-based labels of 7 different labels. Similar to previous tasks, 20% of this data is used for validation and the rest for training purposes.

In many sequence modeling tasks, the bidirectional transformer models outperform other machine learning architectures; therefore, BERT and RoBERTa are used as strong baselines in this task. As a further development, the transformer model is connected with a BiLSTM and a CRF layer as our second architecture. Connecting BiLSTM and CRF to a transformer has shown success in several Named Entity Recognition tasks (Jiang et al., 2019; Dai et al., 2019). The performance of these models over both validation and test sets are presented in Table 8.

Model Name	Validation	Test
BERT	0.70	0.69
RoBERTa	0.72	0.74
BERT-BiLSTM-CRF	0.76	0.75
RoBERTa-BiLSTM-CRF	0.76	0.76

Table 8: Subtask 4: F1 Macro Scores

According to Table 8, RoBERTa outperforms BERT in both validation and test sets. Combining these with BiLSTM-CRF improves both of them. The performance difference between test and validation sets also decreases with this addition.

Even though we achieved good performance, due to a minor format issue at our test submission file, our submissions were not correctly evaluated. Based on our scores at Table 8, with our best model RoBERTa-BiLSTM-CRF, we would have ranked second in the public leaderboard.

Analyzing the individual tag performances revealed that model is doing a better job at identifying the triggers compared to its arguments. This is expected as trigger tag is the second most popular tag at the data after the O tag. Trigger is closely followed by event time, which is easier to predict due to its smaller vocabulary variance and common language patterns, even though its lower presence in the training data.

In order to analyze the weak points of the models, the confusion table of the top performing RoBERTa-BiLSTM-CRF model over the validation data is shown in Figure 2. The confusion matrix specifically focuses on the event trigger and arguments tags.

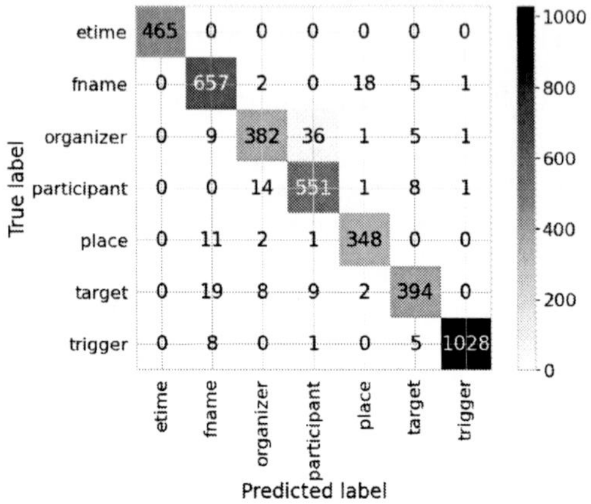

Figure 2: Confusion Table for Event Trigger and Arguments Tags

Based on Figure 2, the *etime* (event time) is the tag which has not been mistaken with any other event specific tags. On the other hand, the highest confusion is between the *organizer* and *participant* tags. That is followed by *place* and *fname* (facility name) which is expected due to use of similar wordings and context around.

5 Conclusion

In this paper, we mainly focus on English, and try to improve the current state-of-the-art on event specific NLP tasks. Source codes of all of our models are available online [9]. Additional details of our models, like hyper-parameters, are also summarized in the Github. As future work, we will focus on other languages and see whether the trends observed with English, exist in those other languages as well.

References

Amit Bagga and Breck Baldwin. 1998. Algorithms for scoring coreference chains. pages 563–566.

[9]https://github.com/furkan-celik/CASE21-SuNLP-Models

Yoshua Bengio, Réjean Ducharme, Pascal Vincent, and Christian Janvin. 2003. A neural probabilistic language model. *The journal of machine learning research*, 3:1137–1155.

Zhenjin Dai, Xutao Wang, Pin Ni, Yuming Li, Gangmin Li, and Xuming Bai. 2019. Named entity recognition using bert bilstm crf for chinese electronic health records. In *2019 12th international congress on image and signal processing, biomedical engineering and informatics (cisp-bmei)*, pages 1–5. IEEE.

Jacob Devlin, Ming-Wei Chang, Kenton Lee, and Kristina Toutanova. 2019. BERT: Pre-training of deep bidirectional transformers for language understanding. In *Proceedings of the 2019 Conference of the North American Chapter of the Association for Computational Linguistics: Human Language Technologies, Volume 1 (Long and Short Papers)*, pages 4171–4186, Minneapolis, Minnesota. Association for Computational Linguistics.

Ali Hürriyetoğlu, Osman Mutlu, Farhana Ferdousi Liza, Erdem Yörük, Ritesh Kumar, and Shyam Ratan. 2021. Multilingual protest news detection - shared task 1, case 2021. In *Proceedings of the 4th Workshop on Challenges and Applications of Automated Extraction of Socio-political Events from Text (CASE 2021)*, online. Association for Computational Linguistics (ACL).

Shaohua Jiang, Shan Zhao, Kai Hou, Yang Liu, Li Zhang, et al. 2019. A bert-bilstm-crf model for chinese electronic medical records named entity recognition. In *2019 12th International Conference on Intelligent Computation Technology and Automation (ICICTA)*, pages 166–169. IEEE.

Zhenzhong Lan, Mingda Chen, Sebastian Goodman, Kevin Gimpel, Piyush Sharma, and Radu Soricut. 2019. Albert: A lite bert for self-supervised learning of language representations. *arXiv preprint arXiv:1909.11942*.

Yinhan Liu, Myle Ott, Naman Goyal, Jingfei Du, Mandar Joshi, Danqi Chen, Omer Levy, Mike Lewis, Luke Zettlemoyer, and Veselin Stoyanov. 2019. Roberta: A robustly optimized bert pretraining approach.

Xiaoqiang Luo. 2005. On coreference resolution performance metrics. pages 6–8.

Tomas Mikolov, Kai Chen, Greg Corrado, and Jeffrey Dean. 2013. Efficient estimation of word representations in vector space. *arXiv preprint arXiv:1301.3781*.

Vincent Ng. 2010. Supervised noun phrase coreference research: The first fifteen years. In *Proceedings of the 48th annual meeting of the association for computational linguistics*, pages 1396–1411.

Faik Kerem Örs, Süveyda Yeniterzi, and Reyyan Yeniterzi. 2020. Event clustering within news articles. In *Proceedings of the Workshop on Automated Extraction of Socio-political Events from News 2020*, pages 63–68, Marseille, France. European Language Resources Association (ELRA).

Jeffrey Pennington, Richard Socher, and Christopher D Manning. 2014. Glove: Global vectors for word representation. In *Proceedings of the 2014 conference on empirical methods in natural language processing (EMNLP)*, pages 1532–1543.

Marc Vilain, John Burger, John Aberdeen, Dennis Connolly, and Lynette Hirschman. 1995. A model-theoretic coreference scoring scheme. pages 45–52.

IBM MNLP IE at CASE 2021 Task 1: Multigranular and Multilingual Event Detection on Protest News

Parul Awasthy, Jian Ni, Ken Barker, and Radu Florian
IBM Research AI
Yorktown Heights, NY 10598
{awasthyp, nij, kjbarker, raduf}@us.ibm.com

Abstract

In this paper, we present the event detection models and systems we have developed for Multilingual Protest News Detection - Shared Task 1 at CASE 2021. [1] The shared task has 4 subtasks which cover event detection at different granularity levels (from document level to token level) and across multiple languages (English, Hindi, Portuguese and Spanish). To handle data from multiple languages, we use a multilingual transformer-based language model (XLM-R) as the input text encoder. We apply a variety of techniques and build several transformer-based models that perform consistently well across all the subtasks and languages. Our systems achieve an average F_1 score of 81.2. Out of thirteen subtask-language tracks, our submissions rank 1st in nine and 2nd in four tracks.

1 Introduction

Event detection aims to detect and extract useful information about certain types of events from text. It is an important information extraction task that discovers and gathers knowledge about past and ongoing events hidden in huge amounts of textual data.

The CASE 2021 workshop (Hürriyetoğlu et al., 2021b) focuses on socio-political and crisis event detection. The workshop defines 3 shared tasks. In this paper we describe our models and systems developed for "Multilingual Protest News Detection - Shared Task 1" (Hürriyetoğlu et al., 2021a). Shared task 1 in turn has 4 subtasks:

- *Subtask 1 - Document Classification*: determine whether a news article (document) contains information about a past or ongoing event.
- *Subtask 2 - Sentence Classification*: determine whether a sentence expresses information about a past or ongoing event.
- *Subtask 3 - Event Sentence Coreference Identification*: determine which event sentences refer to the same event.
- *Subtask 4 - Event Extraction*: extract event triggers and the associated arguments from event sentences.

Event extraction on news has long been popular, and benchmarks such as ACE (Walker et al., 2006) and ERE (Song et al., 2015) annotate event triggers, arguments and coreference. Most previous work has addressed these tasks separately. Hürriyetoğlu et al. (2020) also focused on detecting social-political events, but CASE 2021 has added more subtasks and languages.

CASE 2021 addresses event information extraction at different granularity levels, from the coarsest-grained document level to the finest-grained token level. The workshop enables participants to build models for these subtasks and compare similar methods across the subtasks.

The task is multilingual, making it even more challenging. In a globally-connected era, information about events is available in many different languages, so it is important to develop models that can operate across the language barriers. The common languages for all CASE Task 1 subtasks are English, Spanish, and Portuguese. Hindi is an additional language for subtask 1. Some of these languages are zero-shot (Hindi), or low resource (Portuguese and Spanish) for certain subtasks.

In this paper, we describe our multilingual transformer-based models and systems for each of the subtasks. We describe the data for the subtasks in section 2. We use XLM-R (Conneau et al.,

[1] Distribution Statement "A" (Approved for Public Release, Distribution Unlimited)

Proceedings of the 4th Workshop on Challenges and Applications of Automated Extraction of Socio-political Events from Text (CASE), pages 138–146
August 5–6, 2021, ©2021 Association for Computational Linguistics

Task	Language	Train	Dev	Test
1	English (en)	8392	932	2971
	Spanish (es)	800	200	250
	Portuguese (pt)	1190	297	372
	Hindi (hi)	-	-	268
2	English (en)	20543	2282	1290
	Spanish (es)	2193	548	686
	Portuguese (pt)	946	236	1445
3	English (en)	476	120	100
	Spanish (es)	-	11	40
	Portuguese (pt)	-	21	40
4	English (en)	2565	681	311
	Spanish (es)	106	-	190
	Portuguese (pt)	87	-	192

Table 1: Number of examples in the train/dev/test sets. Subtasks 1 and 3 counts show number of documents, and subtasks 2 and 4 counts show number of sentences.

2020) as the input text encoder, described in section 3. For subtasks 1 (document classification) and 2 (sentence classification), we apply multilingual and monolingual text classifiers with different window sizes (Sections 4 and 5). For subtask 3 (event sentence coreference identification), we use a system with two modules: a classification module followed by a clustering module (section 6). For subtask 4 (event extraction), we apply a sequence labeling approach and build both multilingual and monolingual models (section 7). We present the final evaluation results in section 8. Our models have achieved consistently high performance scores across all the subtasks and languages.

2 Data

The data for this task has been created using the method described in Hürriyetoğlu et al. (2021). The task is multilingual but the data distribution across languages is not the same. In all subtasks there is significantly more data for English than for Portuguese and Spanish. There is no training data provided for Hindi.

As there are no official train and development splits, we have created our own splits. The details are summarized in Table 1. For most task-language pairs, we randomly select 80% or 90% of the provided data as the training data and keep the remaining as the development data. Since there is much less data for Spanish and Portuguese, for some subtasks, such as subtask 3, we use the Spanish and Portuguese data for development only; and for subtask 4, we use the entire Spanish and Portuguese data as training for the multilingual model.

For the final submissions, we use all the provided data, and train various types of models (multilingual, monolingual, weakly supervised, zero-shot) with details provided in the appropriate sections.

3 Multilingual Transformer-Based Framework

For all the subtasks we use transformer-based language models (Vaswani et al., 2017) as the input text encoder. Recent studies show that deep transformer-based language models, when pre-trained on a large text corpus, can achieve better generalization performance and attain state-of-the-art performance for many NLP tasks (Devlin et al., 2019; Liu et al., 2019; Conneau et al., 2020). One key success of transformer-based models is a multi-head self-attention mechanism that can model global dependencies between tokens in input and output sequences.

Due to the multilingual nature of this shared task, we have applied several multilingual transformer-based language models, including multilingual BERT (mBERT) (Devlin et al., 2019), XLM-RoBERTa (XLM-R) (Conneau et al., 2020), and multilingual BART (mBART) (Liu et al., 2020). Our preliminary experiments showed that XLM-R based models achieved better accuracy than other models. Hence we decided to use XLM-R as the text encoder. We use HuggingFace's pytorch implementation of transformers (Wolf et al., 2019).

XLM-R was pre-trained with unlabeled Wikipedia text and the CommonCrawl Corpus of 100 languages. It uses the SentencePiece tokenizer (Kudo and Richardson, 2018) with a vocabulary size of 250,000. Since XLM-R does not use any cross-lingual resources, it belongs to the unsupervised representation learning framework. For this work, we fine-tune the pre-trained XLM-R model on a specific task by training all layers of the model.

4 Subtask 1: Document Classification

To detect protest events at the document level, the problem can be formulated as a binary text classification problem where a document is assigned label "1" if it contains one or more protest event(s) and label "0" otherwise. Various models have been developed for text classification in general and also for this particular task (Hürriyetoğlu et al., 2019).

Model	en-dev	es-dev	pt-dev
XLM-R (en)	91.7	72.1	82.3
XLM-R (es)	85.4	71.9	83.9
XLM-R (pt)	85.5	75.2	84.8
XLM-R (en+es+pt)	90.0	75.2	88.3

Table 2: Macro F_1 score on the development sets for subtask 1 (document classification).

In our approach we apply multilingual transformer-based text classification models.

4.1 XLM-R Based Text Classification Models

In our architecture, the input sequence (document) is mapped to subword embeddings, and the embeddings are passed to multiple transformer layers. A special token is added to the beginning of the input sequence. This BOS token is <s> for XLM-R. The final hidden state of this token, $\mathbf{h}_\mathbf{s}$, is used as the summary representation of the whole sequence, which is passed to a softmax classification layer that returns a probability distribution over the possible labels:

$$\mathbf{p} = \text{softmax}(\mathbf{W}\mathbf{h}_s + \mathbf{b}) \quad (1)$$

XLM-R has $L = 24$ transformer layers, with hidden state vector size $H = 1024$, number of attention heads $A = 16$, and 550M parameters. We learn the model parameters using Adam (Kingma and Ba, 2015), with a learning rate of $2e$-5. We train the models for 5 epochs. Clock time was 90 minutes to train a model with training data from all the languages on a single NVIDIA V100 GPU.

The evaluation of subtask 1 is based on macro-F_1 scores of the developed models on the test data in 4 languages: English, Spanish, Portuguese, and Hindi. We are provided with training data in English, Spanish and Portuguese, but not in Hindi.

The sizes of the train/dev/test sets are shown in Table 1. Note that English has much more training data ($\sim$10k examples) than Spanish or Portuguese ($\sim$1k examples), while Hindi has no training data.

We build two types of XLM-R based text classification models:

- **multilingual model**: a model is trained with data from all three languages, denoted by XLM-R (en+es+pt);
- **monolingual models**: a separate model is trained with data from each of the three languages, denoted by XLM-R (en), XLM-R (es), and XLM-R (pt).

The results of various models on the development sets are shown in Table 2. We observe that:

- A monolingual XLM-R model trained with one language can achieve good zero-shot performance on other languages. For example, XLM-R (en), trained with English data only, achieves 72.1 and 82.3 F_1 score on Spanish and Portuguese development sets. This is consistent with our observations for other information extraction tasks such as relation extraction (Ni et al., 2020).
- Adding a small amount of training data from other languages, the multilingual model can further improve the performance for those languages. For example, with $\sim$1k additional training examples from Spanish and Portuguese, XLM-R (en+es+pt) improves the performance by 3.1 and 6.1 F_1 points on the Spanish and Portuguese development sets, compared with XLM-R (en).

4.2 Final Submissions

For English, Spanish and Portuguese, here are the three submissions we prepared for the evaluation:

S1: We trained five XLM-R based document classification models initialized with different random seeds using provided training data from all three languages (multilingual models). The final output for submission 1 is the majority vote of the outputs of the five multilingual models.

S2: For this submission we also trained five XLM-R based document classification models, but only using provided training data from the target language (monolingual models). The final output is the majority vote of the outputs of the five monolingual models.

S3: The final output of this submission is the majority vote of the outputs of the multilingual models built in (1) and the monolingual models built in (2).

For Hindi, there is no manually annotated training data provided. We used training data from English, Spanish and Portuguese, and augmented the

Model	en-dev	es-dev	pt-dev
XLM-R (en)	89.2	78.0	82.2
XLM-R (es)	84.4	86.4	80.1
XLM-R (pt)	83.2	82.2	85.1
XLM-R (en+es+pt)	89.4	86.2	85.6

Table 3: Macro F_1 score on the development sets for subtask 2 (sentence classification).

data with machine translated training data from English to Hindi ("weakly labeled" data). We trained nine XLM-R based Hindi document classification models with the weakly labeled data, and the final outputs are the majority votes of these models (S1/S2/S3 is the majority vote of 5/7/9 of the models, respectively).

5 Subtask 2: Sentence Classification

To detect protest events at the sentence level, one can also formulate the problem as a binary text classification problem where a sentence is assigned label "1" if it contains one or more protest event(s) and label "0" otherwise. As for document classification, we use XLM-R as the input text encoder. The difference is that for sentence classification, we set max_seq_length (a parameter of the model that specifies the maximum number of tokens in the input) to be 128; while for document classification where the input text is longer, we set max_seq_length to be 512 (for documents longer than 512 tokens, we truncate the documents and only keep the first 512 tokens). We train the models for 10 epochs, taking 80 minutes to train a model with training data from all the languages on a single NVIDIA V100 GPU.

For this subtask we are provided with training data in English, Spanish and Portuguese, and evaluation is on test data for all three languages. The sizes of the train/development/test sets are shown in Table 1.

As for document classification, we build two types of XLM-R based sentence classification models: a multilingual model and monolingual models. The results of these models on the development sets are shown in Table 3. The observations are similar to the document classification task. The multilingual model trained with data from all three languages achieves much better accuracy than a monolingual model on the development sets of other languages that the monolingual model is not trained on.

We prepared three submissions on the test data for each language (English, Spanish, Portuguese), similar to those described in section 4.2.

6 Subtask 3: Event Sentence Coreference Identification

Typically, for the task of event coreference resolution, events are defined by event triggers, and are usually marked in a sentence. Two event triggers are considered coreferent when they refer to the same event. In this task, however, the gold event triggers are not provided; the sentences are deemed coreferent, possibly, on the basis of any of the multiple triggers that occur in the sentences being coreferent, or if the sentences are about the same general event that is occurring. Given a document, this event coreference subtask aims to create clusters of coreferent sentences.

There is good variety in the research for coreference detection. Cattan et al. (2020) rely only on raw text without access to triggers or entity mentions to build coreference systems. Barhom et al. (2019) do joint entity and event extraction using a feature-based approach. Yu et al. (2020) use transformers to compute the event trigger and argument representation for the task.

Following the recent work on event coreference, our system is comprised of two parts: the classification module and the clustering module. The classification module uses a binary classifier to make pair-wise binary decisions on whether two sentences are coreferent. Once all sentence pairs have been classified as coreferent or not, the clustering module clusters the "closest" sentences with each other with agglomerative clustering, using a certain threshold, a common approach for coreference detection (Yang et al. (2015); Choubey and Huang (2017); Barhom et al. (2019)).

Agglomerative clustering is a popular technique for event or entity coreference resolution. At the beginning, all event mentions are assigned their own cluster. In each iteration, clusters are merged based on the average inter-cluster link similarity scores over all mentions in each cluster. The merging procedure stops when the average link similarity falls below a threshold.

Formally, given a document D with n sentences $\{s_1, s_2, ..., s_n\}$, our system follows the procedure outlined in Algorithm 1 while training. The input to the algorithm is a document, and the output is a list of clusters of coreferent event sentences.

Algorithm 1: Event Coreference Training

```
Input: D = {s_1, s_2, ..., s_n}, threshold t
Output: Clusters {c_1, c_2, ..., c_k}
Module Classify(D):
    for (s_i, s_j) ∈ D do
        Compute sim_{i,j}
        SIM ← SIM ∪ sim_{i,j}
    return SIM

Module Cluster(D, SIM, t):
    for (s_i) ∈ D do
        Assign s_i to cluster c_i
        Add c_i → C
    moreClusters = True
    while moreClusters do
        moreClusters = False
        for (c_i, c_j) ∈ C do
            score=0
            for (s_k) ∈ c_i do
                for (s_l) ∈ c_j do
                    score+=sim_{k,l}
            if score > t then
                Merge c_i and c_j
                Update C
                moreClusters = True
    return C
```

6.1 Experiments

The evaluation of the event coreference task is based on the CoNLL coref score (Pradhan et al., 2014), which is the unweighted average of the F-scores produced by the link-based MUC (Vilain et al., 1995), the mention-based B^3 (Bagga and Baldwin, 1998), and the entity-based CEAF$_e$ (Luo, 2005) metrics. As there is little Spanish and Portuguese data, we use it as a held out development set.

Our system uses XLM-R large pretrained model to obtain token and sentence representations. Pairs of sentences are concatenated to each other along with the special begin-of-sentence token and separator token as follows:

$$\text{BOS} < s_i > \text{SEP} < s_j >$$

We feed the BOS token representation to the binary classification layer to obtain a probabilistic score of the two sentences being coreferent. Once we have the score for all sentence pairs, we call the clustering module to create clusters using the coreference scores as clustering similarity scores.

We use XLM-R large pre-trained models. We trained our system for 20 epochs with learning rate of 1e-5. We experimented with various thresholds and chose 0.65 as that gave the best performance on development set. It takes about 1 hour for the model to train on a single V100 GPU.

Model	en-dev	es-dev	pt-dev
S1	83.4	93.3	80.4
S2	87.7	82.4	85.5
S3	88.8	81.7	91.7

Table 4: CoNLL F_1 score on the development sets for subtask 3: Event Coreference.

6.2 Final Submissions

For the final submission to the shared task we explore variations of the approach outlined in 6.1. They are:

S1: This is the multilingual model. To train this we translate the English training data to Spanish and Portuguese and train a model with original English, translated Spanish and translated Portuguese data. The original Spanish and Portuguese data is used as the development set for model selection.

S2: This is the English-only model, trained on English data. Spanish and Portuguese are zero-shot.

S3: This is an English-only coreference model where the event triggers and place and time arguments have been extracted using our subtask 4 models (section 7). These extracted tokens are then surrounded by markers of their type, such as <trigger>, <place>, etc. in the sentence. The binary classifier is fed the sentence representation.

The performance of these techniques on the development set is shown in table 4.

7 Subtask 4: Event Extraction

The event extraction subtask aims to extract event trigger words that pertain to demonstrations, protests, political rallies, group clashes or armed militancy, along with the participating arguments

Model	en-dev	es-dev	pt-dev
S1	80.57	-	-
S2	80.25	64.09	69.67
S3	80.87	-	-

Table 5: CoNLL F_1 score on the development sets for subtask 4: Event Extraction.

in such events. The arguments are to be extracted and classified as one of the following types: time, facility, organizer, participant, place or target of the event.

Formally the Event Extraction task can be summarized as follows: given a sentence $s = \{w_1, w_2, .., w_n\}$ and an event label set $T = \{t_1, t_2..., t_j\}$, identify contiguous phrases $(w_s, ..., w_e)$ such that $l(w_s, .., w_e) \in T$.

Most previous work (Chen et al. (2015); Nguyen et al. (2016); Nguyen and Grishman (2018)) for event extraction has treated event and argument extraction as separate tasks. But some systems (Li et al., 2013) treat the problem as structured prediction and train joint models for event triggers and arguments. Lin et al. (2020) built a joint system for many information extraction tasks including event trigger and arguments.

Following the work of M'hamdi et al. (2019); Awasthy et al. (2020), we treat event extraction as a sequence labeling task. Our models are based on the stdBERT baseline in Awasthy et al. (2020), though we extract triggers and arguments at the same time. We use the IOB2 encoding (Sang and Veenstra, 1999) to represent the triggers and the argument labels, where each token is labeled with its label and an indicator of whether it starts or continues a label, or is outside the label boundary by using *B-label, I-label* and *O* respesctively.

The sentence tokens are converted to token-level contextualized embeddings $\{h_1, h_2, .., h_n\}$. We pass these through a classification block that is comprised of a dense linear hidden layer followed by a dropout layer, followed by a linear layer mapped to the task label space that produces labels for each token $\{l_1, l_2, .., l_n\}$.

The parameters of the model are trained via cross entropy loss, a standard approach for transformer-based sequence labeling models (Devlin et al., 2019). This is equivalent to minimizing the negative log-likelihood of the true labels,

$$L_t = -\sum_{i=1}^{n} \log(P(l_{w_i})) \quad (2)$$

7.1 Experiments

The evaluation of the event extraction task is the CoNLL macro-F_1 score. Since there is little Spanish and Portuguese data, we use it either as train in our multilingual model or as a held out development set for our English-only model.

For contextualized word embeddings, we use the XLM-R large pretrained model. The dense layer output size is same as its input size. We use the out-of-the-box pre-trained transformer models, and fine-tune them with the event data, updating all layers with the standard XLM-R hyperparameters. We ran 20 epochs with 5 seeds each, learning rate of $3 \cdot 10^{-5}$ or $5 \cdot 10^{-5}$, and training batch sizes of 20. We choose the best model based on the performance on the development set. The system took 30 minutes to train on a V100 GPU.

7.2 Final Submission

For the final submission to the shared task we explore the following variations:

S1: This is the multilingual model trained with all of the English, Spanish and Portuguese training data. The development set is English only.

S2: This is the English-only model, trained on English data. Spanish and Portuguese are zero-shot.

S3: This is an ensemble system that votes among the outputs of 5 different systems. The voting criterion is the most frequent class. For example, if three of the five systems agree on a label then that label is chosen as the final label.

The results on development data are shown in table 5. There is no score for S1 and S3 for *es* and *pt* as all provided data was used to train the S1 model.

8 Final Results and Discussion

The final results of our submissions and rankings are shown in Table 6. Our systems achieved consistently high scores across all subtasks and languages.

To recap, our S1 systems are multilingual models trained on all three languages. S2 are monolingual

Task - Language	Our Scores			Best Competitor	Our
	S1	S2	S3	Score	Rank
1 (Document Classification) - English	83.60	83.87	83.93	**84.55**	2
1 (Document Classification) - Portuguese	82.77	**84.00**	83.88	82.43	1
1 (Document Classification) - Spanish	73.86	**77.27**	74.46	73.01	1
1 (Document Classification) - Hindi	78.17	77.76	78.53	**78.77**	2
2 (Sentence Classification) - English	84.17	84.56	83.22	**85.32**	2
2 (Sentence Classification) - Portuguese	88.08	84.87	**88.47**	87.00	1
2 (Sentence Classification) - Spanish	**88.61**	87.59	88.37	85.17	1
3 (Event Coreference) - English	79.17	**84.44**	77.63	81.20	1
3 (Event Coreference) - Portuguese	89.77	92.84	90.33	**93.03**	2
3 (Event Coreference) - Spanish	82.81	**84.23**	81.89	83.15	1
4 (Event Extraction) - English	75.95	77.27	**78.11**	73.53	1
4 (Event Extraction) - Portuguese	**73.24**	69.21	71.5	68.14	1
4 (Event Extraction) - Spanish	**66.20**	62.02	66.05	62.21	1

Table 6: Final evaluation results and rankings across the subtasks and languages. Scores for subtasks 1 and 2 are macro-average F_1; subtask 3 are CoNLL average F_1; subtask 4 are CoNLL macro-F_1. The ranks and best scores are shared by the organizers. Bold score denotes the best score for the track.

models: for subtasks 1 and 2 they are language-specific, but for subtasks 3 and 4 they are English-only. S3 is an ensemble system with voting for subtasks 1, 2 and 4, and an extra-feature system for subtask 3. Among our three systems, the multilingual models achieved the best scores in three tracks, the monolingual models achieved the best scores in six tracks, and the ensemble models achieved the best scores in four tracks.

For subtask 1 (document-level classification), the language-specific monolingual model (S2) performs better than the multilingual model (S1) for English, Portuguese and Spanish; while for subtask 2 (sentence-level classification), the multilingual model outperforms the language-specific monolingual model for Portuguese and Spanish. This shows that building multilingual models could be better than building language-specific monolingual models for finer-grained tasks.

The monolingual English-only model (S2) performs best on all three languages for subtask 3. This could be because the multilingual model (S1) here was trained with machine translated data. Adding the trigger, time and place markers (S3) did not help, even when these features showed promise on the development sets.

The multilingual model (S1) does better for Spanish and Portuguese on subtask 4. This is consistent with our findings in Moon et al. (2019) where training multilingual models for Named Entity Recognition, also a token-level sequence labelling task, helps improve performance across languages. As there is much less training data for Spanish and Portuguese, pooling all languages helps.

9 Conclusion

In this paper, we presented the models and systems we developed for Multilingual Protest News Detection - Shared Task 1 at CASE 2021. We explored monolingual, multilingual, zero-shot and ensemble approaches and showed the results across the subtasks and languages chosen for this shared task. Our systems achieved an average F_1 score of 81.2, which is 2 F_1 points higher than best score of other participants on the shared task. Our submissions ranked 1st in nine of the thirteen tracks, and ranked 2nd in the remaining four tracks.

Acknowledgments and Disclaimer

This research was developed with funding from the Defense Advanced Research Projects Agency (DARPA) under Contract No. FA8750-19-C-0206. The views, opinions and/or findings expressed are those of the author and should not be interpreted as representing the official views or policies of the Department of Defense or the U.S. Government.

References

Parul Awasthy, Tahira Naseem, Jian Ni, Taesun Moon, and Radu Florian. 2020. Event presence prediction helps trigger detection across languages. *CoRR*, abs/2009.07188.

Amit Bagga and Breck Baldwin. 1998. Algorithms for scoring coreference chains. In *In The First International Conference on Language Resources and Evaluation Workshop on Linguistics Coreference*, pages 563–566.

Shany Barhom, Vered Shwartz, Alon Eirew, Michael Bugert, Nils Reimers, and Ido Dagan. 2019. Revisiting joint modeling of cross-document entity and event coreference resolution. In *Proceedings of the 57th Annual Meeting of the Association for Computational Linguistics*, pages 4179–4189, Florence, Italy. Association for Computational Linguistics.

Arie Cattan, Alon Eirew, Gabriel Stanovsky, Mandar Joshi, and Ido Dagan. 2020. Streamlining cross-document coreference resolution: Evaluation and modeling.

Yubo Chen, Liheng Xu, Kang Liu, Daojian Zeng, and Jun Zhao. 2015. Event extraction via dynamic multi-pooling convolutional neural networks. In *Proceedings of the 53rd Annual Meeting of the Association for Computational Linguistics and the 7th International Joint Conference on Natural Language Processing (Volume 1: Long Papers)*, pages 167–176, Beijing, China. Association for Computational Linguistics.

Prafulla Kumar Choubey and Ruihong Huang. 2017. Event coreference resolution by iteratively unfolding inter-dependencies among events. In *Proceedings of the 2017 Conference on Empirical Methods in Natural Language Processing*, pages 2124–2133, Copenhagen, Denmark. Association for Computational Linguistics.

Alexis Conneau, Kartikay Khandelwal, Naman Goyal, Vishrav Chaudhary, Guillaume Wenzek, Francisco Guzmán, Edouard Grave, Myle Ott, Luke Zettlemoyer, and Veselin Stoyanov. 2020. Unsupervised cross-lingual representation learning at scale. In *Proceedings of the 58th Annual Meeting of the Association for Computational Linguistics*, pages 8440–8451, Online. Association for Computational Linguistics.

Jacob Devlin, Ming-Wei Chang, Kenton Lee, and Kristina Toutanova. 2019. BERT: Pre-training of deep bidirectional transformers for language understanding. In *Proceedings of the 2019 Conference of the North American Chapter of the Association for Computational Linguistics: Human Language Technologies, Volume 1 (Long and Short Papers)*, pages 4171–4186, Minneapolis, Minnesota. Association for Computational Linguistics.

Ali Hürriyetoğlu, Osman Mutlu, Farhana Ferdousi Liza, Erdem Yörük, Ritesh Kumar, and Shyam Ratan. 2021a. Multilingual protest news detection - shared task 1, CASE 2021. In *Proceedings of the 4th Workshop on Challenges and Applications of Automated Extraction of Socio-political Events from Text (CASE 2021)*, online. Association for Computational Linguistics (ACL).

Ali Hürriyetoğlu, Hristo Tanev, Vanni Zavarella, Jakub Piskorski, Reyyan Yeniterzi, and Erdem Yörük. 2021b. Challenges and applications of automated extraction of socio-political events from text (CASE 2021): Workshop and shared task report. In *Proceedings of the 4th Workshop on Challenges and Applications of Automated Extraction of Socio-political Events from Text (CASE 2021)*, online. Association for Computational Linguistics (ACL).

Ali Hürriyetoğlu, Erdem Yörük, Deniz Yüret, Çağrı Yoltar, Burak Gürel, Fırat Duruşan, Osman Mutlu, and Arda Akdemir. 2019. Overview of clef 2019 lab protestnews: Extracting protests from news in a cross-context setting. In *Experimental IR Meets Multilinguality, Multimodality, and Interaction*, pages 425–432, Cham. Springer International Publishing.

Ali Hürriyetoğlu, Vanni Zavarella, Hristo Tanev, Erdem Yörük, Ali Safaya, and Osman Mutlu. 2020. Automated extraction of socio-political events from news (AESPEN): Workshop and shared task report. In *Proceedings of the Workshop on Automated Extraction of Socio-political Events from News 2020*, pages 1–6, Marseille, France. European Language Resources Association (ELRA).

Ali Hürriyetoğlu, Erdem Yörük, Osman Mutlu, Fırat Duruşan, Çağrı Yoltar, Deniz Yüret, and Burak Gürel. 2021. Cross-Context News Corpus for Protest Event-Related Knowledge Base Construction. *Data Intelligence*, pages 1–28.

Diederik P. Kingma and Jimmy Ba. 2015. Adam: A method for stochastic optimization. In *Proceedings of the 3rd International Conference on Learning Representations (ICLR)*, ICLR '15.

Taku Kudo and John Richardson. 2018. SentencePiece: A simple and language independent subword tokenizer and detokenizer for neural text processing. In *Proceedings of the 2018 Conference on Empirical Methods in Natural Language Processing: System Demonstrations*, pages 66–71, Brussels, Belgium. Association for Computational Linguistics.

Qi Li, Heng Ji, and Liang Huang. 2013. Joint event extraction via structured prediction with global features. In *Proceedings of the 51st Annual Meeting of the Association for Computational Linguistics (Volume 1: Long Papers)*, pages 73–82.

Ying Lin, Heng Ji, F Huang, and L Wu. 2020. A joint neural model for information extraction with global features. In *Proc. The 58th Annual Meeting of the Association for Computational Linguistics (ACL2020)*.

Yinhan Liu, Jiatao Gu, Naman Goyal, Xian Li, Sergey Edunov, Marjan Ghazvininejad, Mike Lewis, and Luke Zettlemoyer. 2020. Multilingual denoising pre-training for neural machine translation. *CoRR*, abs/2001.08210.

Yinhan Liu, Myle Ott, Naman Goyal, Jingfei Du, Mandar Joshi, Danqi Chen, Omer Levy, Mike Lewis, Luke Zettlemoyer, and Veselin Stoyanov. 2019. Roberta: A robustly optimized BERT pretraining approach. *CoRR*, abs/1907.11692.

Xiaoqiang Luo. 2005. On coreference resolution performance metrics. In *Proceedings of Human Language Technology Conference and Conference on Empirical Methods in Natural Language Processing*, pages 25–32, Vancouver, British Columbia, Canada. Association for Computational Linguistics.

Meryem M'hamdi, Marjorie Freedman, and Jonathan May. 2019. Contextualized cross-lingual event trigger extraction with minimal resources. In *Proceedings of the 23rd Conference on Computational Natural Language Learning (CoNLL)*, pages 656–665, Hong Kong, China. Association for Computational Linguistics.

Taesun Moon, Parul Awasthy, Jian Ni, and Radu Florian. 2019. Towards lingua franca named entity recognition with BERT. *CoRR*, abs/1912.01389.

Thien Huu Nguyen, Kyunghyun Cho, and Ralph Grishman. 2016. Joint event extraction via recurrent neural networks. In *Proceedings of the 2016 Conference of the North American Chapter of the Association for Computational Linguistics: Human Language Technologies*, pages 300–309.

Thien Huu Nguyen and Ralph Grishman. 2018. Graph convolutional networks with argument-aware pooling for event detection. In *Thirty-second AAAI conference on artificial intelligence*.

Jian Ni, Taesun Moon, Parul Awasthy, and Radu Florian. 2020. Cross-lingual relation extraction with transformers. *CoRR*, abs/2010.08652.

Sameer Pradhan, Xiaoqiang Luo, Marta Recasens, Eduard Hovy, Vincent Ng, and Michael Strube. 2014. Scoring coreference partitions of predicted mentions: A reference implementation. In *Proceedings of the 52nd Annual Meeting of the Association for Computational Linguistics (Volume 2: Short Papers)*, pages 30–35, Baltimore, Maryland. Association for Computational Linguistics.

Erik F. Tjong Kim Sang and Jorn Veenstra. 1999. Representing text chunks. In *Proceedings of the Ninth Conference on European Chapter of the Association for Computational Linguistics*, EACL '99, page 173–179, USA. Association for Computational Linguistics.

Zhiyi Song, Ann Bies, Stephanie Strassel, Tom Riese, Justin Mott, Joe Ellis, Jonathan Wright, Seth Kulick, Neville Ryant, and Xiaoyi Ma. 2015. From light to rich ERE: Annotation of entities, relations, and events. In *Proceedings of the The 3rd Workshop on EVENTS: Definition, Detection, Coreference, and Representation*, pages 89–98, Denver, Colorado. Association for Computational Linguistics.

Ashish Vaswani, Noam Shazeer, Niki Parmar, Jakob Uszkoreit, Llion Jones, Aidan N. Gomez, Lukasz Kaiser, and Illia Polosukhin. 2017. Attention is all you need. In *NIPS*, pages 6000–6010.

Marc Vilain, John Burger, John Aberdeen, Dennis Connolly, and Lynette Hirschman. 1995. A model-theoretic coreference scoring scheme. In *Proceedings of the 6th Conference on Message Understanding*, MUC6 '95, page 45–52, USA. Association for Computational Linguistics.

Christopher Walker, Stephanie Strassel, Julie Medero, and Kazuaki Maeda. 2006. Ace 2005 multilingual training corpus. *Linguistic Data Consortium, Philadelphia*, 57.

Thomas Wolf, Lysandre Debut, Victor Sanh, Julien Chaumond, Clement Delangue, Anthony Moi, Pierric Cistac, Tim Rault, Rémi Louf, Morgan Funtowicz, and Jamie Brew. 2019. Huggingface's transformers: State-of-the-art natural language processing. *ArXiv*, abs/1910.03771.

Bishan Yang, Claire Cardie, and Peter Frazier. 2015. A Hierarchical Distance-dependent Bayesian Model for Event Coreference Resolution. *Transactions of the Association for Computational Linguistics*, 3:517–528.

Xiaodong Yu, Wenpeng Yin, and Dan Roth. 2020. Paired representation learning for event and entity coreference.

ALEM at CASE 2021 Task 1: Multilingual Text Classification on News Articles

Alaeddin Selçuk Gürel
selcuk.gurel@bilgiedu.net

Emre Emin
emreemin@sabanciuniv.edu

Abstract

We participated CASE shared task in ACL-IJCNLP 2021. This paper is a summary of our experiments and ideas about this shared task. For each subtask we shared our approach, successful and failed methods and our thoughts about them. We submit our results once for every subtask, except for subtask3, in task submission system and present scores based on our validation set formed from given training samples in this paper. Techniques and models we mentioned includes BERT, Multilingual BERT, oversampling, undersampling, data augmentation and their implications with each other. Most of the experiments we came up with were not completed, as time did not permit, but we share them here as we plan to do them as suggested in the future work part of document.

1 Introduction

This paper includes review and explanations about our ideas and experiments for the CASE shared task in ACL-IJCNLP 2021. The main purpose and goal for this shared task is to identify and classify sociopolitical and crisis event information at multiple levels and languages.

Main categories for subtasks are document classification (subtask1), sentence classification (subtask2), event sentence coreference identification (subtask3) and event extraction (subtask4). Each subtask has three batches of training data which are in English, Spanish and Portuguese (Hürriyetoğlu et al., 2020, 2019a,b).

Document classification and sentence classification tasks are binary classification tasks which aim to classify news articles and sentences respectively. The classification criteria of the document classification task is whether news article contains at least one past or ongoing event. Sentence classification is also a binary classification task, sentences are labeled as 1 if they contain event triggers within them. Event sentence coreference identification task aims to identify which event sentences are referring the same event. The objective of the event extraction task is to gather event trigger information and event information from given news article.

We participated in subtask1, subtask2 and subtask4. The training data for subtask3 was not sufficient for us to build and optimize the model for the given time schedule, since it was not possible to get exact results for test data. Our results are based on validation data that we constructed from given training data.

We propose a multilingual BERT Model (Devlin et al., 2018) for the shared task 1 (Hürriyetoğlu et al., 2021a,b). We trained and measured the performance of our model which is fine-tuned in English, Spanish and Portuguese. The model is formed by using and modifying multiple pretrained BERT models for each subtask and language we participated for [1].

2 Data

2.1 Training Data

Training data includes three languages for each subtask, English, Spanish and Portuguese. The data distributions are given below for each level. For both document classification and sentence classification tasks, training data was shared in JSON Lines text format. In this data, each document/sentence has an ID, text and label. The data of event extraction task was shared in similar format to CoNLL format. In token level data, documents are starting with SAMPLE_START token, document and sentences are separated by empty lines and [SEP] token respectively.

[1] Code that we used for this shared task submission can be found at https://github.com/alaeddingurel/ALEM-CASE2021

Proceedings of the 4th Workshop on Challenges and Applications of Automated Extraction of Socio-political Events from Text (CASE), pages 147–151
August 5–6, 2021, ©2021 Association for Computational Linguistics

Language	0	1	Total
English	7412	1912	9324
Spanish	802	198	1000
Portuguese	1184	303	1487

Table 1: Label distribution of training data in document level

The total number of documents, sentences and tokens provided for the English Language was much larger than other source languages.

Language	0	1	Total
English	18602	4223	22825
Spanish	2232	509	2741
Portuguese	961	221	1182

Table 2: Label distribution of training data in sentence level

There are seven different categories in event extraction dataset which are etime (Event time), fname (Facility name), organizer, participant, place, target and trigger.

3 Methodology

We used Huggingface's transformers (Wolf et al., 2020) library in order to fine-tune our BERT model for each subtask. We fine-tuned separate BERT models, each model pre-trained using a corpus in their respective language. The training data provided was quite unbalanced for every language in terms of both sample size and label distribution. We have tried over and under sampling techniques using imbalanced-learn package (Lemaître et al., 2017) to form a better training split. Both of the methods for our case affected the results in a negligible amount. So we decided to use naive random sampling for our experiments.

One other obstacle we worked on is BERT's maximum token size for its inputs. Tokenized input given to BERT is trimmed if it includes more than 512 tokens. This is a huge data loss for our subtasks, especially for document level classification. Many documents are trimmed by default configuration, so we tried a populating method to avoid losing any data with cost of extra labelling process. The idea is to split the data to be trimmed into chunks less than 512 tokens and label each one as it was labeled before splitting. This may cause a incorrect labeling process since the document is now cut into texts and each one of them may be against its parent label by its own in the training process. As a practical example of this method, let's say we have a text $Z = X_0 \cdot X_1 \cdot ... \cdot X_n$, where each X_i are strings that form Z when concatenated. Tokenized length of Z is greater than 512 and it is labeled as 0 in training set. We split Z into X_is to obtain less than 512 tokens for each part and set the labels of each X_i as 0. This blind labelling process may cause incorrectly assigned labels for some X_is, since label 1 may be more suitable for their individual meanings. However we did not observe a significant change on the results for any of the languages. Considering this method did not improve the results, we did not use it for our final tests.

We also used this method in the prediction phase. The texts were splitted similarly as in the given example. The final prediction was decided by majority of votes method e.g. if 3 texts are labeled as 1,1,0, then their parent prediction is 1 as it has higher vote.

- English - BERT
- Spanish - BETO (Cañete et al., 2020)
- Portuguese - BERTimbau Base (Souza et al., 2020)

For the multilingual BERT experiments we have used the pretrained mBERT model in order to fine-tune our data for subtasks. We used BERT tokenizer which is based on WordPiece tokenization algorithm. We splitted training data with the purpose of forming a test set before submitting the final results to shared task system. The split for train and test data distributed 80% to 20% respectively. The method we use concatenates all English, Spanish and Portuguese data and train them altogether. The split is deterministic and stayed same for all of our experiments for all models in order to obtain results for the same test data.

4 Experiments

The scores we demonstrate on the document classification and sentence classification are based on f1-macro metric. The evaluation criteria that we used in event extraction for validation data is f1 score. We experimented with various epoch numbers and batch sizes with the intent of optimizing the hyper-parameters. We made our decisions to use these epoch numbers and batch sizes based on

Language	etime	fname	organizer	participant	place	target	trigger
English	1209	1201	1261	2663	1570	1470	4595
Spanish	40	49	25	88	15	64	157
Portuguese	41	48	19	73	61	32	122

Table 3: Label distribution of training data in token level

our experimental setup. The epoch and batch parameters given to training phase for BERT Base for document classification task with epoch as 5 and batch as 32, sentence classification task with epoch as 3 and batch as 64. For Multilingual BERT we fine-tuned parameters as 3 epochs and 32 batches for document classification task and 5 epochs and 32 batches for sentence classification task.

Language	mBERT	BERT
English	84.17%	**84.26%**
Spanish	**76.32%**	73.82%
Portuguese	79.78%	**80.20%**

Table 4: Results for document level

English BERT gives better results in comparison with multilingual BERT model by 0.09%. In our experiments we observed that multilingual BERT model has superior results for Spanish Language by 2.5% when compared to Spanish BERT model used in terms of our measurement criteria. Portuguese BERT has a higher f1-macro score by 0.42% when we compare it with its counterpart, multilingual BERT. There is no significant gap between the f1-macro scores of multilingual BERT and BERT Base models which are pretrained with their respective languages.

Language	mBERT	BERT
English	84.70%	**87.68%**
Spanish	76.53%	**83.95%**
Portuguese	82.01%	**82.72%**

Table 5: Results for sentence level

BERT models pretrained with respective languages has greatest scores with comparison with multilingual BERT for all languages in sentence classification task.

Token	**f1-Score**
etime	77.95
fname	54.65
organizer	65.89
participant	75.40
place	83.86
target	55.10
trigger	84.32

Table 6: Results for token level

There isn't enough data points for Spanish and Portuguese languages for training and evaluation of event extraction task. We think that we need different approaches in order to train and evaluate this data for further testing, but we share the evaluation performance results for English language since it has enough data points to form an acceptable model when compared to the other languages. We made our document, sentence and event extraction submissions based on BERT base models which are trained with their respective languages for each . We used f1-score metric with the purpose of analysing event extraction performance for each token category.

5 Conclusion and Future Work

This paper describes our system description for submission for CASE @ ACL-IJCNLP 2021: Socio-Political and Crisis Events Detection shared task. In training phase, we performed our experiments using separate pretrained language models with different training data. We report their performance for 3 tasks with the addition of the results for multilingual BERT model. We also compared our models with the other BERT models which are trained with their respective language data. We tested our fine-tuned language models with the test data provided by shared task organizers and made our submissions for document classification and sentence classification tasks. We achieved 80.82, 72.98 and 46.47 f1-macro scores in document classification. f1-macro scores of the sentence classification task are 79.67, 42.79 and 45.30 for English, Portuguese and Spanish respectively. We didn't make submission for token classification task due time limitations, but shared the results we observed in tests on our validation set.

One of the important issues with BERT is to optimize the training data in order to align with its maximum token size while training. In some tasks, especially in document level classification, this is a significant factor for pre-processing, since the length of the input texts are too long for being tokenized to fit BERT as whole. This situation leads to an experiment devoted for managing this limitation.

Following our experiments in over- and under-sampling methods, we would like to use data augmentation for future training methods in order to achieve an equilibrium in terms of training data labels. Augmenting method may be text generation from already given documents and sentences, but we do not expect this method being successful for languages other than English since our sample data is not as much for the other languages.

One another method we considered applying for future experiments was ensemble learning. The idea is training different models for the same task and observe their differentiated scores and group them by their success on predicting particular inputs. This method has a cost of training many models and measuring their prediction success with respect to the others, however after forming an optimal set of models, we can use them to unite on a cumulative score on a single input by assigning a weight for each of their individual output. This idea of combining many models can be also used for BERT initiated environment by constructing a system where the structure is built on top of BERT and inserting custom networks into its embedding layers.

There are many improvements and analysis to be done in order to understand strengths and weaknesses of this system and further improvements might be added on top of it.

References

José Cañete, Gabriel Chaperon, Rodrigo Fuentes, Jou-Hui Ho, Hojin Kang, and Jorge Pérez. 2020. Spanish pre-trained bert model and evaluation data. In *PML4DC at ICLR 2020*.

Jacob Devlin, Ming-Wei Chang, Kenton Lee, and Kristina Toutanova. 2018. BERT: pre-training of deep bidirectional transformers for language understanding. *CoRR*, abs/1810.04805.

Ali Hürriyetoğlu, Osman Mutlu, Farhana Ferdousi Liza, Erdem Yörük, Ritesh Kumar, and Shyam Ratan. 2021a. Multilingual protest news detection - shared task 1, case 2021. In *Proceedings of the 4th Workshop on Challenges and Applications of Automated Extraction of Socio-political Events from Text (CASE 2021)*, online. Association for Computational Linguistics (ACL).

Ali Hürriyetoğlu, Hristo Tanev, Vanni Zavarella, Jakub Piskorski, Reyyan Yeniterzi, and Erdem Yörük. 2021b. Challenges and applications of automated extraction of socio-political events from text (case 2021): Workshop and shared task report. In *Proceedings of the 4th Workshop on Challenges and Applications of Automated Extraction of Socio-political Events from Text (CASE 2021)*, online. Association for Computational Linguistics (ACL).

Ali Hürriyetoğlu, Erdem Yörük, Deniz Yüret, Osman Mutlu, Çağrı Yoltar, Fırat Duruşan, and Burak Gürel. 2020. Cross-context news corpus for protest events related knowledge base construction. In *Automated Knowledge Base Construction*.

Ali Hürriyetoğlu, Erdem Yörük, Deniz Yüret, Çağrı Yoltar, Burak Gürel, Fırat Duruşan, and Osman Mutlu. 2019a. A task set proposal for automatic protest information collection across multiple countries. In *Advances in Information Retrieval*, pages 316–323, Cham. Springer International Publishing.

Ali Hürriyetoğlu, Erdem Yörük, Deniz Yüret, Çağrı Yoltar, Burak Gürel, Fırat Duruşan, Osman Mutlu, and Arda Akdemir. 2019b. Overview of clef 2019 lab protestnews: Extracting protests from news in a cross-context setting. In *Experimental IR Meets Multilinguality, Multimodality, and Interaction*, pages 425–432, Cham. Springer International Publishing.

Guillaume Lemaître, Fernando Nogueira, and Christos K. Aridas. 2017. Imbalanced-learn: A python toolbox to tackle the curse of imbalanced datasets in machine learning. *Journal of Machine Learning Research*, 18(17):1–5.

Fábio Souza, Rodrigo Nogueira, and Roberto Lotufo. 2020. BERTimbau: pretrained BERT models for Brazilian Portuguese. In *9th Brazilian Conference on Intelligent Systems, BRACIS, Rio Grande do Sul, Brazil, October 20-23 (to appear)*.

Thomas Wolf, Lysandre Debut, Victor Sanh, Julien Chaumond, Clement Delangue, Anthony Moi, Pierric Cistac, Tim Rault, Rémi Louf, Morgan Funtowicz, Joe Davison, Sam Shleifer, Patrick von Platen, Clara Ma, Yacine Jernite, Julien Plu, Canwen Xu, Teven Le Scao, Sylvain Gugger, Mariama Drame, Quentin Lhoest, and Alexander M. Rush. 2020. Transformers: State-of-the-art natural language processing. In *Proceedings of the 2020 Conference on*

Empirical Methods in Natural Language Processing: System Demonstrations, pages 38–45, Online. Association for Computational Linguistics.

Team "NoConflict" at CASE 2021 Task 1: Pretraining for Sentence-Level Protest Event Detection

Tiancheng Hu **Niklas Stoehr**
ETH Zurich, Switzerland
tianhu@student.ethz.ch niklas.stoehr@inf.ethz.ch

Abstract

An ever-increasing amount of text, in the form of social media posts and news articles, gives rise to new challenges and opportunities for the automatic extraction of socio-political events. In this paper, we present our submission[1] to the Shared Tasks on Socio-Political and Crisis Events Detection, Task 1, Multilingual Protest News Detection, Subtask 2, Event Sentence Classification, of CASE @ ACL-IJCNLP 2021. In our submission, we utilize the RoBERTa model with additional pretraining, and achieve the best F1 score of 0.8532 in event sentence classification in English and the second-best F1 score of 0.8700 in Portuguese via simple translation. We analyze the failure cases of our model. We also conduct an ablation study to show the effect of choosing the right pretrained language model, adding additional training data and data augmentation.

1 Introduction

With the growing volume of online news from both traditional news media and social media, large amounts of texts are being created every day. These text data contain information about events happening around the world. For social science and policy making, the event information in these texts can be extremely valuable. Due to the sheer volume of data available, there is a strong demand for tools to automatically extract and analyze socio-political events. Automatic event extraction enables governments, non-governmental organizations and society as a whole to take more timely, proportional and appropriate actions in changing circumstances.

Event sentence classification is an important step in the event extraction pipeline (Hürriyetoğlu et al., 2019a). In this work, we present our submission to the CASE 2021 Shared Task, hosted jointly with the workshop on Challenges and Applications of Automated Extraction of Socio-political Events from Text (CASE) @ ACL-IJCNLP 2021 (Hürriyetoğlu et al., 2021). The shared task consists of two main tasks: Multilingual Protest News Detection and Fine-Grained Classification of Socio-Political Events. In the first shared task, there are four subtasks: event document classification, event sentence classification, event sentence coreference resolution and event extraction. In this paper, we focus on Task 1, Subtask 2, namely event sentence classification. For a detailed description of the shared task, please refer to Hürriyetoğlu et al. (2021). Prior iterations of the workshop can be found in Hürriyetoğlu et al. (2019b, 2020).

Within this subtask, we further narrow down our scope by focusing on the English event descriptions only. We train a classifier to solve the binary classification problem to identify whether a sentence contains a protest event, as defined in Hürriyetoğlu et al. (2021). Given the huge success of pretrained language models such as BERT (Devlin et al., 2019), RoBERTa (Liu et al., 2019), XLNet (Yang et al., 2019) and ELECTRA (Clark et al., 2020), we adopt RoBERTa as the backbone of our model. Inspired by the good result achieved through additional pretraining (Gururangan et al., 2020), we harness the POLUSA dataset (Gebhard and Hamborg, 2020) of political news articles to second-pretrain our model with a masked language modeling (MLM) objective. Further, we conduct a series of ablation studies to justify our design choices. We first run experiments to choose a suitable base model. Then, we conduct experiments on using additional training data from other subtasks. Given the limited amount of training data available, we experiment with data augmentation techniques, including back translation, embedding augmentation, and checklist augmentation (Ribeiro et al., 2020). The rest of this paper is organized

[1] Code available at https://github.com/pitehu/CASE_2021

Proceedings of the 4th Workshop on Challenges and Applications of Automated Extraction of Socio-political Events from Text (CASE), pages 152–160
August 5–6, 2021, ©2021 Association for Computational Linguistics

as follows: Section 2 describes the dataset of the subtask. Section 3 discusses the method of our best-performing submission. Section 4 presents quantitative results achieved by our model as well as a failure case analysis. In Section 5, we present additional experiments as part of an ablation study. In Section 6, we discuss observations of the dataset and models trained on this dataset from the perspective of named entities before concluding the paper in Section 7.

2 Dataset

We are provided with a dataset of labeled sentences which was introduced in Hürriyetoğlu et al. (2021). Each sentence has a binary label indicating if the sentence contains a protest event. While the dataset comprises sentences in English, Spanish and Portuguese, we solely focus on English sentences. The English version of this dataset contains 22,825 sentences, out of which 18,602 (81.50%) have label 0 and 4223 (18.50%) have label 1. Since no official train-validation split is provided, we divide the dataset into a training set (80%) and a validation set (20%).

3 Proposed Method

We utilize the RoBERTa base model (Liu et al., 2019) as the backbone of our model. Throughout this work, we refer to the pretrained RoBERTa model (Liu et al., 2019) as "RoBERTa default". We use the term language model to refer to *Transformer*-based (Vaswani et al., 2017) cloze language models.

Second Pretraining We start by conducting an additional round of pretraining of RoBERTa, initialized with the already pretrained weight, following Gururangan et al. (2020). To this end, we pretrain on the POLUSA dataset (Gebhard and Hamborg, 2020) in an MLM setting with a masking probability of 0.15. We denote this pretraining step as *Second Pretraining*. Intuitively, language models are usually trained on large and diverse datasets of different domains. Thus, their language modeling capacity may not be optimal in specific domains such as protest event classification.

POLUSA Dataset The POLUSA dataset (Gebhard and Hamborg, 2020) is a dataset containing political news covering policy topics published between January 2017 and August 2019. It contains about 0.9M news articles from 18 outlets representing the political spectrum.

Finetuning Once the *second pretraining* is completed, we feed the [CLS] embedding of the last hidden layer to a fully-connected layer, which serves as the classification head. The [CLS] embedding encodes information of the whole sentence.

4 Results

We conduct *second pretraining* for only 42,000 steps, with a batch size of 16 and a maximum sequence length of 256, due to time and resource constraints. For the downstream task, we train for 25 epochs and take the best epoch based on validation F1 score.

4.1 Quantitative Results

Second Pretraining In this section, we discuss the effect of the *second pretraining*. We take a checkpoint every 4000 steps and finetune for the event sentence classification task, and report the best F1 score and the MLM loss during the pretraining in Figure 1. Additionally, we manually select 10 representative sentences from the Subtask 2 dataset and measure the average change of their representations in embedding space during *second pretraining*. To this end, we compute the Euclidean distance between the embedding of a sentence yield by the RoBERTa default model and by our model during *second pretraining* at every checkpoint.

Finetuning Our model with the *second pretraining* strategy achieves a 0.8395 F1 score on the validation set of this subtask. On the evaluation server, we achieve the best performance among all submissions of the shared task with an F1 score of 0.8532 on the testing set. Since our focus is on the English version of the event sentence classification task, we translate the event sentences of other languages into English using Argos Translate (Finlay, 2021). This simple method achieves the second best F1 score of 0.8670 in Portuguese.

Failure Cases Investigating cases in which our model fails to classify sentences correctly offers helpful insights. The model's failure cases broadly fall into the following categories:

Semantic Error: the model makes a clear semantic error. An example is provided in Table 1. Sentence 1 does not contain a protest event but the model predicts one.

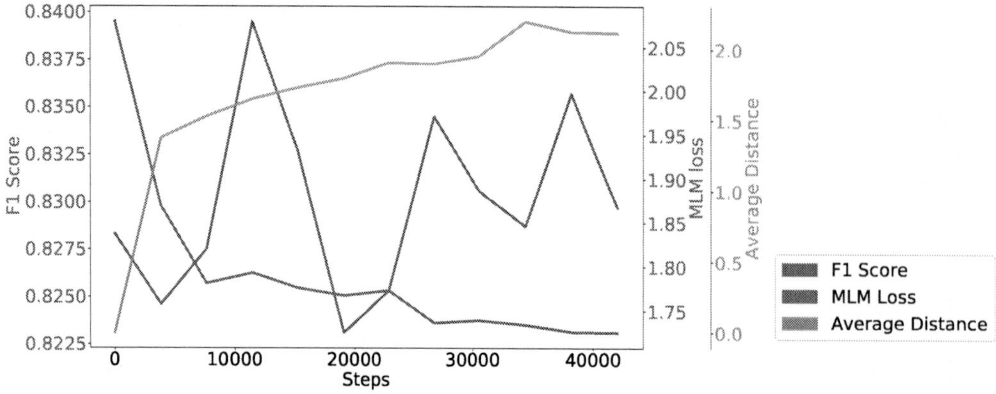

Figure 1: F1 Score, MLM loss, and embedding shift at different steps during the *second pretraining* phase. We take a checkpoint at every 4000 steps. The figure displays the MLM loss from the pretraining objective for each checkpoint as well as the validation F1 score from finetuning for the sentence classification task with this checkpoint. Additionally, we track how much the embeddings change by manually selecting 10 sentences. We measure the Euclidean distance between their vector representations from the RoBERTa default model and our model at each checkpoint. Best viewed in color.

Rule Error: this happens when the sentence could be seen as a protest event sentence in commonsense but is not considered one according to the annotation manual (Hürriyetoğlu et al., 2021). In Sentence 2 in Table 1, there is no indication that the event has happened already or is ongoing. Therefore, based on the annotation manual, it should be classified as negative while the model gives a positive prediction.

Uncertain Reference: The event that a sentence is referring to is ambiguous. We show two examples in Table 1 in sentences 3 and 4. "The act" and "this" refer to an event that we do not have knowledge of without context. In this subtask, we do not have access to any context and thus the labels for these two sentences are uncertain. However, they have opposite labels in the ground truth. This may pose difficulty for model training.

Indirect Mention: There are cases of label inconsistency when an event is indirectly mentioned. In Table 1, sentences 5 and 6 should both receive a positive label as they both pertain to a clear conflict event, but only sentence 6 has a positive label.

5 Ablation Study

In this section, we explore different base models to finetune on, using additional training data from other subtasks and data augmentation techniques. All results reported in this section are on the validation set, without *second pretraining*.

5.1 Base Model

First, we compare the performance of different base models. We consider BERT (Devlin et al., 2019), RoBERTa (Liu et al., 2019), XLNet (Yang et al., 2019) and ELECTRA(Clark et al., 2020) as they represent some of the best-performing language models. Due to resource limitations, we only consider the base version of these models. We follow the same procedure as introduced in Section 3 but without the *second pretraining* step. We present the results in Table 2. We find that RoBERTa achieves the best results while BERT, XLNet and ELECTRA perform similarly or worse.

5.2 Additional Training Data

In this subsection, we explore adding data from other languages of Subtask 2 as well as from other subtasks. When we add data not originally in English, we translate the sentences into English using Argos Translate (Finlay, 2021). We present the result in Table 4. For example, "Sub1 ES&PT+" means Spanish and Portuguese data from Subtask 1 with positive labels. While some settings result in better performance, when we use them in conjunction with *second pretraining*, the performance gain disappears. Thus, we do not include any additional training data in training our model for final submission.

#	Sentence	P	L
	Semantic Error		
1	___ 9:05 a.m. Democratic presidential candidate Bernie Sanders is disavowing remarks made by a campaign surrogate who said voters shouldn't "continue to elect corporate Democratic whores" during a large New York City rally.	1	0
	Rule Error		
2	On Tuesday, a group of aviation staff called for a protest at Hong Kong airport on Friday to condemn the government and police for "ignoring the random attacks on citizens in Yuen Long".	1	0
	Uncertain Reference		
3	The act was captured by CCTV cameras and witnesses using smartphones.	1	0
4	"This has happened across the state.	0	1
	Indirect Mention		
5	He did not give details, but a local independent daily, O Pais, said six people were injured in the attack in Ancuabe in Mozambique's northern Cabo Delgado province.	1	0
6	Spokesman Keith Khoza said they had decided to March to Prime Media because the cartoon had raised various concerns.	0	1

Table 1: Example failure cases. We divide the failure cases into four categories and give example sentences of each category. "P" refers to the model's prediction and "L" refers to the ground truth label.

Base Model	F1 Score
BERT	0.8117
RoBERTa	**0.8283**
XLNet	0.8097
ELECTRA	0.8113

Table 2: Effect of Base Models. We keep all other settings fixed while changing the base models and conduct finetuning on event sentence classification.

Augmentation Methods	F1 Score
None	0.8283
Back Translation	0.8206
Embedding + Checklist	**0.8294**
Paraphrase	0.8026

Table 3: Effect of Data Augmentation. We train the event sentence classification model with augmented data from the data augmentation methods of Subtask 2 data, in addition to the original training data.

Multilingual Data from Subtask 2 In Experiment 2, we add Subtask 2 data from Spanish and Portuguese. We show the result in Experiment 2. The result nearly does not change.

Data from Subtask 3 and 4 In Experiment 3, we add data from Subtask 3 and 4. Subtask 3 is a event coreference resolution task and Subtask 4 is a event trigger detection task, both with data from protest events. As both are downstream tasks of Subtask 2 as shown in (Hürriyetoğlu et al., 2021), we assume that all sentences from the two subtasks contain event sentences and thus may help our Subtask 2 model. Upon manual inspection, there are some overlaps between Subtask 2 and Subtask 3 and 4 data but many new training samples exist. We see small gains compared to Experiments 1 and 2.

Combine Data from Subtask 2, 3 and 4 In Experiment 4, we combine the training data from Experiment 2 and 3, namely Subtask 2 data from all three languages and Subtask 3 data from English only. We see that the F1 score increases from 0.8303 to 0.8363. In Experiment 5, we also include Spanish and Portuguese Subtask 3 and 4 data. The F1 score is nearly the same as Experiment 4.

Negative Samples from Subtask 1 In Experiment 6, we add negative samples from the data of Subtask 1, in addition to the data from Experiment 5. Subtask 1 is a document classification task, in which "positive" indicates that the document contains a protest event. According to Hürriyetoğlu et al. (2020), a positive document contains protest event(s) but it does not imply that all sentences in that document should be labeled positive. On the other hand, any negative document is certain to contain no protest event. Therefore, we experiment with adding the negative documents first. The F1 score drops from 0.8362 to 0.8275. This is even worse than the baseline of considering only the

#	Sub1				Sub2		Sub3+4		F1
	EN+	EN-	ES&PT+	ES&PT-	EN	ES&PT	EN	ES&PT	
1					✓				0.8283
2					✓	✓			0.8282
3					✓		✓		0.8303
4					✓	✓	✓		**0.8363**
5					✓	✓	✓	✓	0.8362
6		✓			✓	✓	✓	✓	0.8275
6		✓		✓	✓	✓	✓	✓	0.8254
7	✓				✓	✓	✓	✓	0.7646
8	✓		✓		✓	✓	✓	✓	0.7439

Table 4: Effect of Training Data. In this table, we show the impact of having different combinations of training data from different subtasks. EN, ES and PT mean the English, Spanish, and Portuguese versions of the training data from a specific subtask, respectively. In Subtask 1, we consider the positive class and negative class separately. "+" indicates data from the positive class while "-" indicates data from the negative class.

English Subtask 2 data (Experiment 1). In Experiment 7, we add the translated negative samples from Spanish and Portuguese. The resulting F1 score further drops to 0.8254.

Positive Samples from Subtask 1 In Experiment 7, we add positive samples from the English version of Subtask 1, assuming that a positive document implies that every sentence in the document has a positive label. In Experiment 8, we add positive samples from the Spanish and Portuguese versions of Subtask 1. As we suspected, this assumption does not hold and the F1 scores drop significantly, to well below 0.8 in both cases.

5.3 Effect of Data Augmentation

In addition to adding more training data directly, we also consider data augmentation methods: back translation, checklist augmentation, embedding augmentation and paraphrasing. We point the reader to Section A.2 in the appendix for a description of these methods and example sentences generated with these augmentation methods. Some augmentation methods result in better performance. When combined with *second pretraining*, however, the performance gain disappears. Thus, we do not include any augmented data in training our model for final submission.

Results We show the result of the models trained with data augmentations in Table 3. We notice a drop in performance in back translation. This may be due to the subtle differences between translated sentences and task sentences native in English, similar to what we discussed in Section 5.2. We find a small improvement in embedding and checklist augmentations. We believe performing these two augmentations makes the model more robust to changes in contextual information. Paraphrasing results in a large drop in the model performance from 0.8283 without augmentation to just above 0.8 in F1 score. After inspecting the paraphrased sentences, we find that the paraphrasing model changes the input sentences very dramatically. In some cases, pieces of information that do not exist in the source text are even created.

Training Data	Initialization	F1 Score
No NE	RoBERTa	0.8210
No NE	second-pretrain	0.8277
Only NE	RoBERTa	0.3959
Only NE	second-pretrain	0.4190
Random	None	0.1896
All	RoBERTa	0.8283
All	second-pretrain	**0.8395**

Table 5: Effect of named entities. We finetune models with data without NEs and data with only NEs, with both RoBERTa default and RoBERTa *second pretraining*. We modify the validation data accordingly. The result shown is on the validation set. We include a random guessing baseline model for comparison. We also include the model performances with no modification to the data for reference.

6 Effect of Named Entities

In this section, we analyse the effect of named entities (NE) on the results. We train models with two modifications of the Subtask 2 data: 1. we remove all named entities in all sentences; 2. we remove all text tokens except for named entities in each sentence. For each data modification setting, we train two models, one model initialized with the RoBERTa default weight, one initialized with the second-pretrained weight as mentioned in Section 3. For comparison, we include a random guessing baseline model. It draws label from the same distribution of the ground truth labels in the training set, without considering the sentences at all. We report the average F1 score of 100 such random assignments. We also include the result of the model trained with the original Subtask 2 training data using RoBERTa default weight and second-pretrain weight for reference. The result is shown in Table 5. We notice that without NEs, the model performs worse than the model trained with full data, in both RoBERTa default weight case and *second pretraining* case, suggesting that NEs contribute to the model's ability to correctly classify protest sentences. We also see that by only relying on NEs, the model is able to achieve an F1 score of around 0.4, more than double that of the random baseline, further suggesting that in this dataset, there are statistics about NEs that the model may utilize to make its decision, in addition to capturing linguistic clues. For example, due to the situation in Hong Kong in recent years, any sentence related to Hong Kong may have an above-average likelihood of containing an event. Additionally, we notice better performance in both the No NE setting and the Only NE setting when we finetune models with second pretrained weight. This emphasizes the importance of *second pretraining* in our approach.

7 Conclusion

In this paper, we present our submission to task 1, subtask 2 at CASE @ ACL-IJCNLP 2021. Our model is based on RoBERTa with a *second pretraining* step done on the POLUSA dataset. We inspect the failure cases of our model on the validation set and provide some explanations. To justify our design choices, we conduct an ablation study. Overall, we achieve the highest F1 score in the English version of this subtask and the second highest F1 score in Portuguese on the evaluation server. In future work, we plan to incorporate knowledge from the annotation manual into the model and incorporate richer semantic context by means of topological graph structures (Stoehr et al., 2019, 2020).

References

Richard W. Brislin. 1970. Back-translation for cross-cultural research. *Journal of Cross-Cultural Psychology*, 1(3):185–216.

Kevin Clark, Minh-Thang Luong, Quoc V. Le, and Christopher D. Manning. 2020. ELECTRA: Pre-training text encoders as discriminators rather than generators. In *ICLR*.

Jacob Devlin, Ming-Wei Chang, Kenton Lee, and Kristina Toutanova. 2019. BERT: Pre-training of deep bidirectional transformers for language understanding. In *Proceedings of the 2019 Conference of the North American Chapter of the Association for Computational Linguistics: Human Language Technologies, Volume 1 (Long and Short Papers)*, pages 4171–4186, Minneapolis, Minnesota. Association for Computational Linguistics.

Sergey Edunov, Myle Ott, Michael Auli, and David Grangier. 2018. Understanding back-translation at scale. *arXiv preprint arXiv:1808.09381*.

P.J. Finlay. 2021. Argos translate. Open source neural machine translation software.

Lukas Gebhard and Felix Hamborg. 2020. The polusa dataset: 0.9 m political news articles balanced by time and outlet popularity. In *Proceedings of the ACM/IEEE Joint Conference on Digital Libraries in 2020*, pages 467–468.

Suchin Gururangan, Ana Marasović, Swabha Swayamdipta, Kyle Lo, Iz Beltagy, Doug Downey, and Noah A. Smith. 2020. Don't stop pretraining: Adapt language models to domains and tasks. In *Proceedings of ACL*.

Sepp Hochreiter and Jürgen Schmidhuber. 1997. Long short-term memory. *Neural computation*, 9(8):1735–1780.

Ali Hürriyetoğlu, Osman Mutlu, Farhana Ferdousi Liza, Erdem Yörük, Ritesh Kumar, and Shyam Ratan. 2021. Multilingual protest news detection - shared task 1, case 2021. In *Proceedings of the 4th Workshop on Challenges and Applications of Automated Extraction of Socio-political Events from Text (CASE 2021)*, online. Association for Computational Linguistics (ACL).

Ali Hürriyetoğlu, Erdem Yörük, Deniz Yüret, Çağrı Yoltar, Burak Gürel, Fırat Duruşan, and Osman Mutlu. 2019a. A task set proposal for automatic protest information collection across multiple countries. In *Advances in Information Retrieval*, pages 316–323, Cham. Springer International Publishing.

Ali Hürriyetoğlu, Erdem Yörük, Deniz Yüret, Çağrı Yoltar, Burak Gürel, Fırat Duruşan, Osman Mutlu, and Arda Akdemir. 2019b. Overview of clef 2019 lab protestnews: Extracting protests from news in a cross-context setting. In *Experimental IR*

Meets Multilinguality, Multimodality, and Interaction, pages 425–432, Cham. Springer International Publishing.

Ali Hürriyetoğlu, Vanni Zavarella, Hristo Tanev, Erdem Yörük, Ali Safaya, and Osman Mutlu. 2020. Automated extraction of socio-political events from news (AESPEN): Workshop and shared task report. In *Proceedings of the Workshop on Automated Extraction of Socio-political Events from News 2020*, pages 1–6, Marseille, France. European Language Resources Association (ELRA).

Ali Hürriyetoğlu, Erdem Yörük, Osman Mutlu, Fırat Duruşan, Çağrı Yoltar, Deniz Yüret, and Burak Gürel. 2021. Cross-Context News Corpus for Protest Event-Related Knowledge Base Construction. *Data Intelligence*, pages 1–28.

Yinhan Liu, Myle Ott, Naman Goyal, Jingfei Du, Mandar Joshi, Danqi Chen, Omer Levy, Mike Lewis, Luke Zettlemoyer, and Veselin Stoyanov. 2019. Roberta: A robustly optimized bert pretraining approach. *arXiv preprint arXiv:1907.11692*.

Nikola Mrkšić, Diarmuid O Séaghdha, Blaise Thomson, Milica Gašić, Lina Rojas-Barahona, Pei-Hao Su, David Vandyke, Tsung-Hsien Wen, and Steve Young. 2016. Counter-fitting word vectors to linguistic constraints. *arXiv preprint arXiv:1603.00892*.

Arpit Rajauria. 2020. Pegasus fine-tuned for paraphrasing. Open source neural machine translation software.

Marco Tulio Ribeiro, Tongshuang Wu, Carlos Guestrin, and Sameer Singh. 2020. Beyond accuracy: Behavioral testing of nlp models with checklist. *arXiv preprint arXiv:2005.04118*.

Rico Sennrich, Barry Haddow, and Alexandra Birch. 2015. Improving neural machine translation models with monolingual data. *arXiv preprint arXiv:1511.06709*.

Niklas Stoehr, Fabian Braesemann, Michael Frommelt, and Shi Zhou. 2020. Mining the automotive industry: A network analysis of corporate positioning and technological trends. In *Complex Networks XI*, pages 297–308. Springer International Publishing.

Niklas Stoehr, Marc Brockschmidt, Emine Yilmaz, and Jan Stühmer. 2019. Disentangling interpretable generative parameters of random and real-world graphs. In *arXiv*, volume 1910.05639.

Ashish Vaswani, Noam Shazeer, Niki Parmar, Jakob Uszkoreit, Llion Jones, Aidan N. Gomez, Lukasz Kaiser, and Illia Polosukhin. 2017. Attention is all you need. In *Advances in Neural Information Processing Systems*.

Zhilin Yang, Zihang Dai, Yiming Yang, Jaime Carbonell, Russ R Salakhutdinov, and Quoc V Le. 2019. Xlnet: Generalized autoregressive pretraining for language understanding. In *Advances in Neural Information Processing Systems*, volume 32. Curran Associates, Inc.

Jingqing Zhang, Yao Zhao, Mohammad Saleh, and Peter Liu. 2020. Pegasus: Pre-training with extracted gap-sentences for abstractive summarization. In *International Conference on Machine Learning*, pages 11328–11339. PMLR.

Xiang Zhang, Junbo Zhao, and Yann LeCun. 2015. Character-level convolutional networks for text classification. *arXiv preprint arXiv:1509.01626*.

A Appendix

A.1 Second Pretraining Considerations

Gururangan et al. (2020) propose two types of additional pretraining: domain-adaptive pretraining (DAPT) and task-adaptive pretraining (TAPT). DAPT involves a *second pretraining* on large corpus of text from a specific domain (e.g news paper articles) while TAPT uses unlabeled training data for the downstream task. We consider the second-pretrained DAPT and TAPT model for AG News (Zhang et al., 2015) and finetune them for our task of event sentence classification. The results are shown in Table 6. We see that the F1 score of the DAPT model is almost 0.01 lower than the finetuned RoBERTa default model and TAPT performs even worse. We believe that training on a general news corpus would not help improve the embedding quality for our task because the AG News dataset contains articles of different categories (e.g business, technology and sports) while our subtask only deals with political news. This is consistent with our observation in Section 5.2 when we see worse result as we add negative data from Subtask 1. Ideally, we would perform TAPT using unlabeled training data, which involves protest news articles from Indian Express, New Indian Express, The Hindu, Times of India, South China Morning Post, and People's Daily, according to (Hürriyetoğlu et al., 2021). This would ensure no domain gap between our data for *second pretraining* and finetuning. Due to time and resource constraint, however, we cannot gain access to articles from these outlets. Thus, we resort to POLUSA (Gebhard and Hamborg, 2020). While it is not from the same outlets, the fact that it only contains political news make it suitable for our purpose.

Initialization	F1 Score
RoBERTa	**0.8283**
DAPT	0.8195
TAPT	0.8155

Table 6: Validation performance of finetuning DAPT and TAPT models, second pretrained on AG News, compared to the finetuned RoBERTa default model

A.2 Data Augmentation

In this section, we discuss the four different data augmentation methods we consider in the main paper.

Back-translation Back-translation means translating the source text into a different language, and translate back to the source language. This method have been used since the 1970s in translation quality research (Brislin, 1970) and have recently been used to improve machine translation models (Sennrich et al., 2015; Edunov et al., 2018). In our implementation, we use Chinese as the intermediate language.

Embedding Augmentation Embedding Augmentation performs augmentation by replacing words with neighbors in the counter-fitted embedding space (Mrkšić et al., 2016).

Checklist Augmentation Checklist Augmentation is based on Ribeiro et al. (2020). This method augments texts by replacing names, locations, and numbers detected in the text as well as performing contraction and extension.

Paraphrasing Paraphrasing refers to augmenting text by generating a paraphrased version of the text. We use the Pegasus (Zhang et al., 2020) model finetuned for paraphrasing (Rajauria, 2020) to generate paraphrased text. We include both the original training set and the paraphrased training set for finetuning our model.

Example We show example sentences of data augmentation methods in Table 7. We see that back-translation, checklist and embedding augmentation perform their intended functions, while paraphrasing seems to create facts that are not present in the original sentence.

A.3 Other Finetuning Setting

We explore other finetuning settings and show the results in Table 8. This experiment is done using the RoBERTa default weight without *second pretraining*. We consider the following setting: 1. We add two more fully connection (FC) layers before the output. We still finetune the entire model; 2. We consider setting 1 but freeze the RoBERTa backbone; 3. We consider the output of all tokens in the last hidden layer, and pass them through an LSTM (Hochreiter and Schmidhuber, 1997) layer before the classification head; 4. Setting 3 but with frozen RoBERTa backbone. We see that more FC layers does not help, and that when we only consider the [CLS] embedding, freezing the main model would result in very bad performance. At the same time, when we consider embeddings from all tokens with

Method	Sentence
Original Sentence	"Purandeswari, who on Tuesday said when it was certain that Telangana would be a reality there was no point in demanding something that was not going to be delivered, reiterated her new stance on Wednesday."
Back-translation	"Tuesday said that Prandeswari was aware that Teangana would be a reality without any requirement to do so, and she therefore reiterated her new position on Wednesday."
Checklist + Embedding	"Mareli, who on Tuesday said when it was certain that Telangana would be a reality there was no point in demanding something that was not going to be delivered, reiterated her new stance on Wednesday."
Paraphrasing	"Thousands of students are writing their National Senior Certificate (matric) exams and could fail to arrive on time."

Table 7: Example sentences from each data augmentation method that we consider: back-translation, embedding augmentation, checklist augmentation and paraphrasing.

an LSTM layer, we get a small boost in performance. Freezing the main model does not hurt nearly as much in this setting, suggesting a possible way of finetuning large language models in resource-constrained situations. Given that using embeddings from all tokens is not the conventional setup of a RoBERTa model for downstream classification tasks, we still use the conventional setting by connecting the [CLS] embedding to an FC layer in our submission.

Setting	F1 Score
Default	0.8283
1	0.8280
2	0.5631
3	**0.8301**
4	0.8155

Table 8: Performance of the model under other finetuning settings. Setting Default: the standard way - RoBERTa model with a FC layer connected to [CLS] embedding for classsification. Setting 1: two more fully connection (FC) layers before the classification head. Setting 2: Setting 1 with the backbone model frozen. Setting 3: Pass embeddings of all tokens to an LSTM before the output layer. Setting 4: Setting 3 with the backbone model frozen.

AMU-EURANOVA at CASE 2021 Task 1: Assessing the stability of multilingual BERT

Léo Bouscarrat[1,2], Antoine Bonnefoy[1], Cécile Capponi[2], Carlos Ramisch[2]
[1]EURA NOVA, Marseille, France
[2]Aix Marseille Univ, Université de Toulon, CNRS, LIS, Marseille, France
{leo.bouscarrat, antoine.bonnefoy}@euranova.eu
{leo.bouscarrat, cecile.capponi, carlos.ramisch}@lis-lab.fr

Abstract

This paper explains our participation in task 1 of the CASE 2021 shared task. This task is about multilingual event extraction from news. We focused on sub-task 4, event information extraction. This sub-task has a small training dataset and we fine-tuned a multilingual BERT to solve this sub-task. We studied the instability problem on the dataset and tried to mitigate it.

1 Introduction

Event extraction is becoming more and more important as the number of online news increases. This task consists of extracting events from documents, especially news. An event is defined by a group of entities that give some information about the event. Therefore, the goal of this task is to extract, for each event, a group of entities that define the event, such as the place and time of the event.

This task is related but still different from named entity recognition (NER) as the issue is to group the entities that are related to the same event, and differentiate those related to different events. This difference makes the task harder and also complicates the annotation.

In the case of this shared task, the type of events to extract is protests (Hürriyetoğlu et al., 2021a,b). This shared task is in the continuation of two previous shared tasks at CLEF 2019 (Hürriyetoğlu et al., 2019) and AESPEN (Hürriyetoğlu et al., 2020). The first one deals with English event extraction with three sub-tasks: document classification, sentence classification, and event information extraction. The second focuses on event sentence co-reference identification, whose goal is to group sentences related to the same events.

This year, task 1 is composed of the four aforementioned tasks and adds another difficulty: multilinguality. This year's data is available in English, Spanish, and Portuguese. Thus, it is important to note that there is much more data in English than in the other languages. For the document classification sub-task, to test multilingual capabilities, Hindi is available on the testing set only.

We have mainly focused on the last sub-task (event information extraction), but we have also submitted results for the first and second sub-tasks (document and sentence classification). We used multilingual BERT (Devlin et al., 2019), henceforth M-BERT, which is a model known to obtain near state-of-the-art results on many tasks. It is also supposed to work well for zero-or-few-shot learning on different languages (Pires et al., 2019). We will see the results on these sub-tasks, especially for sub-task 4 where the training set available for Spanish and Portuguese is small.

Thus, one of the issues with transformer-based models such as M-BERT is the instability on small datasets (Dodge et al., 2020; Ruder, 2021). The instability issue is the fact that by changing some random seeds before the learning phase but using the same architecture, data and hyper-parameters the results can have a great variance. We will look at some solutions to mitigate this issue, and how this issue is impacting our results for sub-task 4.[1]

2 Tasks and data

Sub-tasks 1 and 2 can be seen as binary sequence classification, where the goal is to say if a given sequence is part of a specific class. In our case, a classifier must predict whether a document contains information about an event for sub-task 1 or if a sentence contains information about an event for sub-task 2.

Document and sentence classification tasks, sub-tasks 1 and 2, are not our main research interest.

[1]Our code is available here: https://github.com/euranova/AMU-EURANOVA-CASE-2021

Proceedings of the 4th Workshop on Challenges and Applications of Automated Extraction of Socio-political Events from Text (CASE), pages 161–170

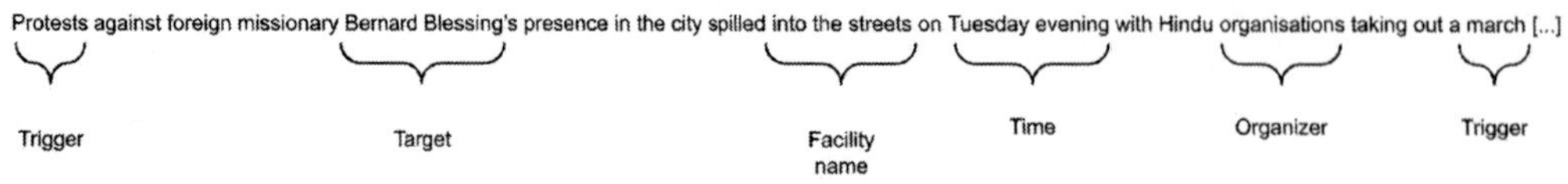

Figure 1: Example of a snippet from sub-task 4.

Moreover, the datasets provided for these tasks are less interesting (reasonable amount of training data).

On the other hand, sub-task 4 not only has less training data available but also requires more fine-grained token-based prediction. The goal of sub-task 4 is to extract event information from snippets that contain sentences speaking about the same event. Hürriyetoğlu et al. (2019) have defined that an event has the following information classes (example in Figure 1):

- Time, which indicates when the protest took place,
- Facility name, which indicates in which facility the protest took place,
- Organizer, which indicates who organized the protest,
- Participant, which indicates who participated in the protest,
- Place, which indicates where the protest took place in a more general area than the facility (city, region, ...),
- Target, which indicates against whom or what the protest took place,
- Trigger, which is a specific word or group of words that indicate that a protest took place (examples: protested, attack, ...),

Thus, not all the snippets contain all the classes, and they can contain several times the same classes. Each information can be composed of one or several adjacent words. Each snippet contains information related to one and only one event.

As the data is already separated into groups of sentences related to the same event, our approach consists of considering a task of named entity recognition with the aforementioned classes. Multilingual BERT has already been used for multilingual named entity recognition and showed great results compared to state-of-the-art models (Hakala and Pyysalo, 2019).

The data is in BIO format (Ramshaw and Marcus, 1995), where each word has a B tag or an I tag of a specific class or an O tag. The B tag means beginning and marks the beginning of a new entity. The tag I means inside, which has to be preceded by another I tag or a B tag, and marks that the word is inside an entity but not the first word of the entity. Finally, the O-tag means outside, which means the word is not part of an entity.

3 System overview

Our model is based on pre-trained multilingual BERT (Devlin et al., 2019). This model has been pretrained on multilingual Wikipedia texts. To balance the fact that the data is not equally distributed between all the languages the authors used exponential smoothed weighting to under-sample the most present languages and over-sample the rarest ones. This does not perfectly balance all the languages but it reduces the impact of low-resourced languages.

The authors of the M-BERT paper shared the weights of a pretrained model that we use to do fine-tuning. Fine-tuning a model consists of taking an already trained model on a specific task and using this model as a starting point of the training for the task of interest. This approach has reached state-of-the-arts in numerous tasks. In the case of M-BERT, the pre-training tasks are Masked Language Modeling (MLM) and Next Sentence Prediction (NSP).

To be able to learn our task, we add a dense layer on top of the outputs of M-BERT and learn it during the fine-tuning. All our models are fine-tuning all the layers of M-BERT.

The implementation is the one from HuggingFace's 'transformers' library (Wolf et al., 2020). To train it on our data, the model is fine-tuned on each sub-task.

3.1 Sub task 1 and 2

For sub-tasks 1 and 2, we approach these tasks as binary sequence classification, as the goal is to predict whether or not a document (sub-task 1) or sentence (sub-task 2) contains relevant information about a protest event. Thus the size of the output of the dense layer is 2. We then perform an argmax on these values to predict a class. We use the base parameters in HuggingFace's 'transformers' library. The loss is a cross-entropy, the learning rate is handled by an AdamW optimizer (Loshchilov and Hutter, 2019) and the activation function is a gelu (Hendrycks and Gimpel, 2016). We use a dropout of 10% for the fully connected layers inside M-BERT and the attention probabilities.

One of the issues with M-BERT is the limited length of the input, as it can only take 512 tokens, which are tokenized words. M-BERT uses the wordpiece tokenizer (Wu et al., 2016). A token is either a word if the tokenizer knows it, if it does not it will separate it into several sub-tokens which are known. For sub-task 1, as we are working with entire documents, it can be frequent that a document is longer than this limit and has to be broken down into several sub-documents. To retain contexts in each sub-documents we use an overlap of 150 tokens, which means between two sub-documents, they will have 150 tokens in common. Our method to output a class, in this case, is as follows:

- tokenize a document,
- if the tokenized document is longer than the 512-tokens limit, create different sub-documents with 150-tokens overlaps between each sub-document,
- generate a prediction for each sub-document,
- average all the predictions from sub-documents originated from the same document,
- take the argmax of the final prediction.

3.2 Sub-task 4

For sub-task 4, our approach is based on word classification where we predict a class for each word of the documents.

One issue is that as words are tokenized and can be transformed into several sub-tokens we have to choose how to choose the prediction of a multi-token word. Our approach is to take the prediction of the first token composing a word as in Hakala and Pyysalo (2019).

We also have to deal with the input size as some documents are longer than the limit. In this case, we separate them into sub-documents with an overlap of 150. Our approach is:

- tokenize a document,
- if the tokenized document is longer than the 512-tokens limit, create different sub-documents with 150-tokens overlaps between each sub-document,
- generate a prediction for each sub-document,
- reconstruct the entire document: take the first and second sub-documents, average the prediction for the same tokens (from the overlap), keep the prediction for the others, then use the same process with the obtained document and the next sub-document. As the size of each sequence is 512 and the overlap is only 150, no tokens can be in more than 2 different sequences,
- take the argmax of the final prediction for each word.

3.2.1 Soft macro-F1 loss

We used a soft macro-F1 loss (Lipton et al., 2014). This loss is closer than categorical cross-entropy on BIO labels to the metric used to evaluate systems in the shared task. The main issue with F1 is its non-differentiability, so it cannot be used as is but must be modified to become differentiable. The F1 score is based on precision and recall, which in turn are functions of the number of true positives, false positives, and false negatives. These quantities are usually defined as follows:

$$tp = \sum_{i \in tokens} (pred(i) \times true(i))$$

$$fp = \sum_{i \in tokens} (pred(i) \times (1 - true(i)))$$

$$fn = \sum_{i \in tokens} ((1 - pred(i)) \times true(i))$$

With:

- *tokens*, the list of tokens in a document,
- *true(i)*, 0 if the true label of the token i is of the negative class, 1 if the true label is of the positive class
- *pred(i)*, 0 if the predicted label of the token i is of the negative class, 1 if the predicted label is of the positive class

As we use macro-F1 loss, we compute the F1 score for each class where the positive class is the current class and negative any other class, e.g. if the reference class is B-trigger, then true(i)=1 for B-trigger and *true(i)=0* for all other classes when macro-averaging the F1.

We replace the binary function *pred(i)* by a function outputting the predicted probability of the token i to be of the positive class:

$$soft\_tp = \sum_{i \in tokens} (proba(i) \times true(i))$$

$$soft\_fp = \sum_{i \in tokens} (proba(i) \times (1 - true(i)))$$

$$soft\_fn = \sum_{i \in tokens} ((1 - proba(i)) \times true(i))$$

With *proba(i)* outputting the probability of the token i to be of the positive class, this probability is the predicted probability resulting from the softmax activation of the fine-tuning network.

Then we compute, in a similar fashion as a normal F1, the precision and recall using the soft definitions of the true positive, false positive, and false negative. And finally we compute the F1 score with the given precision and recall. As a loss function is a criterion to be minimized whereas F1 is a score that we would like to maximize, the final loss is $1 - F1$.

3.2.2 Recommendation for improved stability

A known problem of Transformers-based models is the training instability, especially with small datasets (Dodge et al., 2020; Ruder, 2021). Dodge et al. (2020) explain that two elements that have much influence on the stability are the data order and the initialization of the prediction layer, both controlled by pseudo-random numbers generated from a seed. To study the impact of these two elements on the models' stability, we freeze all the randomness on the other parts of the models and change only two different random seeds:

- the data order, i.e. the different batches and their order. Between two runs the model will see the same data during each epoch but the batches will be different, as the batches are built beforehand and do not change between epochs,
- the initialization of the linear layer used to predict the output of the model.

Another recommendation to work with Transformers-based models and small data made by Mosbach et al. (2021) is to use smaller learning rates but compensating with more epochs. We have taken this into account during the hyper-parameter search.

Ruder (2021) recommend using behavioral fine-tuning to reduce fine-tuning instabilities. It is supposed to be especially helpful to have a better initialization of the final prediction layer. It has also already been used on named entity recognition tasks (Broscheit, 2019) and has shown that it has improved results for a task with a very small training dataset. Thus, to do so, we need a task with the same number of classes, but much larger training datasets. As we did not find such a task, we decided to fine-tune our model on at least the different languages we are working with, English, Spanish and Portuguese. We used named entity recognition datasets and kept only three classes in common in all the datasets: person, organization, and location. These three types of entities can be found in the shared task.

To perform this test, the training has been done like that:

- the first fine-tuning is done on the concatenation of NER datasets in different languages, once the training is finished we save all the weights of the model,
- we load the weights of the previous model, except for the weights of the final prediction layer which are randomized with a given seed,
- we train the model on the dataset of the shared task.

4 Experimental setup

4.1 Data

The dataset of the shared task is based on articles from different newspapers in different languages. More information about this dataset can be found in (Hürriyetoğlu et al., 2021a)

For the final submissions of sub-tasks 1, 2, and 4 we divided the dataset given for training purposes into two parts with 80% for training and 20% for evaluation during the system training phase. We then predicted the data given for testing purposes during the shared task evaluation phase. The quantity of data for each sub-task and language can be found in Table 1. We can note that the majority of

Sub-task	English	Spanish	Portuguese
Sub-task 1	9,324	1,000	1,487
Sub-task 2	22,825	2,741	1,182
Sub-task 4	808	33	30

Table 1: Number of elements for each sub-task for each language in the data given for training purposes. Documents for sub-task 1, sentences for sub-task 2, snippet (group of sentences about one event) for sub-task 4.

Dataset	Train	Eval	Test
CoNLL 2003	14,041	3,250	3,453
CoNLL 2002	8,324	1,916	1,518
HAREM	121	8	128

Table 2: Number of elements for each dataset used in the behavioral fine-tuning in each split.

the data is in English. Spanish and Portuguese are only a small part of the dataset.

For all the experiments made on sub-task 4, we divided the dataset given for training purposes into three parts with 60% for training, 20% for evaluating and 20% for testing.

To be able to do our approach of behavioral fine-tuning, we needed some Named Entity Recognition datasets in English, Spanish and Portuguese. For English we used the CoNLL 2003 dataset (Tjong Kim Sang and De Meulder, 2003), for Spanish the Spanish part of the CoNLL 2002 dataset (Tjong Kim Sang, 2002) and for Portuguese the HAREM dataset (Santos et al., 2006). Each of these datasets had already three different splits for training, development and test. Information about their size can be found in Table 2.

The dataset for Portuguese is pretty small compared to the two others, but the impact of the size can be interesting to study.

4.2 Hyper-parameter search

For sub-task 4, we did a hyper-parameter search to optimize the results. We used Ray Tune (Liaw et al., 2018) and the HyperOpt algorithm Bergstra et al. (2013). We launched 30 different trainings, all the information about the search space and the hyper-parameters can be found in A.1. The goal is to optimize the macro-F1 on the evaluation set.

Our goal was to find a set of hyper-parameters that performs well to use always the same in the following experiments. We also wanted to evaluate the impacts of the hyper-parameters on the training.

4.3 Behavioral fine-tuning

For the first part of the behavioral fine-tuning, we trained an M-BERT model on the three NER datasets for one epoch. We only learn for one epoch for timing issues, as the learning on this datasets takes several hours. We then fine-tune the resulting models with the best set of hyper-parameters found with the hyper-parameter search.

4.4 Stability

To study the stability of the model and the impact of behavioral fine-tuning we made 6 sets of experiments with 20 experiments in each set:

- normal fine-tuning with random data order and frozen initialization of final layer,
- normal fine-tuning with frozen data order and random initialization of final layer,
- normal fine-tuning with random data order and random initialization of final layer,
- behavioral fine-tuning with random data order and frozen initialization of final layer,
- behavioral fine-tuning with frozen data order and random initialization of final layer,
- behavioral fine-tuning with random data order and random initialization of final layer,

Once again it is important to note that what we called behavioral fine-tuning is different from behavioral fine-tuning as proposed by Ruder (2021), as we reset the final layer. Only the weights of all the layers of M-BERT are modified.

For each set of experiments we will look at the average of the macro-F1, as implemented in Nakayama (2018), and the standard deviation of the macro-F1 on the training dataset, on the evaluation dataset, and on three different test datasets, one for each language. Thus we will be able to assess the importance of the instability, if our approach to behavioral fine-tuning helps to mitigate it and if it has similar results across the languages.

We can also note that in our implementation the batches are not randomized. They are built once before the learning phase and do not change, neither in content nor order of passage, between each epoch.

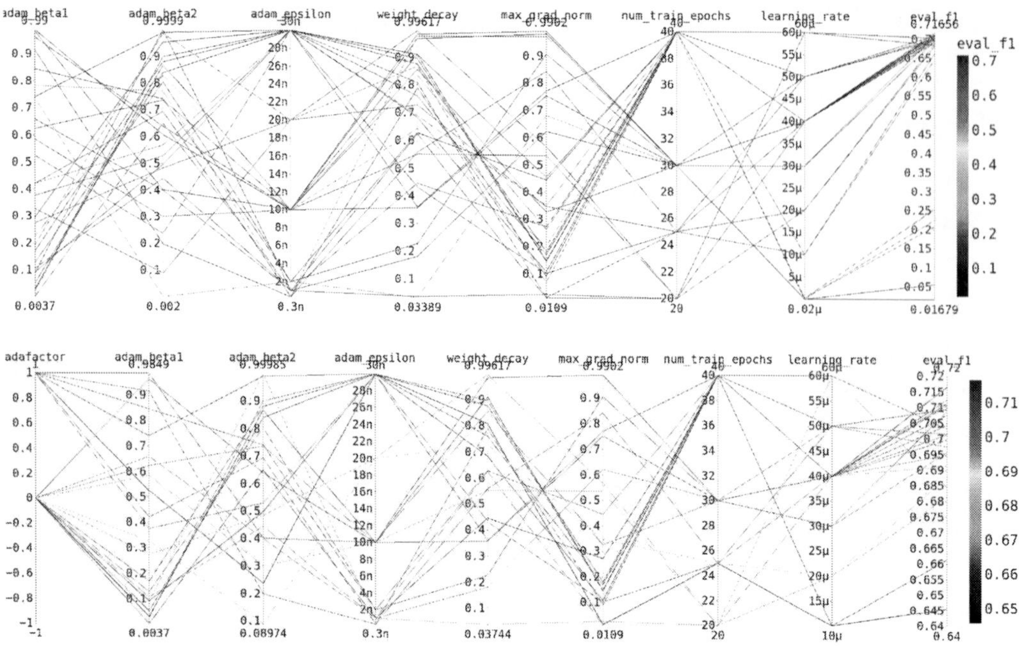

Figure 2: (Top) Parallel coordinates plot of the 30 experiments on sub-task 4 during the hyper-parameter search in function of the value of the hyper-parameters and the value of the F1 on the evaluation set. Each line represents an experiment, and each column a specific hyper-parameter, except the last which is the value of the metric. (Bottom) Same plot with the worst results removed to have a better view of the best results.

5 Results

5.1 Hyper-parameter search

The results of the hyper-parameter search can be seen in Figure 2. On the top pictures which represent the 30 experiments, we can see that a specific hyper-parameter seems to impact the worst results (in blue). This parameter is the learning rate, we can see it in the red box on the top image, all the blue lines are at the bottom, which means these experiments had a small learning rate. It seems that we obtain the best results with a learning rate around 5e-05 (0.00005), lower than 1e-06 seems to give bad results.

We can then focus on the bottom picture, with the same type of plot but with the worst results removed. Another hyper-parameter that seems to have an impact is the number of training epochs, 40 seems better than 20. We use a high number of epochs as recommended by Mosbach et al. (2021) to limit the instability. Beyond the learning rate and number of epochs, it is then hard to find impactful hyper-parameters.

Finally, the set of hyper-parameters that has been selected is:

- Adafactor: True
- Number of training epochs: 40
- Adam beta 2: 0.99
- Adam beta 1: 0.74
- Maximum gradient norm: 0.17
- Adam epsilon: 3e-08
- Learning rate: 5e-05
- Weight decay: 0.36

For the stability experiments, the number of training epochs have been reduced to 20 for speed purposes. For the first part of the behavioral fine-tuning, the learning rate has been set to 1e-05 as more data were available.

5.2 Behavioral fine-tuning

The results on the test dataset of each model after one epoch of training can be found in Table 5.

We could not compare to state-of-the-art NER models on these three datasets as we do not take all the classes (classes such as MISC were removed

	Data	Init layer	Train	Eval	Test EN	Test ES	Test PT
N	Rand	Fix	86.11 (1.08)	69.34 (1.01)	71.80 (.85)	54.33 (3.43)	73.14 (**1.96**)
	Fix	Rand	**86.88** (**.53**)	**70.03** (.63)	71.68 (**.53**)	55.02 (3.28)	74.51 (2.41)
	Rand	Rand	86.63 (1.08)	69.56 (.97)	**71.94** (.72)	54.73 (3.44)	74.08 (3.37)
B	Rand	Fix	85.79 (.97)	69.32 (1.00)	71.60 (.54)	54.69 (2.99)	74.01 (2.92)
	Fix	Rand	86.20 (.55)	69.57 (**.51**)	71.80 (.58)	53.97 (3.90)	74.50 (2.67)
	Rand	Rand	86.11 (.87)	69.40 (.80)	71.85 (.73)	**55.51** (**2.82**)	**74.97** (2.66)

Table 3: Average macro-F1 score, higher is better (standard deviation, lower is better) of the 20 experiments with the specified setup. N means normal fine-tuning and B behavioral fine-tuning. Data means data order and Init layer means initialization of the final layer. Rand means random, and fix refers to frozen.

	English	Spanish	Portuguese	Hindi
Sub-task 1	53.46 (84.55)	46.47 (77.27)	46.47 (84.00)	29.66 (78.77)
Sub-task 2	75.64 (85.32)	76.39 (88.61)	81.61 (88.47)	/
Sub-task 4	69.96 (78.11)	56.64 (66.20)	61.87 (73.24)	/

Table 4: Score of our final submissions for each sub-task, in parenthesis the score achieved by the best scoring team on each sub-task.

Dataset	Test macro-F1
CoNLL 2003	89.8
CoNLL 2002	86.1
HAREM	76.1

Table 5: Macro-F1 score of the NER task on the test split of each dataset used in behavioral fine-tuning after training the base M-BERT for 1 epoch.

before the learning phase). The metrics used on these datasets are not by classes, so the comparison cannot be made. However, the results are already much better than what a random classifier would output, thus the weights of the models should already be better than the weights of the base model.

5.3 Stability

The results of the different sets of experiments can be found in Table 3. First, we can see that the difference between behavioral fine-tuning and normal fine-tuning is not important enough to say one is better than the other. We can also note that the standard deviation is small for English, but not negligible for Spanish and Portuguese.

5.4 Final submission

The results of the final submissions can be found in Table 4. We can see that our results are lower than the best results, especially for sub-task 1 with a difference of between 30 to 50 macro-F1 score depending on the language, whereas for sub-tasks 2 and 4 the difference is close to 10 macro-F1 score for all the languages.

6 Conclusion

6.1 Sub-task 1 and 2

As we can see in Table 4, our final results for sub-task 1 are much lower than the best results, but for sub-task 2 the difference is smaller. This is interesting as the tasks are pretty similar, thus expected the difference between our results and the best results to be of the same magnitude.

One explanation could be our approach to handle documents longer than the input of M-BERT. We have chosen to take the average of the sub-documents, but if one part of a document contains an event the entire document does too. We may have better results looking if one sub-document at least is considered as having an event.

It is then hard to compare to other models as we have chosen to use one model for all the languages and we do not know the other approaches.

6.2 Sub-task 4

For sub-task 4 we have interesting results for all the languages, even for Spanish and Portuguese, as we were not sure that we could learn this task in a supervised fashion with the amount of data available. In a further study, we could compare our results with results obtained by fine-tuning monolingual models, where we fine-tune one model for each language with only the data of one language.

This could show the impact of having data if using a multilingual model instead of several monolingual models improves or not the results. We do not expect good results for Spanish and Portuguese as the training dataset is pretty limited. The results seem to comfort the claim of (Pires et al., 2019) that M-BERT works well for few-shot learning on other languages.

The other question for sub-task 4 was about instability. In Table 3 we can see that the instability is way more pronounced for Spanish and Portuguese. It seems logical as we have fewer data available in Spanish and Portuguese than in English. The standard deviation for Spanish and Portuguese is large and can have a real impact on the final results. Finding good seeds could help to improve the results for Spanish and Portuguese.

Furthermore, our approach of behavioral fine-tuning did not help to reduce the instabilities. It was expected that one of the sources of the instability is the initialization of the prediction, and in our approach, the initialization of this layer is still random. In our approach, we only fine-tune the weights of M-BERT. This does not seem to work and reinforces the advice of Ruder (2021) that using behavioral fine-tuning is more useful for having a good initialization of the final prediction layer.

On the two sources of randomness we studied, data order seems the most impactful for English, where we have more data. Nonetheless, for Spanish and Portuguese, the two sources have a large impact. In a further study, we could see how the quantity of data helps to decrease the impact of these sources of instabilities.

For the final submissions, the macro-F1 score for English and Portuguese is beneath the average macro-F1 score we found during our development phases. This could be due to bad seeds for randomness or because the splits are different. We did not try to find the best-performing seeds for the final submissions.

Acknowledgments

We thank Damien Fourrure, Arnaud Jacques, Guillaume Stempfel and our anonymous reviewers for their helpful comments.

References

James Bergstra, Daniel Yamins, and David Cox. 2013. Making a science of model search: Hyperparameter optimization in hundreds of dimensions for vision architectures. In *International conference on machine learning*, pages 115–123. PMLR.

Samuel Broscheit. 2019. Investigating entity knowledge in BERT with simple neural end-to-end entity linking. In *Proceedings of the 23rd Conference on Computational Natural Language Learning (CoNLL)*, pages 677–685, Hong Kong, China. Association for Computational Linguistics.

Jacob Devlin, Ming-Wei Chang, Kenton Lee, and Kristina Toutanova. 2019. Bert: Pre-training of deep bidirectional transformers for language understanding. In *Proceedings of the 2019 Conference of the North American Chapter of the Association for Computational Linguistics: Human Language Technologies, Volume 1 (Long and Short Papers)*, pages 4171–4186.

Jesse Dodge, Gabriel Ilharco, Roy Schwartz, Ali Farhadi, Hannaneh Hajishirzi, and Noah Smith. 2020. Fine-tuning pretrained language models: Weight initializations, data orders, and early stopping. *arXiv preprint arXiv:2002.06305*.

Kai Hakala and Sampo Pyysalo. 2019. Biomedical named entity recognition with multilingual BERT. In *Proceedings of The 5th Workshop on BioNLP Open Shared Tasks*, pages 56–61, Hong Kong, China. Association for Computational Linguistics.

Dan Hendrycks and Kevin Gimpel. 2016. Gaussian error linear units (gelus). *arXiv preprint arXiv:1606.08415*.

Ali Hürriyetoğlu, Osman Mutlu, Farhana Ferdousi Liza, Erdem Yörük, Ritesh Kumar, and Shyam Ratan. 2021a. Multilingual protest news detection - shared task 1, case 2021. In *Proceedings of the 4th Workshop on Challenges and Applications of Automated Extraction of Socio-political Events from Text (CASE 2021)*, online. Association for Computational Linguistics (ACL).

Ali Hürriyetoğlu, Hristo Tanev, Vanni Zavarella, Jakub Piskorski, Reyyan Yeniterzi, and Erdem Yörük. 2021b. Challenges and applications of automated extraction of socio-political events from text (case 2021): Workshop and shared task report. In *Proceedings of the 4th Workshop on Challenges and Applications of Automated Extraction of Socio-political Events from Text (CASE 2021)*, online. Association for Computational Linguistics (ACL).

Ali Hürriyetoğlu, Erdem Yörük, Deniz Yüret, Çağrı Yoltar, Burak Gürel, Fırat Duruşan, Osman Mutlu, and Arda Akdemir. 2019. Overview of clef 2019 lab protestnews: Extracting protests from news in a cross-context setting. In *Experimental IR Meets Multilinguality, Multimodality, and Interaction*, pages 425–432, Cham. Springer International Publishing.

Ali Hürriyetoğlu, Vanni Zavarella, Hristo Tanev, Erdem Yörük, Ali Safaya, and Osman Mutlu. 2020. Automated extraction of socio-political events from news (AESPEN): Workshop and shared task report. In *Proceedings of the Workshop on Automated Extraction of Socio-political Events from News 2020*, pages 1–6, Marseille, France. European Language Resources Association (ELRA).

Richard Liaw, Eric Liang, Robert Nishihara, Philipp Moritz, Joseph E Gonzalez, and Ion Stoica. 2018. Tune: A research platform for distributed model selection and training. *arXiv preprint arXiv:1807.05118*.

Zachary C Lipton, Charles Elkan, and Balakrishnan Naryanaswamy. 2014. Optimal thresholding of classifiers to maximize f1 measure. In *Joint European Conference on Machine Learning and Knowledge Discovery in Databases*, pages 225–239. Springer.

Ilya Loshchilov and Frank Hutter. 2019. Decoupled weight decay regularization. In *International Conference on Learning Representations*.

Marius Mosbach, Maksym Andriushchenko, and Dietrich Klakow. 2021. On the stability of fine-tuning {bert}: Misconceptions, explanations, and strong baselines. In *International Conference on Learning Representations*.

Hiroki Nakayama. 2018. seqeval: A python framework for sequence labeling evaluation. Software available from https://github.com/chakki-works/seqeval.

Telmo Pires, Eva Schlinger, and Dan Garrette. 2019. How multilingual is multilingual bert? In *Proceedings of the 57th Annual Meeting of the Association for Computational Linguistics*, pages 4996–5001.

Lance Ramshaw and Mitch Marcus. 1995. Text chunking using transformation-based learning. In *Third Workshop on Very Large Corpora*.

Sebastian Ruder. 2021. Recent Advances in Language Model Fine-tuning. `http://ruder.io/recent-advances-lm-fine-tuning`.

Diana Santos, Nuno Seco, Nuno Cardoso, and Rui Vilela. 2006. Harem: An advanced ner evaluation contest for portuguese. In *quot; In Nicoletta Calzolari; Khalid Choukri; Aldo Gangemi; Bente Maegaard; Joseph Mariani; Jan Odjik; Daniel Tapias (ed) Proceedings of the 5 th International Conference on Language Resources and Evaluation (LREC'2006)(Genoa Italy 22-28 May 2006)*.

Erik F. Tjong Kim Sang. 2002. Introduction to the CoNLL-2002 shared task: Language-independent named entity recognition. In *COLING-02: The 6th Conference on Natural Language Learning 2002 (CoNLL-2002)*.

Erik F. Tjong Kim Sang and Fien De Meulder. 2003. Introduction to the CoNLL-2003 shared task: Language-independent named entity recognition. In *Proceedings of the Seventh Conference on Natural Language Learning at HLT-NAACL 2003*, pages 142–147.

Thomas Wolf, Lysandre Debut, Victor Sanh, Julien Chaumond, Clement Delangue, Anthony Moi, Pierric Cistac, Tim Rault, Rémi Louf, Morgan Funtowicz, Joe Davison, Sam Shleifer, Patrick von Platen, Clara Ma, Yacine Jernite, Julien Plu, Canwen Xu, Teven Le Scao, Sylvain Gugger, Mariama Drame, Quentin Lhoest, and Alexander M. Rush. 2020. Transformers: State-of-the-art natural language processing. In *Proceedings of the 2020 Conference on Empirical Methods in Natural Language Processing: System Demonstrations*, pages 38–45, Online. Association for Computational Linguistics.

Yonghui Wu, Mike Schuster, Zhifeng Chen, Quoc V. Le, Mohammad Norouzi, Wolfgang Macherey, Maxim Krikun, Yuan Cao, Qin Gao, Klaus Macherey, Jeff Klingner, Apurva Shah, Melvin Johnson, Xiaobing Liu, Łukasz Kaiser, Stephan Gouws, Yoshikiyo Kato, Taku Kudo, Hideto Kazawa, Keith Stevens, George Kurian, Nishant Patil, Wei Wang, Cliff Young, Jason Smith, Jason Riesa, Alex Rudnick, Oriol Vinyals, Greg Corrado, Macduff Hughes, and Jeffrey Dean. 2016. Google's neural machine translation system: Bridging the gap between human and machine translation. *CoRR*, abs/1609.08144.

A Appendix

A.1 Hyper-parameter search

The space search for our hyper-parameter search was:

- Number of training epochs: value in [20, 25, 30, 40],
- Weight decay: uniform distribution between 0.001 and 1,
- Learning rate: value in [1e-5, 2e-5, 3e-5, 4e-5, 5e-5, 6e-5, 2e-7, 1e-7, 3e-7, 2e-8],
- Adafactor: value in "True", "False",
- Adam beta 1: uniform distribution between 0 and 1,
- Adam beta 2: uniform distribution between 0 and 1,
- Epsilon: value in [1e-8, 2e-8, 3e-8, 1e-9, 2e-9, 3e-10],
- Maximum gradient norm: uniform distribution between 0 and 1.

For the HyperOpt algorithm we used two set of hyper-parameters to help finding a good subspace. We maximized the macro-F1 on the evaluation dataset, and set the number of initial points before starting the algorithm to 5.

Team "DaDeFrNi" at CASE 2021 Task 1: Document and Sentence Classification for Protest Event Detection

Francesco Ignazio Re   Dániel Végh   Dennis Atzenhofer   Niklas Stoehr
ETH Zurich, Switzerland
{franre, davegh, dennisa}@ethz.ch   niklas.stoehr@inf.ethz.ch

Abstract

This paper accompanies our top-performing submission to the *CASE 2021* shared task, which is hosted at the workshop on *Challenges and Applications of Automated Extraction of Socio-political Events from Text.* Subtasks 1 and 2 of Task 1 concern the classification of newspaper articles and sentences into "conflict" versus "not conflict"-related in four different languages. Our model performs competitively in both subtasks (up to 0.8662 macro F1), obtaining the highest score of all contributions for subtask 1 on Hindi articles (0.7877 macro F1). We describe all experiments conducted with the XLM-RoBERTa (XLM-R) model and report results obtained in each binary classification task. We propose supplementing the original training data with additional data on political conflict events. In addition, we provide an analysis of unigram probability estimates and geospatial references contained within the original training corpus.

1 Introduction

Can natural language processing (NLP) be leveraged to extract information on socio-political events from text? This is an important question for Conflict and Peace Studies, as events like protests or armed conflicts are frequently reported in textual format, yet are costly to extract. The workshop on *Challenges and Applications of Automated Extraction of Socio-political Events from Text* (CASE 2021) aims at bringing together political scientists and NLP researchers to improve methods for automated event extraction[1]. As part of this workshop, a shared task is proposed to advance progress on various problems associated with reliable event detection (Hürriyetoğlu et al., 2021).

We combine the data provided by CASE 2021 with additional data sources to train a XLM-RoBERTa (XLM-R) model for subtasks 1 (document classification) and subtask 2 (sentence classification). Our model reaches competitive F1 scores ranging between 0.730 and 0.866 and is best-performing amongst all submissions for document classification in Hindi. Our exploratory analysis unveils relevant insights into the training data provided in the shared task. We find differences in the use of state versus non-state conflict actors based on conditional probabilities, and we identify an outlier in the English corpus via a Tf-Idf-weighted principal component analysis (PCA). Moreover, we conduct an analysis of the geospatial patterns in the underlying data. This report proceeds as follows: First, we briefly outline the datasets that we use. In sections 3 and 4 we elaborate on our model selection and on various conducted experiments. Finally, we report the results for subtasks 1 and 2. With these results in mind, section 6 delves into an exploratory analysis of the training data to better understand potential pitfalls.

[1]This workshop is a continuation of the shared tasks CLEF 2019 Lab Protest News (Hürriyetoğlu et al., 2019), and event sentence co-reference identification task at AESPEN at LREC 2020 (Hürriyetoğlu et al., 2020).

2 Dataset

In order to train our model, we leverage the data provided by the organizers as well as additional data on political conflict events. In this section, we describe both of these datasets.

2.1 Dataset provided for the shared task

The data for the CASE 2021 shared task derives from the *Global Contention Dataset* (GLOCON Gold) (Hürriyetoglu et al., 2020), a manually annotated dataset containing news articles in various languages. The training data consists of texts in three different languages: English articles from India, China, and South Africa, Spanish articles from Argentina, and Portuguese ones from Brazil. For subtask 1, the texts are labelled on the document level, with a binary label indicating whether the document mentions a political conflict event or not.

Proceedings of the 4th Workshop on Challenges and Applications of Automated Extraction of Socio-political Events from Text (CASE), pages 171–178
August 5–6, 2021, ©2021 Association for Computational Linguistics

For subtask 2, these documents are broken down to individual sentences, again with a binary label indicating whether the particular sentence mentions a political conflict or not. Crucially, the training data does not contain texts in the Hindi language, while Hindi texts are contained within the testing set. With a limited amount of texts to learn from, we consider expanding the training data in multiple ways, which we elaborate on in the following.

2.2 Extension with conflict event datasets

In order to fine-tune our model, we aim to extend the training data. To do so, we rely on two strategies: supplementing with data from other sources and translating the original training data.

For conflict-related texts, we harness a dataset provided by the Europe Media Monitor (EMM) (Atkinson et al., 2017; Pierre et al., 2016). This allows us to not only add more English texts, but also provides more Spanish and Portuguese data instances. Specifically, we rely on the human annotated data of the EMM project[2], thus we can be confident that these texts are indeed conflict-related. In addition, we supplement the English training set with data from the *Armed Conflict Location & Event Data Project (ACLED)* (Raleigh et al., 2010).
In order to obtain more negative examples (sentences not mentioning an event) and to add texts in Spanish and Portuguese, we web-scrape various newspaper articles linked on Twitter[3]. To make sure that these articles do not pertain political conflicts, we select only articles that are featured in tweets mentioning words unrelated to conflict[4].
Our second strategy to increase the available information is to translate the original training data. Using the Google Translate API we translate each text into all languages relevant for the task. This also equips us with texts in Hindi to train our model on. Overall, these efforts enable us to increase the available training data substantially:

- T_0: dataset related to subtask 1 as provided in the shared task.
- T_{mix}: combined dataset of subtask 1 and 2.
- $T_{0_{\text{noNER}}}$ and $T_{mix_{\text{noNER}}}$: The previously defined datasets with named entities removed.
- T_1, T_2, T_3: This data includes the articles from the additional sources. The datasets are constructed in a way so that the ratio between positive and negative labels is the same as in T_0. T_1 does not contain any of additional data obtained through translation, while T_2 and T_3 contain all the additional data. The difference among the two is that T_2 undergoes pre-processing steps (removal of punctuation and tags), whereas T_3 is fed into the model without being manually pre-processed first.

3 Model selection

Informed model selection is crucial for competitively solving the task. We choose pre-trained *Transformer*-based (Vaswani et al., 2017) classification models due to their state-of-the-art performance in various tasks (Devlin et al., 2019; Valvoda et al., 2021). Given the fact that the provided dataset is multilingual, we face a crucial design decision: option (a): select a monolingual model e.g. BERT (Devlin et al., 2019), that is pre-trained on huge, unlabeled text corpora in English with the need to translate all the other languages in the dataset back to English, then fine-tune the model on that. Or option (b): choose a multilingual model e.g. a multilingual version of BERT(mBERT), XLM((Lample and Conneau, 2019) or XLM-Roberta (XLM-R)(Conneau et al., 2020), that handles multiple languages simultaneously and fine-tune the model on the original languages. We ultimately choose the XLM-R model to experiment with. Recent results suggest that multilingual models achieve better performance, especially for low-resource languages.

4 Experiments

To conduct our experiments we rely on implementations provided by the Huggingface library [5,6]. For experiment tracking we make use of Wandb library [7]. After several rounds of hyperparameter search, we select a batch size of 16, learning rate of 2e-5, weight decay of 0.01 and train for 4 epochs. We train models for each of the subtasks separately (T_0), then we experiment with combinations of datasets, mixing subtasks and languages (T_{0mix}).

[2] `https://labs.emm4u.eu/events.html`

[3] We use the Python library *Newspaper3k*

[4] Specifically, we filter for mentions of "fashion", "football", "art","festival","movie". Including news reports on sport events could be particularly useful, since they are often described with language that is reminiscent of conflict

[5] `https://huggingface.co/`

[6] We open-source our code at `https://github.com/denieboy/ACL-IJCNLP_2021_workshop`

[7] `https://https://wandb.ai/site/`

Task 1	Subtask-1					Subtask-2				
Dataset	en	es	pr	hi	avg	en	es	pr	hi	avg
T_0	0.8650	0.8023	0.7572	-	0.8082	0.8717	0.8560	0.8811	-	0.8609
T_{0mix}	0.8711	0.7702	0.7841	-	0.8085	0.8720	0.8217	0.8835	-	0.8591
T_{0noNER}	0.7788	0.8138	0.8430	-	0.8119	0.9007	0.8484	0.8667	-	0.8719
T_{0mix_noNER}	0.8616	0.8056	0.7630	-	0.8101	0.8679	0.8320	0.8565	-	0.8521
T_1	0.8547	0.8011	0.7935	0.8241	0.8183	0.8780	0.8098	0.8785	-	0.8554
T_2	0.9111	0.8718	0.8468	0.8386	0.8671	0.9348	0.8670	0.8896	-	0.8971
T_3	0.8860	0.8895	0.8704	0.8546	0.8751	0.9695	0.9305	0.8948	-	0.9316

Table 1: F1 macro scores for task 1 subtasks 1 and 2 obtained with models fine-tuned on different dataset

Task 1	Subtask-1					Subtask-2				
Dataset	en	es	pr	hi	avg	en	es	pr	hi	avg
submission	0.8069	0.7301	0.7722	0.7877	0.7742	0.7928	0.8517	0.8662	-	0.8369

Table 2: F1 macro scores on the final test set achieved by our best model

We achieve the best results when training on the combined dataset including all the languages.

We try different combinations of extensions (T_1-T_3), e.g. having a balanced dataset or keeping the original imbalance rate of the shared task data. Finding protest events in Hindi language is challenging. Therefore, we translate protest events from English sources. Additionally, we experiment with removing contextual information and basing our classification on linguistic patterns only. To this end, we remove all named entities from the dataset (T_{0noNER}-T_{0mix_noNER}). The results, surprisingly, reveal only a slight degradation compared to the original dataset and even a small increase in performance on subtask 2 on English text.

5 Results

In this subsection we present the results achieved by our XLM-R models fine-tuned on different datasets. Table 1 shows the F1-macro score achieved on the different train / validation splits. Generally, we find that increasing the amount of the training data yields better scores. In Table 2, we present an evaluation of our model on the test set, on which we achieve F1-macro scores up to .867.

6 Discussion

In this section we present and analyse the conflict event data corpus, performing a descriptive analysis on the dataset using unigram probabilities and geo-spatial coordinates.

6.1 Unigram probability estimation

We take a probabilistic perspective and model the relation between the content of each document and its associated label considering texts as bags-of-words. Examining the different datasets provided for subtask 1, we study the three corpora (English, Portuguese and Spanish) independently.

6.1.1 Conditional probability estimates

We treat the terms "unigram" and "word" interchangeably. Given a word w, we denote the probability $P(D = 1|w)$ as the probability that the word w comes from a document . Similarly, we define $P(w|D = 1)$ as the probability that a conflictual document contains the word w. We estimate $P(w|D)$ with $\hat{\pi}_{w|D}$ and $P(D|w)$ with $\hat{\pi}_{D|w}$. Hence, we have

$$\hat{\pi}_{w|D} = \frac{\sum_{d_1 \in \mathcal{D}_1} \mathbb{1}\{w \in d_1\}}{\sum_{j=1}^{|V|} \sum_{d \in \mathcal{D}_1} \mathbb{1}\{w_j \in d_1\}}$$

$$\hat{\pi}_{D|w} = \frac{\sum_{d_1 \in \mathcal{D}_1} \mathbb{1}\{w \in d_1\}}{\sum_{d \in \mathcal{D}} \mathbb{1}\{w \in d\}},$$

with $\mathcal{D}$ being the corpus of all documents in a language, and $\mathcal{D}_1$ the subset of all conflict-related documents in $\mathcal{D}$. $\hat{\pi}_{D|w}$ can also be thought as the accuracy computed on the documents containing w, while predicting all of them as conflict-related.

6.1.2 Discriminative information

In this subsection we compute the probability estimates previously introduced and present them graphically in Figure 1. In the right plot, the words are represented by $P(D = 1|w)$ on the x-axis and by $P(w|D = 1)$ on the y-axis. The words on

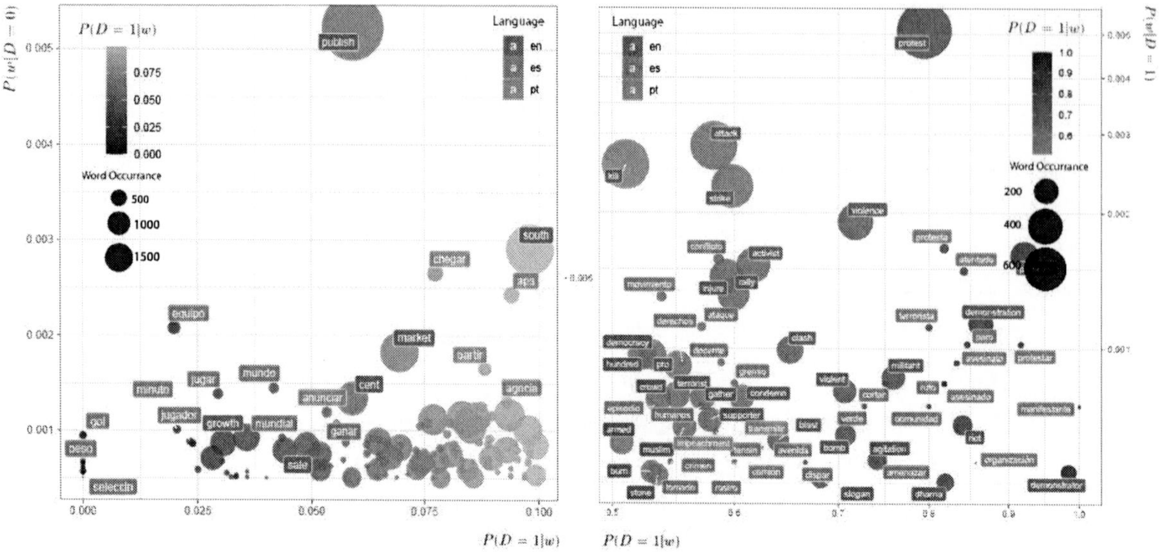

Figure 1: Sample of unigrams in the GLOCON Gold training corpora (English, Spanish, Portuguese); each circle represents a unigram, with circle size corrsponding to term frequency. For each corpus, we compute $P(D|w)$ and $P(w|D)$ as defined in Section 6.1.1. The left plot presents all unigram with low $P(D = 1|w)$ and with $P(w|D = 0) > 0.0005$. $P(w|D = 0)$ indicates how likely a unigram w is to occur in articles that are not conflict-related. Words like "growth" and "peso" contain much discriminate information - having very high $P(D = 0|w)$, but low $P(w|D = 1)$. The reverse logic applies for the right graph, displaying all the unigram with $P(w|D = 1) > 0.0005$.

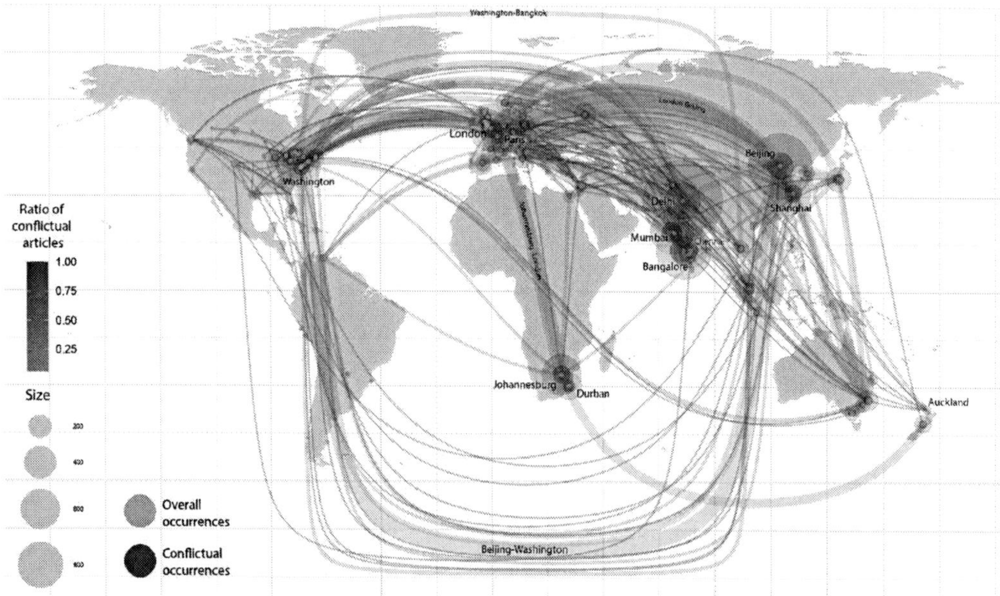

Figure 2: Undirected network of city co-mentions as introduced in Section 6.2.1; the nodes represent all cities present in the English GLOCON Gold training set. The size of the nodes corresponds to the number of occurrences that each city is mentioned. The edges are coloured according to the ratio of articles pertaining "conflict" versus "no conflict" that the cities share. The imbalanced ratio between both classes is well reflected in the map, with the light blue edges being the thickest. Edges related to conflict articles are more, but reveal lower weights.

the left plot have $P(D=1|w)$ as the x-axis and $P(w|D=0)$ y-axis. Indeed, a word would be a good classifier if both $P(w|D)$ and $P(D|w)$ were high. There are however no such words in our corpora. This finding reinforces our presumption that more general words contain less information relevant for our context-dependent task.

6.1.3 Result interpretation

This section summarises the information displayed in Figure 1. The right plot shows that, for words with high $P(w|D=1)$, English ones seem to have higher $P(D=1|w)$ if compared with Spanish and Portuguese. In fact, the Portuguese ones have $P(D=1|w)$ not exceeding 0.7. The right plot also shows an interesting pattern with regard to conflict actors. Rather surprisingly, terms related to state-based conflict actors like `police`, `officer` or `military` do not seem to be the most useful words to identify conflict-related texts. In fact, in terms of conditional probabilities these are not very discriminatory terms for the classification (e.g. we obtain $P(D=1|\text{ military })=0.31$, and accordingly $P(D=0|\text{ military })=0.69$ for the English case, $P(D=1|\text{ militar })=0.37$, and thus $P(D=0|\text{ militar })=0.63$ for the Spanish case). On the other hand, non-state conflict actors are much more indicative of a text covering a conflict event. As seen in the graph, terms like `activist` or `protester` are highly suggestive for a conflict context. We also suspect that polarized sentiment could be a valuable indicator of conflict-related texts, because conflict-news contain negatively associated words - such as `kill`, `violence`, `terrorism` - but also terms that in certain contexts may have positive connotation, like `dharna` (peaceful protest), `democracy`, `pro`, `activist`, `supporter`. The existence of polarized sentiments among words with high $P(D=1|w)$ could be indicative of the narrative style that is adopted for describing conflict events, with stories being usually reduced to oppressors-against-oppressed narratives.

6.2 Geospatial analysis

The analysis described in previous sections mainly focuses on words that appear with relatively high frequency in the corpus. Key contextual information of an article like place, time, actors etc. is usually very specific and thus likely to have lower frequencies. Nevertheless, contextual information plays a major role in detecting conflict events. Thus, we conduct an analysis on the geospatial entities of the English corpus provided by the shared task.

6.2.1 A geospatial undirected network

We construct an undirected network from entity co-mentions as displayed in Figure 2. The network can be seen as a symmetric matrix having as element in position (i,j) the number of times city i appears in an article where also city j is present. Nodes of the network represent the cities prevalent in the English corpus. If a document cites k cities, they will be represented in the network as a k-vertex clique. The network summarizes the relationship among the major locations involved in the events of the English set. The size of each node corresponds to the overall number of articles a city appears in. On an interpretative level, a conflictual edge does not imply that the two cities represent actors standing in conflict with each other. In fact, actors of different cities could as well be partaking in the same protest, hence sharing a common cause, rather than a divisive one. The most frequent cities cited are Indian cities such as Delhi, Bangalore, Chennai and Chinese ones like Beijing and Shanghai. In general, it is interesting to notice how the entire African continent is underrepresented if compared to others, South Africa being the only African state whose cities are mentioned (Braesemann et al., 2019; Stoehr et al., 2020).

6.3 Outlier detection with Tf-Idf

This section investigates the variability of the documents on a term-frequency level. Computing Tf-Idf embeddings for each corpus and reducing their dimensionality with PCA, we are able to detect few outliers. In particular, the document with ID 106495 in the English corpus is written in Afrikaans and not in English. A more detailed analysis can be found in the appendix.

7 Conclusion

In conclusion, the paper outlines two major contributions to the CASE 2021 shared task. Firstly, our XLM-RoBERTa model for classification Task 1.1 and Task 1.2 yields competitive results, especially for the Hindi subtask, where no training data was available. Secondly, we provide a descriptive analysis of idiosyncrasies contained with the provided text corpora. Our analysis qualitatively investigates geographical connotations in the corpora and possible outliers using word probability estimation.

Acknowledgments

Dennis Atzenhofer gratefully acknowledges financial support by the European Research Council (ERC Advanced Grant 787478).

References

Martin Atkinson, Jakub Piskorski, Hristo Tanev, and Vanni Zavarella. 2017. On the creation of a security-related event corpus. In *Proceedings of the Events and Stories in the News Workshop*, pages 59–65. Association for Computational Linguistics.

Fabian Braesemann, Niklas Stoehr, and Mark Graham. 2019. Global networks in collaborative programming. In *Taylor and Francis*.

Alexis Conneau, Kartikay Khandelwal, Naman Goyal, Vishrav Chaudhary, Guillaume Wenzek, Francisco Guzmán, Edouard Grave, Myle Ott, Luke Zettlemoyer, and Veselin Stoyanov. 2020. Unsupervised cross-lingual representation learning at scale. In *Proceedings of the 58th Annual Meeting of the Association for Computational Linguistics*, pages 8440–8451, Online. Association for Computational Linguistics.

Jacob Devlin, Ming-Wei Chang, Kenton Lee, and Kristina Toutanova. 2019. Bert: Pre-training of deep bidirectional transformers for language understanding.

Ali Hürriyetoğlu, Osman Mutlu, Farhana Ferdousi Liza, Erdem Yörük, Ritesh Kumar, and Shyam Ratan. 2021. Multilingual protest news detection - shared task 1, case 2021. In *Proceedings of the 4th Workshop on Challenges and Applications of Automated Extraction of Socio-political Events from Text (CASE 2021)*, online. Association for Computational Linguistics (ACL).

Ali Hürriyetoglu, Erdem Yörük, Deniz Yüret, Osman Mutlu, Çagri Yoltar, Firat Durusan, and Burak Gürel. 2020. Cross-context news corpus for protest events related knowledge base construction. *CoRR*, abs/2008.00351.

Ali Hürriyetoğlu, Erdem Yörük, Deniz Yüret, Çağrı Yoltar, Burak Gürel, Fırat Duruşan, Osman Mutlu, and Arda Akdemir. 2019. Overview of clef 2019 lab protestnews: Extracting protests from news in a cross-context setting. In *Experimental IR Meets Multilinguality, Multimodality, and Interaction*, pages 425–432, Cham. Springer International Publishing.

Ali Hürriyetoğlu, Vanni Zavarella, Hristo Tanev, Erdem Yörük, Ali Safaya, and Osman Mutlu. 2020. Automated extraction of socio-political events from news (AESPEN): Workshop and shared task report. In *Proceedings of the Workshop on Automated Extraction of Socio-political Events from News 2020*, pages 1–6, Marseille, France. European Language Resources Association (ELRA).

Guillaume Lample and Alexis Conneau. 2019. Cross-lingual language model pretraining.

Soille Pierre, Burger Armin, Aseretto Dario, Syrris Vasileios, and Vasilev Veselin. 2016. Towards a JRC earth observation data and processing platform. In *Proceedings of the 2016 conference on Big Data from Space (BiDS'16)*. Publications Office.

Clionadh Raleigh, Andrew Linke, Håvard Hegre, and Joakim Karlsen. 2010. Introducing acled: An armed conflict location and event dataset: Special data feature. *Journal of Peace Research*, 47(5):651–660.

Niklas Stoehr, Fabian Braesemann, Michael Frommelt, and Shi Zhou. 2020. Mining the automotive industry: A network analysis of corporate positioning and technological trends. In *Complex Networks XI*, pages 297–308. Springer International Publishing.

Josef Valvoda, Tiago Pimentel, Niklas Stoehr, Ryan Cotterell, and Simone Teufel. 2021. What about the precedent: An information-theoretic analysis of common law. In *arXiv*, volume 2104.12133.

Ashish Vaswani, Noam Shazeer, Niki Parmar, Jakob Uszkoreit, Llion Jones, Aidan N. Gomez, Lukasz Kaiser, and Illia Polosukhin. 2017. Attention is all you need. In *Advances in Neural Information Processing Systems*.

A Appendix

A.1 Outlier detection with Tf-Idf

This section investigates the variability of the documents of the training corpus provided by the shared task. We try to qualitatively assess possible articles that differ significantly from the rest of the corpus.

A.1.1 Tf-Idf word representation

We produce a Tf-Idf word embedding representation of the corpus in order to gain a deeper understanding on the variability of the documents in terms of term-frequencies. Given a word w and a document d, tf-idf associates a score $\text{tf}(w, d) \cdot \text{idf}(w, \mathcal{D})$ to the word-document pair. The first term refers to how often a word occurs in a document, and the second one refers to how often a word occurs in the overall corpus.

A.1.2 Dimensionality reduction with PCA

After computing the Tf-Idf embeddings, we perform Principal Component Analyis to reduce the dimensionality of the problem. The principal components are calculated on the original Tf-Idf embedding matrix and on its normalized version, with zero mean and unit variance.The results are more interpretable on the normalized matrix, even though it disregards the idf-term of the embeddings. The analysis is carried on the three corpora independently. The representation displays most of the data points as cluttered into one dense cluster, with very few ones standing out. Among these, in the English dataset for example, the data point with ID 108218 is not in English but in Afrikaans. Another article that stands out is the one with ID 106495; it contains 16108 characters whereas the 0.99 quantile of the character length distribution per document is 6290. A graphical representation can be found in the appendix in Figure 3. In Portuguese and Spanish instead, the reason why some articles are isolated from the group is less evident and it is probably more related to the category of content that the articles talk about.

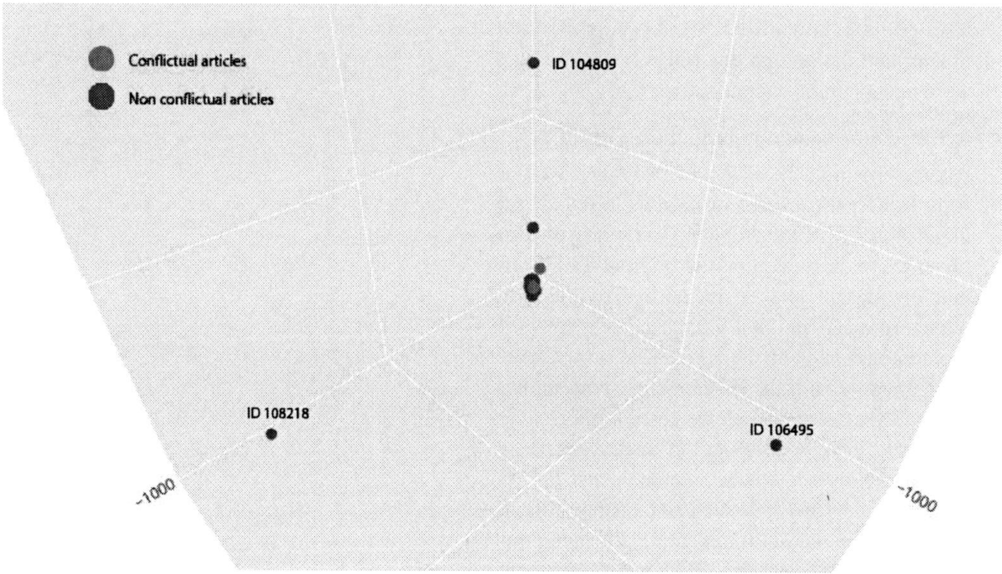

Figure 3: This figure shows the training English set with the first three principal components. Even if most of the data is concentrated in one dense cluster, there are a few points that can be very easily distinguished. They generally are either in a language different than English (ID 108218), or have other very rare characteristics, (ID 106495 having an extremely large character length).

Fine-grained Event Classification in News-like Text Snippets Shared Task 2, CASE 2021

Jacek Haneczok
Erste Digital
Vienna, Austria
jacek.haneczok@gmail.com

Guillaume Jacquet
Joint Research Centre
European Commission
Isrpa, Italy
guillaume.jacquet@ec.europa.eu

Jakub Piskorski
Linguistic Engineering Group
Institute for Computer Science
Polish Academy of Sciences
Warsaw, Poland
jpiskorski@gmail.com

Nicolas Stefanovitch
Joint Research Centre
European Commission
Isrpa, Italy
nicolas.stefanovitch@ec.europa.eu

Abstract

This paper describes the Shared Task on Fine-grained Event Classification in News-like Text Snippets. The Shared Task is divided into three subtasks: (a) classification of text snippets reporting socio-political events (25 classes) for which vast amount of training data exists, although exhibiting different structure and style vis-a-vis test data, (b) enhancement to a generalized zero-shot learning problem, where 3 additional event types were introduced in advance, but without any training data ('unseen' classes), and (c) further extension, which introduced 2 additional event types, announced shortly prior to the evaluation phase. The reported Shared Task focuses on classification of events in English texts and is organized as part of the Workshop on Challenges and Applications of Automated Extraction of Socio-political Events from Text (CASE 2021), co-located with the ACL-IJCNLP 2021 Conference. Four teams participated in the task. Best performing systems for the three aforementioned subtasks achieved 83.9%, 79.7% and 77.1% weighted F_1 scores respectively.

1 Introduction

The task of event classification is to assign to a text snippet an event type using a domain specific taxonomy. It constitutes an important step in the process of event extraction from free texts (Appelt, 1999; Piskorski and Yangarber, 2013) which has been researched since mid 90's and gained a lot of attention in the context of development of real-world applications (King and Lowe, 2003; Yangarber et al., 2008; Atkinson et al., 2011; Leetaru and Schrodt, 2013; Ward et al., 2013; Pastor-Galindo et al., 2020). While vast amount of challenges on automated event extraction, including event classification, has been organised in the past, relatively little efforts have been reported on approaches and shared tasks focusing specifically on fine-grained event classification.

This paper describes the Shared Task on Fine-grained Event Classification in News-like Text Snippets. The task is divided into three subtasks: (a) classification of text snippets reporting socio-political events (25 classes) for which vast amount of training data exists, although exhibiting slightly different structure and style vis-a-vis test data, (b) enhancement to a generalized zero-shot learning problem (Chao et al., 2016), where 3 additional event types were introduced in advance, but without any training data ('unseen' classes), and (c) further extension, which introduced 2 additional event types, announced shortly prior to the evaluation phase. The reported Shared Task focuses on classification of events in English texts and is organized as part of the Workshop on Challenges and Applications of Automated Extraction of Socio-political Events from Text (CASE 2021) (Hürriyetoğlu et al., 2021), co-located with the ACL-IJCNLP 2021 Conference. Four teams actively participated in the

The views expressed in this article are those of the authors and not necessarily those of Erste Digital.

Proceedings of the 4th Workshop on Challenges and Applications of Automated Extraction of Socio-political Events from Text (CASE), pages 179–192
August 5–6, 2021, ©2021 Association for Computational Linguistics

task.

The main rationale behind organising this Shared Task is not only to foster research on fine-grained event classification, a relatively understudied area, but to specifically explore robust and flexible solutions that are of paramount importance in the context of real-world applications. For instance, often available training data is slightly different from the data on which event classification might be applied (data drift). Furthermore, in real-world scenarios one is interested in quickly tailoring an existing solution to frequent extensions of the underlying event taxonomy.

The paper is organized as follows. Section 2 reviews prior work. Section 3 describes the Shared Task in more detail. Section 4 describes the training and test datasets. Next, the evaluation methodology is introduced in Section 5. Baseline and participant systems are described in Section 6. Subsequently, Section 7 presents the results obtained by these systems, whereas Section 8 discusses the main findings of the Shared Task. We present the conclusions in Section 9.

2 Prior Work

The research on event detection and classification in free-text documents was initially triggered by the Message Understanding Contests (Sundheim, 1991; Chinchor, 1998) and the Automatic Content Extraction Challenges (ACE) (Doddington et al., 2004; LDC, 2008). The event annotated corpora produced in the context of the aforementioned challenges fostered research on various techniques of event classification, which encompass purely knowledge-based approaches (Stickel and Tyson, 1997), shallow (Liao and Grishman, 2010; Hong et al., 2011) and deep machine learning approaches (Nguyen and Grishman, 2015; Nguyen et al., 2016).

Multi-lingual Event Detection and Co-reference challenge was introduced more recently in the Text Analysis Conference (TAC) in 2016[1] and 2017[2]. In particular, it included an Event Nugget Detection subtask, which focused on detection and fine-grained classification of intra-document event mentions, covering events from various domains (e.g., finances and jurisdiction).

One could observe in the last decade an ever growing interest in research on fine-grained event classification. Lefever and Hoste (2016) compared SVM-based models against word-vector-based LSTMs for classification of 10 types of company-specific economic events from news texts, whereas Nugent et al. (2017) studied the performance of various models, including ones that exploit word embeddings as features, for detection and classification of natural disaster and crisis events in news articles. Jacobs and Hoste (2020) reports on experiments of exploiting BERT embedding-based models for fine-grained event extraction for the financial domain.

Although most of the reported work in this area focuses on processing English texts, and in particular, news-like texts as presented in Piskorski et al. (2020), some efforts on event classification for non-English language were reported too. For instance, Sahoo et al. (2020) introduced a benchmark corpus for fine-grained classification of natural and man-made disasters (28 types) for Hindi, accompanied with evaluation of deep learning baseline models for this task. Furthermore, an example of fine-grained classification of cyberbullying events (7 classes) in social media posts was presented in Van Hee et al. (2015).

Work on classification of socio-political events and the related shared tasks, although not focusing on fine-grained classification, but covering event types which are in the scope of our task, was presented in Hürriyetoğlu et al. (2021) and Hürriyetoglu et al. (2019).

3 Task Description

The overall objective of this Shared Task is to evaluate the 'flexibility' of fine-grained event classifiers. Firstly, we are interested in the robustness vis-a-vis the input text structure, i.e., how classifiers trained on short texts from a curated database perform on news data taken from diverse sources where this structure is somewhat different. This corresponds to Subtask 1, which can be considered as a regular classification task. Secondly, we wanted to study how classifiers can be made flexible regarding the taxonomy used, with the aim of easily tailoring them for specific needs. This corresponds to Subtask 2 and 3, which were framed as generalized zero-shot learning problems: the label set for Subtask 2 was announced in advance, while the label set for Subtask 3 was announced on the day of the

[1] https://tac.nist.gov//2016/KBP/Event/index.html

[2] https://tac.nist.gov/2017/KBP/Event/index.html

competition.

The aforementioned objectives arise from the practical constraints of working with real data, being exposed to data drift and having different users being interested in different facets of the same events.

In order to train a fine-grained event classifier, we proposed to use ACLED (Raleigh et al., 2010) event database and the corresponding taxonomy described in the ACLED Codebook[3], which has 25 subtypes of events related to socio-political events and violent conflicts. ACLED created a large dataset of events over several years which are manually curated with a common pattern in the way of reporting events and uses a complex event taxonomy: The boundary between the definition of similar classes can be highly intricate, and can seem at point quite arbitrary. Nevertheless, ACLED presented itself as the best possible training material for the specific objectives of this Shared Task.

More precisely, the formal definitions of the different subtasks are as follows:

- **Subtask 1:**
  Classification of text snippets that are assigned to ACLED types only,
- **Subtask 2 (generalized zero-shot):**
  Classification of text snippets that are assigned to all ACLED types plus three unseen (non-ACLED) types, namely: `Organized Crime`, `Natural Disaster` and `Man-made Disaster`, these new types were announced in advance, but no training data was provided,
- **Subtask 3 (generalized zero-shot):**
  Classification of text snippets that are assigned to two additional unseen event types (`Diplomatic Event` and `Attribution of Responsibility`) on top of the ones of Subtask 2, these new types were not announced in advance.

The participating teams had the possibility to submit solutions to any number of subtasks without condition, whereas per subtask up to 5 system responses could be submitted for evaluation. More information on the event types for this Shared Task is provided in Appendix A.

[3] `https://acleddata.com/acleddatanew/wpcontent/uploads/dlm_uploads/2019/01/ACLED_Codebook_2019FINAL.docx.pdf`

4 Data

4.1 Training Data

For the training purposes the participants were allowed to either exploit any freely available existing event-annotated textual corpora and/or to exploit the short text snippets reporting events which are part of the large event database created by ACLED and which can be obtained from ACLED data portal[4] for research and academic purposes. Furthermore, the participants were also recommended to exploit as an inspiration the techniques for text normalization and cleaning of ACLED data, and some baseline classification models trained using ACLED data described in Piskorski et al. (2020).

4.2 Test Data

For the purpose of evaluating the predictive performance of the competing systems a dedicated test set was created based on news-like text snippets. To this end we sourced the web to collect short texts reporting on events either in the form of online news or of a similar style. We posed simple queries with label-specific keywords using conventional search engines to collect relevant text snippets. The most frequent keywords from ACLED datasets have been used a basis to form these queries. The collected set of snippets was cleaned by removing duplicates and further enhanced by adding both manually as well as automatically perturbed short news-like texts. More specifically, for selected snippets the most characteristic keywords were manually replaced by either less common or more vague expressions, so that the event type from the ACLED taxonomy can be still predicted, albeit making it more difficult. Also the reported figures, methods or outcomes of the event were subject to changes. Furthermore, about 15% of the text snippets were automatically perturbed[5] by: (a) replacing all day and month names mentions with another randomly chosen day and month resp., and (b) replacing each occurrence of a toponym referring to a populated place with randomly chosen toponym selected from GEONAMES gazetteer[6] of about 200K populated cities, whose population is at least 500. The perturbed snippets were additionally inspected in order to make sure that the changes allow for guessing the

[4] `https://acleddata.com/data-export-tool`

[5] The choice of 15% was motivated by the willingness to add some (but not too much) additional complexity to the task.

[6] `https://www.geonames.org/`

event type vis-a-vis ACLED taxonomy. Only the perturbed version of the original text snippet were included in the test dataset, the original ones were discarded. An example of original text and the automatically perturbed version thereof is provided in Figure 1.

> *A Catalan pro-independence demonstrator throws a fence into a fire during a protest against police action in Barcelona, Spain, October 26, 2019*
>
> *A Madukkarai pro-independence demonstrator throws a fence into a fire during a protest against police action in Podosinovets, Hohenmölsen, June 26, 2019*

Figure 1: Sample text snippet reporting a violent demonstration event (top) and the perturbed version thereof (bottom).

The distribution of the counts by event type is shown in Figure 3, whereas the distributions of the sequence length by event type is shown in Figure 4. The created test set consists in total of 1019 text snippets, 190 of which were annotated with labels corresponding to the zero-shot classes. An example of text snippet reporting a `Government regains territory` event is provided in Figure 2.

> *Syrian government forces have captured a central town and adjacent villages, boosting security in nearby areas loyal to President Bashar Assad, and marched deeper into a rebel-held neighborhood of Damascus, Syrian state media and an opposition monitoring group said Sunday.*

Figure 2: Sample text snippet reporting an event.

The annotation was performed by two pairs of independent annotators, cross-validating the annotated snippets. The initial disagreement rate was observed to be roughly 10-15%. Most unclear text snippets, for which there were comparably strong arguments for assigning two or more labels, were removed from the test dataset. For text snippets reporting on multiple events, the more recent event was considered to be the main event (and given the priority for determining the type), whereas the remaining events were considered only as background information. Some ambiguities were solved by aligning on common assumptions, e.g. if there is

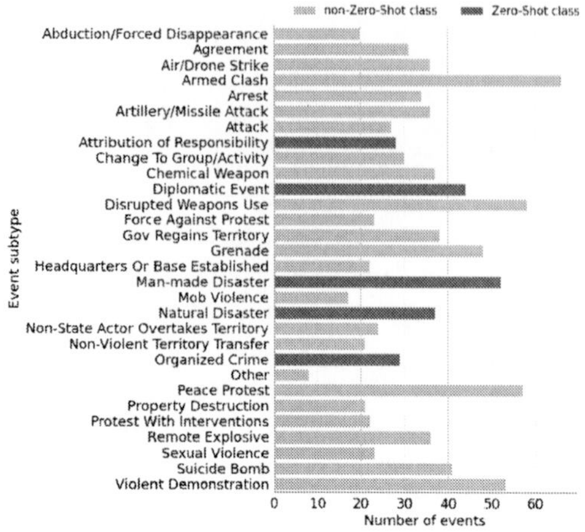

Figure 3: Event type count distribution in the test dataset.

no explicit mention of violence, a protest reported in the snippet was considered to be a peaceful one.

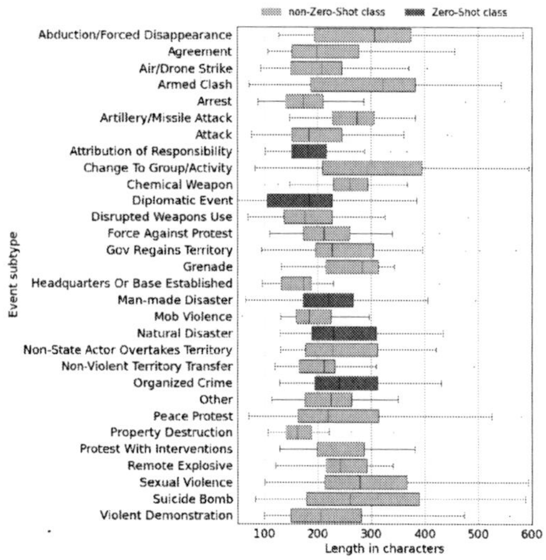

Figure 4: Distribution of the length of the text snippets by event type in the test dataset.

It is important to emphasize that the created test dataset for the Shared Task reported in this paper contains text snippets reporting events, which were prepared solely for the purpose of evaluating solutions for automated fine-grained classification of events reported in short texts.[7]

[7]**Disclaimer:** A significant fraction of the text snippets in the test dataset has no link to any real-world event whatsoever and, in particular, the locations mentioned therein were selected completely at random. As such, even though some of

5 Evaluation methodology

For measuring the event classification performance we used *precision*, *recall*, and the *micro*, *macro* and *weighted* F_1 metric. While the micro version calculates the performance from the classification of individual instances vis-a-vis the all-class model, in macro-averaging, one computes the performance of each individual class separately, and then an average of the obtained scores is computed. The *weighted* F_1 is similar to the *macro* version, but computes the average considering the proportion for each class in the dataset.

6 Systems

6.1 Baseline Systems

We provide two baseline systems: a simple character n-gram based L2-regularized logistic regression model and a system based on two Transformer-based deep neural representation models.

6.1.1 L2-regularized Logistic Regression on character n-grams ($L2LR_{baseline}$)

For Subtask 1 we have trained a L2-regularized Logistic Regression-based model with log-scaled TF-IDF values of 3 to 5 character ngrams found in the text snippets as features[8] (non-optimized, with $C = 1.0$ and $\epsilon = 0.01$) using LIBLINEAR library[9]. In particular, a more balanced subset of ca. 129K event snippets from ACLED-III (Piskorski et al., 2020) was used, i.e., all high-populated classes were under-sampled with a maximum of 10K instances per class.

6.1.2 Combined deep Transformers BERT and BART ($BB_{baseline}$)

As our main baseline model for Subtasks 1-3 we use a combination of two Transformer-based unsupervised language representation models: a multi-layer bidirectional Transformer encoder BERT (Devlin et al., 2019) and a sequence-to-sequence autoencoder BART (Lewis et al., 2019). As a base classifier we employ the BERT-BASE model, pre-trained using two unsupervised tasks: masked language model and next sentence prediction on lower-cased English text of the BooksCorpus (800M words) and English Wikipedia (2,500M words) and fine-tuned for supervised classification using ACLED-III data as described in Piskorski et al. (2020). For Subtasks 2-3 involving a zero-shot learning problem our baseline system relies on the following further steps. The test set observations (text snippets) for which the predicted logits (outputs before the $softmax$ normalization) obtained using fine-tuned BERT fall below the threshold $l = 7$, or for which the predicted label corresponds to the `Other` class, are passed to the second stage of processing using BART. In the second stage with the objective to tackle the zero-shot learning problem we use BART-LARGE-MNLI, pre-trained on the Multi-Genre Natural Language Inference (MNLI) corpus of 433k sentence pairs annotated with textual entailment information (Williams et al., 2018). In this stage, the classification task is reformulated as the natural language inference (NLI) task of determining whether a *hypothesis* is true (entailment) or false (contradiction), given a *premise*. We follow the approach proposed in Yin et al. (2019) and take the text snippet as the *premise* and the descriptive forms of candidate labels as alternative *hypotheses*. The final label is assigned in this stage based on the largest probability of entailment obtained using BART. For each text snippet being processed in this stage the set of candidate labels is defined as consisting of the label predicted in the first stage by the BERT model and all labels of the zero-shot (unseen) classes relevant for the respective subtask.

6.2 Participant Systems

Eight teams registered for the task, whereas four teams submitted their system responses: **ICIP** (Institute of Software Chinese Academy of Sciences), **FKIE-ITF** (Fraunhofer Institute for Communication, Information Processing and Ergonomics), **IBM-MNLP** (IBM Multilingual Natural Language Processing), **UNCC** (University of North Carolina Charlotte). All participants took part in all 3 subtasks, with the exception of FKIE-ITF which took part only in Subtask 1. We provide short overview of these systems.

For Subtask 1 all teams used a fine-tuned ROBERTA as their base classification model. For Subtask 2, most of the teams used a hybrid solution, using a diversity of classifiers, one team did use few shot learning (therefore diverging from the zero shot problem statement). For Subtask 3, where a

the text snippets in the test dataset might have a link to some real-world events the information contained in the snippets may contradict factual information. Consequently, this dataset should not be used as a database of events for the analysis of real-world socio-political developments and conflict events.

[8] An n-gram is considered as a feature only if it appears at least 15 times in the training data.

[9] `https://www.csie.ntu.edu.tw/~cjlin/liblinear`

zero-shot classifier was mandatory, all participants based their system on a Transformer-based model trained on an NLI task, with some variations.

Despite using the same base approaches, each team focused in its submission on different ways to improve it: ICIP tried different attention mechanisms; FKIE-ITF (Kent and Krumbiegel, 2021) explored different text pre-processing techniques and used sub-sampling; IBM-MNLP (Barker et al., 2021) tried re-ranking different combination of few-shot, zero-shot and regular classifiers; UNCC (Radford, 2021) focused on using a single NLI learning approach for all tasks and used a specific sub-sampling.

System	Prec.	Rec.	F_1
$L2LR_{baseline}$	*0.728*	*0.668*	*0.678*
$BB_{baseline}$	*0.861*	*0.837*	*0.838*
FKIE-ITF 1.1	0.824	0.797	0.799
FKIE-ITF 1.2	0.851	0.829	0.830
FKIE-ITF 1.3	0.828	0.808	0.808
FKIE-ITF 1.4	0.841	0.802	0.812
FKIE-ITF 1.5	0.817	0.793	0.793
IBM-MNLP 1.1	0.851	0.830	0.828
IBM-MNLP 1.2	0.856	0.834	0.835
IBM-MNLP 1.3	**0.861**	**0.838**	**0.839**
ICIP 1.1	0.857	0.826	0.829
ICIP 1.2	0.855	0.829	0.831
ICIP 1.3	0.834	0.789	0.796
ICIP 1.4	0.858	0.828	0.832
ICIP 1.5	0.857	0.825	0.829
UNCC 1.1	0.798	0.739	0.736

Table 1: Overall performance overview Subtask 1: weighted average scores.

System	Sys. type	Prec.	Rec.	F_1
$BB_{baseline}$	*Zero-S.*	*0.811*	*0.787*	*0.788*
IBM-MNLP 2.1	Few-S.	0.824	0.782	0.779
IBM-MNLP 2.2	Few-S.	0.817	**0.797**	**0.797**
IBM-MNLP 2.3	Few-S.	0.824	0.794	0.790
IBM-MNLP 2.4	Zero-S.	0.809	0.786	0.785
ICIP 2.1	Zero-S.	0.798	0.744	0.742
ICIP 2.2	Zero-S.	0.823	0.781	0.776
ICIP 2.3	Zero-S.	0.820	0.775	0.769
ICIP 2.4	Zero-S.	0.827	0.781	0.779
ICIP 2.5	Zero-S.	**0.829**	0.784	0.782
UNCC 2.1	Zero-S.	0.670	0.658	0.635
UNCC 2.2	Zero-S.	0.670	0.658	0.635

Table 2: Overall performance overview Subtask 2: weighted average scores.

System	Sys. type	Prec.	Rec.	F_1
$BB_{baseline}$	*Zero-S.*	*0.803*	*0.745*	*0.753*
IBM-MNLP 3.1	Zero-S.	0.793	0.744	0.746
IBM-MNLP 3.2	Few-S.	0.787	0.755	0.756
IBM-MNLP 3.3	Zero-S.	0.793	0.744	0.746
IBM-MNLP 3.4	Few-S.	0.787	0.755	0.756
ICIP 3.1	Zero-S.	0.790	0.741	0.733
ICIP 3.2	Zero-S.	0.818	0.775	0.765
ICIP 3.3	Zero-S.	0.810	0.768	0.757
ICIP 3.4	Zero-S.	0.818	0.775	0.767
ICIP 3.5	Zero-S.	**0.821**	**0.778**	**0.771**
UNCC 3.1	Zero-S.	0.643	0.625	0.602
UNCC 3.2	Zero-S.	0.644	0.629	0.605

Table 3: Overall performance overview Subtask 3: weighted average scores.

7 Evaluation Results

The results for all submitted system responses for all 3 subtasks in terms of precision, recall and F_1 weighted average scores are provided in Table 1, 2 and 3 respectively, detailed results are given in Appendix B. Each team had the possibility to submit a maximum of 5 configurations per subtask, all of which are reported in the table, and identified by a numerical extension. As an overview of the obtained results, the best performing systems for the three subtasks are 83.9%, 79.7% and 77.1% weighted F_1 scores respectively.

The two teams that reported using undersampling due to lack of sufficient computational resources, are also the ones having the overall lowest score on Subtask 1.

In Table 2, all submissions of team IBM-MNLP are few-shots excepts for their last submission: IBM-MNLP 2.4. Both of their few-shot and zero-shot configurations perform better then systems of any other team for Subtask 2. In Table 3, their first and third submissions are zero shot for the 5 new types, while their two other submissions are zero-shot only for the 2 new types.

For Subtask 3, the best weighted F_1 score for zero-shot classifier restricted to the 5 new classes only are the following: 65.1% for ICIC, 52.9% for IBM-MNLP and 26.2% for UNCC, c.f. Table 7 for details.

8 Discussion

8.1 Overall Results

The results of all three subtasks provide interesting insights on fine-grained event classification in the context of real-world applications, where practical constraints can lead to a setup with a drift between the data on which the models were trained and for which predictions are generated, and where unseen classes can naturally pose a zero-shot learning problem. Firstly, we conclude that in Subtask 1 the Transformer-based BERT and ROBERTA were observed to lead to virtually the same level of performance in terms of all considered metrics. This observation is interesting, as e.g. on the GLUE benchmark (Wang et al., 2018) ROBERTA is shown to outperform BERT. Secondly, after enhancing the classification task to a generalized zero-shot learning problems in Subtask 2 and 3, the submitted results suggest that the best solutions are, very similar to our baseline $BB_{baseline}$ described in Section 6.1.2, based on the two-stage approach employing a supervised, fine-tuned Transformer-based classifier and another Transformer-based model instance trained on the MNLI data for tackling the zero-shot classification as the sentence-entailment problem. Interestingly, only one team (UNCC) submitted a single-stage model, trained on the entailment-like reformulation of the classification problem. We hypothesize that compared to the single-stage entailment-like setup, the two-stage approaches might more effectively utilize the information provided in the available training data. The significant differences in performance values between these two paradigms in all three subtasks (73.6% vs. 83.9% in Subtask 1, 63.5% vs. 79.7% in Subtask 2 and 60.5% vs. 77.1% in Subtask 3) might seem to confirm this hypothesis. However, it should be stressed that the submissions following the single-stage entailment-like setup were made with a disclaimer on computational limitations.

In order to provide some flavour of most typical errors and difficulties of automatically labelling event snippets using ACLED taxonomy Figure 5 provides the confusion matrix, normalized over the true conditions (rows), for the $BB_{baseline}$ approach applied to solve Subtask 1.

The most significant type of error is the misclassification of `Force Against Protest` as `Protest With Interventions` (39%), `Property Destruction` as `Mob Violence` (29%) and as `Violent Demonstration` (24%) and `Artillery/Missile Attack` as `Armed Clash` (19%). Given a fine line between these types, the above error rates are not surprising. More generally, one can observe that distinguishing between the sub-types belonging to the same main type (see the ACLED taxonomy in Appendix A), is typically more challenging. Also, it is not surprising that the `Other` class has also a relatively low recall of 50%.

As regards models robustness, in Piskorski et al. (2020), the reported F_1 score of the BERT-based ACLED-trained classifier when evaluated on ACLED data yield about 94.4%. In Subtask 1, using similar Transformer-based classifier lead to a maximal score of 83.9%: we observe approx. 10 percentage point drop in performance. It is important to mention herethat the former model used 80% of the ACLED data for training, whereas the latter used the entire ACLED dataset reported in Piskorski et al. (2020).

Class-wise performance comparison of both classifiers are reported in Table 8.

Such a performance drop can be explained in part by the fact that text snippets in the ACLED follow a pattern that is different than news-like reporting, and as such the classifier struggles to generalize to the real-world news-like reporting style, despite the standard regularization techniques.

The performance drop is not equally distributed over the classes. Actually, when applying to news data, roughly half of the classes have better scores, and half have worse scores.

One possible reason for this performance drop seems to be the three most populated classes in the ACLED dataset (`Armed Clash`, `Attack`, `Artillery/Missile Attack`) which on average lost 18 points when compared with the results of the baseline model $BB_{baseline}$.

8.2 ACLED taxonomy

Having used ACLED taxonomy in the context of this Shared Task have resulted in some reflections, both in terms of experience of using it to annotate text snippets reporting events and its practicality for a real-world application for automatically labelling news-like texts.

As regards the annotation of news-like text snippets great care has been taken to follow strictly the ACLED Codebook. This turned to be a harder task than initially expected, in part due to shortcomings of the Codebook, and, in part due to the nature of how events are reported in the news.

News texts often assume a known global context and do not provide enough information to allow to clearly assign an ACLED event subtype. This is due the high specificity of ACLED subtypes that make it hard, for instance, to classify a text describing a demonstration, if it can not be understood from the text whether the event was violent, and if this was the case, which side started the violence, i.e., the demonstrators or the authority tasked to thwart the demonstration. All such information is needed to select the proper ACLED event class. Having said this, it is worthwhile to mention here that sometimes the nuances between the definitions of the event types are very small and we also found certain inconsistencies between the entries in the ACLED event database itself, e.g. for the `Protest with Intervention` and `Excessive force against the protesters` categories the corresponding text descriptions did not differ much, and at times using certain instrument to intervene was mentioned in the case of both events. Clearly, when encoding an event using ACLED taxonomy based on HUMINT and without considering any source text the human knows the event type upfront, and hence, the resulting text describing the event might not fully reflect/mirror the specific of the particular event type. This poses a certain limitation to what extent the textual descriptions of events in ACLED can be useful for training models to be applied on news-like data, but to have a better picture a full-fledged study of the aforementioned inconsistencies should be carried out, which is out of scope of the Shared Task.

The high specificity of the ACLED taxonomy is also at times problematic as it was not designed for multi-label classification tasks. As such, an attack on a civilian with a suicide bomber can not be classified as suicide bombing event according to ACLED taxonomy if any other interaction took place and is reported, for instance, if the text mentions also assailants attack with firearms first before detonating the bomb or if the police tries to stop them. In such a case the `Armed Clash` event type has to be used. On the other hand, intuitively, it would make sense that the text is tagged with at least two labels: `Attack` (attack on civilian) and `Suicide bombing`, or potentially also a tag that represents an authority intervention. ACLED taxonomy imposes a complex and incomplete set of priorities in order to enforce an event to be labelled using a mono-dimensional classification.

Another issue encountered when using this taxonomy is related to the fact that definitions of some event classes are unclear and not intuitive per-se. For instance, the class `Arrest` which accounts for either mass arrests or arrest of VIPs, but not for arrests of "one or few" people, which fall under a different type. Furthermore, problematic is also the fact that some classes are actually determined not only by what actually happened but also by who was the main actor involved. For instance, the class `Government retakes territory` and `Non-state actor captures territory` are almost indistinguishable when the named entities are shuffled. What is more, the taxonomy does not specify how to handle certain cases, e.g., when a non-government actor is acting on behalf of or is supported by the government in regaining/overtaking territory.

Lastly, disregarding the strictly mono-dimensional nature of ACLED taxonomy, most news text snippets (even single sentences) report on more than one event, and determining which one is the salient one is not always straightforward even to human annotators. One of our observations is that for labelling news reporting on events a multi-class labelling approach would be more intuitive and logical.

9 Conclusions

This paper reported on the outcome of the Shared Task on Fine-grained Event Classification in News-like Text Snippets that has been organized as part of the Workshop on Challenges and Applications of Automated Extraction of Socio-political Events from Text (CASE 2021), co-located with the ACL-IJCNLP 2021 Conference.

8 teams registered to participate in the task, while 4 of them submitted system responses for 3 subtasks, two of which were generalized zero-shot learning tasks. Given the specific set up of the shared task, i.e., the training data being somewhat different from the test data and inclusion of 5 unseen classes the top results obtained can be considered good, however, there is definitely place for improvement. Furthermore, we intend to carry out comparative error analysis across systems, which might reveal some additional insights into the complexity of the task.

Further documentation and related material on the reported Shared Task can be found at `https://github.com/emerging-welfare/case-2021-shared-task/tree/main/task2`, whereas the test dataset alone is also available at: `http://piskorski.waw.pl/resources/case2021/data.zip` for research purposes.

We believe that the reported results, findings and the annotated test dataset will contribute to stimulating further research on fine-grained event classification.

References

Douglas E. Appelt. 1999. Introduction to information extraction. *AI Commun.*, 12(3):161–172.

Martin Atkinson, Jakub Piskorski, Roman Yangarber, and Erik van der Goot. 2011. Multilingual Real-Time Event Extraction for Border Security Intelligence Gathering. In *Open Source Intelligence and Counter-terrorism*. Springer, LNCS, Vol. 2.

Ken Barker, Parul Awasthy, Jian Ni, and Radu Florian. 2021. IBM MNLP IE at CASE 2021 Task 2: NLI Reranking for Zero-Shot Text Classification. In *Proceedings of the* 4th *Workshop on Challenges and Applications of Automated Extraction of Socio-political Events from Text (CASE 2021)*. Association for Computational Linguistics (ACL).

Wei-Lun Chao, Soravit Changpinyo, Boqing Gong, and Fei Sha. 2016. An empirical study and analysis of generalized zero-shot learning for object recognition in the wild. In *European conference on computer vision*, pages 52–68. Springer.

Nancy A. Chinchor. 1998. Overview of MUC-7. In *Seventh Message Understanding Conference (MUC-7): Proceedings of a Conference Held in Fairfax, Virginia, April 29 - May 1, 1998*.

Jacob Devlin, Ming-Wei Chang, Kenton Lee, and Kristina Toutanova. 2019. BERT: Pre-training of Deep Bidirectional Transformers for Language Understanding. In *Proceedings of the 2019 Conference of the North American Chapter of the Association for Computational Linguistics: Human Language Technologies, Volume 1 (Long and Short Papers)*, pages 4171–4186, Minneapolis, Minnesota. Association for Computational Linguistics.

George Doddington, Alexis Mitchell, Mark Przybocki, Lance Ramshaw, Stephanie Strassel, and Ralph Weischedel. 2004. The Automatic Content Extraction (ACE) Program – Tasks, Data, and Evaluation. In *Proceedings of the Fourth International Conference on Language Resources and Evaluation (LREC'04)*, Lisbon, Portugal. European Language Resources Association (ELRA).

Yu Hong, Jianfeng Zhang, Bin Ma, Jianmin Yao, Guodong Zhou, and Qiaoming Zhu. 2011. Using Cross-Entity Inference to Improve Event Extraction. In *Proceedings of the 49th Annual Meeting of the Association for Computational Linguistics: Human Language Technologies*, pages 1127–1136, Portland, Oregon, USA. Association for Computational Linguistics.

Ali Hürriyetoğlu, Hristo Tanev, Vanni Zavarella, Jakub Piskorski, Reyyan Yeniterzi, and Erdem Yörük. 2021. Challenges and Applications of Automated Extraction of Socio-political Events from Text (CASE 2021): Workshop and Shared Task Report. In *Proceedings of the* 4th *Workshop on Challenges and Applications of Automated Extraction of Socio-political Events from Text (CASE 2021)*. Association for Computational Linguistics (ACL).

Ali Hürriyetoglu, Erdem Yörük, Deniz Yuret, Çagri Yoltar, Burak Gürel, Firat Durusan, Osman Mutlu, and Arda Akdemir. 2019. Overview of CLEF 2019 lab protestnews: Extracting protests from news in a cross-context setting. In *Experimental IR Meets Multilinguality, Multimodality, and Interaction - 10th International Conference of the CLEF Association, CLEF 2019, Lugano, Switzerland, September 9-12, 2019, Proceedings*, volume 11696 of *Lecture Notes in Computer Science*, pages 425–432. Springer.

Ali Hürriyetoğlu, Erdem Yörük, Osman Mutlu, Fırat Duruşan, Çağrı Yoltar, Deniz Yüret, and Burak Gürel. 2021. Cross-Context News Corpus for Protest Event-Related Knowledge Base Construction. *Data Intelligence*, pages 1–28.

Gilles Jacobs and Veronique Hoste. 2020. Extracting fine-grained economic events from business news. In *Proceedings of the 1st Joint Workshop on Financial Narrative Processing and MultiLing Financial Summarisation*, pages 235–245, Barcelona, Spain (Online). COLING.

Samantha Kent and Theresa Krumbiegel. 2021. CASE 2021 Task 2: Socio-political Fine-grained Event Classification using Fine-tuned RoBERTa Document Embeddings. In *Proceedings of the* 4th *Workshop on Challenges and Applications of Automated Extraction of Socio-political Events from Text (CASE 2021)*. Association for Computational Linguistics (ACL).

Gary King and Will Lowe. 2003. An Automated Information Extraction Tool For International Conflict Data with Performance as Good as Human Coders. *International Organization*, 57:617–642.

LDC. 2008. Annotation Tasks and Specification. ONLINE: `https://www.ldc.upenn.edu/collaborations/past-projects/ace/annotation-tasks-and-specifications`.

Kalev Leetaru and Philip A Schrodt. 2013. Gdelt: Global data on events, location, and tone, 1979–2012. In *ISA Annual Convention*, volume 2.

Els Lefever and Véronique Hoste. 2016. A Classification-based Approach to Economic Event Detection in Dutch News Text. In *Proceedings of the Tenth International Conference on Language Resources and Evaluation (LREC'16)*, pages 330–335, Portorož, Slovenia. European Language Resources Association (ELRA).

Mike Lewis, Yinhan Liu, Naman Goyal, Marjan Ghazvininejad, Abdelrahman Mohamed, Omer Levy, Ves Stoyanov, and Luke Zettlemoyer. 2019. Bart: Denoising sequence-to-sequence pre-training for natural language generation, translation, and comprehension. *arXiv preprint arXiv:1910.13461*.

Shasha Liao and Ralph Grishman. 2010. Using Document Level Cross-Event Inference to Improve Event Extraction. In *Proceedings of the 48th Annual Meeting of the Association for Computational Linguistics*, pages 789–797, Uppsala, Sweden. Association for Computational Linguistics.

Thien Huu Nguyen, Nicolas Fauceglia, Mariano Rodriguez Muro, Oktie Hassanzadeh, Alfio Massimiliano Gliozzo, and Mohammad Sadoghi. 2016. Joint Learning of Local and Global Features for Entity Linking via Neural Networks. In *Proceedings of COLING 2016, the 26th International Conference on Computational Linguistics: Technical Papers*, pages 2310–2320, Osaka, Japan. The COLING 2016 Organizing Committee.

Thien Huu Nguyen and Ralph Grishman. 2015. Event Detection and Domain Adaptation with Convolutional Neural Networks. In *Proceedings of the 53rd Annual Meeting of the Association for Computational Linguistics and the 7th International Joint Conference on Natural Language Processing (Volume 2: Short Papers)*, pages 365–371, Beijing, China. Association for Computational Linguistics.

Timothy Nugent, Fabio Petroni, Natraj Raman, Lucas Carstens, and Jochen L. Leidner. 2017. A comparison of classification models for natural disaster and critical event detection from news. In *2017 IEEE International Conference on Big Data, BigData 2017, Boston, MA, USA, December 11-14, 2017*, pages 3750–3759.

J. Pastor-Galindo, P. Nespoli, F. Gómez Mármol, and G. Martínez Pérez. 2020. The Not Yet Exploited Goldmine of OSINT: Opportunities, Open Challenges and Future Trends. *IEEE Access*, 8:10282–10304.

Jakub Piskorski, Jacek Haneczok, and Guillaume Jacquet. 2020. New benchmark corpus and models for fine-grained event classification: To BERT or not to BERT? In *Proceedings of the 28th International Conference on Computational Linguistics*, pages 6663–6678, Barcelona, Spain (Online). International Committee on Computational Linguistics.

Jakub Piskorski and Roman Yangarber. 2013. Information extraction: Past, present and future. In Thierry Poibeau, Horacio Saggion, Jakub Piskorski, and Roman Yangarber, editors, *Multi-source, Multilingual Information Extraction and Summarization*, Theory and Applications of Natural Language Processing, pages 23–49. Springer Berlin Heidelberg.

Benjamin Radford. 2021. CASE 2021 Task 2: Zero-Shot Classification of Fine-Grained Sociopolitical Events with Transformer Models. In *Proceedings of the 4th Workshop on Challenges and Applications of Automated Extraction of Socio-political Events from Text (CASE 2021)*. Association for Computational Linguistics (ACL).

Clionadh Raleigh, Andrew Linke, Håvard Hegre, and Joakim Karlsen. 2010. Introducing ACLED: An Armed Conflict Location and Event Dataset: Special Data Feature. *Journal of Peace Research*, 47(5):651–660.

Sovan Kumar Sahoo, Saumajit Saha, Asif Ekbal, and Pushpak Bhattacharyya. 2020. A Platform for Event Extraction in Hindi. In *Proceedings of The 12th Language Resources and Evaluation Conference*, pages 2241–2250, Marseille, France. European Language Resources Association.

Mark Stickel and Mabry Tyson. 1997. Fastus: A cascaded finite-state transducer for extracting information from natural-language text. In *Finite-State Language Processing*, pages 383–406. MIT Press.

Beth M. Sundheim. 1991. Overview of the Third Message Understanding Evaluation and Conference. In *Third Message Uunderstanding Conference (MUC-3): Proceedings of a Conference Held in San Diego, California, May 21-23, 1991*.

Cynthia Van Hee, Els Lefever, Ben Verhoeven, Julie Mennes, Bart Desmet, Guy De Pauw, Walter Daelemans, and Veronique Hoste. 2015. Detection and Fine-Grained Classification of Cyberbullying Events. In *Proceedings of the International Conference Recent Advances in Natural Language Processing*, pages 672–680, Hissar, Bulgaria. INCOMA Ltd. Shoumen, BULGARIA.

Alex Wang, Amanpreet Singh, Julian Michael, Felix Hill, Omer Levy, and Samuel R Bowman. 2018. Glue: A multi-task benchmark and analysis platform for natural language understanding. *arXiv preprint arXiv:1804.07461*.

Michael D Ward, Andreas Beger, Josh Cutler, Matt Dickenson, Cassy Dorff, and Ben Radford. 2013. Comparing GDELT and ICEWS event data. *Analysis*, 21:267–297.

Adina Williams, Nikita Nangia, and Samuel Bowman. 2018. A broad-coverage challenge corpus for sentence understanding through inference. In *Proceedings of the 2018 Conference of the North American Chapter of the Association for Computational Linguistics: Human Language Technologies, Volume 1 (Long Papers)*, pages 1112–1122. Association for Computational Linguistics.

Roman Yangarber, Peter Von Etter, and Ralf Steinberger. 2008. Content Collection and Analysis in the Domain of Epidemiology. In *Proceedings of DrMED 2008: International Workshop on Describing Medical Web Resources at MIE 2008: the 21st International Congress of the European Federation for Medical Informatics 2008*, Goeteborg, Sweden.

Wenpeng Yin, Jamaal Hay, and Dan Roth. 2019. Benchmarking zero-shot text classification: Datasets, evaluation and entailment approach. *arXiv preprint arXiv:1909.00161*.

Appendices

A Event Types

The ACLED event taxonomy comprises of six main event types which are further subdivided into 25 sub-event types as follows:

```
BATTLES
  - Armed clash
  - Government regains territory
  - Non-state actor overtakes territory
EXPLOSION AND REMOTE VIOLENCE
  - Chemical weapon
  - Air/drone strike
  - Suicide bomb
  - Shelling/artillery/missile attack
  - Remote explosive/landmine/IED
  - Grenade
VIOLENCE AGAINST CIVILIANS
  - Sexual violence
  - Attack
  - Abduction/forced disappearance
PROTESTS
  - Peaceful protest
  - Protest with intervention
  - Excessive force against protesters
RIOTS
  - Violent demonstration
  - Mob violence
STRATEGIC DEVELOPMENTS
  - Agreement
  - Arrests
  - Change to group/activity
  - Disrupted weapons use
  - Headquarters or base established
  - Looting/property destruction
  - Non-violent transfer of territory
  - Other
```

For further details on ACLED event taxonomy please refer to the ACLED codebook.

We provide here the description of the 5 new types used in the Shared Task. The first three new types cover contextually important security- and safety-related events and developments that are not related to political violence and not considered to contribute to political dynamics within and across multiple states. The last two new types cover events directly related to security situation, and as such fall under the `Strategic Development` main event type of ACLED, however, they are mainly related to announcements instead of concrete deeds. The 5 additional new types are as follows:

- `Organized crime`: This event type covers incidents related to activities of criminal groups, excluding conflict between such groups: smuggling, human trafficking, counterfeit products, property crime, cyber crime, assassination (for criminal purposes), corruption, etc.
- `Natural Disaster`: This event type covers any kind of natural disasters and hazards where there is a direct or potential harm, including: earthquakes, tsunami, floods, storms, fires, volcano eruptions, landslides, avalanches, infectious disease outbreaks, pandemics, climate related, etc.
- `Man-made Disaster`: This event type covers any kind of disasters caused by humans where there is a direct or potential harm, such as: industrial accidents, traffic incidents, infrastructure failure, foodchain contamination, etc.
- `Diplomatic Event`: This event type covers any kind of diplomatic action or announcement that have a potential impact on the security situation or denoting the attitude of a country towards a conflict. As such this type covers diplomatic measures declaration (e.g. sanctions or closure of embassies), threats, call for actions, praises and condemnations.
- `Attribution of Responsibility`: This event type covers announcements related to the responsibility of attacks and hostile operations. In particular, this event type covers group claiming their own responsibility, accusation of responsibility and denial of responsibility.

B Complete Evaluation Tables

	Micro average			Macro average			Weighted average		
System	Prec.	Rec.	F_1	Prec.	Rec.	F_1	Prec.	Rec.	F_1
$L2LR_{baseline}$	0.668	0.668	0.668	0.702	0.647	0.650	0.728	0.668	0.678
$BB_{baseline}$	0.837	0.837	0.837	0.837	0.804	0.807	0.861	0.837	0.838
FKIE-ITF 1.1	0.797	0.797	0.797	0.790	0.778	0.770	0.824	0.797	0.799
FKIE-ITF 1.2	0.829	0.829	0.829	0.807	0.808	0.794	0.851	0.829	0.830
FKIE-ITF 1.3	0.808	0.808	0.808	0.787	0.779	0.768	0.828	0.808	0.808
FKIE-ITF 1.4	0.802	0.802	0.802	0.788	0.789	0.774	0.841	0.802	0.812
FKIE-ITF 1.5	0.793	0.793	0.793	0.780	0.780	0.766	0.817	0.793	0.793
IBM-MNLP 1.1	0.830	0.830	0.830	0.828	0.787	0.792	0.851	0.830	0.828
IBM-MNLP 1.2	0.834	0.834	0.834	0.849	0.793	0.810	0.856	0.834	0.835
IBM-MNLP 1.3	0.838	0.838	0.838	0.854	0.800	0.814	0.861	0.838	0.839
ICIP 1.1	0.826	0.826	0.826	0.827	0.800	0.796	0.857	0.826	0.829
ICIP 1.2	0.829	0.829	0.829	0.824	0.802	0.798	0.855	0.829	0.831
ICIP 1.3	0.789	0.789	0.789	0.805	0.766	0.765	0.834	0.789	0.796
ICIP 1.4	0.828	0.828	0.828	0.827	0.803	0.799	0.858	0.828	0.832
ICIP 1.5	0.825	0.825	0.825	0.825	0.799	0.795	0.857	0.825	0.829
UNCC 1.1	0.739	0.739	0.739	0.770	0.697	0.698	0.798	0.739	0.736

Table 4: Overall performance overview for Subtask 1.

	Micro average			Macro average			Weighted average		
System	Prec.	Rec.	F_1	Prec.	Rec.	F_1	Prec.	Rec.	F_1
$L2LR_{baseline}$	0.668	0.585	0.624	0.627	0.578	0.581	0.638	0.585	0.593
$BB_{baseline}$	0.79	0.79	0.79	0.797	0.763	0.767	0.811	0.787	0.788
IBM-MNLP 2.1	0.782	0.782	0.782	0.809	0.753	0.752	0.824	0.782	0.779
IBM-MNLP 2.2	0.797	0.797	0.797	0.807	0.761	0.773	0.817	0.797	0.797
IBM-MNLP 2.3	0.794	0.794	0.794	0.811	0.759	0.764	0.824	0.794	0.790
IBM-MNLP 2.4	0.786	0.786	0.786	0.790	0.750	0.758	0.809	0.786	0.785
ICIP 2.1	0.744	0.744	0.744	0.767	0.733	0.718	0.798	0.744	0.742
ICIP 2.2	0.781	0.781	0.781	0.788	0.767	0.750	0.823	0.781	0.776
ICIP 2.3	0.775	0.775	0.775	0.786	0.760	0.743	0.820	0.775	0.769
ICIP 2.4	0.781	0.781	0.781	0.793	0.767	0.752	0.827	0.781	0.779
ICIP 2.5	0.784	0.784	0.784	0.795	0.769	0.755	0.829	0.784	0.782
UNCC 2.1	0.658	0.658	0.658	0.648	0.632	0.613	0.670	0.658	0.635
UNCC 2.2	0.658	0.658	0.658	0.648	0.632	0.613	0.670	0.658	0.635

Table 5: Overall performance overview for Subtask 2.

	Micro average			Macro average			Weighted average		
System	Prec.	Rec.	F_1	Prec.	Rec.	F_1	Prec.	Rec.	F_1
$L2LR_{baseline}$	0.668	0.544	0.600	0.585	0.539	0.542	0.593	0.544	0.551
$BB_{baseline}$	0.745	0.745	0.745	0.771	0.709	0.720	0.803	0.745	0.753
IBM-MNLP 3.1	0.744	0.744	0.744	0.769	0.714	0.720	0.793	0.744	0.746
IBM-MNLP 3.2	0.755	0.755	0.755	0.764	0.723	0.728	0.787	0.755	0.756
IBM-MNLP 3.3	0.744	0.744	0.744	0.769	0.714	0.720	0.793	0.744	0.746
IBM-MNLP 3.4	0.755	0.755	0.755	0.764	0.723	0.728	0.787	0.755	0.756
ICIP 3.1	0.741	0.741	0.741	0.762	0.725	0.708	0.790	0.741	0.733
ICIP 3.2	0.775	0.775	0.775	0.788	0.757	0.738	0.818	0.775	0.765
ICIP 3.3	0.768	0.768	0.768	0.779	0.749	0.729	0.810	0.768	0.757
ICIP 3.4	0.775	0.775	0.775	0.788	0.757	0.741	0.818	0.775	0.767
ICIP 3.5	0.778	0.778	0.778	0.791	0.760	0.744	0.821	0.778	0.771
UNCC 3.1	0.625	0.625	0.625	0.620	0.599	0.580	0.643	0.625	0.602
UNCC 3.2	0.629	0.629	0.629	0.621	0.602	0.582	0.644	0.629	0.605

Table 6: Overall performance overview for Subtask 3.

System	Sys. type	Prec.	Rec.	F_1
IBM-MNLP 3.1	Zero-S.	0.915	0.389	0.529
IBM-MNLP 3.2	Few-S.	0.896	0.553	**0.668**
IBM-MNLP 3.3	Zero-S.	0.915	0.389	0.529
IBM-MNLP 3.4	Few-S.	0.896	0.553	**0.668**
ICIP 3.1	Zero-S.	0.917	0.532	0.599
ICIP 3.2	Zero-S.	**0.941**	0.547	0.621
ICIP 3.3	Zero-S.	0.916	0.521	0.589
ICIP 3.4	Zero-S.	0.928	0.563	0.635
ICIP 3.5	Zero-S.	0.929	**0.579**	0.651
UNCC 3.1	Zero-S.	0.562	0.179	0.244
UNCC 3.2	Zero-S.	0.571	0.200	0.262

Table 7: Performance overview Subtask 3: weighted average scores on the 5 unknown types.

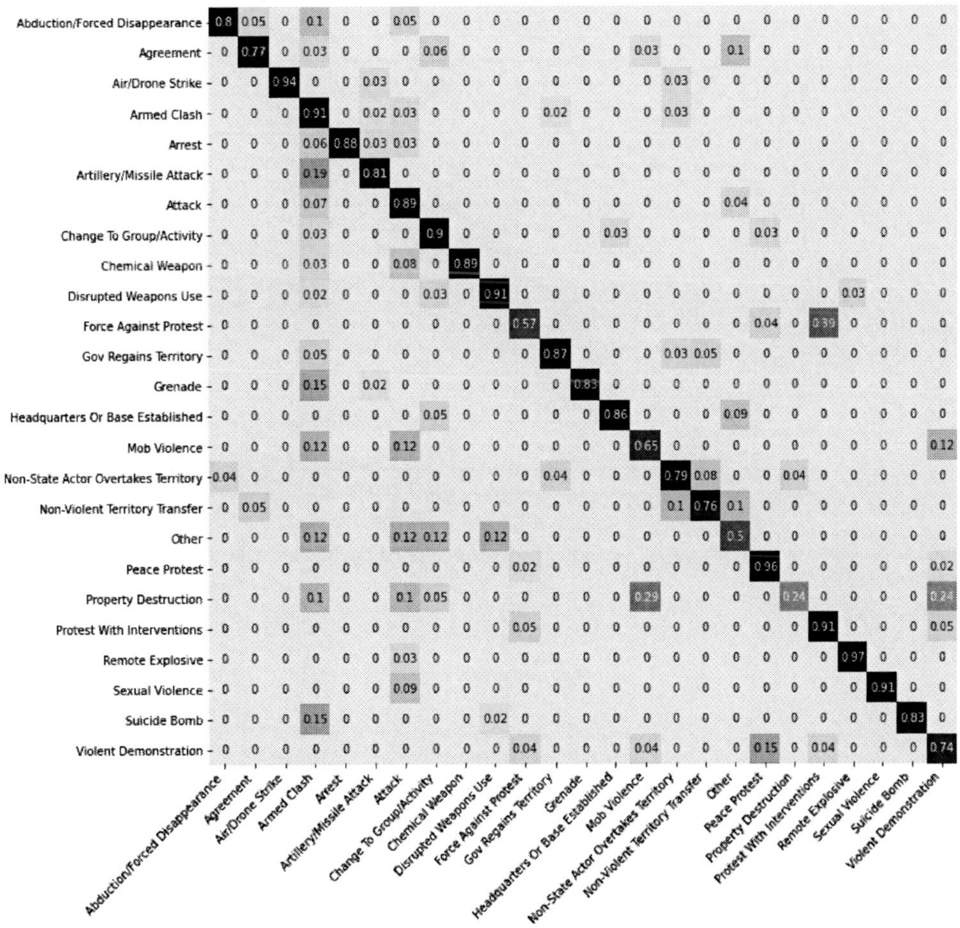

Figure 5: Confusion matrix for $BB_{baseline}$ applied to Subtask 1.

ACLED class	F_1 on ACLED	F_1 on News-like data	ΔF_1
Abduction/forced disappearance	0.903	0.865	-0.04
Agreement	0.831	0.842	0.01
Air/drone strike	0.987	0.971	-0.02
Armed clash	0.956	0.736	-0.22
Arrests	0.89	0.938	0.05
Attack	0.915	0.727	-0.19
Change to group/activity	0.838	0.844	0.01
Chemical weapon	0.829	0.943	0.11
Disrupted weapons use	0.891	0.938	0.05
Excessive force against protesters	0.692	0.650	-0.04
Government regains territory	0.839	0.904	0.07
Grenade	0.893	0.909	0.02
Headquarters or base established	0.758	0.905	0.15
Looting/property destruction	0.808	0.370	-0.44
Mob violence	0.851	0.595	-0.26
Non-state actor overtakes territory	0.784	0.776	-0.01
Non-violent transfer of territory	0.73	0.781	0.05
Other	0.64	0.400	-0.24
Peaceful protest	0.984	0.902	-0.08
Protest with intervention	0.813	0.755	-0.06
Remote explosive/landmine/IED	0.97	0.959	-0.01
Sexual violence	0.93	0.955	0.02
Shelling/artillery/missile attack	0.978	0.841	-0.14
Suicide bomb	0.933	0.907	-0.03
Violent demonstration	0.862	0.772	-0.09

Table 8: Comparison of $BB_{baseline}$ performances when applied on ACLED data vs. news-like data: weighted average scores

IBM MNLP IE at CASE 2021 Task 2: NLI Reranking for Zero-Shot Text Classification

Ken Barker, Parul Awasthy, Jian Ni, and Radu Florian
IBM Research AI
Yorktown Heights, NY 10598
{kjbarker, awasthyp, nij, raduf}@us.ibm.com

Abstract

Supervised models can achieve very high accuracy for fine-grained text classification. In practice, however, training data may be abundant for some types but scarce or even nonexistent for others. We propose a hybrid architecture that uses as much labeled data as available for fine-tuning classification models, while also allowing for types with little (few-shot) or no (zero-shot) labeled data. In particular, we pair a supervised text classification model with a Natural Language Inference (NLI) reranking model. The NLI reranker uses a textual representation of target types that allows it to score the strength with which a type is implied by a text, without requiring training data for the types. Experiments show that the NLI model is very sensitive to the choice of textual representation, but can be effective for classifying unseen types. It can also improve classification accuracy for the known types of an already highly accurate supervised model.[1]

1 Task 2: Fine-grained Classification of Socio-political Events

Fine-grained text classification assigns a type label to a text passage from an extended set of specific types. The types are often domain-specific and more focused than generic, coarse-grained topics. Creating an exhaustive list of such types for a domain or task *a priori* is challenging. Fine-grained type systems for a particular domain and task often evolve, with new, previously unseen types emerging. So some types may have many labeled examples available, some types may have few or none. In such a scenario, a flexible text classifier should be able to use training data when available, but also employ few-shot and zero-shot techniques when training data is limited or absent.

The Fine-grained Classification of Socio-political Events task (Haneczok et al., 2021) at the CASE 2021 workshop (Hürriyetoğlu et al., 2021) simulates the scenario of text classification with an evolving, fine-grained type system. There are 25 core, fine-grained event types capturing political violence, demonstrations, and other politically important events. The 25 types are from the ACLED (Armed Conflict Location & Event Data Project) event taxonomy (Raleigh et al., 2010). Copious training data exists for these types. Subtask 1 evaluates classification to these "seen" or "known" types only. Beyond the core types, subtask 2 identifies three new "unseen" types with no training data. Definitions of these three types were provided to task participants early, allowing exploration of zero-shot techniques on the types, but also few-shot techniques since the development window would allow enough time to annotate a handful of examples. Finally, subtask 3 introduces two additional unseen types revealed only at evaluation time. Subtask 3 evaluates true zero-shot techniques. Table 1 lists the type labels and names for the three subtasks.

For the task evaluation, organizers shared an evaluation set of 1,019 short texts (mostly one or two sentences each) with index numbers. 829 of the texts had gold labels from the 25 ACLED event types; 118 had gold labels from the three subtask2 types; 72 had gold labels from the two unseen subtask3 types. These numbers were not known at submission time. Submissions consisted of pairs of an index number with a single event type prediction for the text associated with the index. For scoring, the organizers removed entries whose gold event type was not among those being tested for the given subtask, and computed micro, macro, and weighted Precision, Recall, and F1-score. Weighted scores are the average of the per-type scores (like macro averages), but with the type scores weighted by the number of gold instances for the type.

[1]Distribution Statement "A" (Approved for Public Release, Distribution Unlimited)

Proceedings of the 4th Workshop on Challenges and Applications of Automated Extraction of Socio-political Events from Text (CASE), pages 193–202
August 5–6, 2021, ©2021 Association for Computational Linguistics

Type Label	Type Name
subtask 1	
ABDUCT_DISSAP	abduction
AGREEMENT	agreement
AIR_STRIKE	air strike
ARMED_CLASH	armed clash
ARREST	arrest
ART_MISS_ATTACK	artillery, missile attack
ATTACK	attack
CHANGE_TO_GRO...	change to group activity
CHEM_WEAP	chemical weapon
DISR_WEAP	disrupted weapons use
FORCE_AGAINST...	excessive force against protesters
GOV_REGAINS_TER...	government regains territory
GRENADE	grenade
HQ_ESTABLISHED	headquarters established
MOB_VIOL	mob violence
NON_STATE_ACT...	non-state actor overtakes territory
NON_VIOL_TERR...	non-violent transfer of territory
PEACE_PROTEST	peaceful protest
PROPERTY_DISTR...	property destruction
PROTEST_WITH_I...	protest with intervention
REM_EXPLOS	remote explosive
SEX_VIOL	sexual violence
SUIC_BOMB	suicide bomb
VIOL_DEMONSTR	violent demonstration
subtask 2	
ORG_CRIME	organized crime
NATURAL_DISAST...	natural disaster
MAN_MADE_DISAS...	man-made disaster
subtask 3	
ATTRIB	attribution of responsibility
DIPLO	diplomatic event

Table 1: Type labels (some truncated) and names for the 25 known types of subtask 1, the three unseen types of subtask 2, and the two unseen types of subtask 3

Our approach to fine-grained text classification mirrors the evolving type system scenario: a hybrid system that is fine-tuned with labeled data when available, but one that can also classify text with types having little or no labeled data. Our approach is first to apply a supervised text classification model to produce a ranked list of predicted, known types. The highest scoring types from the classification model are combined with any unseen types and passed to a Natural Language Inference (NLI) reranking model. The NLI reranker rescores the types on the extent to which they are implied by the input text.

2 System Architecture

We experimented with many different combinations of supervised, few-shot, and zero-shot techniques and submitted multiple such combinations for each of the Case Task 2 subtasks. Despite their differences, all submissions are built on the same cascaded architecture of a supervised neural classification model followed by a neural NLI-based reranking model. The submissions differ on the exact combination of classification model and reranking model.

For each sentence, the classification model produces a ranked list of predicted types with scores, but only for the types the model was trained on. If the score of the top-ranked predicted type is below threshold, or if the top-ranked predicted type is OTHER, the top N predicted types P_N are passed to the reranking model along with all unseen types U. The reranker independently scores each of the types in $P_N \cup U$. The highest scoring type is the final prediction for the sentence.

For each of the known and unseen types $P_N \cup U$ to be submitted to the reranker, we generate a textual representation, based only on the definition of the type (not labeled examples). See section 4.2.1 for details on how we generate textual representations. The NLI reranking model scores each of these representations on the extent to which they are implied by the input text. Figure 1 illustrates the general architecture.

3 Supervised Sequence Classification for Seen Types

For the text classifier we used a standard transformer-based sequence classification model (Vaswani et al., 2017) with a pre-trained language model. Based on previous experience with such text classification systems, we chose RoBERTa (Liu et al., 2019). Specifically, we started with the `roberta-large` model from Hugging Face (Wolf et al., 2020).

3.1 Data

For the 25 known ACLED event types, we used the `ACLED-C-III` dataset derived from the ACLED source data by (Piskorski et al., 2020). This dataset contains 588,940 short text passages each labeled with exactly one of the 25 ACLED event types. The dataset is organized in four folds, where each fold is a different random split of the 588,940 instances into 80% training and 20% test sets. For our 25-type base classifier we fine-tuned `roberta-large` on the training subset (471,152 instances) of fold 1 of the Piskorski dataset. For development experiments to arrive at our final architectures and parameters, we used subsets of the fold 1 test subset (117,788 instances). Piskorski also provides smaller partitions of the dataset used in their learning curve experiments. In our smaller

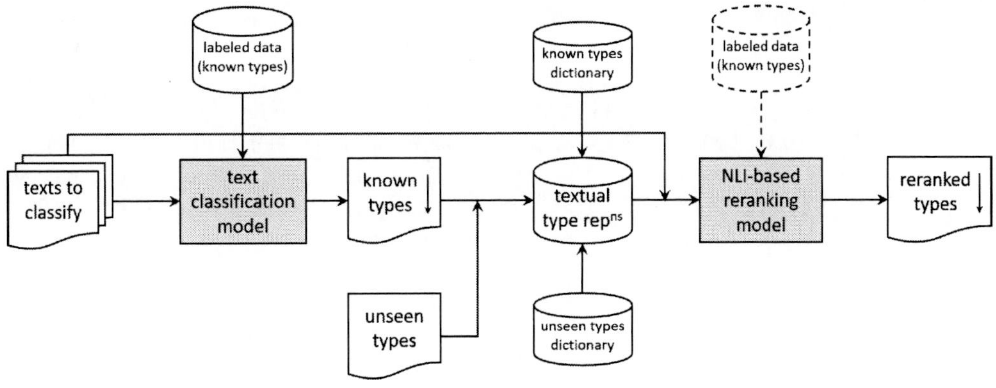

Figure 1: Cascaded Text Classification + NLI Reranking architecture. The classification model is trained on known types only and predicts a ranked list of known types. Any unseen types are added to the top N predicted known types for reranking. The reranking model may be fine-tuned for known types, in which case it is supervised (or few-shot supervised) for those types. The architecture is zero-shot for unseen types.

models (including `roberta-FT28`, see section 3.2), we used the 10% partition of the fold 1 training data.

In addition to the base classifier, we experimented with few-shot supervision for classifying the three unseen event types of subtask 2. We manually created a small training corpus of short texts (one or two sentences each) from Wikipedia and Wikinews. We found relevant documents by browsing the Wikipedia/Wikinews Categories hierarchies (for example, `https://en.wikipedia.org/wiki/Category:Natural_disasters` and `https://en.wikinews.org/wiki/Category:Crime_and_law`). Within relevant documents, we chose short text passages that described a single event of the target type. These passages were often simply the first one or two sentences in the document. An example appears in Figure 2. We originally collected 142 texts total: 56 texts for MAN_MADE_DISASTER; 55 texts for NATURAL_DISASTER; 31 texts for ORG_CRIME. For tuning experiments we created an additional test corpus of 20 short texts each for the three types. For the classification model used for final submissions on the challenge evaluation data, we combined both small corpora (along with an additional 20 texts for ORG_CRIME) for training on a total of 222 texts balanced among the three types.

3.2 Models

We fine-tuned `roberta-large` for sequence classification (with a linear classification layer) on the data described in section 3.1 to produce two classification models:

- `roberta-FT25`: fine-tuned on the 471,152 instances of ACLED training data for the 25 base ACLED event types
- `roberta-FT28`: fine-tuned on the 10% partition of the ACLED training data (47,115 instances) plus additional instances for the three unseen types of subtask 2 (142 instances during development, 222 for the final models)

Given the disparity in the number of training instances, we consider `roberta-FT28` to be supervised for the 25 types and *few-shot* supervised for the three unseen types.

Clock time for training `roberta-FT25` was 30 hours on four v100 GPUs. The time to train `roberta-FT28` was 4.6 hours on four v100 GPUs.

Experiments in (Piskorski et al., 2020) also trained models on the `ACLED-C-III` data, with

> *Search and rescue workers in Arkansas continue to search the Little Missouri and Caddo Rivers for survivors of Friday's flash flood. At least nineteen people were killed when the flood swept through the Albert Pike Recreation Area campground in the Ouachita National Forest in the southwestern portion of the state.*

Figure 2: A short NATURAL_DISASTER text consisting of the first two sentences of a Wikinews article under the Category `https://en.wikinews.org/wiki/Category:Disasters_and_accidents`.

model	trdata	μF	macF	wF
Piskorski	100%	94.3	86.0	94.2
roberta-FT25	100%	94.7	87.3	94.7
Piskorski	10%	>90	>70	>90
roberta-FT28	10%	93.5	77.1	93.5

Table 2: Comparison of micro F_1 score, macro F_1 score, and weighted F_1 score on test fold 1 of the `ACLED-C-III` dataset. Piskorkski refers to the `bert-base` model fine-tuned by Piskorski et al. (2020), which was the top performer on test fold 1 in their experiments. Test scores for the Piskorski model trained on 10% of the training data are estimated from the graphs in Piskorski et al. (2020).

metrics reported on test fold 1. So those results can be compared directly with our models. Performance of our model is consistent with their results fine-tuning `bert-base` (see Table 2).

4 NLI for Unseen Types

Pretrained language models (PLMs) have proven to be very powerful for downstream NLP tasks when they are fine-tuned on data specific to the task. Recently, the research community has begun to observe that PLMs fine-tuned on large amounts of data for complex end-to-end tasks can often be leveraged for new tasks without further fine-tuning. Fine-tuning PLMs on complex tasks such as Question Answering (QA) and Natural Language Inference (NLI) infuses models with high-level knowledge useful for other tasks. By choosing an appropriate task representation, QA models and NLI models can be used as "pre-tuned" models for few-shot (Schick and Schütze, 2021) or even zero-shot (Yin et al., 2019) text classification.

Typically, an NLI model takes two texts (sentence1 and sentence2) and predicts whether sentence1 implies sentence2, with a given confidence score. To re-purpose an NLI model for zero-shot text classification, sentence1 is the text to be classified and sentence2 is some textual representation of a type. The classification score for each type is the NLI score, which represents the extent to which the textual representation of the type is implied by sentence1. Determining implication is not just based on surface lexical overlap between the sentences. In training, the models learn encodings for both sentences, supervised by a large corpus of hand-labeled textual entailment pairs (such as the 433k sentence pairs in the multi-genre RepEval corpus (Williams et al., 2018)).

For the current work, we explored using large, pre-tuned NLI models for few-shot and zero-shot classification. We experimented with NLI extensions to both BART (Lewis et al., 2020) and RoBERTa (Liu et al., 2019) Language Models. For both of these, large models fine-tuned for the NLI task are available from Hugging Face: `bart-large-mnli` and `roberta-large-mnli`. Our experiments tended to favor RoBERTa (see section 4.3.3).

We also experimented with further fine-tuning the NLI models for the 25 subtask 1 types and the three subtask 2 types (sections 4.3.1 and 4.3.2).

4.1 Type Representations

A crucial design choice when using NLI for zero-shot text classification is the choice of representation of the types. We experimented with full English descriptions, keywords, and type names. Examples of each representation for a sample sentence appear in Table 3.

The full English descriptions are the type definitions taken verbatim from source documentation. For the original 25 types, these were taken from ACLED directly. for the five unseen types, definitions were provided by the organizers. The type names were taken from the same source documentation. The keywords were extracted manually from the definitions, with no editing other than deleting text from the definition. The disjoint keywords are exactly the same as the keywords, the difference being how they are submitted to the NLI model.

Table 4 shows how critical the choice of type representation is. The superiority of the name representation over definition and keywords was initially surprising, since it contains so much less information. We hypothesized that having multiple distinct terms covering more of the breadth of a type could help the NLI model, but that specific terms irrelevant to a given text were more harmful in confusing the model than the underspecificity of a single generic phrase. For example, the presence of terms such as "pandemic", "volcano", and "wildfire" would be distracting to a model when trying to determine whether a sentence about avalanches implies a natural disaster. To test the hypothesis, we considered a fourth type representation: *disjunctive keywords*. Rather than a single type representation in which all keywords appear together, with disjunctive keywords, each keyword for a type is considered an independent representation of the

sentence1	*A hacker group called DarkSide is behind the cyberattack on Colonial Pipeline that shut down a major oil pipeline over the weekend.*
Type Rep'n	**sentence2**
definition	*Organized crime: This event type covers incidents related to activities of criminal groups, excluding conflict between such groups: smuggling, human trafficking, counterfeit products, property crime, cyber crime, assassination (for criminal purposes), corruption, etc. (list is non-exhaustive).*
name	*organized crime*
keywords	*organized crime, smuggling, human trafficking, counterfeit products, property crime, cyber crime, assassination, corruption*
disj-kw	*organized crime | smuggling | human trafficking | counterfeit products | property crime | cyber crime | assassination | corruption*

Table 3: Example type representations for a sentence of the type ORG_CRIME. For the disj-kw representation, each phrase in the pipe-delimited list is given separately to the NLI model as sentence2.

Type rep'n	**μAcc**	**macAcc**
definition	0.5461	0.5672
keywords	0.4610	0.5243
name	0.8723	0.8456
disj-kw	0.8936	0.9048

Table 4: Effect of different type representations on zero-shot accuracy for the 142-example dev set for the three unseen types.

type. The extent to which a text implies a type t is the maximum score produced by the NLI model for any of t's keywords $kw(t)_i$.

4.2 Data

The original 25 ACLED event types include the type OTHER, which indicates a closed-world assumption: any event that is not one of the 24 main event types is of type OTHER. In the evolving type system scenario, the closed-world assumption does not hold. Texts labeled OTHER in the classifier training data may describe events of the unseen types. For this reason, we trained our classifiers (section 3) on all known types (including OTHER), but remove OTHER from the top N types submitted to the reranker. We also exclude OTHER instances from any training data used to fine-tune the reranking models.

To compare zero-shot reranking and reranking fine-tuned to known types, we prepared two new datasets.

For the 24 ACLED event types (ignoring OTHER), we created a training dataset derived from a subset of 10% of Piskorki's fold 1 training set (section 3.1). This initial data gave 46,886 positive instances. We added two negative examples for each positive example giving 140,658 total instances. The process for generating both positive and negative examples is described below in section 4.2.1.

To fine tune a few-shot supervised NLI model for the three unseen types of subtask 2, we created a dataset derived from the small dataset described in section 3.1. The 222 instances from that dataset provided the positive examples, to which we again added two negatives each, giving 666 total instances.

4.2.1 Labeling NLI Data

The labeled data for classification (section 3.1) consists of sentences with gold event type labels (REM_EXPLOS, ORG_CRIME, etc.). We need to adapt the data in two ways to use it for fine-tuning NLI models.

First, the labels must be replaced by a textual representation of the class, which will be used as sentence2 by the NLI model. We chose a disjunctive keyword representation as described in section 4.1. To create positive examples, we paired each sentence with each of the disjunctive keywords of the gold label. We then used the untuned `roberta-large-mnli` model to score each of these pairs to determine which of the disjunctive keywords was most strongly implied by the sentence. This gave us the best single keyword to use as sentence 2 for each positive training sentence.

Second, fine-tuning the model requires negative examples. For each positive example, we created two negative examples by replacing the gold type

positive	**s1**	*A hacker group called DarkSide is behind the cyberattack on Colonial Pipeline that shut down a major oil pipeline over the weekend.*
	s2	*cyber crime*
random negative	**s1**	*A hacker group called DarkSide is behind the cyberattack on Colonial Pipeline that shut down a major oil pipeline over the weekend.*
	s2	*forced disappearance*
imposter negative	**s1**	*A hacker group called DarkSide is behind the cyberattack on Colonial Pipeline that shut down a major oil pipeline over the weekend.*
	s2	*attack*

Table 5: Example positive and negative instances generated from a sentence whose gold event type label is ORG_CRIME. Sentence 2 (s2) for the positive instance is the keyword from the gold event type keywords scored highest by `roberta-large-mnli`. Sentence 2 for the imposter instance is the highest-scoring keyword from the non-gold event types.

representation with the type representation of a different event type: one random and one imposter. The random negative example is the original sentence paired with a random keyword selected from all of the keywords of types other than the gold type. The imposter is the keyword most likely to confuse the model. We paired each sentence with each of the disjunctive keywords for all of the types other than the gold type. We used the top scoring pair (the most strongly implied incorrect type representation) as the imposter example.

Table 5 shows positive and negative training instances created for an example sentence.

4.3 Development Experiments and Results

4.3.1 Classification + Reranking

Using an NLI model as described in section 4 is needed for unseen types, since the classification model cannot predict types it was not trained on. But NLI reranking might also improve predictions on the known types. To explore this possibility, we fine-tuned the `bart-large-mnli` model for the 24 non-OTHER ACLED event types using the 140,658 NLI training pairs from the dataset described in section 4.2. We then ran our fine-tuned RoBERTa classifier (`roberta-FT25`) on the 117,788 instances of the ACLED development set and collected its ranked list of predictions for all of the instances where its top-scoring prediction was wrong (6,002 instances, accuracy = 0.0000).

For the 6,002 instances, the average classifier score for the top (wrong) prediction was 0.9644. The average position of the correct type within the list ranked by classifier score was 3.1. When the classifier predicted the correct type, the average classifier top score was 0.9960. When the classifier score was above 0.99, its accuracy was 0.9562. Below that threshold, accuracy was 0.4851.

To explore the benefit of reranking even for known types, we passed the top N classifier predictions for the 6,002 incorrectly classified instances to our fine-tuned BART NLI model for reranking. We first set N to the position of the correct type for each sentence, guaranteeing that the correct type was in the list to be reranked (we refer to this as *setting N to "gold"*). The fine-tuned NLI model predicted the correct type for 2,271 instances (37.8% of the incorrectly classified instances). Setting N to 5 (meaning for some sentences the correct type would not be among the top N), the fine-tuned NLI model predicted 2,027 instances correctly (33.7%). See Table 6.

Surprisingly, using `bart-large-mnli` without fine tuning performed even better on the incorrectly classified instances when the correct type is always in the top N, recovering 2,600 of the correct types (43.3%). When N was 5, however, the untuned model did not perform as well as the tuned model (29.6% recovered). As with other experiments, the untuned `roberta-large-mnli` model performs slightly better than the BART model.

Based on this experiment, it makes sense to pair a fine-tuned classifier with an NLI reranker (fine-tuned or not) even for known types. In practice, we invoke the reranker with the top 5 predictions from the classifier when the classifier's top prediction score is less than 0.99.

4.3.2 Zero-Shot vs. Fine-Tuned Reranking on Unseen Types

We also compared a fine-tuned NLI model to an untuned model on unseen types. To simu-

Model	N	Accuracy
bart-FT24	gold	0.3784
bart-FT24	5	0.3377
bart-large-mnli	gold	0.4332
bart-large-mnli	5	0.2956
roberta-large-mnli	gold	0.4347
roberta-large-mnli	5	0.3121

Table 6: Accuracy of NLI models on the top N predictions from the roberta-FT25 classifier when its top prediction is wrong (6,002 instances). N=gold means that N is the position of the correct type in the ranked list, guaranteeing that it is available to the reranker.

Model	Tune	μAcc	macAcc
bart-large-mnli	none	0.9104	0.7977
bart-mnli-FT24	24	0.9806	0.9708
bart-mnli-FT21	21	0.2396	0.2540

Table 7: Comparison of three NLI models tested on data for three held-out types: an untuned model, a model tuned on all types (including the held-out types), and a model tuned on all types *except* the held-out types.

late the unseen types scenario, we randomly selected three of the original ACLED types and removed their instances (6,080) from the NLI fine-tuning dataset. We then fine-tuned the bart-large-mnli model on the instances for the remaining 21 types. Table 7 shows that fine-tuning an NLI model significantly improves accuracy for types it was tuned on over an untuned NLI model. Fine-tuning an NLI model on known types and then applying to unseen types performs catastrophically worse than even the untuned model. The fine-tuned model is clearly overfitting the 21 types in a way that significantly degrades performance on unseen types. We tried reducing the size of the fine-tuning set and balancing it to 1,000 instances per type to avoid overfitting. The resulting model performed worse by 5-6 micro-averaged accuracy points in all experiments.

Based on this experiment, we conclude that using a fine-tuned NLI model improves reranking for the types on which it was fine-tuned, but for unseen types, it is preferable to use an NLI reranking model not fine-tuned on other types.

4.3.3 BART vs. RoBERTa

We conducted two additional experiments to compare bart-large-mnli and roberta-large-mnli (no fine tuning), using keywords as the textual representation of the types. The first dataset was 457 examples from the ACLED test set, converted to the format needed for the NLI models (section 4.2.1). The 457 examples cover all 24 non-OTHER ACLED types, making this a particularly challenging task for reranking. The second dataset was the 6,080 instances covering the three held out types described in the previous section (4.3.2). Both experiments show a preference for RoBERTa. The experiments also show that the models are much better at distinguishing among smaller numbers of types. This supports the approach of using NLI models as rerankers on the top N classifier predictions (for small N) instead of using them as classifiers themselves on the full inventory of types.

Model	457-all	3heldout
bart-large-mnli	0.2998	0.9104
roberta-large-mnli	0.3129	0.9533

Table 8: Accuracy of BART vs. RoBERTa NLI models with no fine-tuning on two ACLED datasets: 457 random instances covering all event types and 6,080 instances covering three event types.

4.4 Models

Based on the lessons learned from our development experiments, we ultimately fine-tuned two NLI models on the data described in section 4.2

- roberta-mnli-FT24: roberta-large-mnli fine-tuned on the 140,658 instance training set for the base ACLED event types
- roberta-mnli-FT27: roberta-large-mnli fine-tuned on the 140,658 ACLED instances plus 666 instances for the three unseen types of subtask 2

Using the roberta-mnli-FT24 fine-tuned reranker in a system configuration makes that system supervised on the 24 ACLED types of subtask 1. Using roberta-mnli-FT27 makes a system supervised on the ACLED types and few-shot supervised on the three unseen types of subtask 2.

5 Challenge Submissions and Results

Official task results appear in Table 10. The table shows how little difference there was between the top scoring team submissions. Full results and analysis are presented in Haneczok et al. (2021).

Sub#	Classif model	Rerank model	25 classif	25 rerank	3 classif	3 rerank	2 rerank
1.1	roberta-FT25	*none*	sup				
1.2	roberta-FT25	rob-large-mnli	sup	zero			
1.3	roberta-FT25	rob-mnli-FT24	sup	sup			
2.1	roberta-FT28	*none*	sup		few		
2.2	roberta-FT28	rob-large-mnli	sup	zero	few	zero	
2.3	roberta-FT28	rob-mnli-FT27	sup	sup	few	few	
2.4	sub 1.3 output	rob-large-mnli	sup	sup		zero	
3.1	roberta-FT25	rob-large-mnli	sup	zero		zero	zero
3.2	roberta-FT28	rob-large-mnli	sup	zero	few	zero	zero
3.3	sub 1.3 output	rob-large-mnli	sup	sup		zero	zero
3.4	sub 2.2 output	rob-large-mnli	sup	zero	few	zero	zero

Table 9: System configurations for each of the eleven submissions. The combination of classification model and reranking model determines whether classification and reranking are supervised (*sup*), few-shot (*few*), or zero-shot (*zero*) for each category of event types (the 25 seen types, the 3 unseen types of subtask 2, or the 2 unseen types of subtask 3).

task	Our Score	Best Other Score	Our Rank
1	**0.839**	0.832	1
2	**0.797 (0.785)**	0.782	1
3	0.756 (0.746)	**0.771**	2

Table 10: Official challenge results (weighted F_1 scores). Top score is boldface. For subtasks 2 and 3, our highest scoring submission was few-shot fine-tuned for the subtask 2 event types and zero-shot for the subtask 3 event types. The score for our best true zero-shot submission appears in parentheses. Best Other Score is the highest scoring submission from another team.

We now turn to a more detailed discussion of our submissions and more detailed scores.

Combining classifiers and rerankers, we arrived at eleven system configurations for submission to the Challenge evaluation. Table 9 lists these configurations, grouped by Challenge subtask. The table specifies which classification model and which reranking model were used for each submission, as well as an indication of whether the configuration was supervised, few-shot, or zero-shot for each of the subsets of event types.

In every case, the classification model for the known 25 ACLED event types was supervised. For the first three submissions of subtask 2, classification of the three unseen types was few-shot, trained on our small corpus (see Section 3.1). For the fourth subtask 2 submission, we used the output of submission 1.3 as the "classifier". Since submission 1.3 was tuned on data for the 25 known types only, submission 2.4 is zero-shot for the three unseen types. No training data was used for the two new unseen types of subtask 3, so those types were always introduced during the reranking stage only (no classification). These were always zero-shot.

Reranking of the 25 original types was supervised when using the RoBERTa NLI model fine-tuned on the ACLED data (`rob-mnli-FT24` in the table. When using `roberta-large-mnli` off-the-shelf, reranking the 25 was zero-shot. For the 3 unseen types of subtask 2 (and subtask 3), only submission 2.3 reranked using the NLI model fine-tuned on the small amount of data for these types, and is considered few-shot. Otherwise, all reranking of the 3 unseen types and the 2 unseen types of subtask 3 were zero-shot.

6 Observations and Discussion

Table 11 shows results on the official, Task 2 evaluation. For subtask 1, fine-tuning the reranker did better (submission 1.3) than using an untuned reranker (1.2). This is the same result that we saw when passing the top 5 classification predictions to the reranker in the development experiments.

The best performing configuration for subtask 2 overall was supervised classification for all 28 types with untuned (zero-shot) reranking. In particular, the zero-shot reranking (submission 2.2) outperformed the reranker tuned on the three unseen types. This runs counter to what we saw in the development experiments. The configuration that was most successful on the original 25 types was the one whose classifier was the 1.3 submission (which had a fine-tuned reranker). Isolating

		All types			25 types		3 types		2 types	
Sub#	**Sup**	**μF**	**macF**	**wF**	**μF**	**macF**	**μF**	**macF**	**μF**	**macF**
1.1	sup	0.830	0.792	0.828	0.830	0.792				
1.2	sup	0.834	0.810	0.835	0.834	0.810				
1.3	sup	**0.838**	**0.814**	**0.839**	**0.838**	**0.814**				
2.1	few	0.782	0.752	0.779	0.790	0.785	0.712	0.703		
2.2	few	**0.797**	**0.773**	**0.797**	0.800	0.786	**0.779**	**0.756**		
2.3	few	0.794	0.764	0.790	0.799	0.785	0.749	0.746		
2.4	zero	0.786	0.758	0.785	**0.804**	**0.787**	0.621	0.595		
3.1	zero	0.744	0.720	0.746	**0.783**	**0.780**	0.591	0.572	0.362	0.379
3.2	few	**0.755**	**0.728**	**0.756**	0.776	0.765	**0.766**	**0.745**	**0.424**	**0.432**
3.3	zero	0.744	0.720	0.746	**0.783**	**0.780**	0.591	0.572	0.362	0.379
3.4	few	**0.755**	**0.728**	**0.756**	0.776	0.765	**0.766**	**0.745**	**0.424**	**0.432**

Table 11: Detailed scores for the eleven submissions. The "Sup" column denotes whether the submission overall should be considered supervised, few-shot, or zero-shot. μF is micro-averaged F_1 score; macF is macro-averaged F_1 score; wF is the weighted average F_1 score (see section 1). The highest scores for a given subtask and type subset are shown boldface.

the scores on the three unseen types versus the 25 known types shows strong performance in the few-shot case, but significantly weaker performance with zero-shot (2.4).

For subtask 3, submissions 3.1 and 3.3 produced identical predictions (not just scores), as did submissions 3.2 and 3.4. The configurations themselves are not equivalent, with the input to the 3.3 and 3.4 rerankers having already been reranked by the 1.3 and 2.2 rerankers. Interestingly, the configurations built on zero-shot rerankers only performed best, again suggesting NLI models can be used without fine-tuning for reranking classification for both known and unseen types. Performance on the two unseen types of subtask 3 (zero-shot) is significantly weaker than the zero-shot scenario of subtask 2 (2.4). It is possible that the two new types are inherently more difficult to recognize. But we suspect that tweaks to the textual representations for these two types might improve performance. Given the extreme differences that different representations produce (section 4.1), we expect that more carefully chosen representations would help.

7 Conclusion

The CASE 2021 Task 2 challenge accurately simulates a realistic, fine-grained, text classification scenario in which many types in the type inventory have abundant labeled data, some types are recently new and may have a small amount of labeled data, and some types are completely new and have no labeled data. Within these constraints, we proposed a hybrid system that combines supervised classification with NLI-based reranking that can be used in supervised, few-shot, and zero-shot settings. Our results show strong performance on known types with weaker results on unseen types. Nevertheless, the experiments for this challenge have produced some interesting conclusions. First, we confirm that NLI models are useful for zero-shot text classification, but only when distinguishing between a small number of target types. Second, even in a fully supervised scenario, where ample training data can produce classification models with extremely high accuracy, untuned NLI-based reranking can improve classification performance on known types. Third, the choice of textual representation to transform a classification problem into one amenable to an untuned NLI model greatly affects performance. In future work we hope to explore more rigorously what makes a good representation for NLI-based zero-shot text classification, and how to generate these representations more automatically.

Acknowledgments and Disclaimer

This research was developed with funding from the Defense Advanced Research Projects Agency (DARPA) under Contract No. FA8750-19-C-0206. The views, opinions and/or findings expressed are those of the author and should not be interpreted as representing the official views or policies of the Department of Defense or the U.S. Government.

References

Jacek Haneczok, Guillaume Jacquet, Jakub Piskorski, and Nicolas Stefanovitch. 2021. Fine-grained event classification in news-like text snippets - shared task 2, CASE 2021. In *Proceedings of the Workshop on Challenges and Applications of Automated Extraction of Socio-political Events from Text (CASE 2021)*, online. Association for Computational Linguistics (ACL).

Ali Hürriyetoğlu, Hristo Tanev, Vanni Zavarella, Jakub Piskorski, Reyyan Yeniterzi, and Erdem Yörük. 2021. Challenges and applications of automated extraction of socio-political events from text (CASE 2021): Workshop and shared task report. In *Proceedings of the 4th Workshop on Challenges and Applications of Automated Extraction of Socio-political Events from Text (CASE 2021)*, online. Association for Computational Linguistics (ACL).

Mike Lewis, Yinhan Liu, Naman Goyal, Marjan Ghazvininejad, Abdelrahman Mohamed, Omer Levy, Veselin Stoyanov, and Luke Zettlemoyer. 2020. BART: Denoising sequence-to-sequence pre-training for natural language generation, translation, and comprehension. In *Proceedings of the 58th Annual Meeting of the Association for Computational Linguistics*, pages 7871–7880, Online. Association for Computational Linguistics.

Y. Liu, Myle Ott, Naman Goyal, Jingfei Du, Mandar Joshi, Danqi Chen, Omer Levy, M. Lewis, Luke Zettlemoyer, and Veselin Stoyanov. 2019. RoBERTa: A Robustly Optimized BERT Pretraining Approach. *ArXiv*, abs/1907.11692.

Jakub Piskorski, Jacek Haneczok, and Guillaume Jacquet. 2020. New benchmark corpus and models for fine-grained event classification: To BERT or not to BERT? In *Proceedings of the 28th International Conference on Computational Linguistics*, pages 6663–6678, Barcelona, Spain (Online). International Committee on Computational Linguistics.

Clionadh Raleigh, Andrew Linke, Håvard Hegre, and Joakim Karlsen. 2010. Introducing acled: an armed conflict location and event dataset: special data feature. *Journal of peace research*, 47(5):651–660.

Timo Schick and Hinrich Schütze. 2021. Exploiting cloze-questions for few-shot text classification and natural language inference. In *Proceedings of the 16th Conference of the European Chapter of the Association for Computational Linguistics: Main Volume*, pages 255–269, Online. Association for Computational Linguistics.

Ashish Vaswani, Noam Shazeer, Niki Parmar, Jakob Uszkoreit, Llion Jones, Aidan N. Gomez, Lukasz Kaiser, and Illia Polosukhin. 2017. Attention is all you need. In *NIPS*, pages 6000–6010.

Adina Williams, Nikita Nangia, and Samuel Bowman. 2018. A broad-coverage challenge corpus for sentence understanding through inference. In *Proceedings of the 2018 Conference of the North American Chapter of the Association for Computational Linguistics: Human Language Technologies, Volume 1 (Long Papers)*, pages 1112–1122. Association for Computational Linguistics.

Thomas Wolf, Lysandre Debut, Victor Sanh, Julien Chaumond, Clement Delangue, Anthony Moi, Pierric Cistac, Tim Rault, Remi Louf, Morgan Funtowicz, Joe Davison, Sam Shleifer, Patrick von Platen, Clara Ma, Yacine Jernite, Julien Plu, Canwen Xu, Teven Le Scao, Sylvain Gugger, Mariama Drame, Quentin Lhoest, and Alexander Rush. 2020. Transformers: State-of-the-art natural language processing. In *Proceedings of the 2020 Conference on Empirical Methods in Natural Language Processing: System Demonstrations*, pages 38–45, Online. Association for Computational Linguistics.

Wenpeng Yin, Jamaal Hay, and Dan Roth. 2019. Benchmarking zero-shot text classification: Datasets, evaluation and entailment approach. In *Proceedings of the 2019 Conference on Empirical Methods in Natural Language Processing and the 9th International Joint Conference on Natural Language Processing (EMNLP-IJCNLP)*, pages 3914–3923, Hong Kong, China. Association for Computational Linguistics.

CASE 2021 Task 2: Zero-Shot Classification of Fine-Grained Sociopolitical Events with Transformer Models

Benjamin J. Radford
University of North Carolina at Charlotte
benjamin.radford@uncc.edu

Abstract

We introduce a method for the classification of texts into fine-grained categories of sociopolitical events. This particular method is responsive to all three Subtasks of Task 2, *Fine-Grained Classification of Socio-Political Events*, introduced at the CASE workshop of ACL-IJCNLP 2021. We frame Task 2 as textual entailment: given an input text and a candidate event class ("query"), the model predicts whether the text describes an event of the given type. The model is able to correctly classify in-sample event types with an average F_1-score of 0.74 but struggles with some out-of-sample event types. Despite this, the model shows promise for the zero-shot identification of certain sociopolitical events by achieving an F_1-score of 0.52 on one wholly out-of-sample event class.

1 Introduction

We introduce a method for the classification of text excerpts into fine-grained categories of sociopolitical events. This particular method is responsive to all three Subtasks of Task 2, *Fine-Grained Classification of Socio-Political Events*, introduced at the Challenges and Applications of Automated Extraction of Socio-political Events from Text (CASE) workshop of ACL-IJCNLP 2021 (Haneczok et al., 2021). We frame Task 2 as textual entailment: given an input text and a candidate event class ("query"), the model predicts whether the text describes an event of the given type. Because the query is given as an arbitrary sequence of character tokens, the model is open-ended with respect to query and can, theoretically, predict classes completely out-of-sample.

Three shared task challenges were introduced at CASE: (1) Multilingual Protest News Detection, (2) Fine-Grained Classification of Socio-Political Events, and (3) Discovering Black Lives Matter Events in United States. The second of these is further divided into three Subtasks: (1) supervised text classification of 25 event types, (2) unsupervised text classification of three additional event types, and (3) unsupervised text classification of a further two additional event types. No training data were provided by the shared task organizers; teams were given only the 25 initial event type descriptions. These event types were drawn from the Armed Conflict Location and Event Data Project (ACLED) event ontology (Raleigh et al., 2010). The subsequent five event types introduced by Subtasks 2 and 3 were provided by the shared task organizers immediately prior to the response submission deadline.

2 Data

We downloaded all ACLED events and the corresponding source texts within which those events were discovered. Source texts are short excerpts from news articles and are typically no more than a few sentences in length. We use this event-text corpus as training data for our model. These events and sentences represent only the 25 event types of Subtask 1. Event types by subtask are given in the second column of Table 1. The exact text representation of each event class in Table 1 is the query given to the model. No additional event class descriptors are included. Clearly some event types (e.g., *Abduction forced disappearance*) are more descriptive than others (e.g., *Attack*, *Other*). We partition the 1,127,635 ACLED events into training (80%), validation (10%), and test (10%) sets. However, due to time limitations, neither the validation set nor full test set were used.

To generate training data for the model, we pair every text excerpt with all 24 of the Subtask 1 event types that are not described by the excerpt and assign these artificial pairs a value of zero. We then

Proceedings of the 4th Workshop on Challenges and Applications of Automated Extraction of Socio-political Events from Text (CASE), pages 203–207
August 5–6, 2021, ©2021 Association for Computational Linguistics

Subtask	Event class	Precision	Recall	F_1-score	Support
1	Disrupted weapons use	0.971	0.569	0.717	58
1	Abduction forced disappearance	0.714	0.750	0.732	20
1	Agreement	1.000	0.516	0.681	31
1	Air drone strike	0.786	0.917	0.846	36
1	Armed clash	0.449	0.924	0.604	66
1	Shelling artillery missile attack	0.646	0.861	0.738	36
1	Attack	0.333	0.852	0.479	27
1	Change to group activity	0.571	0.533	0.552	30
1	Chemical weapon	0.867	0.703	0.776	37
1	Arrests	0.684	0.382	0.491	34
1	Excessive force against protesters	0.833	0.652	0.732	23
1	Government regains territory	0.780	0.842	0.810	38
1	Grenade	0.949	0.771	0.851	48
1	Headquarters or base established	0.870	0.909	0.889	22
1	Mob violence	0.314	0.647	0.423	17
1	Non state actor overtakes territory	0.810	0.708	0.756	24
1	Non violent transfer of territory	0.714	0.476	0.571	21
1	Other	0.000	0.000	0.000	8
1	Peaceful protest	0.689	0.895	0.779	57
1	Looting property destruction	0.143	0.048	0.071	21
1	Protest with intervention	0.548	0.773	0.642	22
1	Remote explosive landmine IED	0.522	0.972	0.680	36
1	Sexual violence	0.955	0.913	0.933	23
1	Suicide bomb	0.946	0.854	0.897	41
1	Violent demonstration	0.642	0.642	0.642	53
1	*micro avg*	*0.739*	*0.739*	*0.739*	*829*
1	*macro avg*	*0.770*	*0.697*	*0.698*	*829*
1	*weighted avg*	*0.798*	*0.739*	*0.736*	*829*
2	Organized crime	0.500	0.103	0.171	29
2	Natural disaster	0.562	0.243	0.340	37
2	Man made disaster	0.167	0.019	0.034	52
2	*micro avg*	*0.658*	*0.658*	*0.658*	*947*
2	*macro avg*	*0.648*	*0.632*	*0.613*	*947*
2	*weighted avg*	*0.670*	*0.658*	*0.635*	*947*
3	Attribution of responsibility	0.167	0.071	0.100	28
3	Diplomatic event	0.511	0.523	0.517	44
3	*micro avg*	*0.629*	*0.629*	*0.629*	*1019*
3	*macro avg*	*0.621*	*0.602*	*0.582*	*1019*
3	*weighted avg*	*0.644*	*0.629*	*0.605*	*1019*

Table 1: Event types by subtask. Precision, recall, F_1-score, and support given by class. Averages are given by subtask. Class-wise values are all derived from the single result set for Subtask 3. Averages per subtask are derived from the result set for each particular subtask.

```
('<s> On 16 June, AQAP armed
men peacefully took control and
deployed on Al-Rawdah district
from Houthi forces. No further
info was provided. </s> Non
violent transfer of territory
</s>', 1.0)
```

Figure 1: A correct input text-query pair from ACLED. The first tuple element is a single text string containing a special token <s>, the input sentence, a delimiter </s>, the query, and a final delimiter </s>. The second tuple element is the target value for the text-query pair: 1.0 if correct, 0.0 if incorrect.

assign all observed pairs, text excerpts paired with the correct event type, a value of one. The model's job is to take a text-query pair and predict whether it is a correct pair or an incorrect pair. An example text-query pair from an ACLED event is given in Figure 1.

3 Model

We select a pre-trained RoBERTa model as the base of our solution.[1] RoBERTa is a transformer-based language model that is initially trained on a very large English language corpus and can then be fine-tuned to specific tasks with fewer training examples (Liu et al., 2019). We take the final layer hidden states for each token and apply global max pooling (i.e., find the element-wise maximum for each dimension of the hidden states). We add a fully-connected dense layer with a single neuron and sigmoid activation function to this pooled value. We use Adam to minimize the binary cross-entropy loss of our model (Kingma and Ba, 2015). We train the model for a single epoch with a learning rate of 5×10^{-5} and use a variable batch size to manage memory usage.

During the inference stage, the model must select a single class to best represent each text. All possible queries are appended to an input text and every pair is passed to the model independently. The model produces a prediction between 0.0 and 1.0 for each pair and the event class associated with the text-query pair that receives the highest predicted value is chosen. However, the *Other* category may result in misclassifications: can the model distinguish an out-of-sample class, like those from Subtasks 2 and 3, from the in-sample class *Other*? A second aggregation rule is therefore applied: if the greatest predicted value is associated with the *Other* class, the next highest probability class is inspected. If this runner-up class is out-of-sample (i.e., not present in Subtask 1), then it is chosen. If the runner-up class is present in Subtask 1, then the class *Other* is chosen. Results presented for Subtasks 2 and 3 are derived from this second aggregation method.

4 Results

Model performance is given in Table 1. When constrained to the initial 25 event types (Subtask 1), the model achieves average F_1-scores of between 0.70 and 0.74 depending on the method chosen for averaging. These values drop with the introduction of additional out-of-sample event types, averaging between 0.58 and 0.66 for Subtasks 2 and 3. Zero-shot performance on the five out-of-sample event types varies substantially: the F_1-scores for *Natural disaster* and *Diplomatic event* are 0.34 and 0.52, respectively, values that that fall within the typical range of in-sample event types. The model fares relatively poorly on the remaining out-of-sample types. The results are nearly identical when using the first aggregation method that does not correct for the *Other* category present in Subtask 1.

Comparison of predictions against target classes reveals that class overlap may to be blame for some of the poor out-of-sample performance. For example, the model correctly identifies *Organized crime* only 10% of the time and often misclassifies it as *Arrest* (21%), *Mob violence* (21%), and *Looting property destruction* (17%). One example of this, drawn from the test set, is given in Table 2 row a. The excerpt describes the detention of 34 persons by border guards as part of an enforcement action against an international gang. The model predicts *Arrest* but the given label is *Organized crime*. Another example given in Table 2 row b describes an event in which police recovered $500,000 in stolen property after an investigation into a breaking and entering event. The model predicted *Looting property destruction* but the given label is once again *Organized crime*. The model often misclassifies *Man made disaster* as one of *Remote explosive landmine IED* (37%), *Attack* (19%), and *Natural disaster* (12%). One such example relating to the 2020 Beirut port explosion is given in Table 2 row c. Clearly this is a *Man made disaster*, but it also

[1] Available here: `https://huggingface.co/roberta-base`.

ID	Text	Prediction	True Label
a.	Polish border guards have detained 34 people from the Middle East, including four women and four children, who were traveling in a trailer of the lorry that came from Turkey via Slovakia, authorities said on Saturday. The event is linked to a known international gang involved in facilitating illegal migration.	Arrest	Organized crime
b.	Toronto police identified five suspects in connection to a residential break and enter investigation dubbed 'Project High Class.' Police said in a media release they recovered $500,000 in stolen property. Toronto police Inspector Joanne Rudnick is expected to provide further information on the investigation at 10:30 a. [sic]	Looting property destruction	Organized crime
c.	On 4 August, two large explosions hit the city of Beirut, reportedly caused by large quantities of ammonium nitrate being stored in a warehouse in Beirut Port.	Remote explosive landmine IED	Natural disaster

Table 2: Examples of incorrectly classified texts.

describes an explosion that is conceivably "remote" (though not intentional).

5 Conclusion

Failure to account for ambiguity between event classes is likely to be an issue for the next generation of automated fine-grained event classification models. In the case of the model presented here, predictions are not necessarily calibrated properly: the model has no ability to specify that a text does not describe one and only one event type. This is enforced by the fact that a final classification is chosen by identifying the maximum value among all text-query pair predictions. Were the model calibrated by class, we would hope that predicted values greater than 0.5 denote a positive class membership and values below this threshold denote non-membership. In that case, multiple classes (or no class) could be indicated by the model for a single text. However, given the zero-shot nature of Subtasks 2 and 3, we were unable to calibrate those particular classes. Furthermore, the organizers have specified that all texts should be assigned one and only one label. However, it seems clear from inspection of the errors that the given ontology does not describe a mutually exclusive set of classes. Accounting for hierarchical or complementary classes within the ontology may help to produce more useful or consistent event coding models. Doing so will require a novel technique for selecting predicted classes in which each class prediction is not made independently of the other classes (as is the case here).

One solution may be to pose all queries to the model simultaneously. A single input example would comprise the source text concatenated with every possible event class: `<s> text </s> cat1 cat2... </s>`. The model would then output a vector of probabilities the same length (in tokens) as the input sequence. Classes for the source text would be chosen by inspecting this probability vector and selecting categories corresponding to relatively high probability-valued sub-sequences. When appropriate, the model may weight multiple (or no) class tokens very highly. Queries could be shuffled per source text to prevent the model from learning offset values for common classes rather than attending to the query texts themselves.

Despite the poor out-of-sample performance of this particular model on certain zero-shot event categories, the model's performance in-sample and on *Natural disaster* and *Diplomatic event* suggests that transformers will play a major role in future event coding systems. With additional time and resources, it is likely that substantial improvements are possible to the model described here. In fact, the performance of this model, given zero hyper-parameter tuning or model search, suggests that the upper limit for transformer performance on this task is likely very high.[2]

Acknowledgments

We thank the organizers of CASE 2021 and three anonymous reviewers for their thoughtful feedback.

References

J Haneczok, G Jacquet, J Piskorsk, and N Stefanovitch. 2021. Fine-grained event classification in news-like text snippets shared task 2, case 2021. *Proceedings of the Workshop on Challenges and Applications of Automated Extraction of Socio-political Events from Text (CASE 2021), co-located with the Joint Conference of the 59th Annual Meeting of the Association for Computational Linguistics and the 11th International Joint Conference on Natural Language Processing (ACL-IJCNLP 2021).*

Diederik P. Kingma and Jimmy Ba. 2015. Adam: A method for stochastic optimization. In *3rd International Conference on Learning Representations, ICLR 2015, San Diego, CA, USA, May 7-9, 2015, Conference Track Proceedings.*

Yinhan Liu, Myle Ott, Naman Goyal, Jingfei Du, Mandar Joshi, Danqi Chen, Omer Levy, Mike Lewis, Luke Zettlemoyer, and Veselin Stoyanov. 2019. Roberta: A robustly optimized BERT pretraining approach. *CoRR*, abs/1907.11692.

Clionadh Raleigh, Andrew Linke, Håvard Hegre, and Joakim Karlsen. 2010. Introducing acled-armed conflict location and event data. *Journal of Peace Research*, 47:651–660.

[2]Due to time and resource constraints, we trained only one model and performed no out-of-sample evaluation prior to test set submission.

CASE 2021 Task 2: Socio-political Fine-grained Event Classification using Fine-tuned RoBERTa Document Embeddings

Samantha Kent
Fraunhofer FKIE
Fraunhoferstraße 20
53343 Wachtberg
samantha.kent@fkie.fraunhofer.de

Theresa Krumbiegel
Fraunhofer FKIE
Fraunhoferstraße 20
53343 Wachtberg
theresa.krumbiegel@fkie.fraunhofer.de

Abstract

We present our submission to Task 2 of the Socio-political and Crisis Events Detection Shared Task at the CASE @ ACL-IJCNLP 2021 workshop. The task at hand aims at the fine-grained classification of socio-political events. Our best model was a fine-tuned RoBERTa transformer model using document embeddings. The corpus consisted of a balanced selection of sub-events extracted from the ACLED event dataset. We achieved a macro F-score of 0.923 and a micro F-score of 0.932 during our preliminary experiments on a held-out test set. The same model also performed best on the shared task test data (weighted F-score = 0.83). To analyze the results we calculated the topic compactness of the commonly misclassified events and conducted an error analysis.

1 Introduction

Event detection and classification as Natural Language Processing (NLP) tasks can be used to analyze data gathered in the information space. The findings of this analysis can then be connected to events in the physical world and contribute to situational awareness, particularly when they are related to socio-political events. The sheer amount of data that is generated and stored in the information space every day, means that strategies need to be developed to be able to efficiently and effectively process this data. Given the large amounts of data, deep learning strategies are often preferred. However, time and computational constraints may play a role in deciding how to extract and analyze data.

Task 2 in the Socio-political and Crisis Events Detection Shared Task at the CASE @ ACL-IJCNLP 2021 workshop aims at the fine-grained classification of events (Haneczok et al., 2021). The task is based on data extracted from the Armed Conflict Location & Event Data (ACLED) database (Raleigh et al., 2010). It consist of socio-political events that have been annotated based on the ACLED event taxonomy, and includes 6 event types and 25 event subtypes. The aim of this task is to label event snippets using a model trained on data from the ACLED dataset, in order to see how robust models are when presented with data that is not directly covered by ACLED or contains unseen event classes. The results presented in this paper pertain only to subtask 1, where the task is the classification of 25 different event subtypes with ACLED-compliant labels. In other words, all the classes are seen classes from the ACLED dataset. The second and third subtasks are zero-short learning tasks that contain unseen classes.

This paper proceeds by first describing the data collection process in section 3. Section 4 contains the system description and the following section contains the experimental results. Section 6 provides an overview of the results based on the test data provided by the organizers. Finally, in section 7 the error analysis provides an insight into the system results and the data.

2 Related Work

Previous research in event detection and classification shows that there are numerous approaches to solve the problem of detecting events in texts. Xiang and Wang (2019) give a coherent overview of suitable strategies, starting with earlier approaches like pattern matching, and describing methods of machine learning as well as deep learning. There have been a number of shared tasks that have taken place in previous years that contribute to research conducted in this area. Specifically, the shared tasks CLEF 2019 Protest News (Hürriyetoğlu et al., 2019), AESPEN 2020 (Hürriyetoğlu et al., 2020), and CASE 2021 (task 1) (Hürriyetoğlu et al., 2021) focus on event detection at both the sentence and

Proceedings of the 4th Workshop on Challenges and Applications of Automated Extraction of Socio-political Events from Text (CASE), pages 208–217
August 5–6, 2021, ©2021 Association for Computational Linguistics

document level, as well as event co-reference resolution.

Currently, not much research has been conducted that further analyzes event data once the events have been identified. There are a handful of studies across different domains. Peng et al. (2019) achieve state of the art results detecting and classifying social event data with a Pairwise Popularity Graph Convolutional Network (PP-GCN) with an external knowledge base. Nugent et al. (2017) compare different supervised classification methods for detecting a range of different events, and achieve good results with Support Vector Machines (SVM) and Convolutional Neural Networks (CNN). A benchmark corpus for fine-grained political event classification was created by the organizers of this task and an initial exploration and classification of the data is reported on in Piskorski et al. (2020) and Piskorski and Jacquet (2020). The findings reported that BERT transformer models achieved a micro F1 of (0.943-0.949) and a macro F1 of (0.860-0.889). More simple TF-IDF-weighted character n-gram models also achieved good results. A large dataset of 600,000 annotated ACLED event snippets was used as training data.

3 Data collection

Due to copyright reasons, the data used in this paper was collected directly from the ACLED website.[1] To create the corpus, all data from each available region was downloaded and then filtered using the following steps.

Firstly, all events with less than 25 tokens and more than 1000 tokens were removed. The next step was to balance the corpus based on the 25 different fine-grained event classes. Originally, the largest class in the corpus consisted of 36.69% of the events, compared to the smallest with 0.001%. To create a more balanced version of the corpus, we extracted a sample of events per class, with the smallest classes being fully represented and extracting only a percentage of the largest classes. Note that it was not possible to fully balance all of the classes as there was only a very small amount of data for classes such as CHEM_WEAP. A random sample of this balanced corpus was then split into a train (n=94000), development (n=9000), and test (n=2500) corpus, which also all contain the balanced class distribution. We observed that randomizing the order of events was crucial, to avoid introducing a bias based on the different ACLED regions. Figure 2 illustrates the distribution of the corpus. A more detailed table can be found in appendix A.

In a further step, we created three different versions of the original corpus. The first version, referred to as ACLED_N, contains the original text from the ACLED download, an example of which can be found below.

```
{text:  CPI(M) activists attacked
    a BJP rally in Hrishyamukh on
    18 January 2018.,
 subtype: FORCE_AGAINST_PROTEST}
```

Based on the results presented by Piskorski et al. (2020), where the BERT transformer model performed slightly better on the corpus with less pre-processing, we decided to include a version with little to no pre-processing. In ACLED_L, we replaced all locations from the text using the Flair Named Entity Recognition (NER) tagger (Akbik et al., 2018) with the generic token 'LOC'. The third version, ACLED_T, contains a pre-processed version of the original text, but without any time stamps. All dates and times were removed from the text and replaced with 'TIME'. These two alternative versions of the corpus were created to analyse whether or not the information specific to one particular event or set of events would be transferable to the classification of other events.

4 System Description

We submitted five system runs for evaluation. The systems differ slightly from each other, either in the model or the way the used data was pre-processed. The general approach for all submitted systems was to use fine-tuned pre-trained transformer document embeddings. All experiments were conducted using the Flair framework (Akbik et al., 2019).

4.1 System 1 - RoBERTa ACLED_L

For system 1, we fine-tuned the RoBERTa base model (Liu et al., 2019), and trained the embeddings using a learning rate of 3e-5, a batch size of 16. Based on our experiments, we trained the model for 2 epochs, because we found that the model overfits if we trained for more than 2 epochs. After each epoch the training data was shuffled and this was also done in the subsequent systems. Additionally, we assigned weights to the different event classes. This was done to smooth out any

[1]https://acleddata.com/data-export-tool/

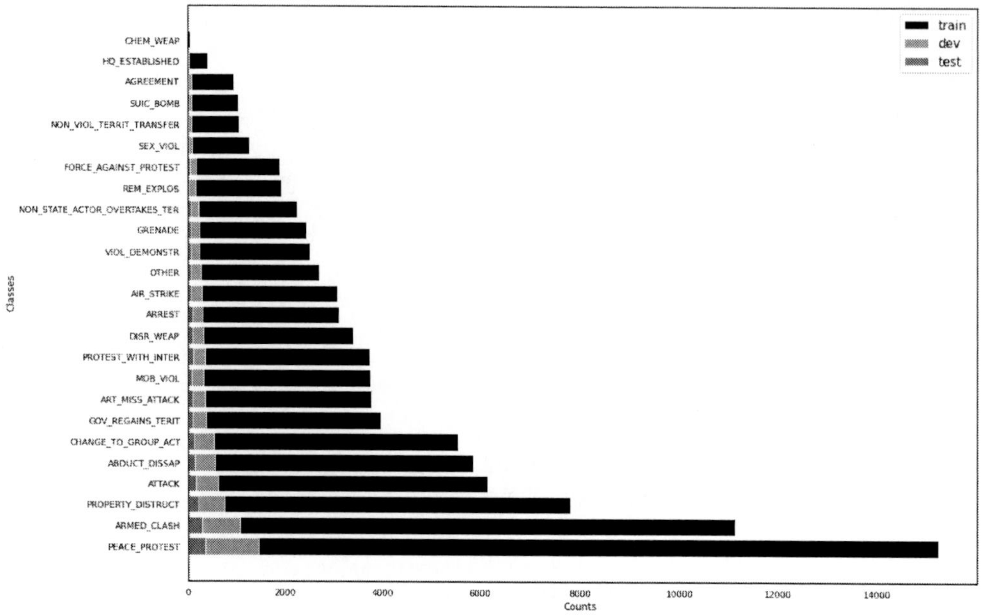

Figure 1: Class distribution

remaining differences in class sizes. We used the ACLED_L version of the corpus as text input.

4.2 System 2 - RoBERTa ACLED_N

System 2 again uses the RoBERTa base model (Liu et al., 2019) and the previously mentioned parameters for learning rate (3e-5), batch size (16) and number of epochs (2). The difference to system 1 is, that the text that was used during the fine-tuning of the model was not pre-processed. This means that the text snippets that were obtained from the ACLED (Donnay et al., 2019) database were fed into the system in their original state and, therefore, all information included in the text was kept.

4.3 System 3 - BERT ACLED_L

For system 3, we used the pre-trained BERT base-cased model (Devlin et al., 2019) along with a learning rate of 3e-5, a batch size of 16 and 2 epochs for training. As in system 1, we used the ACLED_L corpus.

4.4 System 4 - BERT ACLED_N

System 4 used the same settings as system 3, meaning, the pre-trained BERT base-cased model (Devlin et al., 2019), a learning rate of 3e-5, a batch size of 16 and 2 epochs for training. The input data for system 4 consisted of the original text from ACLED_N.

4.5 System 5 - BERT ACLED_T

Our last system, system 5, made use of the pre-trained BERT base-cased model (Devlin et al., 2019). The learning rate was set to 3e-5, the batch size to 32. It was trained for 2 epochs. For the text input we used the text from ACLED_T, where all time and date stamps have been removed.

5 Preliminary experiments

Preliminary model evaluations on 10 held-out test sets show that each of the systems performed comparatively well. The RoBERTa model with the normal ACLED text as input performed slightly better than the other systems. Table 1 below shows the range of Macro and Micro F1 scores across the 10 test sets. Model performance increased or decreased slightly, depending on the samples in the individual test sets. The results also illustrate that the removal of the location or time mentions in the event snippets, does not greatly influence system performance. Rather, the preliminary tests indicate that the fine-tuned RoBERTa embeddings benefit from the inclusion of the more detailed ACLED specific information.

An analysis of the results of the individual classes, shows that each of the 25 subtypes achieve f1-scores of over 0.800. The two lowest scoring classes are HQ_ESTABLISHED and

	Macro F1	Micro F1	Weighted F1
RoBERTa ACLED_L	0.887 - 0.919	0.917 - 0.929	0.917 - 0.929
RoBERTa ACLED_N	0.894 - **0.923**	0.916 - **0.932**	0.918 - **0.931**
BERT ACLED_L	0.868 - 0.911	0.913 - 0.928	0.913 - 0.928
BERT ACLED_N	0.869 - 0.900	0.907 - 0.925	0.907 - 0.925
BERT ACLED_T	0.889 - 0.918	0.913 - 0.929	0.913 - 0.929

Table 1: Preliminary Evaluation Results

VIOL_DEMONSTR, with an F-score of 0.814 and 0.819 respectively. The highest scoring class is CHEM_WEAP (F-score = 1), however there are only two instances present in this test set. PEACE_PROTEST and ABDUCT_DISSAP also score highly, achieving an F-score of 0.978 and 0.975 respectively. A table containing a detailed overview of each class can be found in appendix A.

6 Results

Table 7 shows the results of our five system submissions. The systems were tested on a test set provided by the organizers, consisting of 829 samples for subtask 1. We find that System 2, using the RoBERTa base model (Liu et al., 2019) and ACLED_N as input, performs best with an average weighted F-score of 0.83, average macro F-score of 0.794 and average micro F-score of 0.829. A more detailed overview can be found in appendix A.

Additionally, the second model that uses original ACLED text, System 4, achieves the second best result. As was the case in our preliminary experiments, we see that the inclusion of specific location and timestamps in the training data, does not greatly influence the ability of the system to predict the different classes correctly or incorrectly.

	Macro F1	Micro F1	Weighted F1
RoBERTa ACLED_L	0.797	0.770	0.799
RoBERTa ACLED_N	**0.829**	**0.794**	**0.830**
BERT ACLED_L	0.808	0.768	0.808
BERT ACLED_N	0.802	0.774	0.812
BERT ACLED_T	0.793	0.766	0.793

Table 2: System Results

7 Error Analysis

To get a better insight into the workings of our systems, we conducted an error analysis on the test data provided by the organizers for all five submissions. In order to investigate misclassifications made by the models, we decided to look at the performance of the system with regard to the individual classes.

7.1 Analysis of Word Frequencies

As can be seen in Table 3, all models score low F-scores for either the class OTHER or the class PROPERTY_DISTRUCT, or both. The results obtained for these classes substantially lower the overall average F-scores of the models.

	Worst Class	F1
RoBERTa ACLED_L	OTHER	0.42
RoBERTa ACLED_L	PROPERTY_DISTRUCT	0.46
RoBERTa ACLED_N	PROPERTY_DISTRUCT	0.35
RoBERTa ACLED_N	OTHER	0.40
BERT ACLED_L	PROPERTY_DISTRUCT	0.30
BERT ACLED_L	OTHER	0.34
BERT ACLED_N	OTHER	0.28
BERT ACLED_N	MOB_VIOL	0.49
BERT ACLED_T	PROPERTY_DISTRUCT	0.41
BERT ACLED_T	NON_STATE_ACTOR _OVERTAKES_TER	0.49

Table 3: Event Type Error Analysis

All models achieve the highest scores for the classes SUIC_BOMB, GRENADE and CHEM_WEAP. We looked at the word distribution these classes have in our training data as can be seen in figure 2 and 3.

Considering these distributions, it can be stated that a specific vocabulary, as can be found in the class SUIC_BOMB, is advantageous for a correct classification, while a heterogeneous vocabulary, as can be found in the class OTHER, is disadvantageous. One can tell that while the by far most frequently occurring word in texts regarding the event type SUIC_BOMB, namely "suicide", is clearly indicative for the given class, the most frequently used words in connection with the event type OTHER, namely "activity", "violent", "area" and "force" are rather generic. Furthermore, they can also be found frequently in a number of texts connected

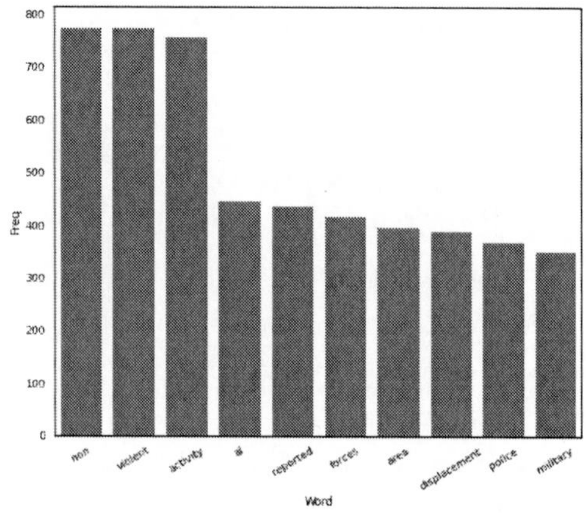

Figure 2: Top 10 words in the class OTHER

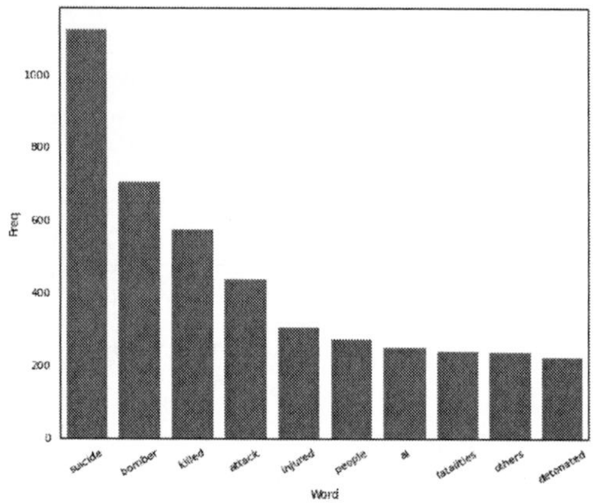

Figure 3: Top 10 words in the class SUIC_BOMB

to other classes (e.g., "area": AIR_STRIKE, CHANGE_TO_GROUP_ACT, "force": NON_STATE _ACTOR_OVERTAKES_TER, NON_VIOL_TERRIT_TRANSFER). This does not hold true for the word "suicide".

7.2 Frequent Errors

Looking further at the errors, we see that 65 samples of the test data were classified incorrectly by all five models. This makes up between 37% and 45% of errors for the respective systems. It is noticeable that all five models frequently predict the class MOB_VIOL for sentences that are gold labeled as PROPERTY_DISTRUCT (between 5 and 9 times for the respective systems). No other two classes are confused this often, and to investigate further we analysed these two classes with regard to their topic compactness. We calculated the topic distances of the sentences in comparison to the topic centroids per class in the training data. Figures 4 and 5 show the results of the topic compactness analysis.

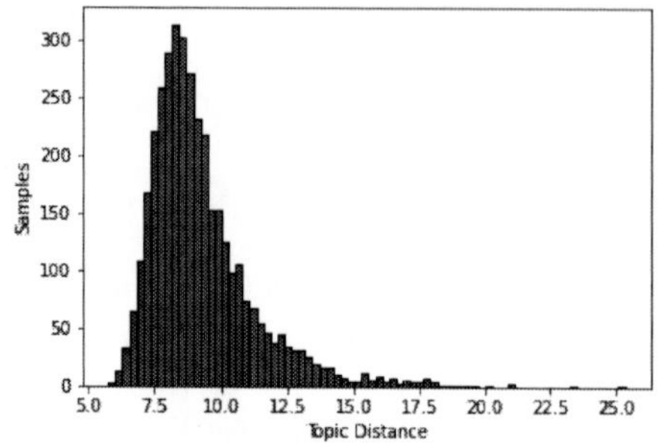

Figure 4: Distribution of document vectors to topic centroid in class MOB_VIOL

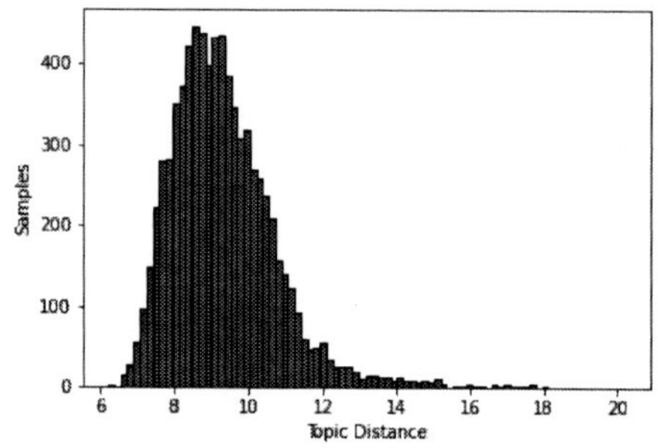

Figure 5: Distribution of document vectors to topic centroid in class PROPERTY_DISTRUCT

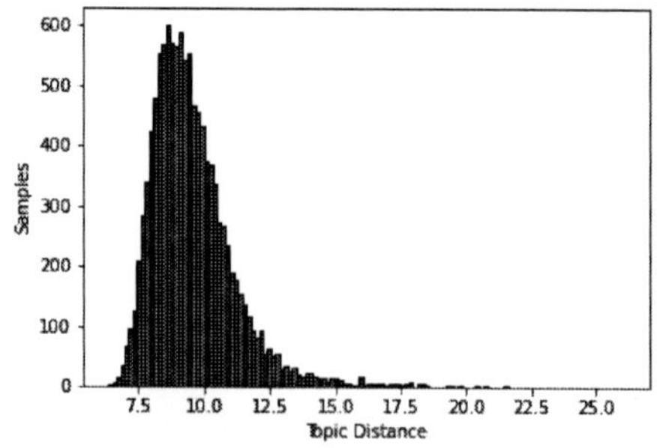

Figure 6: Distribution of document vectors to topic centroid in the combined class PROPERTY_DISTRUCT and MOB_VIOL

We see that both classes, MOB_VIOL and PROPERTY_DISTRUCT, are quite compact. There are some outliers, but most of the document vectors are clustered close to each other and the topic centroid. However, if we combine the classes into one topic and again analyse the distribution of document vectors to the topic centroid, we find that there are also very few outliers, as can be seen in figure 6. This means that the examples for MOB_VIOL and PROPERTY_DISTRUCT in our training data are similar to each other, which may explain why our models consistently confuse these two classes with regard to the test data provided by the organizers.

Looking at the test samples, we further find that due to the large number of classes, it is also difficult for human annotators to distinguish between the different classes in some cases. An example for this is the following:

```
{text: Police said two groups
   from different communities in
   Chhabra town of Rajasthan's
   Baran district pelted stones
   on each other and torched
   vehicles parked around after
   putting six shops afire,
 guess: MOB_VIOL,
 gold: PROPERTY_DISTRUCT}
```

All our models consistently predict the event class MOB_VIOL for this example, the gold standard annotation is, however, PROPERTY_DISTRUCT. It can be argued that the given example actually includes both event classes, with the first part of the sentence, "Police said two groups from different communities in Chhabra town of Rajasthan's Baran district pelted stones on each other" being an instance of MOB_VIOL, while the second part, "and torched vehicles parked around after putting six shops afire", belongs to the class PROPERTY_DISTRUCT. Test instances like this pose a challenge for the models.

8 Conclusion

In this study we proposed the use of fine-tuned RoBERTa transformer document embeddings for the fine-grained classification of socio-political events. We balanced the corpus to ensure that the 25 subtypes were represented as equally as possible. Compared to the results that were achieved during the preliminary experiments, we observed a drop in performance on the test set provided by the organizers. However, compared to the baseline figures provided by the organizers in (Piskorski et al., 2020), we achieved very similar results with less training data. This suggests that balancing the training data data had a positive effect on model performance.

Our analysis of the results of both different test sets, the set created for preliminary experiments and the set provided by the organizers for system evaluation, show that there is definitely a difference in performance in the various classes. It also highlighted the issue of events that could be classed as more than one different subtype, and the challenge that these events pose for fine-grained classification. Depending on the given use case, parts of our system could already be implemented in a real world setting in order to analyze the flow of data in the information space and achieve situational awareness in the physical world, as clear cut classes like CHEM_WEAP and GRENADE are identified reliably. In a military setting, for example, these classes are far more relevant than occurrences of PROPERTY_DISTRUCT.

In future work, it would be interesting to evaluate if the use of more training data, while still trying to obtain a more even distribution of classes, would further increase performance. Particularly, it raises the question if more training data would increase performance for the classes that currently do not perform as well. A more thorough class analysis, which would contribute to understanding why there seem to be systematic errors in specific classes, could provide insight into answering this question.

Acknowledgments

This research has been supported through funding from Philip Morris Impact as part of the Fraud Information Fusion Intelligence Project.

References

Alan Akbik, Tanja Bergmann, Duncan Blythe, Kashif Rasul, Stefan Schweter, and Roland Vollgraf. 2019. Flair: An easy-to-use framework for state-of-the-art nlp. In *NAACL 2019, 2019 Annual Conference of the North American Chapter of the Association for Computational Linguistics (Demonstrations)*, pages 54–59.

Alan Akbik, Duncan Blythe, and Roland Vollgraf. 2018. Contextual string embeddings for sequence labeling. In *COLING 2018, 27th International Conference on Computational Linguistics*, pages 1638–1649.

Jacob Devlin, Ming-Wei Chang, Kenton Lee, and Kristina Toutanova. 2019. BERT: Pre-training of deep bidirectional transformers for language understanding. In *Proceedings of the 2019 Conference of the North American Chapter of the Association for Computational Linguistics: Human Language Technologies, Volume 1 (Long and Short Papers)*, pages 4171–4186, Minneapolis, Minnesota. Association for Computational Linguistics.

Karsten Donnay, Eric T. Dunford, Erin C. McGrath, David Backer, and David E. Cunningham. 2019. Integrating conflict event data. *Journal of Conflict Resolution*, 63(5):1337–1364.

J Haneczok, G Jacquet, J Piskorski, and N Stefanovitch. 2021. Fine-grained event classification in news-like text snippets shared task 2, case 2021. In *Proceedings of the Workshop on Challenges and Applications of Automated Text Extraction of Socio-Political Event from Text (CASE 2021), co-located with the Joint Conference of the 59th Annual Meeting of the Association for Computational Linguistics and the 11th International Joint Conference on Natural Language Processing (ACL-IJCNLP 2021)*.

Ali Hürriyetoğlu, Osman Mutlu, Erdem Yörük, Ritesh Kumar, and Shyam Ratan. 2021. Multilingual protest news detection - shared task 1, case 2021. In *Proceedings of the Workshop on Challenges and Applications of Automated Extraction of Socio-political Events from Text (CASE 2021)*, online. Association for Computational Linguistics (ACL).

Ali Hürriyetoğlu, Erdem Yörük, Deniz Yüret, Çağrı Yoltar, Burak Gürel, Fırat Duruşan, Osman Mutlu, and Arda Akdemir. 2019. Overview of clef 2019 lab protestnews: Extracting protests from news in a cross-context setting. In *Experimental IR Meets Multilinguality, Multimodality, and Interaction*, pages 425–432, Cham. Springer International Publishing.

Ali Hürriyetoğlu, Vanni Zavarella, Hristo Tanev, Erdem Yörük, Ali Safaya, and Osman Mutlu. 2020. Automated extraction of socio-political events from news (AESPEN): Workshop and shared task report. In *Proceedings of the Workshop on Automated Extraction of Socio-political Events from News 2020*, pages 1–6, Marseille, France. European Language Resources Association (ELRA).

Yinhan Liu, Myle Ott, Naman Goyal, Jingfei Du, Mandar Joshi, Danqi Chen, Omer Levy, Mike Lewis, Luke Zettlemoyer, and Veselin Stoyanov. 2019. Roberta: A robustly optimized bert pretraining approach. Cite arxiv:1907.11692.

Tim Nugent, Fabio Petroni, Natraj Raman, Lucas Carstens, and Jochen L. Leidner. 2017. A comparison of classification models for natural disaster and critical event detection from news. In *2017 IEEE International Conference on Big Data (Big Data)*, pages 3750–3759.

Hao Peng, Jianxin Li, Qiran Gong, Yangqiu Song, Yuanxin Ning, Kunfeng Lai, and Philip S. Yu. 2019. Fine-grained event categorization with heterogeneous graph convolutional networks. In *Proceedings of the Twenty-Eighth International Joint Conference on Artificial Intelligence, IJCAI-19*, pages 3238–3245. International Joint Conferences on Artificial Intelligence Organization.

Jakub Piskorski, Jacek Haneczok, and Guillaume Jacquet. 2020. New benchmark corpus and models for fine-grained event classification: To BERT or not to BERT? In *Proceedings of the 28th International Conference on Computational Linguistics*, pages 6663–6678, Barcelona, Spain (Online). International Committee on Computational Linguistics.

Jakub Piskorski and Guillaume Jacquet. 2020. TF-IDF character N-grams versus word embedding-based models for fine-grained event classification: A preliminary study. In *Proceedings of the Workshop on Automated Extraction of Socio-political Events from News 2020*, pages 26–34, Marseille, France. European Language Resources Association (ELRA).

Clionadh Raleigh, Andrew Linke, Håvard Hegre, and Joakim Karlsen. 2010. Introducing acled: An armed conflict location and event dataset: Special data feature. *Journal of Peace Research*, 47(5):651–660.

Wei Xiang and Bang Wang. 2019. A survey of event extraction from text. *IEEE Access*, 7:173111–173137.

A Class Distribution and Results

Class	Train Nr. %	Dev Nr. %	Test Nr. %
PEACE_PROTEST	15229 (16.04)	1452 (16.13)	362 (14.48)
ARMED_CLASH	11132 (11.72)	1055 (11.73)	291 (11.64)
PROPERTY_DISTRUCT	7802 (8.22)	732 (8.13)	216 (8.64)
ATTACK	6153 (6.48)	610 (6.78)	166 (6.64)
ABDUCT_DISSAP	5871 (6.18)	550 (6.11)	154 (6.16)
CHANGE_TO_GROUP_ACT	5548 (5.84)	529 (5.88)	135 (5.40)
GOV_REGAINS_TERIT	3974 (4.18)	366 (4.07)	104 (4.16)
ART_MISS_ATTACK	3770 (3.97)	360 (4.00)	103 (4.12)
MOB_VIOL	3755 (3.95)	320 (3.56)	92 (3.68)
PROTEST_WITH_INTER	3740 (3.94)	354 (3.94)	109 (4.36)
DISR_WEAP	3388 (3.57)	330 (3.67)	99 (3.97)
ARREST	3098 (3.26)	311 (3.46)	97 (3.89)
AIR_STRIKE	3061 (3.22)	299 (3.32)	73 (2.92)
OTHER	2701 (2.84)	276 (3.07)	63 (2.52)
VIOL_DEMONSTR	2507 (2.64)	246 (2.73)	75 (3.00)
GRENADE	2439 (2.57)	238 (2.64)	70 (2.80)
NON_STATE_ACTOR_OVERTAKES_TER	2252 (2.37)	220 (2.44)	67 (2.68)
REM_EXPLOS	1938 (2.04)	170 (1.89)	44 (1.76)
FORCE_AGAINST_PROTEST	1900 (2.00)	178 (1.98)	56 (2.24)
SEX_VIOL	1260 (1.33)	106 (1.18)	30 (1.20)
NON_VIOL_TERRIT_TRANSFER	1033 (1.09)	90 (1.00)	27 (1.08)
SUIC_BOMB	1023 (1.08)	82 (0.91)	30 (1.20)
AGREEMENT	927 (0.98)	78 (0.86)	22 (0.89)
HQ_ESTABLISHED	406 (0.43)	40 (0.44)	13 (0.52)
CHEM_WEAP	57 (0.06)	8 (0.08)	2 (0.08)
Total	94964	9000	2500

Table 4: Corpus class distribution of the 25 event subtypes.

System	Avg Type	Avg Prec	Avg Recall	Avg F-score
System 1	micro avg	0.797	0.797	0.797
System 1	macro avg	0.790	0.778	0.770
System 1	weighted avg	0.824	0.797	0.799
System 2	micro avg	0.829	0.829	**0.829**
System 2	macro avg	0.807	0.808	**0.794**
System 2	weighted avg	0.851	0.829	**0.830**
System 3	micro avg	0.808	0.808	0.808
System 3	macro avg	0.787	0.779	0.768
System 3	weighted avg	0.828	0.808	0.808
System 4	micro avg	0.802	0.802	0.802
System 4	macro avg	0.788	0.789	0.774
System 4	weighted avg	0.841	0.802	0.812
System 5	micro avg	0.793	0.793	0.793
System 5	macro avg	0.780	0.780	0.766
System 5	weighted avg	0.817	0.893	0.793

Table 5: Detailed System Results

Class	Precision	Recall	F1-score	Support
ABDUCT_DISSAP	0.9787	0.9718	0.9753	142
AGREEMENT	0.8974	1.0000	0.9459	35
AIR_STRIKE	1.0000	0.9333	0.9655	75
ARMED_CLASH	0.9429	0.8771	0.9088	301
ARREST	0.9500	0.9500	0.9500	80
ART_MISS_ATTACK	0.9515	0.9608	0.9561	102
ATTACK	0.8361	0.9217	0.8768	166
CHANGE_TO_GROUP_ACT	0.9716	0.9648	0.9682	142
CHEM_WEAP	1.0000	1.0000	1.0000	2
DISR_WEAP	0.9444	0.9659	0.9551	88
FORCE_AGAINST_PROTEST	0.8302	0.9167	0.8713	48
GOV_REGAINS_TERIT	0.8900	0.8900	0.8900	100
GRENADE	0.9744	0.9870	0.9806	77
HQ_ESTABLISHED	0.6875	1.0000	0.8148	11
MOB_VIOL	0.8598	0.8846	0.8720	104
NON_STATE_ACTOR_OVERTAKES_TER	0.8889	0.9014	0.8951	71
NON_VIOL_TERRIT_TRANSFER	0.8966	0.8387	0.8667	31
OTHER	0.9531	0.8971	0.9242	68
PEACE_PROTEST	0.9863	0.9703	0.9782	370
PROPERTY_DISTRUCT	0.9700	0.9417	0.9557	206
PROTEST_WITH_INTER	0.9082	0.8990	0.9036	99
REM_EXPLOS	0.9107	0.9273	0.9189	55
SEX_VIOL	0.9630	0.8966	0.9286	29
SUIC_BOMB	0.9643	0.9643	0.9643	28
VIOL_DEMONSTR	0.7722	0.8714	0.8188	70
weighted avg	0.9338	0.9312	0.9318	2500

Table 6: RoBERTa ACLED_N Detailed Class Evaluation - Prelim. Test Data

Class	Precision	Recall	F1-score	Support
DISR_WEAP	0.915	0.931	0.923	58
ABDUCT_DISSAP	0.792	0.950	0.864	20
AGREEMENT	1.000	0.774	0.873	31
AIR_STRIKE	1.000	0.833	0.909	36
ARMED_CLASH	0.817	0.742	0.778	66
ART_MISS_ATTACK	0.838	0.861	0.849	36
ATTACK	0.806	0.926	0.862	27
CHANGE_TO_GROUP_ACT	0.731	0.633	0.679	30
CHEM_WEAP	1.000	0.865	0.928	37
ARREST	1.000	0.676	0.807	34
FORCE_AGAINST_PROTEST	0.692	0.783	0.735	23
GOV_REGAINS_TERIT	0.822	0.974	0.892	38
GRENADE	0.958	0.958	0.958	48
HQ_ESTABLISHED	0.724	0.955	0.824	22
MOB_VIOL	0.414	0.706	0.522	17
NON_STATE_ACTOR_OVERTAKES_TER	0.625	0.833	0.714	24
NON_VIOL_TERRIT_TRANSFER	0.800	0.762	0.780	21
OTHER	0.333	0.500	0.400	8
PEACE_PROTEST	0.864	0.895	0.879	57
PROPERTY_DISTRUCT	0.714	0.238	0.357	21
PROTEST_WITH_INTER	0.514	0.864	0.644	22
REM_EXPLOS	1.000	0.917	0.957	36
SEX_VIOL	0.957	0.957	0.957	23
SUIC_BOMB	0.976	0.976	0.976	41
VIOL_DEMONSTR	0.881	0.698	0.779	53
weighted avg	0.851	0.829	0.830	829

Table 7: RoBERTa ACLED_N Detailed Class Evaluation - Task Test Data

Discovering Black Lives Matter Events in the United States: Shared Task 3, CASE 2021

Salvatore Giorgi[1,2], Vanni Zavarella[3], Hristo Tanev[3], Nicolas Stefanovitch[3], Sy Hwang[1], Hansi Hettiarachchi[4], Tharindu Ranasinghe[5], Vivek Kalyan[6], Paul Tan[6], Shaun Tan[6], Martin Andrews[6], Tiancheng Hu[7], Niklas Stoehr[7], Francesco Ignazio Re[7], Daniel Vegh[7], Dennis Atzenhofer[7], Brenda Curtis[2], Ali Hürriyetoğlu[8]

[1]University of Pennsylvania, [2]Nation Institute on Drug Abuse,
[3]European Commission, [4]Birmingham City University, [5]University of Wolverhampton,
[6]Handshakes, [7]ETH Zurich, [8]Koc University

sgiorgi@sas.upenn.edu, ahurriyetoglu@ku.edu.tr

Abstract

Evaluating the state-of-the-art event detection systems on determining spatio-temporal distribution of the events on the ground is performed unfrequently. But, the ability to both (1) extract events "in the wild" from text and (2) properly evaluate event detection systems has potential to support a wide variety of tasks such as monitoring the activity of socio-political movements, examining media coverage and public support of these movements, and informing policy decisions. Therefore, we study performance of the best event detection systems on detecting Black Lives Matter (BLM) events from tweets and news articles. The murder of George Floyd, an unarmed Black man, at the hands of police officers received global attention throughout the second half of 2020. Protests against police violence emerged worldwide and the BLM movement, which was once mostly regulated to the United States, was now seeing activity globally. This shared task asks participants to identify BLM related events from large unstructured data sources, using systems pretrained to extract socio-political events from text. We evaluate several metrics, assessing each system's ability to evolution of protest events both temporally and spatially. Results show that identifying daily protest counts is an easier task than classifying spatial and temporal protest trends simultaneously, with maximum performance of 0.745 (Spearman) and 0.210 (Pearson r), respectively. Additionally, all baselines and participant systems suffered from low recall (max.5.08), confirming the high impact of media sourcing in the modelling of protest movements.

1 Introduction

Typically, performance evaluations of automated event coding engines are carried out with respect to benchmarks made of annotated linguistic units (e.g. clause, sentence or document). While this is crucial in order to factorize the individual, linguistic subtasks composing the event extraction process, it does not estimate the overall usability of machine-coded event data sets for micro-level modelling of social processes, particularly in the domain of socio-political and armed conflict, where spatial analysis has become standard.

The complex dynamics of the Black Lives Matter movement and its varied media coverage by news outlets and social media make it a particularly relevant use case for assessing the capability of automated, Event Extraction systems to model socio-political processes. The Task 3: "Discovering Black Lives Matter Events"[1] organized in the context of the Challenges and Applications of Automated Extraction of Socio-political Events from Text (CASE) 2021 workshop aims at doing so by challenging Event Extraction (EE) engines to extract a collection of protest events from two heterogeneous text collections (i.e., news and social media) and then measuring a number of spatio-temporal correlation coefficients against a curated Gold Standard data set of protest incidents from the BLM movement.

During May and June of 2020, protests occurred across the globe in response to the murder of George Floyd, an unarmed Black man, by Derek Chauvin, a white police officer. In the U.S., the number of locations holding demonstrations related to this murder outnumbered any other demonstration in U.S. history (Putnam et al., 2020). These events were more often than not associated with the Black Lives Matter (BLM) movement, either (1) directly through organizing or (2) indirectly through the slogan "Black Lives Matter" or shared political agendas such as police abolition and protests against police violence towards Black communi-

[1]https://github.com/emerging-welfare/case-2021-shared-task

Proceedings of the 4th Workshop on Challenges and Applications of Automated Extraction of Socio-political Events from Text (CASE), pages 218–227
August 5–6, 2021, ©2021 Association for Computational Linguistics

ties. Since its inception in 2013, the Black Lives Matter movement, a loose network of affiliated organizations, has organized demonstrations around a large number of police shootings and killings and sought to raise awareness of systematic violence against Black communities. While support for Black Lives Matter has varied over its lifetime (Horowitz, 2020), the work done over the past years laid the foundation for the global response seen in the wake of George Floyd's murder.

This task is the third in a series of tasks at CASE 2021 workshop (Hürriyetoğlu et al., 2021b). The first task is concerned with protest news detection at multiple text resolutions (e.g., the document and sentence level) and in multiple languages: English, Hindi, Portuguese, and Spanish (Hürriyetoğlu et al., 2021a). Teams which participated in Task 1 were invited to participate in this third task: "Discovering Black Lives Matter Events in the United States". This task is an evaluation only task, where all models are (1) trained on the data supplied in Task 1, (2) applied to the news and social media data (i.e, New York Times and Twitter data), and (3) evaluated on a manually curated, Gold Standard BLM protest event list. Each team's system is compared to simple baselines in order to properly evaluate their accuracy.

2 Related Work

Summary measures such as precision, recall, and F1 are limited in their capacity to inform about the quality of the predictions of an automated system (Derczynski, 2016; Yacouby and Axman, 2020). Moreover, evaluating capabilities of a system on detecting socio-political events from text requires additional metrics such as spatio-temporal correlation of the system output and the actual distribution of the events (Wang et al., 2016; Althaus et al., 2021).

Several studies focused on assessing the correlation of machine-coded event data sets with Gold Standards based on disaggregated event counts, for example Ward et al. (2013) and Schrodt and Analytics (2015). Hammond and Weidmann (2014) applied disaggregation of events incidents across PRIO-GRID geographical cells (Tollefsen et al., 2012) to assess the Global Database of Events, Language and Tone (GDELT) data approximation of the spatio-temporal pattern of conflicts. Zavarella et al. (2020) adapted this method to administrative units for measuring the impact of event de-duplication on increasing correlation with the Armed Conflict Location and Event Data (ACLED) data sets for a number of conflicts in Africa. In this report we report on an evaluation task, which we refer as Task 3, we provide a detailed analysis of the capabilities of the best performing systems on Task 1 (Hürriyetoğlu et al., 2021a) in this respect. We believe this effort will shed light on system performances beyond precision, recall, and F1.

3 Data

The goal of this task is to evaluate the performance of automatic event detection systems on modeling the spatial and temporal pattern of a social protest movement. We evaluate the capability of participant systems to reproduce a manually curated BLM-related protest event data set, by detecting BLM event reports, enriched with location and date attributes, from a news corpus collection, a Twitter collection, and from the union of the two.

3.1 Training Data

As a usability analysis, no training data were provided for this Task. Namely, the event definition applied for coding the reference event data set is the same as the one adopted for Shared Task 1 (Hürriyetoğlu et al., 2021a) and any data utilized for Task 1 and Task 2, such as the one from Hürriyetoğlu et al. (2021), or any additional data could be used to build a system/model run on the input data.

3.2 Input Data

We provide two types of input data. The first is a generic, not topic filtered collection of all news items (Title and Lead Paragraph) from the New York Times for the target time range May 25th - June 30th. The second is a collection of Black Lives Matter related tweets (Giorgi et al., 2020).

New York Times The New York Times (NYT) data sets consists of 5,347 articles published between May, 25 and June 30, 2020. The data associated with each article includes published date, print headline, lead paragraph, web URL, authors, and an abstract, among other meta-data. This is a general set of NYT articles (i.e., articles may or may not be related to BLM), unlike the Twitter data set which only contains tweets related to BLM or counter protests (e.g., All Lives Matter and Blue Lives Matter).

Twitter We used an open source data set of tweets containing keywords related to Black Lives Matter and the counter protests: All Lives Matter and Blue Lives Matter. While this data set contains tweets dating back to the origins of the Black Lives Matter movement, the tweets used in this task are limited to the date range: May 25, 2020 (the date of George Floyd's murder) to June 30, 2020. These tweets were pulled in real time using the Twitter API's keyword matching with the following three keywords: *BlackLivesMatter*, *AllLivesMatter*, and *BlueLivesMatter*. This data set consists of 30,160,837 tweets. Participants were given full access to each tweet's meta-data (including the tweet's text), which could include URLs, location information, and dates.

3.3 Gold Standard Data

For the Gold Standard data (i.e., the BLM events list we wish to automatically detect) we considered two online sources of Black Lives Matter protest events: Creosote Maps [2] and Race and Policing[3]. Starting with these two data sets, we first checked if the source URL link was still active. If not, we referenced other data sets for the event in question: Wikipedia (a list of George Floyd protests in and outside of the U.S.) and the New York Times. If a valid article was not found matching this protest date and location, then we performed a Google search for the specific event. If still nothing was found, then the event was removed from the data set. If at any point, we discovered a valid URL for the event, we ran a validation check. This check asked: (1) is the source a tweet or Facebook post; (2) does the source describe an upcoming event; (3) is the source irrelevant to the protest at the location; (4) does the source have enough information; and (5) is the source not accessible because of a paywall. If the source passed this check, we then scraped the source for the publication date and days of the week in the article text. If the publication date and the day of the week *do not* match, we then inferred the date of the protest by the mention of the day of the week closest to the publication date. Finally, we manually checked the scraped or inferred dates and record this as the event date.

In the end, this produced 3,463 distinct U.S. events between May 25 and June 30, 2020 with date, city, and state information. Of these events, only 537 (approximately 15% of the events) occurred after the first week of June. To compensate for the lack of coverage across all of June, we used the open source data set from the The Crowd Counting Consortium (CCC)[4]. From our original data set of 3,463 events, 754 events also occurred in the CCC data, matching on (1) URL or (2) both date and city. We then combined the two data sets (i.e., the CCC events with our original list) and removed duplicates. This resulted in 7,976 protest events in our final Gold Standard data. The U.S. map in Figure 1 shows the spatial distribution of these events (yellow dots).

4 Evaluation

System performance is evaluated by computing correlation coefficients on event counts aggregated on cell-days, using uniform grid cells of approximately 55 kilometers sides from the PRIO-GRID data set (Tollefsen et al., 2012). We use these analytical measures as a proxy to the spatio-temporal pattern of the BLM protest movement.

4.1 Data Normalization

In order to be joined with PRIO-GRID shapefiles, string-like location information of system output data had to be normalized to coordinate pairs. To do this we used the OpenStreetMap Nominatim search API[5]. For structured location name representations (i.e., *city, state, country*) we used a parametric search, otherwise we used free-form query strings. We note that geographical coordinate conversion from Nominatim places the event at the geographical centroid of the polygon of the assigned administrative unit. In our evaluation, we discarded the system output event records with no source location information or whose string-like location attribute returned null results in Nominatim API.

4.2 Metrics

We use the cell-days counts for two different analysis: the correlation with the total daily "protest cell" counts (i.e., time trends alone) and the event counts for each cell-day (i.e., spatial and temporal trends together).

Temporal Trends The first analysis only considers the total number of "activated" cells (i.e., for

[2] https://www.creosotemaps.com/

[3] http://raceandpolicing.com/

[4] https://sites.google.com/view/crowdcountingconsortium/home

[5] https://nominatim.org/release-docs/develop/api/Search/#parameters

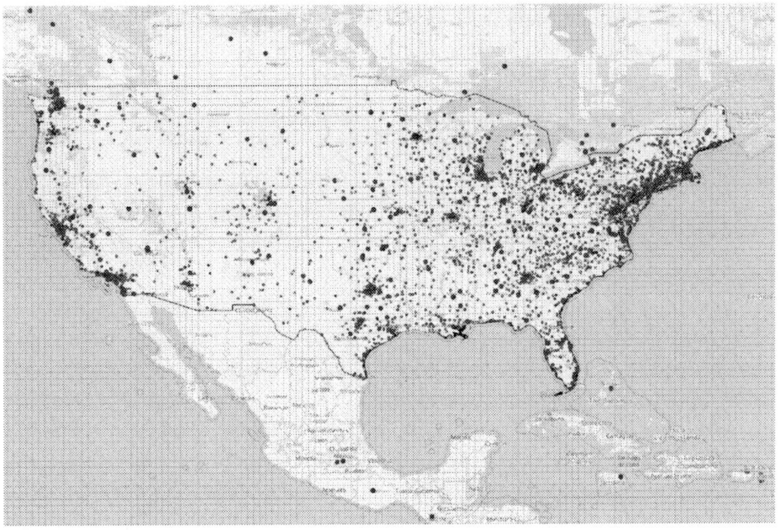

Figure 1: The geo-referenced BLM protest event records from Gold Standard (small yellow dots) overlaid with the PRIO-GRID cells over the US. The larger red and blue dots represent events recognized by the Baseline system from NYT and Twitter, respectively.

which at least one Protest event was recorded), in the system output and Gold Standard data set. This time series analysis is sufficient to estimate how well the automatic systems capture the time trends of the protest movement. However, it does not compute accuracy of system data in estimating the spatial variation of the target process.

Spatial and Temporal Trends To this purpose, we also measure the correlation coefficients on the absolute event counts with respect to Gold Standard, over each single cell-day.

For both analyses, we use two types of correlation coefficients to assess variable's relationship: Pearson coefficient r and Spearman's rank correlation coefficient ρ. Moreover, we used Root Mean Squared Error (RMSE) to measure the absolute value of the error on estimating cell/event counts from the Gold Standard.

4.3 Baseline

As a baseline, we used the output from NEXUS, a state-of-the-art engine for events detection from news (Tanev et al., 2008) that has been used in the area of security and disaster management[6]. We denote this system as *Baseline* throughout. Nexus is based on a blend of rule-based cascaded grammars for detection event slots (i.e. perpetrator, various types of affected people, infrastructure and vehicle targets and weapons used), and a combination of keyword-based and statistical classifiers for detection of event classes. The dictionaries underlying the extraction grammars of the system have been learned using weakly supervised lexical learning on generic news corpora (Tanev and Zavarella, 2014; Zavarella et al., 2014). No learning was performed on domain corpora in protest movements or related themes. Details on Nexus full taxonomy of event categories can be found in Atkinson et al. (2017). For this task, we filter the events belonging to the following type set: Disorder/Protest/Mutiny, Boycott/Strike, Public Demonstration, Riot/Turmoil, Sabotage/Impede, Mutiny. NEXUS performs event geocoding by (1) matching populated place names from the GeoNames gazetteer[7] in the news item; (2) resolving them into unique location entities via disambiguation heuristics (Pouliquen et al., 2006); and (3) selecting a single main event location based on the text proximity with the matched event components (see the slots above) in the news article. In order to mitigate the lack of geographical context in the tweet body, when processing the Twitter data, we ran Nexus on an enriched text, which included the String value of the *full_name* field in the *Place* child object of the tweet, whenever that

[6] A spin-off of the NEXUS system is the Medical NEXUS, an event detection system for disease outbreaks and food poisoning (Linge et al., 2012)

[7] `http://www.geonames.org`

was available[8]. This resulted in a small fraction of 32,085 tweets with geographical information (out of the roughly 30 million tweets originally sampled). For the sake of comparison, we shared with participants this subset of tweets, together with the assigned location.

4.4 Nexus Deduplication

This system, developed by the Task organizers and denoted *NexusDdpl*, is an extension of the Baseline system, where an event deduplication has been integrated as a post-processing module. The algorithm uses two metrics based on geographical distance between two event points and semantic distance, respectively. The semantic distance is computed using the cosine between the projections of the sentence embeddings of the texts of the events records. The LASER embeddings (Schwenk and Douze, 2017) were used for that purpose. Twitter data has been cleaned of hashtags, URLs, and accounts names, as these have a negative impact on the semantic similarity measure. In order to be considered duplicate two events must have both distance measures under a fixed threshold, which were set to 2km for spatial distance, 0.20 for semantic distance on NYT data, 0.30 for semantic distance on Twitter data. The reason of these different threshold depending on the data sets is that Twitter data are noisier than NYT data, with higher variations in text size and style when describing a single event. As such looser threshold was required. When applying on the combination of both data sets, we use a compromise threshold of 0.35 was used.

4.5 Team Systems

Four teams participated in this event: *DaDeFrNi*, *EventMiner*, *Handshakes*, and *NoConflict*. We briefly describe the systems below and ask the reader to refer to their systems papers for additional details.

DaDeFrNi This team considered two slightly different procedures for this task. For the NYT data set, they first extracted geo-entities from each article using the Python library geography, which was used to classify each entity in one of the three categories "city", "country", and "region". For the cases where an article contained the name of a city but did not provide any region or country reference, *DaDeFrNi* retrieved the necessary information by checking the city name against a worldwide cities database. When the name of a city was associated with several locations, we filtered the city with the highest population, along with its corresponding "region" and "country". For the Twitter data set, given the large size of the data, the above procedure was computationally expensive. Thus, the Python library spaCy (Honnibal et al., 2020) for retrieving NER/GPE entities, given its much smaller computational cost. The complete system details can be found in Ignazio Re et al. (2021).

EventMiner Team *EventMiner*'s approach for Task 3 is mainly based on transformer models (Hettiarachchi et al., 2021). This approach involved three steps: (1) event document identification, (2) location detail extraction, (3) and event filtering to identify the spatial and temporal pattern of the targeted social protest movement. Event documents are identified using the winning solution submitted to CASE 2021 Task 1-Subtask 1: event document classification (Hettiarachchi et al., 2021). Next, the location details in event described tweets are extracted. Since this team only focused on the Twitter corpus, they used tweet metadata to extract location details. However, since the majority of the tweets are not geotagged and to extract the location details mentioned in the text, they used a NER approach too. For NER, a transformer model is fine-tuned for token classification using the data set released with the WNUT 2017 Shared Task on Novel and Emerging Entity Recognition (Derczynski et al., 2017). The BERTweet model is used since it is pretrained on Tweets (Nguyen et al., 2020). To convert the location details into an unique format and fill the missing details (e.g. region, country), locations are geocoded using the GeoPy library[9]. For the final step, event tweets with location details are grouped based on their created dates and locations and removed the groups with fewer tweets assuming that important events generate a high number of tweets. Three systems were submitted. For the first system, denoted by †, only the new events are included (i.e., events with locations which are identified in the previous day are removed). The second system ††, includes all the extracted events (i.e., no filtering as in †). Finally, the third system ††† further filters the events from † to include U.S. events only. Please see Hettiarachchi et al. (2021) for more details

[8] https://developer.twitter.com/en/docs/twitter-api/data-dictionary/object-model/tweet

[9] https://geopy.readthedocs.io

Handshakes This model is a pretrained XLM-RoBERTa model, fine-tuned on the multi-language article data from Task 1 Subtask 1 and sentence data from Subtask 2, with a classification head that predicts if the input text is a protest or not. We make use of the provided location data in the data sets, where available. Please see Kalyan et al. (2021) for further details.

NoConflict Team *NoConflict* used their model of protest event sentence classification from the winning submission of the English version of Task 1 Subtask 2. Their model is based on a RoBERTa (Liu et al., 2019) backbone with a second pretraining (Gururangan et al., 2020) stage done on the POLUSA (Gebhard and Hamborg, 2020) data set before finetuned on Subtask 2 data. For the NYT data set, they first filtered the articles based on the section name. They then ran their model on the abstract of each article to identify ones containing protest events. For each remaining article, they run a transformer-based (Vaswani et al., 2017) named entity recognition from spaCy (Honnibal et al., 2020) to identify the location and date of the events. They covert the location to absolute location using the Geocoder library and convert the date of the event to the absolute date based on the article's publication date. If the relative location or date is unavailable, they default to those included in the metadata. The event sentence classification system details can be found in Hu and Stoehr (2021). Three systems were submitted for the NYT data, denoted $\diamond$, $\diamond\diamond$, and $\diamond\diamond\diamond$. Each system used a set of manually curated keywords applied to different parts of each data point. Theses rules are included in the Appendix. For the Twitter data set, Team *NoConflict* ran their model on the full text of each tweet to identify protest events. For each potential event tweet, they identify the location and time based on the metadata of the tweet itself and the main tweet if it is a retweet.

5 Results

Table 1 shows the Pearson r, Spearman correlation coefficient ρ, and Root Mean Squared Error (RMSE) for the total daily protest cell counts of the Baseline and participant systems, over the 35 days target time range. When a run for both source types exists for a system, we also evaluate the union of the two event sets (noted as "Merged" in Tables). Here, the correlations are between the total number of cells per day where the system found an event vs. the number of cells where event happened according to the Gold Standard (i.e., temporal patterns and not spatial patterns). These correlation measures are tolerant to errors in geocoding (as far as the events are located in U.S.) and evaluate the capability of the system to detect protest events in the news and social media, independent of their location. We see the following: (1) *NoConflict* surpasses the *Baseline* with the NYT, Twitter, and Merged data in both Pearson r and Spearman ρ, and (2) *EventMiner* and *HandShakes* surpasses *Baseline* with Twitter data in Pearson r (both systems have lower Spearman ρ than *Baseline*). Additionally, *NoConflict* surpasses the *NexusDdpl* system (using NYT, Twitter, and Merged data), and the *HandShakes* system surpasses the *NexusDdpl* system using Twitter data.

	Data	r	ρ	RMSE
	NYT	0.646	0.626	301.98
Baseline	Twitter	0.337	0.367	291.01
	Merged	0.353	0.334	288.04
	NYT	0.646	0.626	301.98
NexusDdpl	Twitter	0.337	0.367	291.01
	Merged	0.357	0.334	287.85
	NYT	-0.366	-0.264	287.04
DaDeFrNi	Twitter	-0.202	-0.280	306.77
	Merged	-0.408	-0.365	287.26
	Twitter†	0.451	0.327	300.15
EventMiner	Twitter††	0.427	0.312	299.59
	Twitter†††	0.453	0.343	300.83
HandShakes	Twitter	0.424	0.254	**276.13**
	NYT$^{\diamond}$	0.725	0.669	302.14
	NYT$^{\diamond\diamond}$	**0.745**	**0.762**	302.96
NoConflict	NYT$^{\diamond\diamond\diamond}$	0.601	0.658	303.407
	Twitter	0.534	0.524	287.88
	Merged	0.522	0.537	286.59

Table 1: Correlation coefficients and error rates for daily protest cell counts: r represents Pearson correlation coefficient, ρ is Spearman's rank correlation coefficient, and RMSE is the Root Mean Squared Error computed on day-cell units. Superscripts refer to the various systems submitted by *EventMiner* and *NoConflict*, as described in Section 4.5.

Table 2 reports Pearson r, Spearman correlation coefficient ρ, and Root Mean Squared Error (RMSE) over cell-day event counts of the Baseline and participant systems with respect to Gold Standard, for the 35 days time range. Here the variables range over the whole set of PRIO-GRID cells included in the US territory and, thus, shows the correlation of event numbers across geo-cells, thus evaluating the system's geolocation capabilities. *NoConflict* (NYT$^{\diamond}$) had the highest Pearson r and lowest RMSE across all systems, as well as the highest Spearman ρ (with the Merged data). Using

Twitter data alone, the *Baseline* and *NexusDdpl* systems outperformed all others in terms of Pearson r, however *NexusDdpl* had a higher Spearman ρ. However, when looking at both correlation metrics simultaneously, no system is above the *NexusDdpl* baseline.

In Figure 2 we plot the time series of total daily protest cells for the best performing instance of each system on New York Times (left) and Twitter (right) data, respectively. We see the systems evaluated on the NYT data failing to pick up both variation in the temporal patterns (i.e., a large number of protests early in late May and early June, which gradually declines with weekly spikes) and the magnitude of the events (i.e, most systems pick up less than 100 events per day). Systems evaluated on Twitter data pick up more events in late May and early June, but still fail to pick up the magnitude of the events.

A more lenient representation of the agreement with Gold Standard is shown in Table 3. Here we report the confusion matrix between grid cells that Gold Standard and system runs code as experiencing at least a protest event. It can be observed that only few of the cells classified as Protest by Gold Standard are detected by the automatic systems, which on the other hand incorrectly classified as Protest several additional cells.

	Data	r	ρ	RMSE
	NYT	0.096	0.089	0.732
Baseline	Twitter	0.171	0.127	0.785
	Merged	0.181	0.132	0.724
	NYT	0.100	0.088	0.725
NexusDdpl	Twitter	0.193	0.124	0.777
	Merged	0.192	0.129	0.715
	NYT	0.165	0.136	0.711
DaDeFrNi	Twitter	0.002	-0.004	69.171
	Merged	0.003	0.122	87.422
	Twitter†	0.155	0.077	0.715
EventMiner	Twitter††	0.147	0.077	0.715
	Twitter†††	0.157	0.076	0.715
HandShakes	Twitter	0.109	0.105	0.783
	NYT$^{\diamond}$	**0.210**	0.095	**0.712**
	NYT$^{\diamond\diamond}$	0.196	0.086	0.714
NoConflict	NYT$^{\diamond\diamond\diamond}$	0.184	0.082	0.715
	Twitter	0.020	0.138	148.18
	Merged	0.018	**0.145**	148.20

Table 2: Correlation coefficients and error rates for *cell-day* event counts of the Baseline and participant systems with respect to Gold Standard. Superscripts refer to the various systems submitted by *EventMiner* and *NoConflict*, as described in Section 4.5.

6 Conclusions

The goal of the "Discovering Black Lives Matter Events" Shared Task was to explore novel performance evaluations of pretrained event detection systems. These systems were applied to large noisy, multi-modal text data sets (i.e., news articles and social media data) related to a specific protest movement, namely, Black Lives Matter. Thus, the systems are being evaluated out-of-domain in terms of both data type (i.e., the systems are trained on news data and evaluated on both news and social media) and protest movement context (i.e., the training data are not necessarily related to BLM). Systems are evaluated in their ability to identify both events across time as well as events their distribution across space. This evaluation scenario proved difficult for all systems participating in the shared task. A major problem, as shown on Table 3, is the system's low recall. No system was able to outperform the *NexusDdpl* baseline both in precision and recall together. The only system which outperformed the baseline in either recall or F1 is the *DaDeFrNi* (Ignazio Re et al., 2021), with a recall of 5.08 and F1 of 8.86. On the other hand, two systems surpass the baseline in precision: *EventMiner* (Hettiarachchi et al., 2021) and *NoConflict* (Hu and Stoehr, 2021), with precisions of 56.0 and 73.6, respectively.

The low recall at this years shared task may well be due to the low coverage of protest events of the highly diffused BLM movement both in the NYT and Twitter corpus, so the upper bound of the recall may turn out not to be much higher than the system performance. One possible explanation for this is that a significant part of the BLM events in the Gold standard are located in small towns, for which NYT has a limited coverage and also they were not in the focus of social media, due to their small scale. *NexusDdpl* turned out to be quite high both in terms of event detection accuracy, as well as geo-coding correlation. While no single system outperformed all others in tracking both temporal and spatial trends, *NoConflict* had a clear advantage (i.e., the highest scoring system in 2 out of 3 metrics) in terms of tracking daily events.

Acknowledgments

The author from Koc University was funded by the European Research Council (ERC) Starting Grant 714868 awarded to Dr. Erdem Yörük for his project Emerging Welfare. The authors from the National

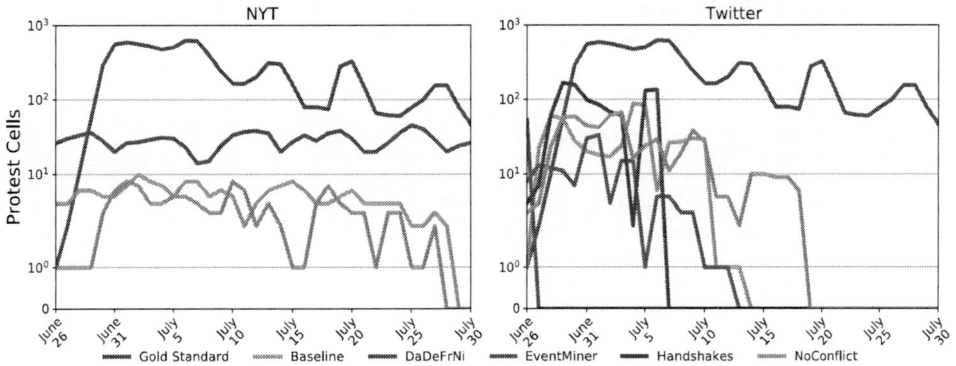

Figure 2: Time series of total daily protest cells from the Gold Standard (in blue), against system runs on New York Times (left) and Twitter (right) input data. Protest cell counts are on a log scale. *Baseline* and *NexusDdpl* systems produce the same cell count numbers (see Table 2), so the *NexusDdpl* system was omitted.

		Gold Standard		Precision	Recall	F1
		true	false			
Baseline	true	330	341	49.2	3.87	7.20
	false	8163	195790			
NexusDdpl	true	326	353	48.0	3.84	7.11
	false	8167	195778			
DaDeFrNi	true	431	802	35.0	**5.08**	**8.86**
	false	8062	195329			
EventMiner[†††]	true	94	74	56.0	1.11	2.17
	false	8399	196057			
Handshakes	true	328	631	34.2	3.86	6.94
	false	8165	195500			
NoConflict[◇◇◇]	true	81	29	**73.6**	0.95	1.88
	false	8412	196102			

Table 3: Confusion matrix of grid cells experiencing at least one Protest event (true) versus inactive cells (false), for the Gold Standard, Baseline and participant systems. Unless denoted by a superscript, all systems use the "merged" version (i.e., both NYT and Twitter data sets) except for *HandShakes* system which uses only Twitter data.

Institute on Drug Abuse were supported in part by the Intramural Research Program of the NIH, National Institute on Drug Abuse (NIDA).

References

Scott Althaus, Buddy Peyton, and Dan Shalmon. 2021. A total error approach for validating event data. *American Behavioral Scientist*, 3(2).

Martin Atkinson, Jakub Piskorski, Hristo Tanev, and Vanni Zavarella. 2017. On the creation of a security-related event corpus. In *Proceedings of the Events and Stories in the News Workshop*, pages 59–65.

Leon Derczynski. 2016. Complementarity, F-score, and NLP evaluation. In *Proceedings of the Tenth International Conference on Language Resources and Evaluation (LREC'16)*, pages 261–266, Portorož, Slovenia. European Language Resources Association (ELRA).

Leon Derczynski, Eric Nichols, Marieke van Erp, and Nut Limsopatham. 2017. Results of the WNUT2017 shared task on novel and emerging entity recognition. In *Proceedings of the 3rd Workshop on Noisy User-generated Text*, pages 140–147, Copenhagen, Denmark. Association for Computational Linguistics.

Lukas Gebhard and Felix Hamborg. 2020. The polusa dataset: 0.9 m political news articles balanced by time and outlet popularity. In *Proceedings of the ACM/IEEE Joint Conference on Digital Libraries in 2020*, pages 467–468.

Salvatore Giorgi, Sharath Chandra Guntuku, Muhammad Rahman, McKenzie Himelein-Wachowiak, Amy Kwarteng, and Brenda Curtis. 2020. Twitter corpus of the #blacklivesmatter movement and counter protests: 2013 to 2020. *arXiv preprint arXiv:2009.00596*.

Suchin Gururangan, Ana Marasović, Swabha Swayamdipta, Kyle Lo, Iz Beltagy, Doug Downey, and Noah A. Smith. 2020. Don't stop pretraining: Adapt language models to domains and tasks. In *Proceedings of ACL.*

Jesse Hammond and Nils B Weidmann. 2014. Using machine-coded event data for the micro-level study of political violence. *Research & Politics*, 1(2):2053168014539924.

Hansi Hettiarachchi, Mariam Adedoyin-Olowe, Jagdev Bhogal, and Mohamed Medhat Gaber. 2021. DAAI at CASE 2021 task 1: Transformer-based multilingual socio-political and crisis event detection. In *Proceedings of the 4th Workshop on Challenges and Applications of Automated Extraction of Socio-political Events from Text (CASE 2021)*, online. Association for Computational Linguistics (ACL).

Matthew Honnibal, Ines Montani, Sofie Van Landeghem, and Adriane Boyd. 2020. spaCy: Industrial-strength Natural Language Processing in Python.

Juliana Horowitz. 2020. *Amid protests, majorities across racial and ethnic groups express support for the Black Lives Matter movement.* Pew Research Center.

Tiancheng Hu and Niklas Stoehr. 2021. Team noconflict at case 2021 task 1: Pretraining for sentence-level protest event detection. In *Proceedings of the 4th Workshop on Challenges and Applications of Automated Extraction of Socio-political Events from Text (CASE 2021)*, online. Association for Computational Linguistics (ACL).

Ali Hürriyetoğlu, Osman Mutlu, Farhana Ferdousi Liza, Erdem Yörük, Ritesh Kumar, and Shyam Ratan. 2021a. Multilingual protest news detection - Shared Task 1, CASE 2021. In *Proceedings of the 4th Workshop on Challenges and Applications of Automated Extraction of Socio-political Events from Text (CASE 2021)*, online. Association for Computational Linguistics (ACL).

Ali Hürriyetoğlu, Hristo Tanev, Vanni Zavarella, Jakub Piskorski, Reyyan Yeniterzi, Erdem Yörük, Osman Mutlu, Deniz Yüret, and Aline Villavicencio. 2021b. Challenges and Applications of Automated Extraction of Socio-political Events from Text (CASE 2021): Workshop and Shared Task Report. In *Proceedings of the 4th Workshop on Challenges and Applications of Automated Extraction of Socio-political Events from Text (CASE 2021)*, online. Association for Computational Linguistics (ACL).

Ali Hürriyetoğlu, Erdem Yörük, Osman Mutlu, Fırat Duruşşan, Çağrı Yoltar, Deniz Yüret, and Burak Gürel. 2021. Cross-Context News Corpus for Protest Event-Related Knowledge Base Construction. *Data Intelligence*, 3(2):308–335.

Francesco Ignazio Re, Daniel Vegh, Dennis Atzenhofer, and Niklas Stoehr. 2021. Team dadefrni at case 2021 task 1: Document and sentence classification for protest event detection. In *Proceedings of the 4th Workshop on Challenges and Applications of Automated Extraction of Socio-political Events from Text (CASE 2021)*, online. Association for Computational Linguistics (ACL).

Vivek Kalyan, Paul Tan, Shaun Tan, and Martin Andrews. 2021. Handshakes ai research at case 2021 task 1: Exploring different approaches for multilingual tasks. In *Proceedings of the 4th Workshop on Challenges and Applications of Automated Extraction of Socio-political Events from Text (CASE 2021)*, online. Association for Computational Linguistics (ACL).

Jens P Linge, Marco Verile, Hristo Tanev, Vanni Zavarella, Flavio Fuart, and Erik van der Goot. 2012. Media monitoring of public health threats with medisys. *C. WILLIAM, CWR. WEB-STER, D. BALAHUR, et al*, pages 17–31.

Yinhan Liu, Myle Ott, Naman Goyal, Jingfei Du, Mandar Joshi, Danqi Chen, Omer Levy, Mike Lewis, Luke Zettlemoyer, and Veselin Stoyanov. 2019. Roberta: A robustly optimized bert pretraining approach. *arXiv preprint arXiv:1907.11692.*

Dat Quoc Nguyen, Thanh Vu, and Anh Tuan Nguyen. 2020. BERTweet: A pre-trained language model for English tweets. In *Proceedings of the 2020 Conference on Empirical Methods in Natural Language Processing: System Demonstrations*, pages 9–14, Online. Association for Computational Linguistics.

Bruno Pouliquen, Marco Kimler, Ralf Steinberger, Camelia Ignat, Tamara Oellinger, Ken Blackler, Flavio Fuart, Wajdi Zaghouani, Anna Widiger, Ann-Charlotte Forslund, et al. 2006. Geocoding multilingual texts: Recognition, disambiguation and visualisation. *arXiv preprint cs/0609065.*

Lara Putnam, Erica Chenoweth, and Jeremy Pressman. 2020. The floyd protests are the broadest in us history—and are spreading to white, small-town america. *Washington Post*, 6.

Philip A Schrodt and Parus Analytics. 2015. Comparing methods for generating large scale political event data sets. In *Text as Data meetings, New York University, 16–17, 2015*, pages 1–32.

Holger Schwenk and Matthijs Douze. 2017. Learning joint multilingual sentence representations with neural machine translation. *arXiv preprint arXiv:1704.04154.*

Hristo Tanev, Jakub Piskorski, and Martin Atkinson. 2008. Real-time news event extraction for global crisis monitoring. In *Natural Language and Information Systems*, pages 207–218, Berlin, Heidelberg. Springer Berlin Heidelberg.

Hristo Tanev and Vanni Zavarella. 2014. Multilingual lexicalisation and population of event ontologies: A case study for social media. In *Towards the Multilingual Semantic Web*, pages 259–274. Springer.

Andreas Forø Tollefsen, Håvard Strand, and Halvard Buhaug. 2012. Prio-grid: A unified spatial data structure. *Journal of Peace Research*, 49(2):363–374.

Ashish Vaswani, Noam Shazeer, Niki Parmar, Jakob Uszkoreit, Llion Jones, Aidan N. Gomez, Lukasz Kaiser, and Illia Polosukhin. 2017. Attention is all you need. In *Advances in Neural Information Processing Systems*.

Wei Wang, Ryan Kennedy, David Lazer, and Naren Ramakrishnan. 2016. Growing pains for global monitoring of societal events. *Science*, 353(6307):1502–1503.

Michael D Ward, Andreas Beger, Josh Cutler, Matthew Dickenson, Cassy Dorff, and Ben Radford. 2013. Comparing gdelt and icews event data. *Event Data Analysis*, 21(1):267–297.

Reda Yacouby and Dustin Axman. 2020. Probabilistic extension of precision, recall, and f1 score for more thorough evaluation of classification models. In *Proceedings of the First Workshop on Evaluation and Comparison of NLP Systems*, pages 79–91, Online. Association for Computational Linguistics.

Vanni Zavarella, Jakub Piskorski, Camelia Ignat, Hristo Tanev, and Martin Atkinson. 2020. Mastering the media hype: Methods for deduplication of conflict events from news reports. In *Proceedings of AI4Narratives — Workshop on Artificial Intelligence for Narratives*.

Vanni Zavarella, Hristo Tanev, Ralf Steinberger, and Erik Van der Goot. 2014. An ontology-based approach to social media mining for crisis management. In *SSA-SMILE@ ESWC*, pages 55–66. Citeseer.

A Additional System Details

The *NoConflict* team produced three separate rule-based systems for the NYT data. NYT$^{\diamond}$: include keywords "Police Brutality, Misconduct and Shootings", "Attacks on Police", "George Floyd Protests (2020)", "Demonstrations, Protests and Riots", "Black Lives Matter Movement"; excluded keywords: "Hong Kong Protests (2019)"; include section name: "U.S.", "Politics", "New York", "World"; exclude News Desk: "Arts & Leisure", "Gender", "Investigative", "Special Sections", "Sports", "Science", "Magazine", "Video", "Podcast", "News Desk"; exclude if present in abstract or lead paragraph: "Hong Kong". NYT$^{\diamond\diamond}$: include keywords: "Police Brutality, Misconduct and Shootings", "Attacks on Police", "George Floyd Protests (2020)", "Demonstrations, Protests and Riots", "Black Lives Matter Movement"; exclude keywords: "Hong Kong Protests (2019)"; include section name: "U.S.", "Politics", "New York", "World"; exclude News Desk: "Arts & Leisure", "Gender", "Investigative", "Special Sections", "Sports", "Science", "Magazine", "Video", "Podcast", "News Desk", "Washington", "Politics"; exclude if present in abstract or lead paragraph: "Hong Kong". NYT$^{\diamond\diamond\diamond}$: include keywords: "Police Brutality, Misconduct and Shootings", "Attacks on Police", "George Floyd Protests (2020)", "Demonstrations, Protests and Riots", "Black Lives Matter Movement"; exclude keywords: "Coronavirus (2019-nCoV)", "Quarantines", "Hong Kong Protests (2019)"; include section name: "U.S.", "Politics", "New York"; exclude News Desk: "Arts & Leisure", "Gender", "Investigative", "Special Sections", "Sports", "Science", "Magazine", "Video", "Podcast", "News Desk", "Washington", "Politics", "Foreign"; exclude if present in abstract or lead paragraph: "Hong Kong".

Author Index

Association for Computational Linguistics
209 N. Eighth Street
Stroudsburg, Pennsylvania 18360

CURRAN ASSOCIATES INC.
proceedings.com

ISBN 978-1-7138-3313-0
9 781713 833130